ADVANCES IN SOCIAL NETWORK ANALYSIS

*Research in the Social
and Behavioral Sciences*

**Stanley Wasserman
Joseph Galaskiewicz**
editors

SAGE PUBLICATIONS
International Educational and Professional Publisher
Thousand Oaks   London   New Delhi

For information address:

 SAGE Publications, Inc.
2455 Teller Road
Thousand Oaks, California 91320

SAGE Publications Ltd.
6 Bonhill Street
London EC2A 4PU
United Kingdom

SAGE Publications India Pvt. Ltd.
M-32 Market
Greater Kailash I
New Delhi 110 048 India

Printed in the United States of America

Library of Congress Cataloging-in-Publication Data

Main entry under title:
Advances in social network analysis: Research in the social and behavioral
   sciences / edited by Stanley Wasserman, Joseph Galaskiewicz.
      p. cm. — (Sage focus editions ; 171)
   Includes bibliographical references.
   ISBN 0-8039-4302-4 (cl). — ISBN 0-8039-4303-2 (pb)
   1. Social networks—Research. I. Wasserman, Stanley.
II. Galaskiewicz, Joseph.
HM131.A318   1994
300'.72—dc20   94-3378

94 95 96 97 98   10 9 8 7 6 5 4 3 2 1

Sage Production Editor: Astrid Virding

To Andrew and Eliot

Contents

Part II. Anthropology and Communication

Part III. Politics and Organizations

Acknowledgments

We would like to thank the National Science Foundation, and particularly Jim Blackman, Cheryl Eavey, and Bill Bainbridge, who have supported our research over the past years. We thank Scott Long for inviting us to edit a special issue of his journal, *Sociological Methods & Research*, and for proposing the idea of this edited volume to us. Five of the papers in this volume originally appeared in Volume 22, Issue 1, of *SMR*. C. Deborah Laughton at Sage Publications deserves a large thank you for her patience while we were slowly pushing our authors to finish their chapters for this volume. We also appreciate her encouragement over the 3 years that this volume was "in the works." But, most important, we would like to thank our authors for their diligence and cooperation. We are truly pleased that they have all written marvelous chapters and that we are able to bring this collection to you, the reader.

Readers can contact us via electronic mail (*stanwass@uiuc.edu* and *galaskie@soc.umn.edu*) if correspondence is desired.

Introduction

Advances in the Social and Behavioral Sciences From Social Network Analysis

JOSEPH GALASKIEWICZ
STANLEY WASSERMAN

We put together this edited volume to show how social network analysis has been used to advance substantive research in the social and behavioral sciences. The "instructions" given to our authors asked them to describe how social network concepts and methods have helped to advance their specific substantive disciplines. These disciplines, from social psychology and diffusion research, to anthropology and communications, and to politics and organization studies, span the range of present-day social network analysis applications.

The range of applications using the social network paradigm has grown exponentially since major methodological breakthroughs in the 1970s and early 1980s. Although important social network research is still being done in the small group laboratory and field sites as it was in the 1940s and 1950s, there has been an explosion of research since the early 1970s on social networks in modern societies. Much of this

AUTHORS' NOTE: We thank Laura Koehly and Pip Pattison for comments on this short introduction. Our research is supported by grants from the National Science Foundation to the University of Minnesota and the University of Illinois.

research relies heavily on survey methods. No doubt the social network perspective has grown in popularity because it enables researchers to study not only social actors but the social relationships among these actors. Of all the research using the network perspective, one fundamental finding stands out: Many important aspects of societal life are organized as networks. The importance of networks in society has put social network analysis at the forefront of social and behavioral science research.

The authors in this volume write for many different audiences, yet they all work within the common network tradition. We hope that this volume will give the reader insight into what the network perspective can do to advance our understanding of individual and institutional behavior.

Before going further, we should note that this volume is not a collection of papers presenting new methods; rather, we have asked the authors to write primarily about substantive areas and only about network methods secondarily. We view each chapter as the "expert" opinion on the particular area—such opinions that we ourselves could not write. Thus the collection allows the reader to gain a complete understanding of the importance of network analysis directly from the experts. Books on network methodology are far more common than such collections. We view this collection as a complement to such methodology texts (particularly Wasserman & Faust, 1994).

The Network Perspective

What constitutes the social network perspective? The most distinguishing feature is that social network analysis focuses on relationships among social entities and on the patterns and implications of these relationships (Wasserman & Faust, 1994, p. 6). Instead of analyzing individual behaviors, attitudes, and beliefs, social network analysis focuses its attention on social entities or actors in interaction with one another and on how these interactions constitute a framework or structure that can be studied and analyzed in its own right. These principles distinguish social network analysis from other research approaches (see Wellman, 1988).

In addition to the use of relational concepts that quantify these interactions, the social network perspective makes a variety of assumptions about actors, relations, and the resulting structure (Wasserman & Faust, 1994, p. 7) such as the following:

- Actors and their actions are viewed as interdependent rather than independent, autonomous units.
- Relational ties (linkages) between actors are channels for transfer or "flow" of resources (either material, like money, or nonmaterial, like information, political support, friendship, or respect).
- Network models focusing on individuals view the network structural environment as providing opportunities for or constraints on individual action.
- Network models conceptualize structure (whether social, economic, political, and so forth) as enduring patterns of relations among actors.

Clearly, then, a central item on the network agenda is to bridge the gap between the micro- and macro-order. At the micro level, network analysts examine dyads, triads, other small subgroups, and ego-centered networks. Such structures are unique to the network perspective. At the macro level, attention is often given to the examination of configurations of entire networks and the identification of structural positions and components of the network.

One way that network analysis provides a "bridge" between the micro- and macro-orders is that successive levels are "embedded" in one another. Individual relational ties are the crucial components of dyads; dyads constitute triads; triads are contained in higher order subgraphs; and all are embedded in complete networks. The network itself is often embedded in a larger institutional context (whether social, political, economic, epidemiological, or whatever); further, even the institutional order is embedded in myriad networks that connect it to other institutional sectors in a national and international context. The beauty of network analysis is that it allows a researcher to tie together so many interdependent parts that constitute micro- and macro-social orders. One can understand how changes in one level of social organization (for example, the dyadic) affects another level (for example, the network as a whole), which in turn affects the institutional order. A useful way to think about this is to envision society as a giant "Tinkertoy" creation where the blocks are actors and the sticks are the relationships between them. There are many ways to study the resulting structural creation. Social network analysis provides a ready framework for linking the micro- and macro-orders.

Another way that network analysis bridges the gap between the micro- and the macro-order is that it allows the researcher to pay attention to individual action or behavior within the context of larger structural configurations. Individual actors can be viewed as passive players, captives of the structures that they are embedded in. A great deal of work configured network effects in this way. More recently, researchers have been looking at actors as "network entrepreneurs," exploiting their network position to further their own interests. Groups and institutions similarly are sometimes portrayed as "victims" of the networks that operate within them, but they also can exploit structural conditions for their own gain. The appeal of this new approach is that, while the former merely reaffirms the configuration of the macro-social order, the latter allows for change. As network entrepreneurs strategically use their networks to further their own interests, they will in turn change the network itself.

This Edited Volume

The chapters in this volume may at first appear to be a disjointed lot, yet they all speak the language of network analysis. All focus on how the network perspective has improved research and given new theoretical insights. The language of network analysis, which allows a researcher to optimally exploit the network perspective, is quite unique; social network analysis has a code all its own. Because our space in this introduction is limited, we cannot give a careful, detailed history of network analysis, nor can we spend pages defining terms and developing the many methods of network analysis. Instead, we refer the reader to several sources that present a lucid description of the key concepts and terms of the field. Historical overviews are given by Galaskiewicz and Wasserman (1993), Wasserman and Faust (1994), Berkowitz (1982), Wellman (1988), Wellman and Berkowitz (1988), Burt (1982), and many others. Methodological reviews can be found in the texts of Wasserman and Faust (1994), Scott (1992), Marsden (1990), and Knoke and Kuklinski (1982).

For those of you who are "doing networks" for the first time, we recommend that you peruse these overviews and reviews before you venture into this volume. Although most authors take considerable care to explain all their terms, they, like us, had a page limit and they had to take some knowledge of network analysis for granted. We recommend that this volume be used in conjunction with a network methodological text, to give the network novice a complete, substantive, and methodological introduction to social network analysis. We do note that this volume is unique—no other collection has presented social network analysis from the perspective of such a wide variety of disciplines. Space prevents us from describing at length the chapters in this volume. As one can see, the chapters fall naturally into three parts:

1. Social psychology and diffusion
2. Anthropology and communication
3. Politics and organizations

In Part I, the chapter by Peter V. Marsden and Noah E. Friedkin explores the way network analysts have studied social influence processes. They argue that social relations provide a basis through which one actor alters the behavior or attitudes of another. Martina Morris shows how the spread of disease through human populations can be better understood by looking at the patterned networks of social contact. There are obvious implications here for understanding the spread of sexually transmitted diseases. Michael E. Walker, Stanley Wasserman, and Barry Wellman review the research on social support networks. They focus explicitly on the flow of resources (from information to money to whatever) among individuals and the consequences this has for individual well-being. Finally, Philippa Pattison describes how network concepts have advanced the field of cognitive psychology. She is particularly excited about the prospects of using different definitions of structural position to define social contexts or "locales."

The second part of the volume presents three papers on anthropology and communication. Jeffrey C. Johnson reviews the many contributions made by anthropology to network analysis, taking as a start Clyde Mitchell's wonderful review in the 1974 *Annual Review of Anthropology*. Highlighted in this chapter are advances in social cognition, kinship, and especially ethnography. Donald Stone Sade and Malcolm M. Dow describe nonhuman primate networks, giving a brief history of such studies, focusing on dominance hierarchies and social roles and structure. Finally, Ronald E. Rice reviews research on computer-mediated communication systems, such as computers and telecommunication systems. Network analysis has helped answer many research questions about such systems, such as whether systems cause certain outcomes, how actors interact to process resources and information, and what kind of system data to gather (including questions of accuracy and validity). The third part of the volume focuses on politics and organizations. Much of this work has been done in sociology and management science. David Krackhardt and Daniel Brass argue that many of the topics now under the umbrella of organizational behavior (for example, motivation, leadership, job design, turnover/absenteeism, and work attitudes) can be enlightened and extended using a network approach. They review several works on intraorganizational relations and power and influence in the workplace. Mark S. Mizruchi and Joseph Galaskiewicz focus on interorganizational relations. They show how network concepts have contributed greatly to resource dependency theory, the social class framework, and the "new" institutional analysis. Phipps Arabie and Yoram Wind review the work that has been done on social networks and marketing. In addition to the marketing channel and buying center literatures, marketing researchers are now using network analysis to better understand consumer behavior. Finally, David Knoke describes the voluminous work on social networks and elite decision making. In addition to reviewing the early work on elite networks, he describes recent research on interest group "networking" and the social construction of policy domains.

We hope all these chapters will soon be "dated." Our strategy for this volume is to send a "wake-up call" to researchers in different substantive areas and disciplines and to show them how theory and research in their fields can be extended using the social network approach. If our effort is a success, then all of these chapters will have to be revised in 5 years or so as a new generation of network analysts revolutionize the social and behavioral sciences once again.

References

Berkowitz, S. D. (1982). *An introduction to structural analysis: The network approach to social research*. Toronto: Butterworths.

Burt, R. S. (1982). *Towards a structural theory of action: Network models of social structure, perceptions, and action*. New York: Academic Press.

Galaskiewicz, J., & Wasserman, S. (1993). Social network analysis: Concepts, methodology, and directions for the 1990s. *Sociological Methods & Research, 22*, 3-22.

Knoke, D., & Kuklinski, J. H. (1982). *Network analysis*. Beverly Hills, CA: Sage.

Marsden, P. V. (1990). Network data and measurement. *Annual Review of Sociology, 16*, 435-463.

Scott, J. (1992). *Social network analysis.* Newbury Park, CA: Sage.

Wasserman, S., & Faust, K. (1994). *Social network analysis: Methods and applications.* New York: Cambridge University Press.

Wellman, B. (1988). Structural analysis: From method and metaphor to theory and substance. In B. Wellman & S. D. Berkowitz, (Eds.), *Social structures: A network approach* (pp. 19-61). Cambridge: Cambridge University Press.

Wellman, B., & Berkowitz, S. D. (1988). Introduction: Studying social structures. In B. Wellman & S. D. Berkowitz (Eds.), *Social structures: A network approach* (pp. 1-14). Cambridge: Cambridge University Press.

PART I

Social Psychology and Diffusion

1

Network Studies
of Social Influence

PETER V. MARSDEN
NOAH E. FRIEDKIN

The study of social influence is a strategic arena for social network research; it links the structure of social relations to attitudes and behaviors of the actors who compose a network. Such research is crucial to demonstrating the explanatory potential of the network approach by exhibiting what Laumann (1979) takes to be "the hallmark of a network analysis . . . to explain, at least in part, the behavior of network elements . . . by appeal to specific features of the interconnections among the elements" (p. 394).

Network analysts have developed a distinctive approach to social influence that entails a structural conceptualization of social proximity. The general hypothesis is that the proximity of two actors in social networks is associated with the occurrence of interpersonal influence between the actors. Thus, for example, in the context of a study of innovation diffusion, Burt (1987) describes the structural basis of influence as "something about the social structural circumstances of ego and alter [that] makes them proximate such that ego's evaluation of the innovation is sensitive to alter's adoption" (p. 1288).

Following March (1955) and Simon (1957), Cartwright (1965) argues that influence is "simply a special instance of causality, namely, the modification of one person's responses by the actions of another" (p. 3). The particular substantive processes that underlie influence are diverse and include relations of authority, identification, expertise, and compe-

3

tition. As we use the term, *influence* does not require face-to-face interaction; indeed, the only precondition for social influence is information (which allows social comparison) about the attitudes or behaviors of other actors. Influence does not require deliberate or conscious attempts to modify actors' attitudes or behaviors. It encompasses what Lippitt, Polansky, and Rosen (1952) term *behavioral contagion* involving "the spontaneous pickup or imitation by other . . . [actors] of a behavior initiated by one member of the group where the initiator did not display any intention of getting the others to do what he did" as well as *direct influence* "in which the actor initiates behavior which has the manifest objective of affecting the behavior of another member of the group" (p. 37).

Noteworthy tasks to be addressed by the network approach to social influence include (a) elucidating the substantive processes that underlie claims that there should be structural effects on the attitudes and behaviors of actors, (b) defining interpersonal proximity in a network in an appropriate manner given these processes, and (c) assessing the predictive success of the approach using available mathematical and statistical models of social influence processes. In this chapter, we contrast two perspectives on the environments in which interpersonal influence may be transmitted and the substantive processes that underlie such transmission. We review mathematical models of social influence and their implications; these lead toward statistical models for data analysis. Particular attention is given to the "network effects" or "mixed regressive-autoregressive" model. A number of applications of this and related statistical models are highlighted. The chapter concludes with comments on issues of research design, measurement, and conceptualization.

Two Perspectives on Social Influence

Two ways of measuring social proximity—structural cohesion and equivalence—have provided contrasting approaches to the study of social influence. The first, stemming from the sociometric tradition and its generalizations concerned with the definition of solidary network environments, emphasizes the network connectivity present among actors. The second, emanating from the factor-analytic tradition and its generalizations concerned with the definition of equivalent network positions, describes the similarity of actors in terms of their profiles of interpersonal relations. In this section, we review, compare, and contrast the structural features and substantive foundations of the two approaches.

Substantive Bases of Social Influence

Erickson (1988) organized her discussion of network foundations for attitude similarity around the theme of social comparison. This framework posits that, in a situation involving ambiguity, people obtain normative guidance by comparing their attitudes with those of a reference group of similar others. Attitudes are confirmed and reinforced when they are shared with the comparison group but altered when they are discrepant. This view of the process of attitude change is consistent with Moscovici's (1985) argument that the resolution of intra- and interpersonal conflict is the driving force in social influence processes.[1]

A difficult question, one on which network studies differ, is that of how reference groups—that is, sets of others regarded as similar—are determined. There are many different grounds that could lead one actor to treat a subset of other actors as a comparison point. The most rudimentary requirement is the possession of information about the attitude or behavior of another actor. Such information is sometimes a sufficient basis for influence, but it is necessary to the operation of all influence processes. Simmel (1950) and Merton (1968), among others, have acknowledged the key importance of interpersonal visibility as a condition of reference group behavior and social control; see, for example, Friedkin (1983), Skolnick and Woodworth (1967), and Raub and Weesie (1990). Obviously, this informational basis of influence may exist in the absence of face-to-face communication.

Social psychological studies emphasize the occurrence of some form of social power in the alteration of actors' views or actions. French and Raven (1959) identified five sources of social power: the capacity to coerce, the ability to reward, incumbency in a position of legitimacy or authority, recognized expertise, and referent power—which rests on identification, charisma, or esteem. Control over information has come to be seen as a sixth basis (Pettigrew, 1972; Raven, 1965).

Festinger (1954) proposed that influence between two actors declines as a function of the discrepancy of their opinions or behaviors. The assertion that actors are most influenced by similar others is a somewhat broader restatement of this fundamental proposition of social comparison theory. Actors tend to couple opinions with the expressed or imputed interests of the opinion holders; when discrepant opinions suggest substantially divergent interests, the basis of interpersonal influence is eroded. Thus influence tends to occur among actors with consistent interests.

Many views of influence assume that it is founded on solidary relations, such as friendship, or hierarchical ones, such as authority. An alternative view, most forcefully articulated by Burt (1987), emphasizes competition. Burt claims that those seeking normative guidance in the face of uncertainty engage in a process of role taking as they seek behavioral models appropriate to actors in their social location. They therefore come to imitate the actions of their competitors, to whom they need not be joined directly. The resulting influence process resembles the "mimetic isomorphism" discussed by DiMaggio and Powell (1983).

Interpersonal influences may contribute to uniformity, but so may other mechanisms. Cartwright (1965) describes a mechanism, ecological influence, whereby alter influences ego indirectly by affecting the conditions to which ego responds. The direct effect is not interpersonal. Along the same lines, actors may become homogeneous as a consequence of entirely independent responses to circumstances. Thus occupants of a given social position or environmental niche may come to share similar attitudes or behaviors if they respond similarly to their conditions. The common conditions, which may be material or cognitive, include economic circumstances and normative guidelines associated with the position or niche.

Usually the bases of interpersonal influence are intertwined. Two actors may simultaneously be friends and competitors, with each basis contributing to the responsiveness of one actor to the other. Actors who jointly occupy a social position are more likely to be tied by social relations than are actors who do not jointly occupy any social position; such ties allow a variety of interpersonal bases of social influence. Multiplex ties and multiple bases of power provide a stable context for the exertion of influence on a variety of attitudes and behaviors.

Characteristic features of the local environments of actors are sometimes indicative of contexts in which social influence is likely. Geographic proximity is a well-documented indicator of influence opportunities (e.g., Festinger, Schachter, & Back, 1950). Roles also powerfully shape their occupants' attitudes and behaviors via social influence mechanisms when they bring role occupants into regular interaction with other actors who have expectations about appropriate role behaviors. In this vein, social network analysis provides two broad approaches to indicating environments in which influence between particular pairs of actors is more or less likely.

Structural Cohesion

Structural cohesion defines social proximity in terms of the number, length, and strength of paths that connect actors in networks. The most restrictive definition of structural cohesion is simple adjacency whereby two actors are proximate if, and only if, they are directly tied in a network. Defining proximity in this way implies that reference groups are composed of those to which an actor has intense (usually affective) ties.

Generalizations of this definition permit two actors to be proximate, while not directly tied, if they are connected by numerous short connections via intermediaries. These include both generalizations pertaining to binary networks and refinements of these approaches that permit valued relations to enter into the definition of structural cohesion; for a review of these, see Wasserman and Faust (1994, chap. 7).

Generalizations of adjacency, as measures of social proximity, retain the idea that actors are proximate to the extent that they are jointly located in structurally cohesive regions of networks. The generalizations differ by emphasizing particular structural features. For example, the *n*-clique concept (Mokken, 1979) focuses on path distances among actors, while the *k*-plex concept (Seidman & Foster, 1978) is sensitive to the number and pattern of direct ties among actors.

Equivalence

The second approach defines social proximity in terms of the similarity of actors' *profiles* of network relations. The most restrictive definition within this approach defines two actors as proximate when they are structurally equivalent—that is, when they have identical relations with other actors (Lorrain & White, 1971). Under this definition, for example, two actors would be considered proximate—and thus influential on each other—only if they have exactly the same set of friends. The profile similarity approach to proximity has methodological ties with numerical taxonomy (Arabie & Hubert, 1992) and early factor-analytic approaches to cluster analysis (e.g., Lankford, 1974). It became prominent in the 1970s with the publication of several articles that illustrated the utility of these methods for sociological research (see, especially, White, Boorman, & Breiger, 1976).

Vigorous efforts to generalize this restrictive definition of structural equivalence have produced two lines of work. First, the qualitative definition of equivalence has been relaxed so that actors' *extent* of profile similarity can be assessed (e.g., Burt, 1976). Second, the concentration on relations to and from *particular* actors has been relaxed to allow definitions of "equivalent" network environments, in which members are tied to the same *types* of actors; for example, two actors are regarded as proximate if they are located in similar positions in the authority structures of two separate organizations. The contributions to this latter line of work are numerous; see Borgatti and Everett (1992) and the literature cited therein.

Social Processes in Cohesive and
Equivalent Network Environments

Measures of social proximity based on structural cohesion and equivalence are conceptually, if not empirically, independent. Neither approach subsumes the other as a special case. Both appear successful in locating clusters of actors with relatively homogeneous behaviors and attitudes, as we will see below. Cohesive and equivalent cluster memberships intersect in most networks, however, and corresponding overlap in the underlying social processes is therefore likely. Thus, without suitable statistical controls, it is difficult to assess the relative contributions of those processes, if any, that are operative only between actors who are structurally cohesive or equivalent, as the case may be.

Hypothetically, if two actors are not connected by any social network (including, in particular, interpersonal awareness), then a large number of substantive processes may be eliminated as plausible grounds for any behavioral or attitudinal homogeneity observed. In such a setting, actors in equivalent positions might exhibit a degree of homogeneity as a consequence of common material circumstances, cultural norms, or social roles. Role expectations will be "sent" by disjoint sets of actors who are connected to the occupants of the position. Hence army lieutenants may behave similarly because of the uniform military code and training that governs their behavior or because of the uniform role expectations among their immediate superiors and subordinates who also are governed by that code and training. Diverse material circumstances or role expectations should substantially reduce the homogeneity of relationally equivalent actors.

Similarly positioned actors, who are not connected by an interpersonal social network, nonetheless may be aware of each other's attitudes or behaviors; mass and local communication media (e.g., newspapers, professional journals) may provide such information in ways that do not entail information flow through interpersonal network channels. Given some visibility, a variety of social comparison mechanisms may come into play; such visibility need not involve an awareness of specific actors but may also entail general or aggregate information concerning the behavior of actors in the same or proximate social positions. Thus, for example, a focal actor may not learn that any specific actor has adopted an innovation but only that a large percentage of actors in similar locations (e.g., other farmers in Iowa or other pediatricians in Peoria) have adopted it.

Finally, consider actors who not only are similarly positioned and mutually visible but who also are joined in a structurally cohesive network. All of the bases of social influence discussed previously may be pertinent under those conditions.

Can we imagine a situation in which actors are structurally cohesive but not equivalent? An important and ubiquitous illustration is that of a superior and a subordinate within a single hierarchically organized group. The "lateral" and "vertical" ties of these two actors will tend not to overlap, and the extent to which they are structurally equivalent is likely to decrease as the distance separating them in a chain of command increases. Even actors in an immediate superior-subordinate relationship may differ substantially in their profiles of relations. Nevertheless, a superior's preferences are likely to be influential when they are communicated directly to the subordinate; indeed, this influence is arguably stronger the more distant (i.e., the less equivalent) the two actors are in the chain of command. Such interpersonal influence rests fundamentally on the authority relation, which is based on the superior's ability to punish and reward the subordinate; it also may involve the subordinate's identification with the superior and respect for the superior's expertise in particular domains of action.

Models of Influence

In what follows, we assume the existence of a stable influence network that describes the unmediated effect of one actor on another for all pairs in a set of actors. This section reviews several mathematical models that involve influence networks; these lead toward a model useful for data analysis.

The centerpiece of these models is a deterministic, discrete-time linear process in which an actor's attitudes or opinions are adjusted to those of the others who have some influence on the actor. Following French (1956), Harary (1959), and DeGroot (1974), this can be written

$$y_{t+1} = Wy_t \tag{1}$$

where y_t is an n-element column vector containing the attitudes of network units at time t and W is an n by n matrix of influence coefficients. Elements w_{ij} of W are usually taken to be nonnegative and further constrained such that they give relative influences:

$$\sum_{j=1}^{n} w_{ij} = 1. \tag{2}$$

In studies of social influence, empirical measurements of W are usually based on network indices of social proximity discussed above.

For individual element i, model 1 can be written

$$y_{i,t+1} = \sum_{j=1}^{n} w_{ij} y_{jt} \tag{3}$$

or, by virtue of constraint 2, as

$$y_{i,t+1} = y_{it} + \sum_{\substack{j=1 \\ j \neq i}}^{n} w_{ij} (y_{jt} - y_{it}) \tag{4}$$

Expression 3 shows that adjusted attitudes are a weighted mean of prior attitudes, while model 4 demonstrates that changes in attitudes result from an interaction between influence relations and attitude discrepancies.

In a broad class of influence networks, the influence process of model 1 will result in consensus. More general models allow for both disagreement and consensus as possible outcomes. Toward such generality, Friedkin (1986) elaborates model 1 with the stipulation that influence links are activated with probability γ. Marsden (1981) adds one iteration of an influence process like model 1 to an exchange model of collective decision making. This reduces variation in the outcomes of events under consideration without driving the process toward complete consensus.

Friedkin and Johnsen (1990) generalize model 1 by introducing covariates that determine initial attitudes y_0 and have a persisting effect on subsequent attitudes y_t. The equations of the model are

$$y_0 = Xb, \tag{5}$$

and

$$y_{t+1} = \alpha W y_t + \beta X b \tag{6}$$

where X is an n by p matrix of covariates (usually including a constant vector), b is a p-element column vector of regression coefficients for covariates, and α and β are weights for the endogenous and exogenous (initial) components of attitudes.[2]

Friedkin and Johnsen (1990, p. 197) demonstrate that the equilibrium attitudes under this model are

$$y_e = (I - \alpha W)^{-1} \beta X b = \alpha W y_e + \beta X b \tag{7}$$

Because of the continuing effect of initial conditions, complete consensus is not predicted by the model of equations 5-7 except as a limiting condition for $\alpha \to 1$. This model subsumes many other influence models. For example, by setting α to 1 and β to 0, model 1 is obtained.

Statistical Methods

Model 5-6 is dynamic, but empirical studies of social influence rarely work with longitudinal data; most researchers study data from cross-sectional designs and infer the operation of social influence from homogeneity among network elements that remains after adjusting for effects of covariates. A few studies have made use of over-time data and associated statistical methods. A distinct analytic approach focuses on dyadic homogeneity, relating dyadic network measures to the similarity of two network elements on a response.

The most sustained attention has been given to a statistical model related to model 7.[3] We refer to it as the "network effects model," specifying it as follows:

$$y = \alpha Wy + X\beta + \varepsilon \qquad (8)$$

In model 8, y is an n-element column vector containing measures on a response variable and ε is an n-element column vector of stochastic errors, usually taken to be normally distributed with mean 0 and covariance matrix $\sigma_\varepsilon^2 I$. Model 8 differs from model 7 in that vector b and parameter β in model 7 have been combined into vector β in model 8 and in that model 8 includes an error term while model 7 is deterministic. The model is appealing because it integrates covariate or "attribute" effects of variables in X on the outcome y with network or interdependence effects of Wy.

Because y appears on both sides of equation 8, ordinary least-squares (OLS) estimates are biased and inconsistent. The model can be estimated, however, by both maximum likelihood (ML) and instrumental variable/two-stage least-squares (IV/2SLS) methods. Doreian (1981) reviews the ML approach and provides a detailed derivation of the covariance matrix of parameters α and β (see also Anselin, 1988); Friedkin (1990b) and Anselin (1990) provide software implementing this technique. Anselin (1988) and Land and Deane (1992) outline IV/2SLS estimation procedures.

Findings pertinent to the performance of these estimators have been presented in two Monte Carlo studies. Doreian, Teuter, and Wang (1984) demonstrate that the ML approach is superior to ordinary least-squares (OLS) estimation ignoring the "influence" term Wy and to a "quick and dirty" (QAD) approach that includes Wy as an OLS regressor. Marsden and Andrews (1991) show that, as a result of the interelement dependence in the term Wy, both the ML and the IV/2SLS techniques can yield biased estimates when applied to data on a sample rather than a complete population.

Among alternatives to, and generalizations of, model 8 is the network autocorrelation model (e.g., Doreian, 1980, p. 33), which specifies that error terms are interdependent and that the response y is directly affected only by the covariates X:

$$y = X\beta + \varepsilon \qquad (9)$$

with

$$\varepsilon = \rho W \varepsilon + \upsilon \qquad (10)$$

where ρ is the network autocorrelation parameter and υ is a vector of random perturbations.

The important distinction between model 9-10 and model 8 lies in the way in which they incorporate interelement dependencies. The network effects model 8 includes direct effects of one element's response on another's, which is consistent with the presence of an influence process. In the network autocorrelation model 9-10, by contrast, the source of the interdependence of error terms is unspecified and could be due to various processes, such as ecological influence or environmental molding, that do not involve direct effects of actors on one another. Under model 9-10, the principal statistical consequence of ignoring the interelement dependence in W is inefficiency, whereas in model 8 bias and inconsistency result as well. Doreian (1980) indicates that it may be difficult to choose between these specifications for network interdependence on statistical grounds; substantive considerations may dictate one representation rather than the other. Some analysts, including most of those who study social influence, are intrinsically interested in the substantive process (e.g., influence, contagion) leading to interdependence of elements; they are often inclined toward the network effects model. Others view adjusting for interdependence as a methodological problem to be dealt with in the course of obtaining estimates of covariate effects β; many such researchers are disposed toward the autocorrelation model. Friedkin (1990a) argues that the latter view may be misleading; if interdependencies arise from direct effects among actors on the endogenous variable, then model 9-10 may not be appropriate.

Several authors elaborate on these two basic structures. Doreian (1982) and Anselin (1988) present estimation procedures for a model including both network effects and network autocorrelation, that is, a model specified by equations like 8 and 10, which may include distinct weight matrices W. Dow (1984) gives a biparametric version of the network autocorrelation model, allowing two distinct sources of correlation in the disturbances. Doreian (1989b) gives a similar generalization of the network effects model 8:

$$y = (\alpha_1 W_1 + \alpha_2 W_2)y + X\beta + \varepsilon. \qquad (11)$$

The properties of these formal elaborations warrant further attention. Model 11 seems particularly attractive for multiplex networks where direct effects vary for the different types of ties that may be present. It could also be used to assess the extent of homogeneity attributable to structural cohesion while controlling for equivalence, and vice versa.

Erbring and Young (1979) argue that model 8 is an appropriate structural representation for phenomena studied under the heading "contextual effects." Conventional specifications of contextual-effect models include group-level averages of explanatory variables on the right-hand side; a simple example is

$$y_{ij} = \eta + \beta_1 x_{ij} + \beta_2 \bar{x}_i + \varepsilon_{ij}, \qquad (12)$$

where y_{ij}, x_{ij}, and ε_{ij} are the dependent, independent, and disturbance variables for the jth element in the ith group, $\bar{x}_i$ is the mean level of x_{ij} within group i, and η, β_1, and β_2 are parameters. Erbring and Young claim that an implausible "social telepathy" is involved in the contextual effect β_2; they advocate model 8 in place of model 12.

Friedkin (1990a) elaborates model 8 to include network effects of exogenous conditions, that is, responses of actors to each other's values on an exogenous variable

$$y = \alpha_1 W_1 y + X\beta + \alpha_2 W_2 x_2 + \varepsilon \qquad (13)$$

where x_2 is a column vector for an exogenous variable and W_1 may equal W_2. Model 13 allows the exogenous conditions of significant others to have direct effects on actors. Actors may respond to the conditions of others whenever they are aware of those conditions. For example, views about Social Security could be affected by the ages of one's parents, independent of parental attitudes about Social Security.

A small number of network studies of influence have used longitudinal data. These have used models and methods that allow for time-lagged, rather than simultaneous, influence. Galaskiewicz and Wasserman (1989) analyze a two-wave panel study with a 4-year interval, introducing a number of lagged terms Wy_{t-1} as regressors in a logit analysis of a dichotomous dependent variable. Marsden and Podolny (1990) use event-history methods to examine network effects on rates of adopting an innovation, including lagged regressors with 1-month intervals (see also Strang, 1991; Strang & Tuma, 1993).

The use of lagged regressors to capture influence pressures simplifies estimation greatly; little attention, however, has been given by network analysts to the question of how to determine the appropriate lags. Model 6 is Markov-like and specifies that only the immediately prior time period is directly relevant. Other lag structures are certainly conceivable, and data collection intervals may not mirror lags in the transmission of influence. Furthermore, the discrete-time assumptions of model 5-6 are not necessarily realistic, and the question of how to specify lags for influence processes that take place in continuous time is open.

As noted at the beginning of this section, analysts typically infer the operation of social influence from homogeneity of network elements on the dependent variable of interest. Some argue that the similarity of pairs of actors should be studied directly (Erickson, 1988) rather than deduced from a model such as model 8. Mizruchi (1989), for example, takes this approach, specifying linear models that relate a measure of the behavioral similarity of pairs of corporations to measures of their geographic and social proximity. Because each corporation is involved in multiple dyads, Mizruchi uses a least-squares dummy-variable regression (LSDV) technique that includes dummy variables for the corporations in a dyad among the explanatory variables.

When the research question concerns influence processes affecting a single dependent variable, it would seem preferable to use the network effects model 8 rather than the dyadic approach. The $n(n - 1)/2$ similarities of pairs of network elements are a direct consequence of the n scores of the elements on y; using the dyadic approach, predicted similarity values for pairs need not conform to triadic constraints that dictate, for example, that the similarity of two elements is equal to the difference of their similarities to a third. Moreover, the influence model 5-6 that gives rise to model 8 is a more elaborated account of the influence process underlying similarity than that associated with the dyadic approach.

There may be advantages to the dyadic approach, however, when multiple dependent variables are at issue, as is the case in Mizruchi's study. The LSDV approach permits a more complete control for interunit heterogeneity than is possible in a cross-sectional network effects analysis. Studying an aggregate similarity indicator across m dependent variables may also be less unwieldy than m separate network effects analyses.[4]

Empirical Applications

In this section, we review selected empirical studies of social influence, with special attention to their findings and their measures of social foundations of influence. Virtually all the studies covered are nonexperimental; with the exception of Friedkin and Cook (1990), network researchers interested in influence have given little attention to experiments. Many of the applications mentioned make use of the network effects model. We begin with studies that use measures of social influence based on structural cohesion, turning then to those that involve structural equivalence-based measures.

A number of studies have employed a special case of model 8, specifying that actors are influenced equally by their significant others:

$$y = \alpha\bar{y} + X\beta + \varepsilon, \qquad (14)$$

where $\bar{y}$ is a column vector containing the mean responses of those who influence each actor. Known as the "standard peer effects" model, it has been used by sociologists of education to show that peer groups are important in shaping adolescents' aspirations and educational decisions (e.g., Davies & Kandel, 1981; Epstein, 1983; Sewell, Haller, & Ohlendorf, 1970). Few of these studies estimated model 14 taking into account the endogenous feedback that is implicit in it; see, however, Duncan, Haller, and Portes (1971).

Duke (1991), using ML estimation, applied the network effects model in an analysis of the educational and occupational aspirations, levels of academic performance, and educational attainments of a large sample of adolescents. His measures of influence channels W were based on sociometric citations of others whom a respondent "goes around with most often"; the study thus takes a structural cohesion approach. Duke found appreciable network effects and noted that models including them had greater explanatory power than contextual effect models like model 12.

Several studies focus on dyads. Best known among these is that by Duncan et al. (1971). They estimated nonrecursive structural equation models for dyads consisting of a survey respondent and another person cited as a "best friend," and found moderate reciprocal effects linking the educational and occupational aspirations of peers. Succeeding studies highlight the importance of including crucial covariates. Davies and Kandel (1981) reported weaker reciprocal influences for educational aspirations than those found by Duncan et al. and noted that influences of parents appeared substantially stronger than those of peers. Cohen (1983) argued that much peer homogeneity in educational aspirations is attributable to selection of similarly disposed friends rather than to interpersonal influence. In his panel analysis, peer influences declined by more than 50% once prior aspirations were controlled (see, also, the dyadic study of adolescent marijuana use; Kandel, 1978). Dyadic studies assume a simple influence structure. The study of dyads assumes that, in the population, matrix W in model 8 can be partitioned into isolated, two-element subsets; under such conditions, analyses of dyads will recover network effects (Marsden, 1988a). If, however, one assumes a structure of disjoint dyads when a person is, in fact, influenced by more than one other, or when sets of people influencing one another cannot be partitioned into discrete clusters, bias may be introduced in the estimation of influence effects; the available evidence suggests that such bias is likely to be downward (Marsden & Andrews, 1991).

Several network effects studies have dealt with territorial units. Gould (1991) examines levels of resistance in the Paris Commune of 1871 for *arrondissements*, finding that resistance levels were reinforced by interarrondissement overlaps in enlistment but not by simple geographic adjacency. Doreian (1981) provides two examples in which spatial adjacency is consequential, for diffusion of insurgency among Philippine municipalities and for presidential voting in Louisiana parishes. Land, Deane, and Blau (1991) report spatial effects on church adherence rates for U.S. counties; they measured elements w_{ij} of W as reciprocals of the geographic distances between county centroids. As Doreian (1981) notes, multiple interpretations—only one of which is social influence—are possible for the spatial effects in these studies.

Burt and Doreian (1982) studied perceptions of the significance of journals by prominent sociological methodologists. They estimated model 8 separately, using two alternative measurements of W. To operationalize the cohesion model, they used citations of other scientists as sources of influential comments. They also examined a measure of W based on structural equivalence within the "influential comments" network. Their findings are compatible with both approaches to influence, though estimates of α were slightly higher for the W based on structural equivalence.

Burt (1987) offered additional evidence on the cohesion and equivalence approaches in an analysis of adoptions of a new drug by physicians. There was virtually no indication in OLS results that strongly tied physicians adopted at similar times, while there was a tendency to do so among structurally equivalent pairs. Galaskiewicz and Burt (1991) reported similar findings in a study of corporate philanthropy. Burt and Uchiyama (1989) presented further analyses of the drug-adoption data, suggesting that direct ties become important when social structure is ambiguous, that is, when network elements are only weakly equivalent.

Friedkin's (1984) analyses of agreement among educational policy-makers yield different implications about how structural cohesion and equivalence affect homogeneity. Friedkin reports that joint membership in cohesive social circles and joint occupancy of structurally equivalent positions were both substantially associated, on a bivariate level, with perceived agreement; the stronger of these was for social circles. The association between structural equivalence and agreement persisted only for dyads linked by direct contact, while common circle member-ship led to agreement regardless of whether direct contact was present.

A number of organizational studies examine one or both of the theoretical perspectives on influence. Mizruchi's (1989, 1990) results show that firms in the same primary industry tend to support similar profiles of political candidates. He takes common primary industry as an indicator of structural equivalence, and this may, indeed, be a more direct measure of competition than is a network-based index of equiva-lence. Mizruchi also found that similarity increases if two firms are in strongly related industries and if they are indirectly interlocked through banks or insurance companies.[5] Overall, Mizruchi concludes that influ-ence relations are best indexed by structural equivalence measures. Davis (1991), however, reports contrary findings in an analysis of the adoption of "poison pill" takeover defenses by *Fortune* 500 corpora-tions; corporations heavily interlocked with previous adopters were substantially more likely to adopt poison pills, but the level of prior adoption by competitors (those in a corporation's primary industry) had little association with adoption.

Galaskiewicz and Wasserman (1989), in a two-wave panel study, examined factors influencing corporate charitable contributions. They found that the social foundations of such giving decisions are interper-sonal networks linking the donation officers of corporations, shared membership (boards of directors, social clubs) networks connecting corporate chief executive officers, and interlocking directorates among nonprofits. Adherents of both perspectives on social influence can find support among these findings.

Contributions, Problems, and Open Issues

Network studies have been successful in developing models, methods, and evidence to support the claim that the social structural contexts surrounding actors shape a variety of responses, both attitudinal and behavioral. Theoretical models like 5-6 and models for data analysis like model 8 integrate a key postulate of the network orientation—that units are interdependent—into models that also involve covariates describing the heterogeneity of network elements. Analysts can thus avoid the dichotomy sometimes posed between individual attributes and interunit relations as explanatory factors. Such models relax restrictive assumptions entailed in some previous approaches to the study of influence: Analyses need not be confined to the study of dyads; weights w_{ij} indicating the influences of elements on one another need not be equal; and the elements of W can be chosen to operationalize a variety of hypotheses about the social foundations of influence. Some of these hypotheses do not require that W be based on face-to-face interactions.

In this concluding discussion, we highlight some conceptual and methodological issues faced by network studies of social influence. When influence networks are added to models that predict attitudes and behaviors, specification issues arise that go beyond those commonly encountered in multivariate data analysis.

Claims about effects of social influence networks are based largely on evidence that comes from nonexperimental, cross-sectional studies. Analysts infer the operation of influence processes from associations between interactor homogeneity and network patterns that persist after controls for individual covariates. Such inferences can, of course, be hazardous, for reasons that are among the common threats to validity in nonexperimental designs.

One possibility is that observed homogeneity is a result of selection; the associations could be observed because actors use similarity on the response at issue as a basis for forming relationships, instead of altering their response toward conformity with those of others within their networks.[6] Omitted or erroneously measured covariates could also produce spurious findings; this is a plausible risk given the numerous studies that demonstrate that network ties tend to join similar actors (e.g., Marsden, 1988b). Exposure to alternative sources of influence should receive special consideration. Network models of influence covered here focus on element-to-element transmission within a closed set of actors. Elementary diffusion models (e.g., Lave & March, 1975) also allow transmission from external sources, such as mass media, and nonexperimental studies must consider exposure to such sources if they are to properly assess the extent of internal influence.

The interpretation of findings of patterned homogeneity could be especially subject to ambiguity when equivalence is posited as a social foundation for influence, because there is no direct evidence that equivalent elements are aware of one another. Homogeneity by equivalence could proxy the omission of covariates, or it could be the result of similar responses to environmental constraints rather than of a process of influence. In the latter case—which would seem a plausible account for findings that homogeneity is patterned by role equivalence rather than structural equivalence (Borgatti & Everett, 1992)—interelement dependence might be modeled better as network autocorrelation than as a network effect.

Alternative research designs may be of some aid in clarifying these issues. Longitudinal data sets would yield some control over the selection problem, for example. Experiments could help too, but to yield insight into the social foundations of influence relations, they would have to be different than the experiments reported in the social psychological literature (Moscovici, 1985). In particular, they would have to involve interaction structures that are less than fully connected; Friedkin and Cook's (1990) experiments on opinion consensus do, but were not intended to disentangle the relative merits of structural cohesion and equivalence approaches to influence.

Experiments will not, in any event, yield understanding of how "people choose among their contacts in ongoing social life, as opposed to choosing among hypothetical strangers in a laboratory" (Erickson, 1988, p. 117). Debates about alternative social foundations for influence concern interactional networks, while influence itself necessarily involves some cognitive process after which outward behaviors and/or inner beliefs are adjusted. Some important nonexperimental work is therefore indicated on the interpenetration between interactional networks of social relations and certain cognitive networks involved in social influence processes. Friedkin's (1983) study of awareness networks provides one example. It shows that scientists separated by more than one intermediary in a communication network were rarely aware of one another's research work. Awareness does not imply influence, but it is a necessary condition for it; similar research could profitably be done on reports about flows of influence. This would help to illuminate the foundational question of how interactional networks contribute to constructing reference groups.

If such studies were to examine several interactional networks, they also might provide guidance about the relation contents to be included in measurements of the network weights in W. The assumption of the structural cohesion perspective on influence is that asymmetries in network ties reflect discrepancies in social power; if measures based on a particular form of interaction miss some resource inequalities, then influence effects may be erroneously attributed to covariate or attribute measures. Similar problems arise for the structural equivalence approach if the selection of role models is based on attribute similarities not fully captured by network measures.

Other specification questions arise when one consults the social psychological literature on influence (Moscovici, 1985; Worchel, Cooper, & Goethals, 1991). That literature reports "majority effects": Conformity pressures are much stronger when a subject is confronted by a unanimous social environment than when there is even a single dissenter. Majority influence seems to rise as the majority grows, but the increase is slower once there are three others. These observations suggest that the appropriate specification for influence models might be nonlinear.

Nonlinearity also would be indicated if it is so that "beyond a certain discrepancy [in initial positions] influence should tend to decrease and eventually become nonexistent" (Moscovici, 1985, p. 354). This suggests a nonlinear relationship between the discrepancy term in model 4 and change in the response; such a process might lead to a "separating equilibrium" in which subgroups converge on discrepant attitudes or behavior.

Social psychological studies also might be pertinent to the selection of covariates. Individual differences in commitment, behavioral style, and capacity or susceptibility to influence could prove important in two ways. They might directly affect the response itself. They could also be important bases for differences in the influence weights w_{ij}.

Notes

1. Moscovici, however, deemphasizes the condition of ambiguity on the grounds of experimental evidence showing that social pressure results in change in perceptions even when objective evidence is accessible.

2. Friedkin and Johnsen (1990) begin with a more general model that includes time subscripts for X, W, b, α, and β; model 5-6 gives a version specialized to static conditions.

3. Model 8 is sometimes called the spatial effects model (Doreian, 1981) because it was initially proposed by geostatisticians interested in the study of spatial dependence; Cressie (1991) discusses it among "lattice models" for spatial data analysis. Anselin (1988), following Ord (1975), refers to it as the "mixed regressive-autoregressive model" to emphasize its parallels to econometric models. Terms related to the study of social influence include the "endogenous feedback model of social conformity" (Erbring & Young, 1979), the "network model" (Friedkin, 1990a), and the "network effects model" (Doreian, 1989a).

4. Mizruchi's dependent variable is an aggregate similarity indicator based on a large number of dichotomous measures of whether or not a corporation contributed to a particular candidate, each of which would have to be treated as a separate dependent variable if the network effects model were to be used to analyze the data. A suitable multivariate generalization of the network effects model would be $Y = WYA + XB + E$ where Y and E are n by m matrices of dependent variables and stochastic errors, respectively; A is an m by m matrix of network effects; and B is a p by m matrix of covariate effects. Estimates based on such a model would have implications for interelement similarity; the functional form linking similarity to other dyadic properties is not clear, but is not necessarily linear.

5. See also Clawson and Neustadtl's (1989) findings on corporate interlocks and contributions to political candidates.

6. Just such a selection process is suggested by Festinger's (1954) assertion that actors are most influenced by similar others; this suggests that the size of the influence weight w_{ij} in model 4 is affected by the attitude discrepancy $(y_{jt} - y_{it})$.

References

Anselin, L. (1988). *Spatial econometrics: Methods and models*. Dordrecht, the Netherlands: Kluwer Academic.

Anselin, L. (1990). *SPACESTAT: A program for the statistical analysis of spatial data*. Santa Barbara: University of California, National Center for Geographic Information and Analysis.

Arabie, P., & Hubert, L. J. (1992). Combinatorial data analysis. *Annual Review of Psychology, 43,* 169-203.

Borgatti, S. P., & Everett, M. G. (1992). Notions of position in social network analysis. In P. V. Marsden (Ed.), *Sociological methodology 1992* (pp. 1-35). Oxford: Blackwell.

Burt, R. S. (1976). Positions in networks. *Social Forces, 55,* 93-122.

Burt, R. S. (1987). Social contagion and innovation: Cohesion versus structural equivalence. *American Journal of Sociology, 92,* 1287-1335.

Burt, R. S., & Doreian, P. (1982). Testing a structural model of perception: Conformity and deviance with respect to journal norms in elite sociological methodology. *Quality and Quantity, 16,* 109-150.

Burt, R. S., & Uchiyama, T. (1989). The conditional significance of communication for interpersonal influence. In M. Kochen (Ed.), *The small world* (pp. 67-99). Norwood, NJ: Ablex.

Cartwright, D. (1965). Influence, leadership, control. In J. G. March (Ed.), *Handbook of organizations* (pp. 1-47). Chicago: Rand McNally.

Clawson, D., & Neustadtl, A. (1989). Interlocks, PACs, and corporate conservatism. *American Journal of Sociology, 94*, 749-773.

Cohen, J. (1983). Peer influence on college aspirations with initial aspirations controlled. *American Sociological Review, 48*, 728-734.

Cressie, N. (1991). *Statistics for spatial data.* New York: Wiley.

Davies, M., & Kandel, D. B. (1981). Parental and peer influences on adolescents' educational plans: Some further evidence. *American Journal of Sociology, 87*, 363-387.

Davis, G. F. (1991). Agents without principles? The spread of the poison pill through the intercorporate network. *Administrative Science Quarterly, 36*, 583-613.

DeGroot, M. H. (1974). Reaching a consensus. *Journal of the American Statistical Association, 69*, 118-121.

DiMaggio, P. J., & Powell, W. W. (1983). The iron cage revisited: Institutional isomorphism and collective rationality in organizational fields. *American Sociological Review, 48*, 147-160.

Doreian, P. (1980). Linear models with spatially distributed data: Spatial disturbances or spatial effects. *Sociological Methods and Research, 9*, 29-60.

Doreian, P. (1981). Estimating linear models with spatially distributed data. In S. Leinhardt (Ed.), *Sociological methodology 1981* (pp. 359-388). San Francisco: Jossey-Bass.

Doreian, P. (1982). Maximum likelihood methods for linear models: Spatial effect and spatial disturbance terms. *Sociological Methods and Research, 10*, 243-269.

Doreian, P. (1989a). Network autocorrelation models: Problems and prospects. In D. A. Griffith (Ed.), *Spatial statistics: Past, present, future* (pp. 369-389). Ann Arbor: Michigan Document Services.

Doreian, P. (1989b). Two regimes of network effects autocorrelation. In M. Kochen (Ed.), *The small world* (pp. 280-295). Norwood, NJ: Ablex.

Doreian, P., Teuter, K., & Wang, C. (1984). Network autocorrelation models: Some Monte Carlo results. *Sociological Methods and Research, 13*, 155-200.

Dow, M. M. (1984). A biparametric approach to network autocorrelation. *Sociological Methods and Research, 13*, 201-217.

Duke, J. B. (1991). *The peer context and the adolescent society: Making sense of the context effects paradox.* Unpublished doctoral dissertation, Harvard University.

Duncan, O. D., Haller, A. O., & Portes, A. (1971). Peer influences on aspirations: A reinterpretation. In H. M. Blalock, Jr. (Ed.), *Causal models in the social sciences* (pp. 219-244). Chicago: Aldine.

Epstein, J. L. (1983). The influence of friends on achievement and affective outcomes. In J. L. Epstein & N. Karweit (Eds.), *Friends in school: Patterns of selection and influence in secondary schools* (pp. 177-200). New York: Academic Press.

Erbring, L., & Young, A. A. (1979). Individuals and social structure: Contextual effects as endogenous feedback. *Sociological Methods and Research, 7*, 396-430.

Erickson, B. H. (1988). The relational basis of attitudes. In B. Wellman & S. D. Berkowitz (Eds.), *Social structures: A network approach* (pp. 99-121). New York: Cambridge University Press.

Festinger, L. (1954). A theory of social comparison processes. *Human Relations, 7*, 117-140.

Festinger, L., Schachter, S., & Back, K. (1950). *Social pressures in informal groups: A study of human factors in housing.* New York: Harper.

French, J. R. P., Jr. (1956). A formal theory of social power. *The Psychological Review, 63*, 181-194.

French, J. R. P., & Raven, B. H. (1959). The bases of social power. In D. Cartwright (Ed.), *Studies in social power* (pp. 150-167). Ann Arbor: University of Michigan Press.

Friedkin, N. E. (1983). Horizons of observability and limits of informal control in organizations. *Social Forces, 62*, 54-77.

Friedkin, N. E. (1984). Structural cohesion and equivalence explanations of social homogeneity. *Sociological Methods and Research, 12*, 235-261.

Friedkin, N. E. (1986). A formal theory of social power. *Journal of Mathematical Sociology, 12*, 103-126.

Friedkin, N. E. (1990a). Social networks in structural equation models. *Social Psychology Quarterly, 53*, 316-328.

Friedkin, N. E. (1990b). SNAPS (Social Network Analysis Procedures) for GAUSS. *Social Networks, 12*, 173-178.

Friedkin, N. E., & Cook, K. S. (1990). Peer group influence. *Sociological Methods and Research, 19*, 122-143.

Friedkin, N. E., & Johnsen, E. C. (1990). Social influence and opinions. *Journal of Mathematical Sociology, 15*, 193-205.

Galaskiewicz, J., & Burt, R. S. (1991). Interorganization contagion in corporate philanthropy. *Administrative Science Quarterly, 36*, 88-105.

Galaskiewicz, J., & Wasserman, S. (1989). Mimetic processes within an interorganizational field: An empirical test. *Administrative Science Quarterly, 34*, 454-479.

Gould, R. V. (1991). Multiple networks and mobilization in the Paris Commune, 1871. *American Sociological Review, 56*, 716-729.

Harary, F. (1959). A criterion for unanimity in French's theory of social power. In D. Cartwright (Ed.), *Studies of social power* (pp. 168-182). Ann Arbor, MI: Institute for Social Research.

Kandel, D. B. (1978). Homophily, selection and socialization in adolescent friendships. *American Journal of Sociology, 84*, 427-436.

Land, K. C., & Deane, G. (1992). On the large-sample estimation of regression models with spatial or network effects terms: A two-stage least-squares approach. In P. V. Marsden (Ed.), *Sociological methodology 1992* (pp. 221-248). Oxford: Blackwell.

Land, K. C., Deane, G., & Blau, J. R. (1991). Religious pluralism and church membership: A spatial diffusion model. *American Sociological Review, 56*, 237-249.

Lankford, P. M. (1974). Comparative analysis of clique identification methods. *Sociometry, 37*, 287-305.

Laumann, E. O. (1979). Network analysis in large social systems: Some theoretical and methodological problems. In P. W. Holland & S. Leinhardt (Eds.), *Perspectives on social network research* (pp. 379-402). New York: Academic Press.

Lave, C. A., & March, J. G. (1975). *An introduction to models in the social sciences.* New York: Harper & Row.

Lippitt, R., Polansky, N., & Rosen, S. (1952). The dynamics of power. *Human Relations, 5*, 37-64.

Lorrain, F., & White, H. C. (1971). Structural equivalence of individuals in social networks. *Journal of Mathematical Sociology, 1*, 49-80.

March, J. G. (1955). An introduction to the theory and measurement of influence. *American Political Science Review, 49*, 431-451.

Marsden, P. V. (1981). Introducing influence processes into a system of collective decisions. *American Journal of Sociology, 86*, 1203-1235.

Marsden, P. V. (1988a, February). *Influence models for survey network data: Initial simulation results.* Paper presented at the Sunbelt Social Network Conference, San Diego.

Marsden, P. V. (1988b). Homogeneity in confiding relations. *Social Networks, 10*, 57-76.

Marsden, P. V., & Andrews, S. B. (1991). *Network sampling and the network effects model.* Unpublished manuscript, Harvard University.

Marsden, P. V., & Podolny, J. (1990). Dynamic analysis of network diffusion processes. In J. Weesie & H. Flap (Eds.), *Social networks through time* (pp. 197-214). Utrecht, the Netherlands: University of Utrecht/ISOR.

Merton, R. K. (1968). *Social theory and social structure.* New York: Free Press.

Mizruchi, M. S. (1989). Similarity of political behavior among large American corporations. *American Journal of Sociology, 95*, 401-424.

Mizruchi, M. S. (1990). Cohesion, structural equivalence, and similarity of behavior: An approach to the study of corporate political power. *Sociological Theory, 8*, 16-32.

Mokken, R. J. (1979). Cliques, clubs and clans. *Quality and Quantity, 13*, 161-173.

Moscovici, S. (1985). Social influence and conformity. In G. Lindzey & E. Aronson (Eds.), *The handbook of social psychology* (Vol. 2, pp. 347-412). New York: Random House.

Ord, K. (1975). Estimation methods for models of spatial interaction. *Journal of the American Statistical Association, 70*, 120-126.

Pettigrew, A. M. (1972). Information control as a power resource. *Sociology, 6*, 187-204.

Raub, W., & Weesie, J. (1990). Reputation and efficiency in social interactions: An example of network effects. *American Journal of Sociology, 96*, 626-654.

Raven, B. H. (1965). Social influence and power. In I. D. Steiner & M. Fishbein (Eds.), *Current studies in social psychology* (pp. 371-382). New York: Holt, Rinehart & Winston.

Seidman, S. B., & Foster, B. L. (1978). A graph-theoretic generalization of the clique concept. *Journal of Mathematical Sociology, 6*, 139-154.

Sewell, W. H., Haller, A. O., & Ohlendorf, G. (1970). The educational and early occupational attainment process: Replication and revision. *American Sociological Review, 35*, 1014-1027.

Simmel, G. (1950). *The sociology of Georg Simmel.* New York: Free Press.

Simon, H. A. (1957). *Models of man.* New York: Wiley.

Skolnick, J. H., & Woodworth, J. R. (1967). Bureaucracy, information, and social control: A study of a moral detail. In D. J. Bordua (Ed.), *The police: Six sociological essays* (pp. 99-136). New York: Wiley.

Strang, D. (1991). Adding social structure to diffusion models: An event history framework. *Sociological Methods and Research, 19*, 324-353.

Strang, D., & Tuma, N. B. (1993). Spatial and temporal heterogeneity in diffusion. *American Journal of Sociology, 99*, 614-639.

Wasserman, S., & Faust, K. (1994). *Social network analysis: Methods and applications.* New York: Cambridge University Press.

White, H. C., Boorman, S. A., & Breiger, R. L. (1976). Social structure from multiple networks. I: Blockmodels of roles and positions. *American Journal of Sociology, 81*, 730-781.

Worchel, S., Cooper, J., & Goethals, G. R. (1991). *Understanding social psychology.* Pacific Grove, CA: Brooks/Cole.

2

Epidemiology and Social Networks

Modeling Structured Diffusion

MARTINA MORRIS

Social networks play an important role in the spread of infectious disease, but one that has been largely ignored. Perhaps due to the long and spectacular list of successes produced by medical biology, from vaccines to treatments to cures, disease has come to be framed almost entirely in biological terms. Biological factors clearly play a critical role in the spread of disease, regulating the transmissibility and natural history of the infectious agent. Social factors, however, are also important, as these regulate the patterns of interpersonal contact and thus the structure within which transmission is channeled.

In the field of epidemiology, attention has historically been restricted to biological factors. Modeling efforts have focused almost exclusively on natural history of the infectious agent: the period of infectiousness, the duration of latency or incubation, the duration of the illness, the rate of mortality, the existence of natural or exposure-related immunity, the role of disease-spreading vectors like insects. This tradition of research has produced both a well-integrated framework of statistical estimation from epidemiological and experimental data and simulation models for projection. The standard reference texts are Bailey (1975), Anderson (1982), and Anderson and May (1991). The dominant assumption made

AUTHOR'S NOTE: Supported in part by grant SES-91-10798 from the National Science Foundation. Address reprint requests to M. Morris, Department of Sociology, Columbia University, New York, NY 10027.

regarding social factors has been the assumption of random mixing (also referred to as homogeneous mixing). While this choice of focus might be expected in epidemiology, it is somewhat surprising that sociologists have not really challenged the biologically driven analysis of disease. It is as though we too are convinced that disease is not a proper topic for sociological inquiry.

Most people recognize that infectious disease has played an important role in social history. The most infamous cases include the disastrous effects of introducing European diseases, especially smallpox, into the Native American population, and the sequence of plagues in Europe (see McNeill, 1976).

The flip side of this coin is that various structural aspects of social relations have always served to channel these diseases. Like other exchangeable goods, for example, information, wealth, occupational access, and norms, the diffusion of disease through a human population traces the structure of social networks. Different kinds of diseases travel along different structural routes. The plague, for example, is spread by a mobile vector of rats and fleas. This makes for an efficient, long-lasting infectious vehicle and opens up the potential for spread via long-distance transportation routes; in 14th-century Europe, this meant trade routes. In such cases, macro-economic structures dominate the diffusion path. With the measles, by contrast, there is a relatively short infectious period, and transmission involves either casual or indirect contact. Such diseases are more likely to evolve as geographically localized processes structured by centers of collective activity like schools and supermarkets. Finally, there are diseases spread only by intimate or prolonged contact, such as sexually transmitted diseases. These diseases travel along the most selective forms of social networks, operating on what is comparatively a microstructure.

From a modeling perspective, epidemiologists have made some progress incorporating the first two forms of spatially structured diffusion, but very little on the last. It is in this last area—the patterns of differential association—that the tools of social network analysis are beginning to be used.

Structured Diffusion in Epidemiology

The foundations of modern mathematical epidemiology were laid in the early part of this century. Though, perhaps, never explicitly recognized as such, sociological dynamics have played a part in these models from the beginning. In one of the earliest contributions to formal modeling, the role of social contact in the spread of disease was expressed as a "mass action principle" (Hamer, 1906). This principle defined the population dynamics of an epidemic in a simple and intuitive way, proportional to the product of three factors: the probability that one member of the contact is susceptible, the probability that the other is infected, and the number of effective contacts made between individuals per unit time. The first two factors are conventionally defined as the relative fraction of each group in the population. The third factor is a function of the number of contacts and the probability of transmission per contact. Despite the proliferation of additional terms in modern models of disease dynamics, this mass action principle remains central.

Some of the most important later contributions include the threshold theorem of Kermack and McKendrick (1927), which ties the outbreak of an epidemic to the density of susceptibles, the development of stochastic formulations to mimic the role of chance and variation (Bailey, 1975; Bartlett, 1955, 1956), and the parameterization of models in terms of a "reproductive rate," R, a measure of the number of new cases generated by each infective that serves as a practical index for measuring the rate of spread or for tracking the effectiveness of immunization efforts (Anderson, 1982). Both stochastic and deterministic formulations are used in the field. Mollison (1977, 1991) provides an excellent, though non-social science-oriented, review of the relative strengths, weaknesses, and comparative predictions of deterministic and stochastic models of diffusion. Analytic solutions for the dependence of the epidemic on key parameters are often impossible. With stochastic models, for example, analytic solutions are typically only available for the pure birth versions of the models (known as simple epidemic models); birth-death processes (known as general epidemic models), even the simplest kind, are intractable (Bailey, 1975, pp. 88 ff.). For this reason, much of the work involves either strong simplifying assumptions, asymptotic approximations, or simulation.

The stochastic-deterministic split in epidemic modeling is analogous to the sociometric-egocentric split in network analysis. Stochastic formulations, like sociometric analyses, model each individual node in a system and the links among them. In network analysis, such data are typically represented as a sociomatrix or sociogram. Deterministic formulations, like egocentric analyses, divide the population into relatively homogeneous groups and map the average rates of contact among them. These models are sometimes called "compartmental models" in epidemiology. In network analysis, such data are typically represented in the form of a contact or mixing matrix.

The most systematic work on structured diffusion has been in the area of spatial models (for a social science-oriented review, see Bartholomew, 1973, pp. 323-334). This work is typically based on stochastic models. Selection bias here operates as a simple function of physical proximity: the closer two individuals are, the higher the probability that they will come into contact. The position of individuals is modeled either in continuous space, using distributions from the exponential family (Fisher, 1937; Van den Bosch, Metz, & Diekmann, 1990), or in discrete space, with individuals arrayed on a lattice (Cox & Durrett, 1988; Harris, 1974). Because of their simplicity and ease of simulation, lattices are the most common framework for modeling two-dimensional space, and contacts are often restricted to the "nearest-neighbor" in the lattice (Harris, 1974). The nearest-neighbor epidemic models are equivalent to percolation models under certain conditions (Mollison, 1977, p. 302). The simplicity of the lattice comes at a price, however, as the shape of the grid (e.g., square with four neighbors, square with eight neighbors, or hexagonal) has been shown to affect the type of epidemic patterns observed in simulation (Lloyd, 1991). Continuous diffusion approximations have also been used, and work is beginning to be done on modeling epidemics on random graphs (e.g., Mollison & Barbour, 1989). Models for spatially distributed populations have been considered in Cliff and Ord (1975), Hethcote (1976, 1978), Mollison (1977), and May and Anderson (1984a, 1984b). Other references may be found in these articles.

For most social processes, however, factors other than physical distance contribute to biased mixing. Spatial models can be adapted to make use of some more socially relevant metrics. Hagerstrand (1967), a geographer interested in the spread of innovations, modified a simple spatial model by mapping the frequency of telephone contacts among regions and using these as the basis for probabilities of contact in his simulations. A similar approach has been used more recently in a simulation study of the global spread of influenza (see Longini, Fine, & Thacker, 1986, for a review). Here, the volume of airline travel was used as the metric of distance among regions. A social distance metric could potentially be constructed by several commonly used methods (e.g., multidimensional scaling, factor analysis, log-linear models, and latent class analysis). The potential for spatial models to represent biased mixing is there and, as yet, largely untapped.

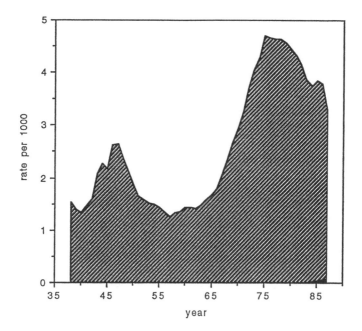

Figure 2.1. U.S. Gonorrhea Rate, 1938-1987
SOURCE: *Morbidity and Mortality Weekly Review, Summary of Notifiable Diseases* (1987).

Outside of spatial models, few attempts were made to model nonrandom mixing until the late 1970s and early 1980s when, despite the relative availability of penicillin and other antibiotics, gonorrhea rates rose precipitously (see Figure 2.1). To understand and potentially control the population dynamics of this sexually transmitted disease, it was recognized that specific forms of selective mixing would have to be modeled.

Compartmental models were typically adopted for modeling selective mixing. In almost all cases, the models were built around contact or mixing matrices, a cross-tabulation of partnerships by the category of the subject and the category of the partner. Typically, both the group definitions and the mixing functions were very simple. Activity level was the most common characteristic used to form groups, distinguishing those with high levels of sexual activity (e.g., prostitutes, highly active homosexuals) from those with low levels. This approach was pioneered by Lajmanovich and Yorke (1976) and popularized by Hethcote and

Yorke (1984) in their modeling of core populations in gonorrhea dynamics. In this early work, the rates of contact between groups were assumed to be governed by proportionate mixing (see also Barbour, 1978; Hethcote & Van Ark, 1987; Nold, 1980). Under this assumption, one group's exposure to another is proportional to the total number of contacts made by each group rather than the total number of people, a small variation on the original random mixing formulation. Letting π_{ij} denote the proportion of group is contacts that are with js,

$$\pi_{ij} = \frac{c_j N_j}{\sum_k c_k N_k} = \pi_j, \tag{1}$$

where $c_{(\cdot)}$ is the group-specific average number of partners per unit time, and $N_{(\cdot)}$ is the number in the group. The π_{ij}s are conditional probabilities that sum to one across the index j. This formulation, while it recognizes population heterogeneity, still assumes homogeneous mixing; every group has the same fraction of their contacts with group j. Proportionate mixing is equivalent to the statistical assumption of independence in the contact matrix. Under this assumption, for example, female prostitutes and highly active male homosexuals, by virtue of their high relative activity levels, would have a great deal of interaction. What is still ignored is social selectivity.[1]

The first real model for selection bias in epidemiology, the "like-with-like" or "preferred mixing" model, introduced a single parameter to reflect the tendency to choose a partner from one's own group (Anderson, Gupta, & Ng, 1990; Hethcote & Van Ark, 1987; Hethcote & Yorke, 1984; Hethcote, Yorke, & Nold, 1982; Jacquez, Simon, Koopman, Sattenspiel, & Perry, 1988; Nold, 1980). The bias parameter in this model is similar in function to the homophily bias parameter used in network analysis (Fararo & Sunshine, 1964). Under this model, the fraction of contacts between group i and group j is given by

$$\pi_{ij} = \begin{cases} \rho + (1 - \rho)\pi_j & i = j \\ (1 - \rho)\pi_j & i \neq j, \end{cases} \tag{2}$$

where ρ is the homophily bias parameter, the fraction of contacts reserved for partners from the same group, and π_j is the proportional mixing fraction defined in equation 1 above, the fraction of all contacts that are made by group j. As the homophily bias varies from 0 to 1, mixing varies from proportional to restricted (within-group contacts only). One of the earliest papers to use this approach was concerned with the role of selection bias in the relative effectiveness of three contact-tracing methods in the control of gonorrhea (Hethcote et al., 1982). Using an eight-group model defined by gender, symptomatic status, and high or low activity level and a single parameter to measure homophily, they found that the relative efficiency of different contact-tracing methods was directly related to the degree of homophily. In simulation models for the spread of AIDS, the introduction of a homophily parameter was found to slow the rise of incidence of the disease (De Gruttola & Mayer, 1988) and to result in the generation of sequential waves of infection as the virus moves through the different groups in the population (Hyman & Stanley, 1988). This approach has also been generalized to allow for differential homophily, group-specific biases with a parameter ρ_i for each group (Jacquez, Simon, & Koopman, 1989). While homophily bias models, uniform and differential, introduce an important form of selective mixing, they do so only on the diagonal of the contact matrix; out-group contacts continue to be allocated proportionally.

Before the early 1980s, there were virtually no models in which preference orderings for out-group contacts could be introduced. One exception is a paper by Lajmanovich and Yorke (1976). Here, no constraints are placed on the variability in contact rates among groups, and there are few specific findings. They do prove that, if the disease does not die out, it will persist at levels in each group that are independent of the levels of initial infection. Another exception is the simulation study by Elveback, Ackerman, Gatewood, and Fox (1971). This study examined the effects of structuring population contact by families, neighborhoods, school, and play groups, with contact rates assumed to vary in each group. School and play groups are shown here to function as bridges between families and neighborhoods, increasing the size of epidemics. The mixing patterns in these studies are not really modeled; they are more a collection of ad hoc assumptions. The attention given to the role of social factors in structuring the mixing process, in contrast to activity levels and disease stages, marks a more sociologically grounded formulation than previous work had shown.

With the emergence of AIDS in the early 1980s, the role of selective mixing became the focus of a sustained modeling effort. Some of this work assumes a particular structure of mixing, but the goal has been to develop more general representations of arbitrarily complicated structures. Sattenspiel (1987a, 1987b), an anthropologist, extended the earlier work of Elveback et al. (1971), systematizing the informal mixing assumptions of the earlier work into migration matrix models. She simulated the spread of hepatitis through a child population with a two-level mixing structure: children mixed within neighborhoods, and some children from each neighborhood mixed in day-care centers. The children who attended day-care centers thus functioned as bridges among the neighborhoods. In these simulations, the size of the epidemic was found to depend on (a) the origin of the outbreak and (b) the density of intragroup relations. In Gail, Preston, and Piantadosi (1989), the contact matrix is constructed by using a mixture of available data or knowledge and an assumption of proportionate mixing where data are absent. The mixture is determined by minimizing the discrimination information (Kullback-Liebler distance) from proportionate mixing matrix to the matrix of known constraints. Again through simulation, Gail found that the degree of heterogeneity in mixing directly affects the optimal testing strategy for the control of AIDS. In the most general formulations (Blythe, Castillo-Chavez, Palmer, & Cheng, 1991; Busenberg & Castillo-Chavez, 1989; Jacquez et al., 1989; Koopman, Simon, Jacquez, & Park, 1989), arbitrarily complicated mixing structures can be represented. These models, however, tend to be highly overparameterized, with little attention paid to either interpretation or estimation of the parameters.

A simpler model has recently been proposed by Gupta and Anderson (1989). As with the homophily bias approach, the level of assortative mixing is summarized here by one parameter, but the parameter can index disassortative as well as assortative mixing. The parameter "Q" is given by

$$Q = \frac{(\sum_{i=1}^{N} w_i - 1)}{(N - 1)}$$

where the w_i are the eigenvalues of an $N \times N$ mixing matrix. At the assortative extreme, this measure tends to unity; at the disassortative extreme to $-\frac{1}{N}$; and for proportional mixing, it takes the value 0. Simulations show that assortative mixing generates the most rapid initial growth, while disassortative generates larger epidemics over the long term. The model has been applied to a sociometric data set from a male homosexual community in Iceland (Haraldsdottir, Gupta, & Anderson, 1992) where activity levels were used to define subgroups. The observed mixing pattern was found to be disassortative and generated a larger epidemic than would be the case under proportional or assortative mixing. While this approach is more tractable than some of the overparameterized models described above, the single parameter it employs is more of a mathematical convenience than a substantive summary. The interpretation of the value of "Q" is meaningful only with respect to 0 and the extreme values. The parameter also does not specify how selection patterns change as the population profile changes (an issue that will be dealt with in detail below). These dynamics thus remain outside the model and must be separately addressed in an ad hoc fashion.

A slightly different focus can be found in models of pair formation and dissolution (Dietz, 1987, 1988; Dietz & Hadeler, 1988; Waldstätter, 1989). Where the classical models of infectious disease assume a constant mixing between males and females, pair-formation models address the issue of temporary monogamous coupling. Such coupling can introduce significant transient effects at the early stage of an epidemic. Couples in which both members are infection-free are effectively "immune" for the duration of the partnership, and a significant number of such couples will slow the spread of the epidemic relative to a noncoupled population. Technically, pairing is introduced by creating new categories for the population reflecting single or paired status, and new parameters for the flows between categories reflecting the pairing and separation rates. Dietz and Hadeler's (1988) primary focus is on deriving analytic solutions for the dependence of the reproductive rate, R, on the pairing parameters. This becomes fairly difficult due to the matching constraints introduced by multigroup pairing, so they divide the mixing population only by gender. The findings from this work suggest that the persistence of the disease (endemic equilibrium) is directly linked to the separation rate and the number of partnerships during the life course. Given a low probability of disease transmission (.001-.002 per contact), the minimum number of lifetime partners needed for persistence of the disease is about 12. For extremely short partnerships (3-4 days), more than 1,000 partners over the lifetime would be needed for persistence.

There are thus several different traditions in epidemiology for modeling structured mixing. An important distinction is between the spatial models, which enumerate all of the nodes and links in a network, and the contact matrix models (of which the pair-formation models are a special case), which operate on aggregate units linked by average rates of contact. As noted above, this distinction is essentially equivalent to the sociometric and egocentric traditions in network analysis. The remainder of this chapter will focus largely on the latter approach. Part of the motivation for this choice of focus is the availability of data. The necessity for completely enumerating the nodes and links in a sociometric analysis makes the collection of such data feasible only for small, bounded communities. In addition, when the "links" involve sensitive information (as with sexually transmitted diseases), contact tracing is intrusive, subject to significant refusal bias, and raises serious confidentiality issues. Egocentric data, while subject to other forms of reporting bias, can be collected using standard survey methods and raise fewer confidentiality issues. While the egocentric approach introduces some heterogeneity within groups and loses information on triad or transitivity bias, it tends to be more appropriate for large-scale epidemic modeling.

In moving from simple to general formulations of a mixing structure, two problems arise. The first is complexity. For an $n \times n$ contact matrix, there are potentially n^2 parameters that must be identified and integrated into the diffusion equation; more if there are changes over time. For example, when the subpopulation sizes are not stable or when activity levels are allowed to change, additional parameters are needed to model the process of selection in a nonequilibrium structure. Thus, in some of the general models cited above, the total number of parameters used to model the process is as much as four times the number of cells in the matrix.

This raises the second problem, that of selecting and justifying the parameter settings. The logical choice would be to base these settings on empirical data, though the lack of network data often makes this impossible. Empirically based parameters require a framework for estimation, however, and a statistically sound estimation framework is noticeably lacking from all of the papers that propose selective mixing models.

These issues, then, provide criteria for judging among competing models. There is no unique representation for a given contact matrix. Some formulations are inherently limited, like proportional or preferred mixing, but even these can be parameterized in different ways. Arbitrary mixing functions, which have proportional or preferred mixing as special cases, can also be represented in many ways. A particular representation, then, cannot claim superiority on the basis of being general. A claim to superiority can, however, be based on a model's ability to solve the two problems identified above: manageable complexity and a framework for estimation. Log-linear models can make this claim. These models make it possible to parsimoniously describe a mixing structure; they generate parameters that have clear and relatively intuitive interpretations; and they provide a sound statistical basis for estimating these parameters from data. The remainder of this chapter reviews a log-linear-based framework for analyzing the effects of networks on diffusion (Morris, 1991a). While the immediate application is to epidemiology, this framework can be used for any socially structured diffusion process. In sociology, as in epidemiology, the issue of structured diffusion has been explored (Coleman, 1964, pp. 492-514; Coleman, Katz, & Menzel, 1966; Granovetter, 1978, 1983; Granovetter & Soong, 1988; Rapoport, 1953, 1957, 1979, 1980; Skvoretz, 1985), but a general analytic framework has been lacking.

A General Framework for Selective Mixing

In almost all models for diffusion that rely on interpersonal contact, transmission is represented by a term resembling

$$\text{Transmission rate} = \beta(t)S(t)I(t), \tag{3}$$

where S and I are the number of susceptibles and infecteds, and β is the "coefficient of conversion" or transmission coefficient.[2] In contagion models, $\beta(t)$ can be decomposed into two components, one representing activity levels or contacts and the other representing the conditional probability of transmission:

$$\beta(t) = \frac{c(t)\tau}{N(t)} \tag{4}$$

and

$c(t)$ = the number of contacts per person per unit time,
τ = the probability of transmission given contact, and
$N(t) = S(t) + I(t)$, the total active population

As formulated here, this term reflects the assumption of random mixing. Susceptibles and infecteds are two otherwise undifferentiated groups that mix in proportion to their numbers in the population. They mix randomly with respect to their disease status and with respect to other social characteristics, such as age, race, and gender. For simplicity, the transmission coefficient, τ, is represented as constant over time. As with other biological assumptions, simplicity is chosen here to focus attention on the mixing issues. These assumptions may be easily relaxed.

To relax the assumption of random mixing, the infection rate term must be modified to reflect the subgroups in the population and the mixing structure among them. A model for selective mixing replaces $\beta(t)S(t)I(t)$ with the term $\sum_{ij} \beta_{ij}(t)S_i(t)I_j(t)$, where the subscripts i and j index the subgroups in the population and $\beta_{ij}(t)$ the transmission coefficient between them:

$$\beta_{ij}(t) = \frac{c_i(t)\pi_{ij}(t)\tau_{ji}}{N_j(t)}, \tag{5}$$

$c_i(t)$ = the average number of contacts per unit time for members of group i,

$\pi_{ij}(t)$ = the conditional probability of a partner from group j given a subject from group i,

τ_{ji} = the per-partner probability of transmission from j to i, and

$N_j(t)$ = the total number in group j.

Note that the transmission coefficient τ_{ji} need not be symmetric. In the case of AIDS, for example, the transmission coefficient from male to female is believed to be higher than the coefficient from female to male. Status asymmetries may be present in other transmission contexts. There is, however, an implicit symmetry constraint in the number of contacts between groups, and this constraint will be addressed at length below.

The level of grouping is flexible. It can be used to index individuals or to index broader categories, such as age, race, gender, religion, and cross-tabulations of these characteristics. Ideally, the level is chosen to ensure homogeneity within the groups created, but the choice of level is also constrained by the type of data available. The partnerships can be displayed as a mixing matrix, with the rows representing subject groups and the columns representing partner groups. The cell entries of this matrix represent dyads rather than individuals, and the subject-group classification is, by convention, identical to the partner-group classification, so the mixing matrix is square. Where the index refers to individuals, this will be a sociomatrix.

Log-linear models are an appropriate method for summarizing the structure of this mixing matrix (Fienberg & Wasserman, 1981; Holland & Leinhardt, 1981). When the data are in the form of a sociomatrix, the models can be used to investigate the effects of in-degree, out-degree, and attribute bias (Wasserman & Faust, 1994, provide a systematic review); to estimate blockmodels for node-group bias (see Wang & Wong, 1987); and to summarize forms of dyad dependence that lead to transitivity bias (Frank & Strauss, 1986; Strauss & Ikeda, 1990). When the data are in the form of a group-mixing matrix, log-linear models can be used to investigate various patterns of within- and between-group selection bias.[3] For nominal parameters, patterns of homophily can be represented by one or more factor levels for diagonal cells (see Marsden, 1988, for an example). Such homophily bias models represent the mixing continuum for the hypotheses most commonly used in epidemiology: proportional, preferred, and restricted mixing. Models for nominal factors also generalize to arbitrary mixing functions, however, so that in-group and out-group preferences of all kinds may be examined. Ordinal models can be used when the location of a cell relative to the main diagonal can be summarized and interpreted as the distance between the two groups. A wide range of ordinal models exists, from a simple one-parameter model to the log-multiplicative models for estimating row and column scores (Goodman, 1984, pp. 66-111).

The estimated parameters are also easily integrated into the diffusion model. Because the cell counts of the contact matrix, x_{ij}, can be expressed as a function of the row total and the conditional row probabilities,

$$x_{ij}(t) = N_i(t)c_i(t)\pi_{ij}(t), \tag{6}$$

the transmission coefficient $\beta_{ij}(t)$ can now be expressed in terms of the mixing matrix cell counts

$$\beta_{ij}(t) = \frac{x_{ij}(t)\tau_{ji}}{N_i(t)N_j(t)} \tag{7}$$

The mixing matrix cell counts, in turn, can be expressed in terms of an appropriate log-linear model, thus linking the summary parameters of the mixing structure to the diffusion process.

The dynamic nature of these processes, however, raises an additional problem. For many reasons, including demographic cycles, changes in behavior, and differential rates of removal from the active population, the relative sizes of subgroups in the population may not be stable over time. The model must therefore specify how people alter their mixing patterns in response to changes in the population profile. What do people do when their preferred partners become more (or less) available? This is an interesting substantive question, and the answer will vary from one context (say, rumor spreading) to the next (say, sexual behavior). For any contact process, however, it is still possible to define the range of possible answers. As a preferred partner group becomes less available, an individual can either substitute with partners from other, less preferred groups or reduce the number of partners he or she has.

This choice is constrained by the behavior of other groups; that is, it must obey a contact consistency constraint: The number of contacts between is and js must equal the number of contacts between js and is,[4] and this implies symmetry in the contact matrix; $x_{ij}(t)$ must equal $x_{ji}(t)$. In practice, any empirical contact matrix will display some departure from symmetry due to a combination of sampling variability and reporting error. In theory, however, the constraint must hold, and empirical matrices will have to be adjusted accordingly. Given equation 6 above, this means

$$N_i(t)c_i(t)\pi_{ij}(t) = N_j(t)c_j(t)\pi_{ji}(t). \qquad (8)$$

Group sizes $[N_{(\cdot)}(t)]$ change independently over time. To ensure that this equation remains satisfied over time, corresponding changes must be made to either or both of the remaining parameters, $c_{(\cdot)}(t)$ and $\pi_{(\cdot\cdot)}(t)$. In substantive terms, as the relative availability of groups changes over time, subjects must either adjust their contact rates or their selection patterns or both.

As the parameterization of the constraint suggests, the possible behavioral responses can be arrayed along a continuum. At one end, the contact rates can be fixed, with all compensation operating through selection patterns, that is, $c_{(\cdot)}(t) = c_{(\cdot)}$. This can be seen as a "pure drive" model of contacts; each individual has an inherent drive or quota to achieve, and as one group becomes less available, partners are simply chosen from more available groups to fill the quota.

The way in which selection patterns change in this model is constrained but not determined by the population changes. This can be seen
by manipulating the contact equation above. Letting α_i be the proportional change in group size and β_{ij} be the proportional change in
selection patterns, substitution into equation 8 gives

$$\alpha_i N_i(t) c_i \beta_{ij} \pi_{ij}(t) = \alpha_j N_j(t) c_j \beta_{ji} \pi_{ji}(t) ,$$

and, with simplification, the dependence of selection on population
changes can be made explicit,

$$\beta_{ij} = \frac{{}^{\prime}\alpha_j}{\alpha_i} \beta_{ji}.$$

At any point in time, two things are fixed: population changes, $\alpha_{(\cdot)}$s, and
the margins of the contact matrix (by virtue of the fixed contact rates).
The compensating changes in selection patterns thus have $n(n-1)/2$
degrees of freedom, the degrees of freedom in a square, symmetric,
fixed-margin matrix. This flexibility means that the model can generate
massive changes in partnership patterns as the population structure
changes, a feature that may not be appropriate when modeling sexual
(or other) partnerships. In fact, the notion of selection "preference" here
is almost misleading, as the model makes selection primarily a function
of drive and availability.

At the other end, the selection patterns can be fixed with all compen-
sation operating through contact rates; that is, $\pi_{(\cdot\cdot)}(t) = \pi_{(\cdot\cdot)}$. This can be
seen as a "pure selection" model of behavior and might reflect some
notion of personal identity. Here, people choose partners in fixed ratios,
the mix rather than the quantity being the important aspect. Using the
approach above, and letting γ_i represent the proportional change in
contact rates (the $c_{(\cdot)}$s) this time, substitution into equation 8 and simplification gives

$$\gamma_i = \frac{\alpha_j}{\alpha_i} \gamma_j.$$

One solution to this will always be $\gamma_i = \alpha_i^{-1}$; the group changes its
contact rate in exact inverse proportion to its change in size, but the
general solution above implies that, for any set of population changes,

choosing one of the contact rate adjustments (γ_j) sets the rest. In other words, while there may be different contact rates for every group, there is only one degree of freedom under the pure selection model for setting them all. It is as if the group with the ability to enforce its sexual activity level drives the rest of the population.

Neither of these models is very satisfying or realistic. In between the two extremes that they define lie what might be called "modified selection" models. In these models, individuals accommodate changes in relative group size by adjusting both contact rates and selection patterns. The way in which this mix is obtained is open to modeling, though, in general, this flexibility entails a loss of direct control over the basic behavioral components, $c_{(\cdot)}$ and $\pi_{(\cdot \cdot)}$. In return, it becomes possible to separate and directly model the effects of population composition and preferences.

The population composition can be regarded as an opportunity structure or market, a constraint within which people negotiate their preferences. This suggests a different decomposition of the contact matrix cell counts. Rather than the traditional margin × conditional probability equation (equation 6), cell counts can be modeled as a function of population structure and mixing preferences. Population structure is then free to change over time, and mixing preferences may be treated as either stable or changing, depending on the substantive context. In simple form, this decomposition might look like

$$x_{ij}(t) = \frac{N_i(t)N_j(t)}{N(t)}\alpha_{ij}, \quad \alpha_{ij} = \alpha_{ji}$$

$$= K_{ij}(t)\alpha_{ij} \tag{9}$$

where $K_{ij}(t)$ represents the population or opportunity structure, and the mixing preference term, α_{ij}, could reflect a mutual signaling dynamic between the two potential partners, for example,

$$\alpha_{ij} = cs_{ij}s_{ji}.$$

The s_{ij} terms can be interpreted as the probability that a member of group i signals yes to a member of group j, a function of activity level preference and selection preferences for members of group i. These are not required to be symmetric. The scale factor c represents the number of contact opportunities, that is, the average number of new people met per unit time. Under this model, behavior now varies over time in response to relative group sizes, and the preferences of both partners contribute to the probability of contact being made. These two features enhance the substantive credibility of the model.

The α_{ij} preference term may be treated as either constant or time-dependent. In the absence of longitudinal data, it would seem reasonable to assume, as a first approximation, that the preferences are constant. The reasonableness of this assumption clearly varies with context. Sexual preferences, for example, are likely to be less volatile than brand loyalties. The assumption of constant preferences, in any case, does not constrain behavior to be constant, as behavior is also a function of changing opportunities, $K_{ij}(t)$.

Perhaps most important, the α_{ij} term from equation 9 can be estimated from data using standard techniques under some reasonable conditions (see Morris, 1991a, app.). Assuming constant preferences, for example, one can estimate the α_{ij} term from contact matrix data at any time point using a log-linear model. Letting m_{ij} represent the expected cell counts under the model,

$$\hat{m}_{ij}(0) = K_{ij}(0)\hat{\alpha}_{ij} \qquad (10)$$

$$= \exp\{\log K_{ij}(0) + \hat{u} + \hat{u}_{1(i)} + \hat{u}_{2(j)} + \sum_{l} \hat{u}_{l(ij)}\}.$$

The first three u terms represent the reference category and the main row and column effects, respectively. The last term, $u_{l(ij)}(0)$, represents the lth interaction term, either the standard row $\times$ column interaction, or a specific contrast, for example, a diagonal parameter. These provide a summary of the mixing preference structure, an estimate of $\hat{\alpha}_{ij}$. The $K_{ij}(0)$ term, which represents only population size, is assumed to be known and to have a coefficient of 1, so it can be fit as an offset (see Aitkin, 1989, p. 127).

The estimates of $\hat{\alpha}_{ij}$ can then be used to incorporate selective mixing into a diffusion model. In a simulation setting, the new subgroup sizes computed at each time step can be used to calculate $K_{ij}(t)$, the population structure. The mixing matrix cell counts can then be updated using the new population structure and the estimates of the preferences obtained by the log-linear model,

$$\hat{m}_{ij}(t) = K_{ij}(t)\hat{\alpha}_{ij}$$

These estimates can then be substituted back into the infection rate term of the diffusion model (equation 7), completing the updating algorithm and establishing the final link in the modeling framework:

$$\hat{\beta}_{ij}(t) = \frac{\hat{m}_{ij}(t)\tau_{ji}}{N_i(t)N_j(t)}$$

$$= \frac{\hat{\alpha}_{ij}\tau_{ji}}{N(t)}. \tag{11}$$

In short, log-linear models can be used to estimate the underlying selection preference structure. These estimates can then be used to update the contact patterns and thus the infection rate, as the population profile changes over time.

The framework reviewed here provides a simple way to model the widest possible variety of mixing patterns and incorporate these patterns into dynamic models of diffusion. Log-linear methods make it possible to systematically explore and summarize network structure. The conditional likelihood ratio statistic can be used to monitor the accuracy-parsimony trade-off, and the size and standard error of the parameter estimates can be used to identify the major sources of differential association. The modified selection model and the updating algorithm allow the estimated mixing parameters to drive a diffusion simulation even as the population profile changes. It is, in short, an integrated and general framework for exploring the role of social structure in the dynamic of social diffusion.

Some Results in Projecting the Spread of AIDS

For diseases that require only casual or unintentional contact, like influenza, the assumption of random mixing may not introduce serious distortion. For a sexually transmitted disease like AIDS, however, this assumption implies that sexual partners are chosen at random and is clearly untenable. The sexual opportunities available to an individual, and the partners deemed appropriate, will vary systematically from one social group to the next. Demographic attributes like age, race, ethnicity, gender, sexual preference, and marital status play an overwhelming role in defining the boundaries of appropriate sexual partner groups. Other attributes, like occupation, education, social status, and religion, play a similarly important role. The evidence for such selective association in friendship (e.g., Fischer, 1982; Laumann, 1973; Verbrugge, 1977) and marriage formation (Centers, 1949; Hunt, 1940; Pagnini & Morgan, 1990) is overwhelming. In projecting the sexual spread of AIDS, therefore, selective mixing cannot be ignored.

While the log-linear framework proposed above solves the methodological challenge posed by selective mixing, the virtual absence of empirical data remains a problem. Reliable data on sexual behavior are rare, sexual network data (either egocentric or sociometric) even more so. A limited range of data are available from various sources, however, including census data on age matching for first marriages, General Social Survey data on contact rates in the general adult population, and one network-oriented AIDS survey. These data have made it possible to use the log-linear modeling framework to explore how selective mixing might potentially affect the spread of the epidemic.

One of the most important findings is that the type of attribute used to define partner selection rules makes a difference. When these attributes are relatively stable over an individual's lifetime, like gender, race, or sexual preference, stable mixing groups are likely to form. The potential for spread between two groups that are not directly connected by sexual interaction then (e.g., gay men and heterosexual women) depends on the existence and size of a bridge population. By contrast, when the attributes that define partner selection rules change over an individual's lifetime (e.g., age or marital status), more fluid mixing groups are formed and the potential for spread is much higher. Here the mixing structure is characterized by a dual transmission regime, with some infections carried into a group by individuals whose group membership changes and other infections passed between groups by sexual contact. This kind of mixing structure makes the epidemic much more likely to spread, even with lower rates of sexual contact. The two attribute types thus generate two distinct transmission regimes. The implication is that the amount of behavioral change required, and the most strategically important subgroups from an intervention standpoint, depend on the type of mixing structure in which people are embedded (Morris, 1989, 1994a).

Another significant finding is that the effects of selective mixing interact strongly with other characteristics of the transmission process—

most important, variations in initial seroprevalence (fraction of the population infected) and subgroup activity levels. Using one of the few available data sets on networks of sexual partners, the AIDS in Multi-Ethnic Neighborhoods Survey (AMEN; Catania, Coates, Kegels, & Fullilove, 1992), the effects of selection patterns based on racial and ethnic boundaries were examined (Morris, 1991b, 1994a). These effects were shown to be fairly complex.

The initial effects of mixing depend strongly on initial prevalence: Mixing has little effect if there is uniform prevalence across all groups, but fairly large effects if initial prevalence varies. Where initial prevalence in a subgroup is high, positive assortative mixing acts to intensify within-group spread, increasing rates of infection relative to proportional mixing. Where initial seroprevalence is low, on the other hand, positive assortative mixing helps to keep it low. These initial effects may be transient, however. If the group has a relatively lower contact rate, the lower rate will be amplified by within-group selection and eventually lead to lower levels of infection under selective mixing. If the group has a relatively higher contact rate, on the other hand, within-group selection amplifies the rate of transmission, leading to higher levels of infection under selective mixing. Where both initial prevalence and activity level are low, and the homophily bias is relatively strong, selective mixing always leads to lower levels of infection.

Finally, these simulations have also shown that, even when the effects of selective mixing are small at the aggregate level, they may still be quite pronounced at the subgroup level. In the AMEN-based analyses described above, the effects of selective mixing on the total number infected at each point in the epidemic path was fairly small: Selective mixing led to about 1% to 2% less infection over time. The effects at the subgroup level, however, tended to be much larger and more variable, with selective mixing generating as much as 15% to 20% more (or less) infection in each subgroup. Such subgroup effects are also critical from an intervention standpoint. They become visible more quickly, and they help to pinpoint where intervention is most needed and most likely to be effective.

Overall, the simulations suggest that there is some potential for a heterosexual epidemic under the conditions examined. These models suggest, however, that the first evidence of such an epidemic will not appear at the aggregate level but at the subpopulation level. If the infection is just beginning to spread in the non-drug-using heterosexual population, noticeable growth in the overall number of AIDS cases will not occur for decades. The overall incidence of AIDS may actually even decline for some period of time, but in the presence of selective mixing, such overall trends will be misleading. Much attention is currently being given to the recent reduction in the *overall* rate of growth in new AIDS cases (see Centers for Disease Control, 1991a, figure 5). The rate of growth in heterosexual cases, however, while still small, continues to rise (see Centers for Disease Control, 1991b, figures 1a and 1b). This type of pattern is consistent with the evolution of an epidemic in a selectively mixing population. To interpret the overall decline as meaning that the epidemic has run its course, therefore, is probably premature. Careful monitoring of sentinel groups, guided by selective mixing models, can help to distinguish between short- and long-term dynamics in this epidemic.

At the same time, it is important to keep in mind the limitations of the simulation approach. The characteristics used to define the mixing groups in these simulations—age, race, ethnicity, and sexual preference—are clearly not the only relevant characteristics used for partner selection. Other characteristics, such as marital status and socioeconomic status, need to be considered, and variation in activity levels within groups is also likely to be significant. Theoretically, this poses no problem for the modeling framework, as one can easily expand the mixing matrix to permit more specific mixing group definitions. Practically, however, increasing the number of mixing groups exponentially raises the number of cells in the mixing matrix that have to be filled, requiring exponential increases in sample size. In addition, the reliability and validity of respondent reports on partner characteristics become problematic when one moves from asking the respondents to report their partner's race/ethnicity to the number of partners their partner has had in the last year.

As a general rule, simulations of the sort presented here are best used for gaining insight into the dynamics of diffusion through typical mixing structures. Demands for realism or accuracy will seldom be satisfied, but understanding may still be enhanced. Finally, it is worth noting, again, that the compartmental model approach adopted here precludes the investigation of certain types of network biases—most important, triad or transitivity bias. It can be expected that triads would function much as the couples in the pair-formation models reviewed above and would reduce the speed of within-group spread. This is an area that should be addressed in future research.

Conclusion

A decade ago, a chapter on epidemiology and social networks would have seemed like a strange idea. Things have changed quickly. In large part, the change has been "disease driven," but this should not obscure the methodological and theoretical gains that both fields now stand to gain from collaboration. At this point, there is great deal of interest among epidemiological modelers in developing methods for analyzing how social networks channel epidemics. Among sociologists, by contrast, the response has been small; practically none have become involved in the modeling effort (Klovdahl, 1985; Klovdahl et al., 1991, 1994; Laumann, Gagnon, Michaels, Michael, & Coleman, 1989; Morris, 1990, 1991a, 1991b, 1994a, 1994b; Morris & Dean, 1994; Morris & Kretzschmar, 1994, are the exceptions). This is unfortunate for two reasons. From a practical perspective, projections for the spread of diseases like AIDS may be very misleading if the effects of selective mixing are ignored. From a theoretical perspective, diffusion processes offer an interesting vantage point for research into the dynamic aspects of social structure. The challenge is to formally represent the way that social structure transforms individual behavior into an often unintended collective outcome.

Both sociology and epidemiology have something to gain from collaboration here, as their strengths and weaknesses are complementary. Where sociology is strong on the theory of selective mixing, and weak on the mathematical depiction of diffusion under these conditions, epidemiology is strong on the mathematics of diffusion, and weak on the modeling of selective mixing. A major barrier between the fields has been the absence of a general analytic framework that bridges the mixing and diffusion processes. The framework reviewed in this chapter provides such a bridge and offers a general method for modeling diffusion through social structures.

Notes

1. Proportionate mixing is assumed by another popular method of incorporating heterogeneity in activity levels, the coefficient of variation approach developed by Anderson, Medley, May, and Johnson (1986).

2. When conversion is a function of both contagion and innovation (a noncontagious process, like an external source), the rate of change in adopters (infecteds) reflects both

components: $(\alpha + \beta I)S$. For a discussion of the stochastic version of this process, see Coleman (1964, pp. 343-353). This kind of model is commonly used in market research (Bass, 1969, pp. 217-218) and is equivalent to the simple contagion model when $\alpha = \beta I(0)$ (Bartholomew, 1973, p. 299).

3. When subjects have more than one partner (a form of clustered sampling), this may introduce some correlation among contacts within persons, raising questions about the statistical independence of the observed dyads. Dependence would result if respondents filled rigid quotas of partner types; the type of partner for the later contacts, then, would not be independent of the type of partner for the earlier contacts. Given the low average number of partners (per year) for most of the population, this problem may not be a serious one. Yamaguchi (1990) presents methods that can be used to assess this assumption.

4. This is essentially equivalent to the "two-sex" problem in demographic modeling (Pollak, 1986; Pollard, 1973). Implicit in the model that will be reviewed here is an alternative solution to the two-sex problem. Note that the transmission coefficient τ_{ij} does not have to be symmetric, so transmission may be more likely in one direction than the other. Only the contact process must be symmetric.

References

Aitkin, M., Anderson, D., Francis, B., & Hind, B. (1989). *Statistical modeling in GLIM.* Oxford: Oxford University Press.

Anderson, R. M. (1982). *The population dynamics of infectious diseases.* London: Chapman Hall.

Anderson, R. M., Gupta, S., & Ng, W. (1990). The significance of sexual partner contact networks for the transmission dynamics of HIV. *Journal of Acquired Immune Deficiency Syndromes, 3,* 417-429.

Anderson, R. M., & May, R. M. (1991). *Infectious diseases of humans: Dynamics and control.* New York: Oxford University Press.

Anderson, R. M., Medley, G. F., May, R. M., & Johnson, A. M. (1986). A preliminary study of the transmission dynamics of the human immunodeficiency virus (HIV), the causative agent of AIDS. *IMA Journal of Mathematics Applied in Medicine and Biology, 3,* 229-263.

Bailey, N. T. J. (1975). *The mathematical theory of infectious diseases.* New York: Hafner.

Barbour, A. (1978). Macdonald's model and the transmission of bilharzia. *Transactions of the Royal Society for Tropical Medicine and Hygiene, 72,* 6-15.

Bartholomew, D. J. (1973). *Stochastic models for social processes.* New York: Wiley.

Bartlett, M. S. (1955). *Stochastic processes.* Cambridge: Cambridge University Press.

Bartlett, M. S. (1956). Deterministic and stochastic models for recurrent epidemics. *Proceedings of the 3rd Berkeley Symposium on Mathematical Statistics and Probability, 4,* 81-109.

Bass, F. M. (1969). A new product growth model for consumer durables. *Management Science, 15,* 215-227.

Blythe, S., Castillo-Chavez, C., Palmer, J. S., & Cheng, M. (1991). Toward a unified theory of sexual mixing and pair formation. *Mathematical Biosciences, 107,* 379-407.

Busenberg, S., & Castillo-Chavez, C. (1989). Interaction, pair formation and force of infection terms in sexually transmitted diseases. In C. Castillo-Chavez (Ed.), *Mathematical and statistical approaches to AIDS epidemiology* (pp. 289-300). Berlin: Springer-Verlag.

Catania, J. A., Coates, T. J., Kegels, S., & Fullilove, M. T. (1992). Condom use in multi-ethnic neighborhoods of San Francisco: The population-based AMEN (AIDS in Multi-Ethnic Neighborhoods) study. *American Journal of Public Health, 82*, 287.

Centers, R. (1949). Marital selection and occupational strata. *American Journal of Sociology, 54*, 530-535.

Centers for Disease Control. (1991a, January). *HIV/AIDS Surveillance Report*, pp. 1-22.

Centers for Disease Control. (1991b). *Morbidity and Mortality Weekly Report (MMWR), 40*, 357-369.

Cliff, A. D., & Ord, J. K. (1975). Model building and the analysis of spatial pattern in geography. *Journal of the Royal Statistical Society* (Series B), *37*, 297-348.

Coleman, J. S. (1964). *Introduction to mathematical sociology.* New York: Free Press.

Coleman, J. S., Katz, E., & Menzel, H. (1966). *Medical innovation.* New York: Bobbs-Merrill.

Cox, J. T., & Durrett, R. (1988). Limit theorems for the spread of epidemics and forest fires. *Stochastic Process and Applications, 30*, 171-191.

De Gruttola, V., & Mayer, K. H. (1988). Assessing and modeling heterosexual spread of the human immunodeficiency virus in the United States. *Review of Infectious Diseases, 10*, 138-150.

Dietz, K. (1987). Epidemiological models for sexually transmitted infections. In the *Proceedings of the First World Congress Bernoulli Society*, Tashkent.

Dietz, K. (1988). On the transmission dynamics of HIV. *Mathematical Biosciences, 90*, 397-414.

Dietz, K., & Hadeler, K. P. (1988). Epidemiological models of sexually transmitted diseases. *Journal of Mathematical Biology, 26*, 1-25.

Elveback, L. R., Ackerman, E., Gatewood, L., & Fox, J. P. (1971). Stochastic two-agent epidemic simulation models for a community of families. *American Journal of Epidemiology, 93*, 267-280.

Fararo, T. J., & Sunshine, M. H. (1964). *A study of a biased friendship net.* Syracuse, NY: Syracuse University Press.

Fienberg, S., & Wasserman, S. (1981). Analyzing data from multivariate directed graphs: An application to social networks. In V. Barnett (Ed.), *Interpreting multivariate data* (pp. 289-306). London: Wiley.

Fischer, C. S. (1982). *To dwell among friends: Personal networks in town and city.* Chicago: University of Chicago Press.

Fisher, R. A. (1937). The wave of advance of advantageous genes. *Annals of Eugenics, 7*, 355-369.

Frank, O., & Strauss, D. (1986). Markov graphs. *Journal of the American Statistical Association, 81*, 832-842.

Gail, M., Preston, D., & Piantadosi, S. (1989). Disease prevention models of voluntary confidential screening for human immunodeficiency virus (HIV) in isolated low risk and high risk populations and in mixed gay/heterosexual populations. *Statistics in Medicine, 8*, 59-81.

Goodman, L. A. (1984). *The analysis of cross-classified data having ordered categories.* Cambridge, MA: Harvard University Press.

Granovetter, M. (1978). Threshold models of collective behavior. *American Journal of Sociology, 83,* 1420-1443.

Granovetter, M. (1983). Threshold models of diffusion and collective behavior. *Journal of Mathematical Sociology, 9,* 165-179.

Granovetter, M., & Soong, R. (1988). Threshold models of diversity: Chinese restaurants, residential segregation, and the spiral of silence. *Sociological Methodology, 18,* 69-104.

Gupta, S., & Anderson, R. (1989). Networks of sexual contacts: Implications for the pattern of spread of HIV. *AIDS, 3,* 807-817.

Hagerstrand, T. (1967). *Innovation diffusion as a spatial process.* Chicago: University of Chicago Press.

Hamer, W. H. (1906). Epidemic disease in England. *Lancet, 1,* 733-739.

Haraldsdottir, S., Gupta, S., & Anderson, R. (1992). Preliminary studies of sexual networks in a male homosexual community in Iceland. *Journal of AIDS, 5,* 374-381.

Harris, T. E. (1974). Contact interactions on a lattice. *Annals of Probability, 2,* 969-988.

Hethcote, H. W. (1976). Qualitative analysis for communicable disease models. *Mathematical Biosciences, 28,* 335-356.

Hethcote, H. W. (1978). An immunization model for a heterogeneous population. *Theoretical Population Biology, 14,* 338-349.

Hethcote, H. W., & Van Ark, J. W. (1987). Epidemiological models for heterogeneous populations: Proportionate mixing, parameter estimation, and immunization programs. *Mathematical Biosciences, 84,* 85-118.

Hethcote, H. W., & Yorke, J. A. (1984). *Gonorrhea transmission dynamics and control.* Berlin: Springer-Verlag.

Hethcote, H. W., Yorke, J. A., & Nold, A. (1982). Gonorrhea modeling: A comparison of control methods. *Mathematical Biosciences, 58,* 93-109.

Holland, P., & Leinhardt, S. (1981). An exponential family of probability distributions for directed graphs. *Journal of the American Statistical Association, 77,* 33-50.

Hunt, T. C. (1940). Occupational status and marriage selection. *American Sociological Review, 5,* 495-504.

Hyman, J. M., & Stanley, E. A. (1988). Using mathematical models to understand the AIDS epidemic. *Mathematical Biosciences, 90,* 415-474.

Jacquez, J. A., Simon, C. P., & Koopman, J. (1989). Structured mixing: Heterogeneous mixing by the definition of activity groups. In C. Castillo-Chavez (Ed.), *Mathematical and statistical approaches to AIDS epidemiology* (pp. 301-315). Berlin: Springer-Verlag.

Jacquez, J. A., Simon, C. P., Koopman, J., Sattenspiel, L., & Perry, T. (1988). Modelling and analyzing HIV transmission: The effect of contact patterns. *Mathematical Biosciences, 92,* 119-199.

Kermack, W. O., & McKendrick, A. G. (1927). A contribution to the mathematical theory of epidemics. *Proceedings of the Royal Society of London* (Series A), *115,* 700-721.

Klovdahl, A. S. (1985). Social networks and the spread of infectious diseases: The AIDS example. *Social Science and Medicine, 21*(11), 1203-1216.

Klovdahl, A. S., Potterat, J. J., & Woodhouse, D. E. (1994). Social networks and infectious disease: The Colorado Springs study. *Social Science & Medicine, 38,* 79-88.

Klovdahl, A. S., Potterat, J., Woodhouse, D., Muth, J., Muth, S., & Darrow, W. W. (1991, February). *HIV infection in an urban social network: A progress report.* Paper presented at the Sunbelt Social Network Conference, Tampa, FL.

Koopman, J., Simon, C. P., Jacquez, J. A., & Park, T. S. (1989). Selective contact within structured mixing with an application to HIV transmission risk from oral and anal sex. In C. Castillo-Chavez (Ed.), *Mathematical and statistical approaches to AIDS epidemiology* (pp. 316-349). Berlin: Springer-Verlag.

Lajmanovich, A., & Yorke, J. A. (1976). A deterministic model for gonorrhea in a nonhomogeneous population. *Mathematical Biosciences, 28,* 221-236.

Laumann, E. O. (1973). *Bonds of pluralism: The form and substance of urban social networks.* New York: Wiley.

Laumann, E. O., Gagnon, J. H., Michaels, S., Michael, R. T., & Coleman, J. S. (1989). Monitoring the AIDS epidemic in the United States: A network approach. *Science, 244,* 1186-1189.

Lloyd, M. (1991). *The effect of grid shape on an epidemic growth model.* Unpublished manuscript.

Longini, I. M., Fine, P. E. M., & Thacker, S. B. (1986). Predicting the global spread of new infectious agents. *American Journal of Epidemiology, 123*(3), 383-391.

Marsden, P. V. (1988). Homogeneity in confiding relations. *Social Networks, 10,* 57-76.

May, R. M., & Anderson, R. M. (1984a). Spatial heterogeneity and the design of immunization programs. *Mathematical Biosciences, 72,* 83-111.

May, R. M., & Anderson, R. M. (1984b). Spatial, temporal and genetic heterogeneity in host populations and the design of immunization programmes. *IMA Journal of Mathematics Applied in Medicine and Biology, 1,* 233-266.

McNeill, W. H. (1976). *Plagues and peoples.* New York: Anchor.

Mollison, D. M. (1977). Spatial contact models for ecological and epidemic spread. *Journal of the Royal Statistical Society* (Series B), *39,* 283-326.

Mollison, D. M. (1991). Dependence of epidemic and population velocities on basic parameters. *Mathematical Biosciences, 170,* 255-287.

Mollison, D. M., & Barbour, A. (1989). Epidemics and random graphs. In J. P. Gabriel, C. Lefevre, & P. H. Picard (Eds.), *Stochastic processes in epidemic theory* (pp. 86-89). Berlin: Springer-Verlag.

Morris, M. (1989). *Networks and diffusion: An application of log-linear models to the population dynamics of disease.* Unpublished doctoral dissertation, University of Chicago.

Morris, M. (1991a). A log-linear modeling framework for selective mixing. *Mathematical Biosciences, 170,* 349-377.

Morris, M. (1991b, February). *Racial and ethnic boundaries in the spread of AIDS.* Paper presented at the Sunbelt Social Network Conference, Tampa, FL.

Morris, M. (1994a). Data driven network models for the spread of infectious disease. In D. Mollison (Ed.), *Epidemic models: Their structure and relation to data.* Cambridge: Cambridge University Press.

Morris, M. (1994b). Behavior change and non-homogeneous mixing. In V. Isham & G. Medley (Eds.), *Models for infectious human diseases: Their structure and relation to data.* Cambridge: Cambridge University Press.

Morris, M., & Dean, L. (1994). The effects of behavior change on long-term HIV seroprevalence in homosexual men. *American Journal of Epidemiology.*

Morris, M., & Kretzschmar, M. (1994). Concurrent partnerships and transmission dynamics in networks. *Social Networks.*

Nold, A. (1980). Heterogeneity in disease-transmission modeling. *Mathematical Biosciences, 52,* 227-240.

Pagnini, D. L., & Morgan, S. P. (1990). Intermarriage and social distance among U.S. immigrants at the turn of the century. *American Journal of Sociology, 96,* 405-432.

Pollak, R. (1986). A reformulation of the two-sex problem. *Demography, 23,* 247-259.

Pollard, J. H. (1973). *Mathematical models for the growth of human populations.* Cambridge: Cambridge University Press.

Rapoport, A. (1953). Spread of information through a population with socio-structural bias: I and II. *Bulletin of Mathematical Biophysics, 15,* 523-533, 535-543.

Rapoport, A. (1957). Contribution to the theory of random and biased nets. *Bulletin of Mathematical Biophysics, 19,* 257-277.

Rapoport, A. (1979). Some problems relating to randomly constructed biased networks. In P. W. Holland & S. Leinhardt (Eds.), *Perspectives on social network research* (pp. 119-136). New York: Academic Press.

Rapoport, A. (1980). A probabilistic approach to networks. *Social Networks, 2,* 1-18.

Sattenspiel, L. (1987a). Epidemics in nonrandomly mixing populations: A simulation. *American Journal of Physical Anthropology, 73,* 251-265.

Sattenspiel, L. (1987b). Population structure and the spread of disease. *Human Biology, 59*(3), 411-438.

Skvoretz, J. (1985). Random and biased networks: Simulations and approximations. *Social Networks, 7,* 225-261.

Strauss, D., & Ikeda, M. (1990). Pseudolikelihood estimation for social networks. *Journal of the American Statistical Association, 85,* 204-212.

Van den Bosch, F., Metz, J. A. J., & Diekmann, O. (1990). The velocity of spatial population expansion. *Journal of Mathematical Biology, 28,* 529-565.

Verbrugge, L. M. (1977). The structure of adult friendship choices. *Social Forces, 56,* 1286-1309.

Waldstätter, R. (1989). Pair formation in sexually-transmitted diseases. In C. Castillo-Chavez (Ed.), *Mathematical and statistical approaches to AIDS epidemiology* (pp. 260-274). Berlin: Springer-Verlag.

Wang, Y. Y., & Wong, G. Y. (1987). Stochastic blockmodels for directed graphs. *Journal of the American Statistical Association, 82,* 8-19.

Wasserman, S., & Faust, K. (1994). *Social network analysis: Methods and applications.* New York: Cambridge University Press.

Yamaguchi, K. (1990). Homophily and social distance in the choice of multiple friends. *Journal of the American Statistical Association, 85,* 356-366.

3

Statistical Models for
Social Support Networks

MICHAEL E. WALKER
STANLEY WASSERMAN
BARRY WELLMAN

Since the 1970s, community psychology researchers (e.g., Cassel, 1974; Cobb, 1976; Dean & Lin, 1977) have used the term *social support* to refer to social relationships in the context of health and well-being (Barrera & Ainlay, 1983). Early researchers conceptualized social support as a generalized resource available from one's network of friends and acquaintances (the *social network*) that helped one to deal with everyday problems or more serious crises. They then studied whether a greater amount of social support led to increased health, happiness, and longevity of life.

More recently, researchers have focused on the composition of the social network and its role in providing social support. These researchers now realize that the mere presence of a tie between two people does not equate with the provision of support. Further, different ties within a network will provide different types of support. This means that an individual cannot rely on merely one or two others for all types of assistance. Rather, the person must maintain relationships with a

AUTHORS' NOTE: Research support provided by an NIMH Training Grant to the Department of Psychology, University of Illinois. We thank Joseph Galaskiewicz and several reviewers for comments on this chapter and Philippa Pattison for her help with this research. Please address correspondence to Michael Walker, Department of Psychology, University of Illinois, 603 East Daniel Street, Champaign, IL 61820. E-mail addresses: mwalker@-s.psych.uiuc.edu, stanwass@uiuc.edu, and wellman@epas.utoronto.ca.

wide variety of individuals to ensure provision of all types of needed support.

As researchers adopt a network approach, they model support as a complex flow of resources among a wide range of actors rather than as just a transaction between two individuals. In doing so, they move away from the nebulous and ill-defined concept of social support, focusing instead on specific resources and the manner in which they flow throughout the network and back to ego. It becomes apparent that the actors' power, influence, and access to resources affect their supportiveness in networks. Researchers can also examine how nonsupportive ties affect supportive ties. By treating the complete network as a complex and unique entity, rather than focusing only on dyads or one or two types of relations, the analyst can discover how the structure of the network and its component parts affect the provision of support. Network analysts in the field of social support are discovering that an understanding of support extends far beyond the mere number of individuals in a personal network. Network methods are proving invaluable in dissecting and understanding the complex mechanisms contributing to overall support (see, also, Wellman, 1992b).

This chapter will examine the use of network methodology in the study of social support. First, it will discuss how the social network has been defined in the context of social support research. Next, it will look at how characteristics of individual ties affect provision of support. Then, the chapter will discuss characteristics of the entire network and their relationship to levels of support. Finally, the chapter will briefly review current advances in the field of network analysis that should prove useful to the study of support.

The Social Support Network

The Composition of the Network

Many studies of social support examine ego's personal network, that is, the members of an individual's ego-centered "universe" and the relationships among them. Researchers operationally define the composition of these networks by using name generators (Burt, 1984; Marsden, 1990). Most often, these name generators specify a role, that is, the purpose of the interaction or the type of support sought. The respondents may, for example, be asked to name those to whom they go for help or with whom they discuss important matters (Campbell & Lee, 1991).

Often, in addition to obtaining the names of the individuals in a personal network, a researcher asks the respondent to describe the relationships among the network members. Usually the respondent simply indicates which of the network members know each other. In this way, the researcher obtains at least partial (and ego-generated) information on the internal structure of the network.

The broadest definition of the personal network would include all those with whom a person interacts on an informal basis (people mutually recognized enough to have a conversation). The average North American has about 1,500 such informal ties (Bernard & Killworth, 1990). Social support studies only examine, at most, the small percentage of ties in the personal network that are active. The average North American has about 20 active ties to *significant* individuals, based on frequent sociable contact, supportiveness, or feelings of connectedness (Bernard & Killworth, 1990; C. Fischer, 1982; Milardo, 1989; Riley & Cochran, 1985; Wellman, Carrington, & Hall, 1988; Wellman & Wortley, 1989, 1990; Willmott, 1986, 1987). Most network studies have looked only at a subset of these strong ties, either socially close intimates or those in frequent contact. Only about a fourth of these ties (i.e., four to seven ties) are close and supportive intimates.

While it may appear to make sense to study only supportive ties, when studying the conditions under which support is given, analysts should take into account the possibility of nonsupportive ties as well (Gottlieb, 1981; Wellman, 1981). Treating the set of supportive ties as an entirely separate and enclosed system makes the assumption that they operate independently of other relationships in the network. Nonsupportive members can be important in several ways, from providing indirect support to discouraging support through their inaction (e.g., Liu & Duff, 1972). Exclusion of nonsupporters could lead to a grossly inaccurate representation of the operation of the network as a whole.

A support network, then, can be seen as embedded in a larger network including nonsupportive ties. At the same time, these larger networks are themselves interconnected, forming a much larger social system. The network approach allows the researcher to study social support as the flow of resources through this entire system rather than as a singular transaction between two individuals.

The Myth of Social Support

As mentioned earlier, researchers originally conceptualized social support as a broad, unidimensional characteristic of relationships, without regard to the nature of these interpersonal ties, and they attempted to show that the mere existence of these ties helped the individual to cope with everyday problems. One large longitudinal study of residents of Alameda County, California, for example, found that respondents "who lacked social and community ties were more likely to die in the follow-up period than those with more extensive contacts" (Berkman & Syme, 1979, p. 186). Several researchers have since shown that social support is not a unitary characteristic of relationships. Rather, different types of relationships provide different kinds of support. Although no standard typology exists, researchers using factor analysis and other multivariate data-analytic techniques have consistently distinguished among emotional aid, material aid (goods, money, and service), information, and companionship (Barrera & Ainlay, 1983; Cutrona & Russell, 1990; Wellman & Wortley, 1989, 1990).

It is highly unlikely that any one member of the ego's network will provide all four types of support. Parents and adult children do provide a broad spectrum of aid, but neighbors and frequently seen network members are more likely to provide material aid, and women are more likely than men to provide emotional support (Campbell & Lee, 1990; Rosenthal, 1985; Wellman, 1985, 1992a; Wellman & Wortley, 1989, 1990). In a study among East Yorkers in southern Ontario, Canada, Wellman and colleagues (see Wellman, 1982; Wellman & Wortley, 1989, 1990; Wellman et al., 1988) found that, of 18 different types of support examined, most members of the ego's network supplied only one to three types of support. Generally, these individuals provided either emotional aid or services, but not both. On the other hand, those who provide major services (such as acute or chronic health care) tended to provide emotional aid as well, but not those who provided lesser services (such as household aid or occasional child care).

The nature of support differs across societies as well. In (post)industrial social systems, support tends to be egalitarian, reciprocally exchanged, and specialized. Such support contributes primarily to domestic needs (Hall & Wellman 1985; Wellman, Carrington, & Hall, 1988). Because they are not generally lacking in basic necessities, people in these societies use support to help with emotional problems, emergencies, and various other crises.

In Third World systems, aid is often nonegalitarian, flowing through parent-child and patron-client relationships (Espinoza, 1992; Roberts, 1991). Because these nations are impoverished, people's need for aid is more survival based than in other societies. Support networks offer broad-based aid, not only providing for domestic needs but also supplying paid work (Radoeva, 1993; Sik, 1993).

Personal Relationships

Different individual ties provide different kinds of social support. This finding has led many researchers to discard the notion of social support as a unitary construct. As they have done so, they have examined the number and characteristics of relationships and how these influence the provision of support.

Tie Strength

Researchers argue that tie strength and support are highly associated. They have found that strong ties exhibit three related characteristics: (a) a sense that the relationship is intimate and special, with a voluntary investment in the tie and a desire for companionship with the partner; (b) an interest in frequent interactions in multiple contexts; and (c) a sense of mutuality of the relationship, with the partner's needs known and supported (e.g., Argyle & Henderson, 1984; Berscheid, Snyder, & Omoto, 1989; Blumstein & Kollock, 1988; Duck, 1983; Maxwell, 1985; Perlman & Fehr, 1987; Reis & Shaver, 1988; Waring, 1985). It may be that individuals who have a strong tie support each other out of a sense of obligation or because they empathize with one another. However, a common problem is that respondents often define someone as intimate because the person routinely offers assistance. Indeed, many respondents in the second East York study defined intimacy in terms of exchanging social support (Leighton, 1986).

Social Resource Theory (Lin, 1982, 1986a) relates tie strength and the provision of resources to the ego's actions. Instrumental actions (e.g., buying goods, looking for a job, looking for a mate) require diverse social resources and are therefore more likely to be accomplished through one's weak ties (see Granovetter, 1973, 1974, 1982). Expressive actions (e.g., sharing life experiences or problems) are mainly undertaken to maintain personal resources and are more likely engaged in with similar others in close or strong relationships. Further, the theory states that, insofar as psychological and emotional well-being requires expressive action, it should be promoted by access to strong ties. Unfortunately, little work has compared a person's most intimate ties with the 1,500 or so other ties in the personal network (but, see Erickson & Nosanchuk, 1985). Instead, most studies of social support have only examined strong ties, trying to link degree of intimacy to level of support. Several studies have demonstrated that, among intimates, the most intimate ties have provided more support than have those that are somewhat less intimate (C. Fischer, 1982; Wellman, 1979). More recently, Wellman and Wortley (1990) used logistic regression to show that strong ties (ties described as being intimate, voluntary, and stretching across multiple contexts) provided more services and emotional aid than other active ties. Further, strong friendship (but not strong kinship) ties provided most companionship.

Several researchers have argued that multiplexity—multiple-role relations between two individuals—is a key characteristic of strong ties. Multiplex ties should be stronger and more supportive because the network members have detailed knowledge of each other's needs and multiple claims on each other's attention (Ferrand, 1989; Mitchell, 1969, 1987; Verbrugge, 1977). Hirsch (1980) found that multiplex relationships were associated with better social support and mental health (see also Wellman & Wortley, 1989, 1990). Lin, Dumin, and Woelfel (1986) found some evidence that the number of multiplex relationships with strong ties was negatively correlated with level of depression.

Kinship Versus Friendship

Most of the active and intimate members of one's network are friends or neighbors and not kin. Friends and neighbors comprise almost half of most active and intimate networks as well as half of the ties providing each kind of support. On the other hand, kin have the densely knit relationships useful for coordinating social events and mobilizing resources in emergencies. Kin are even more effective in this capacity when they are also tied to the friends and neighbors of the focal person (Coe, Wolinsky, Miller, & Prendergast, 1984). Kin are quicker to care for sick relatives, and children often take turns caring for ailing parents (Soldo, Wolf, & Agree, 1986).

Some studies have compared the support provided by friends and different types of kin. Crohan and Antonucci (1989), for example, showed that people are more apt to be dissatisfied with unsupportive friends than unsupportive kin. Several studies have demonstrated that most immediate kin—parents, siblings, and adult children—are supportive. These studies further suggest that friends and kin differ in the quality and the amount of support they provide (Ball, Warheit, Vandiver, & Holzer, 1980; Chatters, Taylor, & Neighbors, 1989; Dressler, 1985; Essock-Vitale & McGuire, 1985; Gerstel, 1988; Milić, 1991; O'Connell, 1984; Wagner, 1987; Warren, 1981; Young, Giles, & Plantz, 1982).

The second East York study (Wellman & Wortley, 1989) used hierarchical cluster analysis to uncover three distinct types of kinship relations (parent-adult child, sibling, and extended kin) and the three additional relations of friend, neighbor, and workmate. The parent-adult child relationship is the most supportive of all intimate and active ties, providing high levels of both emotional and material support. These ties are so broadly supportive that even weaker, but still active, parent-adult child ties provide almost as much support as intimate friendship ties.

Among East Yorkers, siblings are less supportive and vary more in supportiveness than do parents and adult children. Intimate siblings exchange much more support than siblings with weaker ties. Extended kin, even those who have an active relationship with the ego, are only about half as likely to provide support as more immediate kin. They rarely provide support for routine, chronic, or acute problems. They do, however, prove useful in situations where social and spatial dispersion give weak ties a comparative advantage over strong ones, such as moving or finding jobs.

Wellman and Wortley (1989) found that, although friends are less apt to provide emotional and instrumental support than parents and adult children, they are just as likely as siblings to provide support and more likely to provide companionship. Moreover, many people who do not have active kinship ties have intimate friends who act like kin by providing a wide range of support. Neighbors, on the other hand, are a primary source of routine companionship and minor material aid (e.g., minding children or homes, providing a cup of sugar; see, also, Campbell & Lee, 1992).

Proximity and Contact

Although modern transportation has allowed contemporary relationships to move beyond the confines of the immediate environment, proximity continues to play a role in personal networks. Typically, 10% to 25% of active ties are local, even though the individual has access to the larger metropolitan area, the region, and beyond. Most North Americans know about a dozen neighbors well enough to speak to, although they may have only one or no intimates who are neighbors (Campbell & Lee, 1992). The majority of active ties extends beyond the neighborhood. About three fourths of active ties in East York, Ontario, extend beyond the neighborhood; one third are outside the metropolitan area, and one fifth are outside of a 100-mile radius (Wellman et al., 1988). Intimate ties are even less likely to be local. For example, about seven eighths of the intimate ties of East Yorkers are outside of their neighborhood, while one fourth extend beyond the metropolitan area (Wellman, 1979; Wellman et al., 1988). Most kinship ties, as well, are outside the neighborhood but remain within the metropolitan area. Kinship ties generally withstand long distances better than friendship ties.

Proximity is positively correlated with frequency of contact (see reviews in Bulmer, 1986; Hunter & Riger, 1986; Keller, 1968; Olson, 1982; Silverman, 1986; Unger & Wandersman, 1985). Respondents in the second East York study have more frequent contact, both in person and by telephone, with those who live nearby (Wellman & Wortley, 1990). The study does not, however, show much association between frequency of face-to-face contact and strength of the relationship. Respondents are in most frequent contact with weaker ties, such as neighbors and coworkers.

Telephone contact, which is more voluntary than face-to-face contact, is significantly correlated with strength of the relationship. At the same time, however, ties with frequent telephone contact are not more likely to provide support. Instead, the telephone acts as a social catalyst that keeps network members connected.

Some theorists have suggested that frequent contact should lead to more supportive relationships (Galaskiewicz, 1985; Hammer, 1983; Homans, 1961). The effects of contact should be independent of the strength of the relationship, given the lack of correlation between the two (Marsden & Campbell, 1984). However, Homans (1950, 1961) argues that contact develops strong *and* supportive relationships, and thus the two should be related. Recent research offers mixed support for Homans's position. Frequent contact by telephone plays an important role in communicating needs for support and arranging its delivery. Frequent face-to-face contact with strong ties—often socially close neighbors and workmates—fosters the supportive provision of goods and services. However, frequent contact with strong ties is not associated with the provision of emotional support or financial aid, and frequent contact with weaker ties is not associated with the provision of any sort of support (Israel & Antonucci, 1987; Jones, 1982; Kessler & McLeod, 1985; Rook, 1984; Seeman & Berkman, 1988; Wellman & Tindall, 1993; Wellman & Wortley, 1990). As mentioned earlier, the provision of small goods and services is related to both proximity and frequency of contact. Access facilitates the exchange of this type of support, even between individuals with weak ties. Physical access is not related to more important kinds of support, however. Network members can (and do) provide emotional and financial aid over much larger distances.

Similarity

Similarity analysts argue that similar individuals tend to form strong friendships (Lazarsfeld & Merton, 1964). Network members, then, should have similar characteristics. Their shared interests, based on these similarities, should foster empathic understanding and mutual support (Feld, 1982; Marsden, 1988). Dissimilarity analysts, by contrast, argue that people exchange support with those from different social positions (Blau & Schwartz, 1984; Kemper, 1972). Such ties, bridging social milieus, should provide good access to goods and services.

Among East Yorkers, only age dissimilarity and employment similarity are significantly correlated with provision of support. Network members with similar employment status are somewhat more likely to exchange small services than those with different employment status. Younger adults are more likely to provide older adults with physical labor, while older adults provide knowledge and impart skill to younger adults (Wellman & Wortley, 1990). Degree of similarity may also be related to the effectiveness of received support in dealing with crises. Lin, Woelfel, and Light (1986) found that those who receive help from similar others in the face of a stressful life event suffered less from depression than those who interacted with dissimilar others.

Network Characteristics

Thus far, the discussion has focused on the nature of individual ties in a personal network and how the characteristics of these ties affect the provision of support. We now turn to the characteristics of the network as a whole. Although researchers have looked more at ties than at network structure, existing research suggests a connection between the type and quantity of support provided and the patterns of relationships among the network members themselves.

Size

Several studies have shown that larger networks are generally more supportive (Barrera, 1981; Burt, 1987; Fischer, Sollie, Sorell, & Green, 1989; Seeman & Berkman, 1988; Wellman & Gulia, 1993; Wellman & Wortley, 1989, 1990; but see Sandler & Barrera, 1984), especially for women (Sarason, Sarason, & Shearin, 1986; Stokes & Wilson, 1984). For example, Wellman and Gulia (1993) find that, the larger the network, the greater the number of network members who provide emotional aid, goods and services, and companionship. They also find evidence that, the larger the network, the higher the percentage of network members who provide such support. Hence people with large networks may win both ways: Not only do they have more potential providers of support in their networks, each member of their network is more likely to be supportive.

Yet, the greater supportiveness of larger networks may be a mixed blessing. For example, Stokes (1983) found a curvilinear relationship between number of confidants in a network and overall satisfaction with support (but, of course, satisfaction is not synonymous with amount of support). Riley and Eckenrode (1986) found that larger networks provide more support but also lead to more interpersonal problems, and other research found that the quality and not the quantity of support provided was related to greater well-being (Antonucci & Akiyama, 1987; Israel & Antonucci, 1987).

Density

Density of the network is generally measured as the proportion of ties present out of all possible ties. Usually, analysts exclude ties from ego to alter when computing density. The rationale is that one wants to discover how density relates to the network's ability to mobilize support for the focal person. When ties between ego and alter are omitted, the density of active and intimate networks ranges from 0.3 to 0.5. That is, fewer than half of all potential ties among network members actually exist.

Conjectures about how density relates to support ultimately return to Durkheim's (1897/1951) contention that social integration promotes mental health. By extension, socially integrated individuals (those from densely knit networks) should experience less stress and receive more support to cope with what stress they do experience (Pescosolido & Georgianna, 1989; Thoits, 1982). Usually, researchers assume that denser networks facilitate communication and coordination, enhancing support provision.

What little research exists on the relationship between density and support presents a complex picture. Hirsch (1980) found that, among younger widows and mature women (returning to college), low density was more closely associated with satisfaction with support. Similarly, Wilcox (1981) found that people with low-density networks adjusted more easily to divorce. Among East Yorkers, the effects of density appear to depend on the kinds of support provided. High-density (predominantly kin) networks tend to be more conducive to provision of large services such as emergency or chronic health care. Low-density (predominantly friend) networks provide more companionship. Density is not related to provision of small services and emotional aid. Perhaps it is not density but connectivity (the extent to which pairs of alters are at least indirectly linked through ties to others) that facilitates social support. This is suggested by Burt's (1987) finding that expressed happiness is strongly linked to network members not being isolated from each other (see, also, Haines & Hurlbert, 1992, on "network range").

Centrality and Prestige

Centrality and *prestige* refer to the prominence or importance of the individuals in the personal network. An actor is central to the extent that he or she is involved in many relationships (Knoke & Burt, 1983; Faust & Wasserman, 1992). The simplest measure of centrality is the number of ties that a network member has to other members in the respondent's network (also known as the *degree* of the actor). Among East Yorkers, structurally central network members (those with ties to many others in the network) are slightly more likely to provide assistance to the ego (Wellman, 1979). The ability to provide help may, in fact, have led to their centrality. Additionally, central individuals may provide a necessary link between the respondent and other people in the network. In fact, East Yorkers maintain ties with one fifth of all their intimates primarily because of their ties to some third party (Wellman et al., 1988).

Role Structures

There has been very little research on the application of relational-analytic methods (see Boyd, 1990; Pattison, 1993) to social support networks, although such analyses are certainly possible. The goal would be to find similarities and associations among the different types of relational ties, especially as they are compounded with each other; for example, one might like to know how similar one's friends' friends (compounding the friend relation with itself) are to one's friends. Nearly all of the work in this area has involved complete networks, and not the ego-centered, respondent-focused networks typically analyzed in support studies.

One problem that has hindered such analyses is the vast amount of data that support studies can generate. Relational analyses can be applied to a single network, but "aggregating" these analyses across all ego-centered networks would be quite a task. The first step in a good relational analysis of support data must be the development of good aggregation techniques, for, in their absence, role algebras (and similar descriptive summaries arising from relational analyses) are simply not possible.

Reciprocity

Not all of the effects of social support are positive. If the focal person receives aid but does not, in some way, return it, disequilibrium will develop, possibly leading to resentment on the part of the help-givers or destruction of the relationships (DiMatteo & Hays, 1981). The person receiving aid may reciprocate in any of three ways: (a) specific exchange, or repayment in kind to the help-giver; (b) generalized reciprocity, in which the person receiving aid repays the original helper with some other form of aid; or (c) network balancing, in which the recipient of aid, in turn, helps another network member (Wellman et al., 1988).

Specific exchange has been measured as the number or proportion of ties in which a specific type of aid is both given and received by the focal individual. In East York, people who offer small services and emotional aid usually receive the same type of support from the original recipient, eventually. Less common types of aid, such as chronic health care or lending large sums of money, are generally not reciprocated. The latter result could be from lack of an opportunity to return the favor.

Generalized reciprocity has been studied by counting the number of different types of aid sent and received in each tie (or sometimes between the focal person and the network as a whole). Some comparison (the correlation or, alternatively, the difference) between the number of types of aid sent and received has been used as a measure of generalized reciprocity (van Tilburg, van Sonderen, & Ormel, 1991; Wellman et al., 1988). Among East Yorkers, those network members to whom focal persons send many types of aid usually return many types of aid, and those to whom they send few types of aid return few types of aid.

Instead of being concerned with individual ties, network balancing operates at the level of the network. Researchers have investigated network balancing by comparing the number of network members from whom the focal person receives a given type of support with the number to whom the focal person sends support (van Tilburg et al., 1991; Wellman et al., 1988). Alternatively, analysts have disregarded the actual network members and have looked, simply, at the numbers of types of support the focal individual sent to or received from the network as a whole (C. Fischer, 1982; Rook, 1987). Networks of East Yorkers exhibit a high degree of balance. Those who receive little aid also do not help others often, whereas those who help others often also receive much assistance. The former prefer to stand alone, while the networks of the latter are built around sending and receiving resources.

Reciprocity, as discussed thus far, refers to the relationship between the focal individual and the network (or between the focal person and individual network members). In this regard, the usage of the term does not correspond directly to its meaning in traditional network analysis. To study the reciprocity of the network as a whole, one would need to gather information on the flow of support among all network members. Measures, such as those discussed above, could be used to examine the reciprocal or mutual nature of these relationships. To our knowledge, no researchers in the area of social support have yet done so.

Change over Time

In attempting to understand the relationship between social support and mental health, researchers generally rely on one of two views. The first is that social support exerts a positive and direct effect on well-being, independent of other factors. The other is that support acts as a mediator, serving to buffer the effects of stressful life events on mental health. Lin (1986b) has argued that the usual cross-sectional studies cannot adequately test either the direct or the buffering effects of social support. By reviewing existing studies and by collecting longitudinal data, Lin demonstrated that social support has a direct effect on well-being, both contemporaneously and over time. No interactive (mediating) effect of social support was demonstrated.

Hammer (1981, 1983) has argued that the traditional focus on support itself, rather than on social connections, implies a buffering role of social support. Hammer posits that, by studying social connections as they change over time, a researcher can entertain a wider variety of possible relationships between social factors and well-being. Furthermore, such a research strategy allows the effects of social factors (i.e., the characteristics of the personal network) to be separated from the ego's personal characteristics and social behavior (Gottlieb, 1983, p. 37).

Ideally then, one would like to study the flow of support over time. Support networks may indeed change and, perhaps, even approach some sort of quantifiable equilibrium. Methods exist for such a study, assuming that the data gathered from the respondents are rich enough in their longitudinal aspects. We refer the reader to Wasserman and Faust (1994, chap. 15) for an overview of available methodology.

Future Directions

So far, we have discussed several characteristics of social ties and network structure, how they have been measured, and their relationship to other characteristics of the individual. Increased inclusion of these network variables in research on social support in the past decade has greatly extended our knowledge in this area. Naturally, some methodological problems still exist, two of which we will discuss next. The first concerns how well the network indices represent the true characteristics of the personal networks from which the data were sampled. The second has to do with the reliability of these indices.

Validity and Reliability of Network Data

We could imagine that the support network a person reported in an interview or questionnaire would fluctuate from time to time, not because the network composition had changed but simply because of errors in recall or other random situational factors. In this case, the reported network would merely be a sample of the person's actual personal network. The network measures discussed above describe the composition of an individual's reported personal network: the number of network members, the network's demographic characteristics, the density, the reciprocity, and so on. If we think of this reported network as random, a logical question would be this: How well do the characteristics of ego's observed network reflect the characteristics of ego's "true" personal network? (See Bernard, Killworth, & Sailer, 1981, for a critique of respondent accuracy.) Similarly, "personal relationships" psychologists have debated the extent to which respondents' reports of the supportiveness of network members accurately reflect the support network members actually provide (Milardo, 1989, 1991).

A related issue concerns the reliability of these network-derived indices. Cumulative indices of network characteristics, such as size and frequency of contact, appear to be more stable than other measures (Marsden, 1990). Limited evidence suggests that network indices exhibit a moderate amount of test-retest reliability (Neyer, Bien, Marbach, & Templeton, 1991). A test-retest approach to reliability cannot, however, distinguish between error in measurement and actual change over time.

Recent advances in the analysis of network data offer solutions to these two problems. These new methods adopt a statistical approach to network analysis. By making certain assumptions about the underlying distribution of the network itself, a researcher can obtain descriptive measures of the network's characteristics as well as the standard errors associated with these measures. These standard errors provide some indication of the stability or reliability of the measures. In addition, the researcher can perform tests of hypotheses about the characteristics of the entire personal network, of which the measured network is a sample.

Much of the work on the statistical analysis of network data has been advanced by Holland and Leinhardt (1981). These researchers consider a social network as consisting of a set of dyads. Let us consider a directed relation—for example, liking—in which one person in a dyad can like the other without the other reciprocating the sentiment. Then, each dyad (consisting of two actors, say A and B) can contain zero ties (if neither A nor B like each other), one tie (if A likes B or B likes A, but not both), or two ties (if A and B like each other). Holland and Leinhardt assume that the dyads in the social network are all independent of each other and, further, that the number of ties in each dyad (0, 1, or 2) follows a specific discrete distribution. In so doing, the researchers are able to model the probabilities governing the numbers of ties in a dyad (and, indeed, in the social network as a whole) using a traditional log-linear model (see Iacobucci & Wasserman, 1987, for a concise explanation of the procedures for fitting the models; see, also, Iacobucci & Wasserman, 1988; Wasserman & Weaver, 1985).

The log-linear models of Holland and Leinhardt yield a density parameter, indicating the likelihood of a tie in the network; a "popularity" parameter, indicating the tendency of an actor in the network to be chosen (in our example, liked) by another; an "expansiveness" parameter, indicating the tendency of an actor to choose another; and a mutuality or reciprocation index, reflecting the likelihood that both actors in a dyad choose each other. Notice that this definition of reciprocity deals only with the relation that defines the social network (e.g., who likes whom), and not with the flow of support through the network (see the earlier discussion on reciprocity).

In some cases, information gathered on social support networks is nondirected. That is, if Actor A relates to Actor B, then Actor B necessarily relates to Actor A. Usually, the ties in the personal network are defined by which network members know each other. In the case of nondirected data, the log-linear models only yield two parameters: the density parameter mentioned above and a single parameter describing the tendency of a network member to relate to others in the network. This latter parameter can be interpreted as an index of centrality or importance of the actor (see Faust & Wasserman, 1992).

The parameters obtained from the log-linear model parallel the more easily obtained indices discussed above, which have already been used to some extent in studies of social support. The great advantage of log-linear methods is that they yield standard errors with which to judge the reliability or accuracy of these indices in describing the social networks themselves. This reliability information is useful in its own right and also forms a basis for better judging the relationship (or lack of a relationship) of these indices to provision of support.

Independence of Dyads

The dyadic statistical model outlined above assumes that all dyads are independent of each other. Substantively, this means that the fact that two people in the network relate to each other should not influence whether two other people in the network relate to each other. Although Holland and Leinhardt (1981) assert that dyad independence may indeed hold for sets of actors and measured relations studied by social network analysts, others call into question the tenability of this assumption. Particularly in the case of personal networks, given that the members are all linked at least indirectly through the focal person, we can expect that the ties in the network will not be independent of each other. If we base our statistical test on dyadic independence when the data are actually interdependent, we will obtain artificially inflated chi-squared-based statistics. Such a test will be overly liberal, rejecting the model at a level greater than the nominal rejection rate when the model is correct.

Frank and Strauss (1986) consider a class of models that allow a very restricted form of (Markov) dependency between dyads. Under these models, dyads are conditionally dependent if they share a common actor. Otherwise, the dyads are conditionally independent. Although the introduction of dyadic dependence generally rules out obtaining parameter estimates using standard maximum likelihood log-linear techniques, Strauss and Ikeda (1990) have developed a method for approximating the models using a pseudolikelihood technique. These models yield the same parameters as the dyadic independence models and share the advantage of providing standard errors as well.

The statistical models discussed above would prove very useful to the study of social support, augmenting and extending the work to date on the structure of support networks and the relationship of structure to the provision of support. Clearly, the independence models are not readily applicable, as the independence assumption is probably not met.

Although Strauss and Ikeda demonstrate how to model social networks with dyadic dependencies present, they restrict themselves, specifically, to Markov dependency. They offer the observation that more general dependency models are too complicated to be of much use in data analysis. Unfortunately, ego-centered networks very likely do not have simple dependency structures. Because of the way in which such data are obtained, they can actually be considered a cluster sample (Wasserman & Faust, 1994).

One possible area for future research would explore a further relaxation of the dependency of structure in the models mentioned above. Such a relaxation is probably only feasible for networks of small size (say, with six or fewer members; see Frank & Strauss, 1986). Fortunately, in general, only networks of moderate size are studied in the context of social support.

Another possible solution would be a deflation factor that corrects the chi-squared statistic for dependence among the dyads. Reitz and Dow (1989; see, also, Brier, 1980) offer a method that is immediately applicable to support networks, with measures on the attributes of the network members. This is only true, however, if the main interest is in the interrelationships among the attributes themselves. Generally, however, the focus is primarily on the relationships among the actors in the ego network. We are currently examining a deflation factor in the context of log-linear dyadic analyses as applied to ego networks. We suspect that such a method will prove most feasible in the case where actor attributes are included in the analyses.

Conclusion

In this chapter, we have briefly discussed social support from a network perspective. We have shown the types of tie-wise and network characteristics that researchers have measured and have summarized research findings on how these characteristics reflect the supportiveness of the social network. We have indicated a few areas that have not yet fully been explored as well as some current methodological advances that should add to the utility of network methodology for social support researchers.

Many early studies that collected information on personal networks equated simple network indices (e.g., network size) with level of support. By correlating these indices with measures of well-being (e.g., depression inventories) and possibly with measures of stressful life events, researchers demonstrated the direct and indirect effects of "social support" on psychological well-being. As researchers used more sophisticated network analysis, they began to realize that the relationship between support and network structure is much more complex than "bigger is better."

As researchers have focused more on personal networks, they have been able to develop and test more elaborate theories of social support. Many studies have focused on the "direct" and "buffering" effects of support on personal well-being. To illustrate, we turn to Gottlieb (1983, pp. 34-48), who has offered a framework within which to study the effects of social support on health. According to this model, an individual reacts to stressful life events with feelings of strain or disequilibrium. These reactions, in turn, affect the person's affective, cognitive, and behavioral well-being. Personal resources (e.g., personality and coping skills) and social resources (the personal network), themselves mutually influential, act as mediators in the causal chain from stressor to reaction to health state. Although the model includes both personal and social resources, Gottlieb focuses on the effects of social resources. He notes that they can have a direct effect, acting to reduce exposure to stressful events and to enhance the health of the individual. They can also have a buffering effect, preserving positive self-appraisals in stressful situations and protecting against depression when negative reactions occur.

Hammer (1981) has argued that we cannot fully understand the role of social factors in the stress process until we can disentangle them from the effects of personal resources. Hammer cites Cassel's (1976) social feedback model as one possible mechanism underlying the mutual influence of social and personal resources. According to the model, social feedback acts to maintain appropriate behavior and performance, whereas the absence of such feedback leads to behavioral and physiological disturbance, which, in turn, increases susceptibility to disease.

In explaining the relationship of social support to schizophrenia, Hammer (1981) proposes a "social feedback model of cultural predictability, in which one's social orientations and social performance— including one's ways of maintaining and forming connections—are viewed as being shaped over time by the feedback mediated through one's changing networks of connections" (p. 55). She argues that testing such a model requires knowledge of the personal network and the interconnections among the different people within this network. Further, to understand the processes affecting the relationship between the personal network and health, we need to study the connections between this core network and an extended network of all potential contacts. Within this larger framework, we can study how the core network changes over time and how this change affects the adequacy of the network for maintaining the individual's psychological and physical well-being. We can also view the interplay between personal characteristics and network flux.

In a slightly different context, sociologists have long held that we should study interpersonal relationships in the context of the larger social structure. The *Community Question,* as this issue has been termed, concerns how the structure and divisions of labor in large-scale social systems affect the content of interpersonal ties, including the provision of socially supportive resources (Wellman, 1988, offers a recent review). Early discussions of the Community Question began with the premise that a healthy community was a close-knit, broadly supportive neighborhood-as-kinship group that helped individuals navigate life's difficulties. Many scholars feared that industrialization and division of labor had created macrostructural conditions in which community could no longer exist; that is, that community had been "lost." They believed community ties were few, weak, and fragmented. Other researchers argued that people form communities in all social settings. They sought and obtained evidence that community had been "saved," that it still flourished, even in the postindustrial society.

But what if supportive community ties still exist, but as loosely knit networks stretching beyond the neighborhood and kinship group? Then community would look much like the ego-centered networks we have discussed in this chapter. What if, instead of there being broadly supportive relationships in these networks, different ties—and different types of ties—provided different kinds of support? For example, some friends might provide emotional support, while others might be companions; some neighbors might provide many goods and services, while immediate kin might provide both emotional and financial support.

To take into account such possibilities, several analysts have begun to stress the social network rather than the spatial aspects of community. They define community from the standpoint of the focal individual and equate it with the personal network of informal ties. To them, community has not been lost but "liberated" beyond the confines of the neighborhood. Researchers operating from this perspective and collecting personal network data have demonstrated the existence of community in large cities (see the reviews in Wellman, 1988, in press; Wellman et al., 1988). They have also found very strong community ties among ethnic populations stereotypically thought to be fragmented and pathological (Lee, Campbell, & Miller, 1991; Oliver, 1988).

The use of network measures in community research has increased rapidly in the past decade. Already, its use has added greatly to our knowledge in these areas. Especially in the area of social support, it quickly demonstrated its utility and continues to show promise. As social network methodology continues to advance and to be used in a variety of contexts, it should prove a valuable tool to the social researcher.

References

Antonucci, T., & Akiyama, H. (1987). An examination of sex differences in social support among older men and women. *Sex Roles, 17,* 737-749.

Argyle, M., & Henderson, M. (1984). The rules of friendship. *Journal of Social and Personal Relationships, 1,* 209-235.

Ball, R., Warheit, G., Vandiver, J., & Holzer, C., III. (1980). Friendship networks: More supportive of low-income black women? *Ethnicity, 7,* 70-77.

Barrera, M. (1981). Social support in the adjustment of pregnant adolescents. In B. H. Gottlieb (Ed.), *Social networks and social support* (pp. 69-96). Beverly Hills, CA: Sage.

Barrera, M., Jr., & Ainlay, S. L. (1983). The structure of social support: A conceptual and empirical analysis. *Journal of Community Psychology, 11,* 133-143.

Berkman, L., & Syme, S. L. (1979). Social networks, host resistance, and mortality. *American Journal of Epidemiology, 109,* 186-204.

Bernard, H. R., & Killworth, P. (1990). *Report to the anthropology and MMDI programs.* Washington, DC: National Science Foundation.

Bernard, H. R., Killworth, P., & Sailer, L. (1981). Summary of research on informant accuracy in network data and the reverse small world problem. *Connections, 4,* 11-25.

Berscheid, E., Snyder, M., & Omoto, A. (1989). Issues in studying close relationships. In C. Hendrick (Ed.), *Close relationships* (pp. 63-91). Newbury Park, CA: Sage.

Blau, P., & Schwartz, J. (1984). *Crosscutting social circles.* Orlando, FL: Academic Press.

Blumstein, P., & Kollock, P. (1988). Personal relationships. *Annual Review of Sociology, 14,* 467-490.

Boyd, J. P. (1990). *Social semigroups: A unified theory of scaling and blockmodelling as applied to social networks.* Fairfax, VA: George Mason University Press.

Brier, S. S. (1980). Analysis of contingency tables under cluster sampling. *Biometrika, 67,* 591-596.

Bulmer, M. (1986). *Neighbours: The work of Philip Abrams.* Cambridge: Cambridge University Press.

Burt, R. (1984). Network items and the General Social Survey. *Social Networks, 6,* 293-339.

Burt, R. (1987). A note on strangers, friends and happiness. *Social Networks, 9,* 311-331.

Campbell, K. E., & Lee, B. A. (1990). Gender differences in urban neighboring. *The Sociological Quarterly, 31,* 495-512.

Campbell, K. E., & Lee, B. A. (1991). Name generators in surveys of personal networks. *Social Networks, 13,* 203-221.

Campbell, K. E., & Lee, B. A. (1992). Sources of personal neighbor networks: Social integration, need, or time? *Social Forces, 70,* 1077-1100.

Cassel, J. (1974). Psychosocial processes and stress: Theoretical formulations. *International Journal of Health Services, 4,* 471-482.

Cassel, J. (1976). The contribution of the social environment to host resistance. *American Journal of Epidemiology, 104,* 107-123.

Chatters, L., Taylor, R., & Neighbors, J. (1989). Size of informal helper network mobilized during a serious personal problem among black Americans. *Journal of Marriage and the Family, 51,* 667-676.

Cobb, S. (1976). Social support as a moderator of life stress. *Psychosomatic Medicine, 38,* 300-314.

Coe, R., Wolinsky, F., Miller, D., & Prendergast, J. (1984). Social network relationships and use of physician services: A reexamination. *Research on Aging, 6,* 243-256.

74   Social Psychology and Diffusion

Crohan, S., & Antonucci, T. (1989). Friends as a source of social support in old age. In R. Adams & R. Blieszner (Eds.), *Older adult friendship* (pp. 129-146). Newbury Park, CA: Sage.

Cutrona, C. E., & Russell, D. W. (1990). Type of social support and specific stress: Toward a theory of optimal matching. In B. R. Sarason, I. G. Sarason, & G. R. Pierce (Eds.), *Social support: An interactional view* (pp. 319-366). New York: Wiley.

Dean, A., & Lin, N. (1977). The stress buffering role of social support. *Journal of Nervous and Mental Disease, 165,* 403-417.

DiMatteo, M. R., & Hays, R. (1981). Social support and serious illness. In B. Gottlieb (Ed.), *Social networks and social support* (pp. 117-148). Beverly Hills, CA: Sage.

Dressler, W. (1985). Extended family relationships, social support, and mental health in a southern black community. *Journal of Health and Social Behavior, 26,* 39-48.

Duck, S. (1983). *Friends for life.* Brighton, England: Harvester.

Durkheim, É. (1951). *Suicide.* Glencoe, IL: Free Press. (Original work published 1897)

Erickson, B., & Nosanchuk, T. A. (1985). How high is up? Calibrating social comparison in the real world. *Journal of Personality and Social Psychology, 48,* 624-634.

Espinoza, V. (1992). *Networks of informal economy: Work and community among Santiago's urban poor.* Unpublished doctoral dissertation, University of Toronto.

Essock-Vitale, S., & McGuire, M. (1985). Women's lives viewed from an evolutionary perspective: II. Patterns of helping. *Ethology and Sociobiology, 6,* 155-173.

Faust, K., & Wasserman, S. (1992). Centrality and prestige: A review and synthesis. *Journal of Quantitative Anthropology, 4,* 23-78.

Feld, S. (1982). Social structural determinants of similarity among associates. *American Sociological Review, 47,* 797-801.

Ferrand, A. (1989, February). *A holistic approach to interpersonal relations.* Paper presented to the Sunbelt Social Network Conference, Tampa, FL.

Fischer, C. (1982). *To dwell among friends.* Berkeley: University of California Press.

Fischer, J., Sollie, D., Sorell, G., & Green, S. (1989). Marital status and career stage influences on social networks of young adults. *Journal of Marriage and the Family, 51,* 521-534.

Frank, O., & Strauss, D. (1986). Markov graphs. *Journal of the American Statistical Association, 81,* 832-842.

Galaskiewicz, J. (1985). *Social organization of an urban grants economy: A study of business philanthropy and nonprofit organizations.* Orlando, FL: Academic Press.

Gerstel, N. (1988). Divorce and kin ties: The importance of gender. *Journal of Marriage and the Family, 50,* 209-219.

Gottlieb, B. H. (1981). Preventive interventions involving social networks and social support. In B. H. Gottlieb (Ed.), *Social networks and social support* (pp. 201-232). Beverly Hills, CA: Sage.

Gottlieb, B. H. (1983). *Social support strategies.* Beverly Hills, CA: Sage.

Granovetter, M. (1973). The strength of weak ties. *American Journal of Sociology, 78,* 1360-1380.

Granovetter, M. (1974). *Getting a job.* Cambridge, MA: Harvard University Press.

Granovetter, M. (1982). The strength of weak ties: A network theory revisited. In P. Marsden & N. Lin (Eds.), *Social structure and network analysis* (pp. 105-130). Beverly Hills, CA: Sage.

Haines, V., & Hurlbert, J. (1992). Network range and health. *Journal of Health and Social Behavior, 33,* 254-256.

Hall, A., & Wellman, B. (1985). Social networks and social support. In S. Cohen & S. L. Syme (Eds.), *Social support and health* (pp. 23-41). Orlando, FL: Academic Press.

Hammer, M. (1981). Social supports, social networks, and schizophrenia. *Schizophrenia Bulletin, 7*, 45-57.

Hammer, M. (1983). 20 "core" and "extended" social networks in relation to health and illness. *Social Science and Medicine, 17*, 405-411.

Hirsch, B. J. (1980). Natural support systems and coping with major life changes. *American Journal of Community Psychology, 8*, 159-172.

Holland, P. W., & Leinhardt, S. (1981). An exponential family of probability distributions for directed graphs. *Journal of the American Statistical Association, 76*, 33-65.

Homans, G. (1950). *The human group.* New York: Harcourt, Brace & World.

Homans, G. (1961). *Social behavior: Its elementary forms.* New York: Harcourt Brace Jovanovich.

Hunter, A., & Riger, S. (1986). The meaning of community in community mental health. *Journal of Community Psychology, 14*, 25-69.

Iacobucci, D., & Wasserman, S. (1987). Dyadic social interactions. *Psychological Bulletin, 102*, 293-306.

Iacobucci, D., & Wasserman, S. (1988). A general framework for the statistical analysis of sequential dyadic interaction data. *Psychological Bulletin, 103*, 379-390.

Israel, B., & Antonucci, T. (1987). Social network characteristics and psychological well-being. *Health Education Quarterly, 14*, 461-481.

Jones, W. (1982). Loneliness and social behavior. In L. A. Peplau & D. Perlman (Eds.), *Loneliness* (pp. 238-252). New York: Wiley.

Keller, S. (1968). *The urban neighborhood.* New York: Random House.

Kemper, T. (1972). The division of labor: A post-Durkheimian analytical view. *American Sociological Review, 37*, 739-753.

Kessler, R., & McLeod, J. (1985). Social support and mental health in community samples. In S. Cohen & S. L. Syme (Eds.), *Social support and health* (pp. 219-240). Orlando, FL: Academic Press.

Knoke, D., & Burt, R. S. (1983). Prominence. In R. S. Burt & M. J. Minor (Eds.), *Applied network analysis: A methodological introduction.* Beverly Hills, CA: Sage.

Lazarsfeld, P., & Merton, R. (1964). Friendship as a social process. In M. Berger, T. Abel, & C. Page (Eds.), *Freedom and control in modern society* (pp. 18-66). New York: Octagon.

Lee, B. A., Campbell, K. E., & Miller, O. (1991). Racial differences in urban neighboring. *Sociological Forum, 6*, 525-550.

Leighton, B. (1986). *Experiencing personal network communities.* Unpublished doctoral dissertation, University of Toronto.

Lin, N. (1982). Social resources and instrumental action. In P. Marsden & N. Lin (Eds.), *Social structure and network analysis* (pp. 131-146). Beverly Hills, CA: Sage.

Lin, N. (1986a). Conceptualizing social support. In N. Lin, A. Dean, & W. Ensel (Eds.), *Social support, life events, and depression* (pp. 17-30). New York: Academic Press.

Lin, N. (1986b). Modeling the effects of social support. In N. Lin, A. Dean, & W. Ensel (Eds.), *Social support, life events, and depression* (pp. 173-209). New York: Academic Press.

Lin, N., Dumin, M. Y., & Woelfel, M. (1986). Measuring community and network support. In N. Lin, A. Dean, & W. Ensel (Eds.), *Social support, life events, and depression* (pp. 153-170). New York: Academic Press.

Lin, N., Woelfel, M., & Light, S. C. (1986). Buffering the impact of the most important life event. In N. Lin, A. Dean, & W. Ensel (Eds.), *Social support, life events, and depression* (pp. 307-332). New York: Academic Press.

Liu, W., & Duff, R. (1972). The strength in weak ties. *Public Opinion Quarterly, 78,* 361-366.

Marsden, P. (1988). Homogeneity in confiding relations. *Social Networks, 10,* 57-76.

Marsden, P. (1990). Network data and measurement. *Annual Review of Sociology, 16,* 435-463.

Marsden, P., & Campbell, K. (1984). Measuring tie strength. *Social Forces, 63,* 482-501.

Maxwell, G. (1985). Behaviour of lovers: Measuring the closeness of relationships. *Journal of Social and Personal Relationships, 2,* 215-238.

Milardo, R. (1989). Theoretical and methodological issues in the identification of the social networks of spouses. *Journal of Marriage and the Family, 51,* 165-174.

Milardo, R. (1991, May). *Comparative methods for delineating social networks.* Paper presented at the International Network Conference on Personal Relationships.

Milić, A. (1991). *Family social network and social stratification.* Unpublished manuscript, University of Beograd.

Mitchell, J. C. (Ed.). (1969). *Social networks in urban situations.* Manchester: Manchester University Press.

Mitchell, J. C. (1987). The components of strong ties among homeless women. *Social Networks, 9,* 37-48.

Neyer, F., Bien, W., Marbach, J., & Templeton, R. (1991). Obtaining reliable network data about family life: A methodological examination concerning reliability of ego-centered networks in survey research. *Connections, 14,* 14-26.

O'Connell, L. (1984). An exploration of exchange in three relationships: Kinship, friendship and the marketplace. *Journal of Social and Personal Relationships, 1,* 333-345.

Oliver, M. (1988). The urban black community as network. *Sociological Quarterly, 29,* 623-645.

Olson, P. (1982). Urban neighborhood research. *Urban Affairs Quarterly, 17,* 491-518.

Pattison, P. E. (1993). *Algebraic models for social networks.* Cambridge: Cambridge University Press.

Perlman, D., & Fehr, B. (1987). The development of intimate relationships. In D. Perlman & S. Duck (Eds.), *Intimate relationships* (pp. 13-42). Newbury Park, CA: Sage.

Pescosolido, B., & Georgianna, S. (1989). Durkheim, suicide, and religion: Toward a network theory of suicide. *American Sociological Review, 54,* 33-48.

Radoeva, D. (1993, February). *Networks of informal exchange in state-socialist societies.* Paper presented at the International Sunbelt Social Network Conference, Tampa, FL.

Reis, H., & Shaver, P. (1988). Intimacy as an interpersonal process. In S. Duck (Ed.), *Handbook of interpersonal relationships* (pp. 367-390). Chicester, U.K.: Wiley.

Reitz, K. P., & Dow, M. M. (1989). Network interdependence of sample units in contingency tables. *Journal of Mathematical Sociology, 14,* 85-96.

Riley, D., & Cochran, M. (1985). Naturally occurring childrearing advice for fathers: Utilization of the personal social network. *Journal of Marriage and the Family, 47,* 275-286.

Riley, D., & Eckenrode, J. (1986). Social ties: Subgroup differences in costs and benefits. *Journal of Personality and Social Psychology, 51,* 770-778.

Roberts, B. (1991). Household coping strategies and urban poverty in a comparative perspective. In M. Gottdiener & C. Pickvance (Eds.), *Urban life in transition* (pp. 135-168). Newbury Park, CA: Sage.

Rook, K. (1984). The negative side of social interaction: Impact on psychological well-being. *Journal of Personality and Social Psychology, 46,* 1097-1108.

Rook, K. (1987). Reciprocity of social exchange and social satisfaction among older women. *Journal of Personality and Social Psychology, 52,* 145-154.

Rosenthal, C. (1985). Kinkeeping in the familial division of labor. *Journal of Marriage and the Family, 47,* 965-974.

Sandler, I. N., & Barrera, M. (1984). Toward a multimethod approach to assessing the effects of social support. *American Journal of Community Psychology, 12,* 37-52.

Sarason, I., Sarason, B., & Shearin, E. N. (1986). Social support as an individual difference variable. *Journal of Personality and Social Psychology, 50,* 845-855.

Seeman, T., & Berkman, L. (1988). Structural characteristics of social networks and their relationship with social support in the elderly. *Social Science and Medicine, 26,* 737-749.

Sik, E. (1993, February). *Networking in capitalist, communist and post-communist societies.* Paper presented at the International Sunbelt Social Network Conference, Tampa, FL.

Silverman, C. (1986). Neighboring and urbanism: Commonality versus friendship. *Urban Affairs Quarterly, 22,* 312-328.

Soldo, B., Wolf, D., & Agree, E. (1986, November). *Family, household and care arrangements of disabled older women.* Paper presented at the annual meeting of the Gerontological Society of America, Chicago.

Stokes, J. (1983). Predicting satisfaction with social support from social network structure. *American Journal of Community Psychology, 11,* 141-152.

Stokes, J., & Wilson, D. G. (1984). The inventory of socially supportive behaviors: Dimensionality, prediction, and gender differences. *American Journal of Community Psychology, 12,* 53-69.

Strauss, D., & Ikeda, M. (1990). Pseudolikelihood estimation for social networks. *Journal of the American Statistical Association, 85,* 204-212.

Thoits, P. (1982). Conceptual, methodological and theoretical problems in studying social support as a buffer against life stress. *Journal of Health and Social Behavior, 23,* 145-159.

Unger, D., & Wandersman, A. (1985). The importance of neighbors. *American Journal of Community Psychology, 13,* 139-169.

van Tilburg, T., van Sonderen, E., & Ormel, J. (1991). The measurement of reciprocity in ego-centered networks of personal relationships: A comparison of various indices. *Social Psychology Quarterly, 54,* 54-66.

Verbrugge, L. (1977). The structure of adult friendship choices. *Social Forces, 56,* 576-597.

Wagner, R. (1987). Changes in the friend network during the first year of single parenthood for Mexican American and Anglo women. *Journal of Divorce, 11,* 89-102.

Waring, E. M. (1985). Measurement of intimacy. *Psychological Medicine, 15,* 9-14.

Warren, D. (1981). *Helping networks.* Notre Dame, IN: University of Notre Dame Press.

Wasserman, S., & Faust, K. (1994). *Social network analysis: Methods and applications.* New York: Cambridge University Press.

Wasserman, S., & Weaver, S. O. (1985). Statistical analysis of binary relational data: Parameter estimation. *Journal of Mathematical Psychology, 29,* 406-427.

Wellman, B. (1979). The community question. *American Journal of Sociology, 84,* 1201-1231.

Wellman, B. (1981). Applying network analysis to the study of support. In B. H. Gottlieb (Ed.), *Social networks and social support* (pp. 171-200). Beverly Hills, CA: Sage.

Wellman, B. (1982). Studying personal communities. In P. Marsden & N. Lin (Eds.), *Social structure and network analysis* (pp. 61-80). Beverly Hills, CA: Sage.

Wellman, B. (1985). Domestic work, paid work and net work. In S. Duck & D. Perlman (Eds.), *Understanding personal relationships* (pp. 159-191). Beverly Hills, CA: Sage.

Wellman, B. (1988). The community question re-evaluated. In M. P. Smith (Ed.), *Power, community and the city* (pp. 81-107). New Brunswick, NJ: Transaction.

Wellman, B. (1992a). Men in networks: Private communities, domestic friendships. In P. Nardi (Ed.), *Men's friendships* (pp. 74-114). Newbury Park, CA: Sage.

Wellman, B. (1992b). Which types of ties and networks give what kinds of social support? In E. Lawler, B. Markovsky, C. Ridgeway, & H. Walker (Eds.), *Advances in group processes* (Vol. 9, pp. 207-235). Greenwich, CT: JAI.

Wellman, B. (in press). An egocentric network tale. *Social Networks.*

Wellman, B., Carrington, P., & Hall, A. (1988). Networks as personal communities. In B. Wellman & S. D. Berkowitz (Eds.), *Social structures: A network approach* (pp. 130-184). Cambridge: Cambridge University Press.

Wellman, B., & Gulia, M. (1993, February). *Which types of networks provide what kinds of social support?* Paper presented at the International Sunbelt Social Network Conference, Tampa, FL.

Wellman, B., & Tindall, D. (1993). Reach out and touch some bodies: How social networks connect telephone networks. In G. Barnett & W. Richards, Jr. (Eds.), *Advances in communication networks* (pp. 63-99). Norwood, NJ: Ablex.

Wellman, B., & Wortley, S. (1989). Brothers' keepers: Situating kinship relations in broader networks of social support. *Sociological Perspectives, 32,* 273-306.

Wellman, B., & Wortley, S. (1990). Different strokes from different folks: Community ties and social support. *American Journal of Sociology, 96,* 558-588.

Wilcox, B. (1981). Social support in the adjusting to marital disruptions: A network analysis. In B. Gottlieb (Ed.), *Social networks and social support* (pp. 97-116). Beverly Hills, CA: Sage.

Willmott, P. (1986). *Social networks, informal care and public policy.* London: Policy Studies Institute.

Willmott, P. (1987). *Friendship networks and social support.* London: Policy Studies Institute.

Young, C., Giles, D., Jr., & Plantz, M. (1982). Natural networks: Help-giving and help-seeking in two rural communities. *American Journal of Community Psychology, 10,* 457-469.

4

Social Cognition in Context

Some Applications of
Social Network Analysis

PHILIPPA PATTISON

Social cognition[1] is the study of individuals' mental representations of the social world, especially of other individuals and social events. It is concerned with the ways in which mental representations and judgment processes interact in a dynamic way with information that a person receives about persons and events in his or her social environment (e.g., M. B. Brewer, 1988). The area has traditionally encompassed the study of phenomena such as impression formation, person memory, social persuasion, attribution processes, and attitude change (e.g., Fiske & Taylor, 1990). Although many of these processes have been argued to depend on the context of social relationships in which they occur, relatively little systematic examination has been undertaken of the relationship between social cognition and this aspect of social context. Instead, a great deal of experimental work has been conducted in relative isolation so as to reduce the anticipated contextual effects as far as possible.

No doubt the difficulty of specifying and measuring the relevant aspects of social context have contributed to its status as an acknowledged but rarely studied component of social cognition (e.g., Fiske & Taylor, 1990; Levine, Resnick, & Higgins, 1993; Morgan & Schwalbe, 1990; Schneider, 1991). In this chapter, I outline some of the possibilities for conceptualizing social context that are offered by the concepts and methods of social network analysis. The chapter is divided into two parts. The first introduces some concepts from network analysis that are useful for describing social context or social "locale." The second reviews the arguments that have been made about the nature of the relationship between cognition and social locale and describes some illustrative empirical studies. It is proposed that different aspects of social context are invoked by these arguments and that we can construct a general framework for combining methods of network analysis with insights into the nature of contextual effects.

Describing Social Locale

The notion that individuals are arranged by their social relationships into interconnected social "positions" has a long history in social science, but attempts to identify concrete social positions from observed relational data are more recent. The work of Harrison White and his colleagues (e.g., Lorrain & White, 1971; White, Boorman, & Breiger, 1976) was instrumental in this development. It elaborated the insights of Nadel (1957), who argued that "we arrive at the structure of a society through abstracting from the concrete population and its behaviour the pattern or network (or 'system') of relationships obtaining between actors in their capacity of playing roles relative to one another" (p. 12). White and his colleagues developed the first means of identifying, from observed network data, those individuals who held similar patterns of social relationships to other individuals, and so who operated in a similar environment of social relationships. They argued that persons with similar patterns of social relations held the same social *position* and therefore that they played similar social *roles*. Implicit in the discussion that follows is the notion that social positions and roles identified from network data contribute to an understanding of an individual's social context. The term *position* is used here to refer to a form of social "location," and *role* is used to denote the pattern of relationships in terms of which a position is described (Faust, 1988, and Faust & Wasserman, 1992, adopt the same convention). This use of the terms is not entirely standard in the literature; in particular, a role is

Table 4.1 A Network on Seven Models

Relation	Element						
	1	*2*	*3*	*4*	*5*	*6*	*7*
P	1	1	0	0	0	1	0
	1	1	0	0	0	0	0
	0	0	1	0	0	0	0
	0	1	0	1	1	0	0
	1	1	0	1	1	1	0
	0	1	0	0	1	1	0
	0	0	0	0	0	0	0
N	0	0	1	1	1	1	1
	0	0	0	0	1	0	0
	1	0	0	0	1	1	1
	1	0	0	0	0	0	0
	0	0	0	0	0	0	0
	1	0	1	0	1	0	1
	0	0	0	0	0	1	0

often identified with a *label* signifying a form of social location and associated relationships, such as teacher, mother, and friend, and both positions and roles are often assumed to convey a collection of implied rights and obligations. Here, though, we will use the terms in the more technical sense adopted by White et al., characterizing them in terms of collections of observed social relationships.

Two types of network are described in the discussion that follows. The first is a *complete* network, comprising a collection of individuals and a set of relations representing their interpersonal ties of one or more kinds. A complete network may be presented in matrix form (as in Table 4.1) with the rows and columns of each matrix corresponding to the individuals in the network and each matrix representing a particular type of tie. For instance, in Table 4.1, one matrix represents friendship links while another represents relations of negative affect. The entries in the matrix record the presence or absence of a link of the given type from the row person to the column person; $R_h(i, j)$ is equal to 1 if the link of type h from person i to person j is present, and 0 otherwise. The scheme may be generalized to accommodate valued links indicating the strength of relation; for details, see Pattison (1993a).

The second type of network is a *local* (or *ego-centered*) one. It records the relations among a focal individual (termed *ego*) and those in *ego*'s immediate social circle. The members of this social circle may all be *direct* associates of *ego* or they may be *indirect* associates. The network constituting *ego*, individuals to whom *ego* is directly connected, and all the ties among *ego* and these individuals are termed the *first-order zone* for *ego*. The *second-order zone* contains individuals connected to *ego* by a path of no more than two relations, together with all their interrelations. More generally, the *kth-order zone* includes all individuals connected to *ego* by a path of no more than k relations. (There is a *path* $T_1 T_2 \ldots T_k$ of *length* k in a complete or local network if there is a sequence $x_1, x_2, \ldots, x_{k+1}$ of network members such that $T_h(x_h, x_{h+1}) = 1$, for each $h = 1, 2, \ldots, k$.) A local network may also be represented in matrix form; for instance, the network in Table 4.1 can be seen as a local network constructed from the first-order zone of node 1. The representation is the same as that for a complete network except that we adopt the convention of using the first row and column of each matrix for the relations of *ego*. (As for complete networks, the links in a local network may be either dichotomous or valued; the valued case is described by Pattison, 1993a.) There are some complex and, as yet, unresolved issues in the measurement of network data, including questions of how best to identify the nodes in the network, how to determine which relations are relevant, and how to assess network ties; for discussion of the issues, see Batchelder (1989), Marsden (1990), and Wasserman and Faust (1994).

Social Positions in Complete Networks

White et al.'s (1976) original notion was that two individuals occupied the same social position if they were related by the same types of relations to exactly the same individuals. The notion is captured by the relation of *structural equivalence* defined as follows: Persons i and j are *structurally equivalent* if (a) $R_h(i, m) = R_h(j, m)$ for all relations R_h and for all network members m; and (b) $R_h(m, i) = R_h(m, j)$ for all relations R_h and for all m. A social position is then defined by a group of individuals who are structurally equivalent, and the members of any network can be divided into a collection of such groups. As might be expected, the conditions of structural equivalence are rarely satisfied exactly for observed network data; instead, groups, or *blocks*, of individuals who are *approximately* structurally equivalent are usually sought, often with the help of a numerical algorithm (e.g., Breiger, Boorman, & Arabie, 1975; Burt, 1976; also Arabie, Hubert, & Schleutermann, 1990; Batagelj, Ferligoj, & Doreian, 1992). White et al. defined a *blockmodel* for an observed network as an assignment of each network member to one of a collection of blocks, together with a specification of the relations among the blocks. The block to which a person was assigned represented his or her *social position*; the person's *role set* was defined as the collection of relations between his or her block and all the other blocks. When an assignment of individuals to blocks has been determined from empirical data using some clustering algorithm, relations between blocks may be specified by some type of rule. For instance, the *zeroblock criterion* specifies that there is a relation between two blocks whenever *any* person in the first block is linked by the relation to *any* person in the second block, while a *density criterion* requires that such relations exist for a specified *proportion* of pairs of members from the two blocks (Arabie, Boorman, & Levitt, 1978; Breiger et al., 1975). A blockmodel can be represented in the same form as the original network, that is, as a collection of matrices, one for each type of relation, specifying the ties among the blocks (for instance, $B_h[i, j]$ = 1 if there is a link from block i to block j on relation R_h, and $B_h[i, j]$ = 0, otherwise).

The problem of finding blocks of individuals who are approximately structurally equivalent may be tackled in a number of different ways and continues to attract attention (e.g., Batagelj et al., 1992; Borgatti, Everett, & Freeman, 1992). The relative virtues of numerical algorithms for identifying blockmodels from network data are discussed by Batagelj et al. (1992), Faust and Wasserman (1992), and Wasserman and Faust (1994), among others; algorithms are available in the UCINET IV package (Borgatti et al., 1992). Stochastic generalizations of structural equivalence have also been defined (e.g., Anderson, Wasserman, & Faust, 1992; Fienberg & Wasserman, 1981; Holland, Laskey, & Leinhardt, 1983; Wasserman & Anderson, 1987), with persons who are *stochastically equivalent* having links to others with the same probability distribution (where the links between persons i and j are viewed as constituents of a random dyadic vector).

Persons who are structurally equivalent have the same social position in the sense that they are related by the same types of relations to *exactly* the same other individuals. Winship (1988) argued in 1974 that it was useful to conceive of a more abstract notion of social position. He observed that two individuals can be related in similar ways to similar *types* of individuals without having any associates in common. For example, the principals of two schools may relate in similar ways to their supervisors and to their teaching staffs, yet there may be no relationship between staff at the two schools. Winship argued that, although the two principals occupy different concrete positions and roles, they may be playing the same *abstract* social *role* (also Winship & Mandel, 1983). He and Mandel proposed characterizations of role that depended on the *pattern* of relationships between an individual and his or her associates.

A number of attempts have been made to develop Winship's conception of an abstract role, beginning with Winship's own observations about the possible application of network automorphisms. An automorphism of a network is a mapping that relabels the network members but preserves the network structure. Formally, an *automorphism* α of a network **R** comprising relations $R_1, R_2, \ldots, R_p$ among a set of network members X is a one-to-one mapping of the members in X such that

$$R_h(i, j) = R_h[\alpha(i), \alpha(j)]$$

for all members i and j and for all relations R_h. Two persons i and j are *automorphically equivalent* if there is an automorphism α of the network for which $\alpha(i) = j$. Any automorphism of a network partitions the network members into classes of individuals who are automorphically equivalent: The classes are termed *orbits* and the partitioning is termed an *automorphic equivalence* relation. An algorithm for finding all of the orbits of a network is described by Everett (1985); the algorithm, as well as methods for identifying partitions that are approximate automorphic equivalences (Everett & Borgatti, 1988), are also available in UCINET IV (Borgatti et al., 1992). Borgatti et al.'s approximate measures of automorphic equivalence exploit the observation that automorphically equivalent nodes share the same label-independent properties (such as the dyad census, triad census, and various path properties); Burt (1990) has also described a similar strategy.

Winship (1988) argued that individuals who are automorphically equivalent have the same abstract roles; they are related to others by identical *patterns* of relationships. Indeed, this is a very strict definition of abstract role, because relationships involving automorphically equivalent individuals must be strictly parallel, in both form and quantity. As a result, several attempts to relax the conditions of the definition have been proposed. The first was by Winship (1988) and was based on the idea of a "role relation." Consider two people i and j in a network **R** comprising network relations $R_1, R_2, \ldots, R_p$. There may exist direct paths from i to j, labeled by some of the relations in **R**, as well as indirect paths passing through other network members. Imagine a binary vector X_{ij} recording the presence or absence of all possible direct and indirect paths from i to j, with the paths recorded in some fixed order and limited to some maximum length. (Winship & Mandel, 1983, claimed that there is probably no need to consider paths of length greater than 3 or 4.) The vector X_{ij} is termed a *role relation* and characterizes all of the relationships from i to j, both direct and indirect, that result from "the roles that they occupy with respect to each other" (p. 321). For example, paths labeled N, PN, and NN link node 1 to node 7 in the network of Table 4.1. Thus, if the paths of length 2 or less are listed in the order P, N, PP, PN, NP, NN, then the role relation X_{17} is [0 1 0 1 0 1 0]. Person i's *role set* is the set of all distinct role relations that emanate from person i. Winship and Mandel defined as *role equivalent* any two people who have identical role sets. Because any two individuals who are automorphically equivalent have the same role sets, role equivalence is a generalization of automorphic equivalence. As in the case of structural equivalence, collections of people who are approximately role equivalent may be sought using a numerical procedure (e.g., Pattison, 1980, 1988; Winship & Mandel, 1983).

Another generalization of automorphic equivalence has been termed *extended* (Pattison, 1980) or *iterated* (Borgatti, Boyd, & Everett, 1989) automorphic equivalence and leads to the definition of *iterated roles*. The generalization is based on the observation that a reduced network defined on the orbits of an automorphic equivalence relation may itself possess nontrivial automorphisms. (The reduced network has the orbits of the automorphic equivalence as its nodes, and a relation of type R_h from orbit i to orbit j if any member of orbit i is related to any member of orbit j by R_h.) As a result, a new reduced network can be constructed, which again may possess a nontrivial automorphism. The process can be continued until no nontrivial automorphisms can be found; the collection of network members represented by the same node in the final reduced network are said to stand in the same *iterated role* or to be related by an *extended* automorphic equivalence relation.

The generalization of automorphic equivalence that has become most widely adopted is that of "regular" equivalence introduced by White and Reitz (1989). A *regular* equivalence relation on a network **R** among members of a set X is a partition P of X for which persons i and j are in the same class of P if and only if (a) $R_h(i, m) = 1$ implies that $R_h(j, l) = 1$ for some person l in the same class of P as m, and (b) $R_h(m, i) = 1$ implies that $R_h(l, j) = 1$ for some person l in the same class of P as m.

It is clear from the definition that any automorphic equivalence relation is a regular equivalence but that the converse does not necessarily hold. As for automorphic equivalence, individuals in the same class have relationships of the same types to occupants of other classes; here, though, the number of such relationships may vary from one class member to another. White and Reitz devised an algorithm to derive partitions of the set of network members that is an approximate regular equivalence; other algorithms have since been developed as well (also see Batagelj, Doreian, & Ferligoj, 1992; Borgatti et al., 1992; Doreian, 1988). The problem of identifying exact regular equivalence relations in a network is discussed by Borgatti and Everett (1988).

Other relational generalizations of structural, automorphic, and regular equivalence have also been developed, although these have not yet been proposed as general-purpose characterizations of social positions (see, for instance, Kim & Roush, 1984; Pattison, 1982, 1988, 1993a). One of these generalizations to which we refer later is the *central representatives* condition (Pattison, 1982). A partition P satisfies the central representatives condition if each class of P containing a node i of X possesses an element i_c (termed the *central representative* of the class) whose relations satisfy $R_h(i, j) = 1$ implies $R_h(i_c, j_c) = 1$, for all nodes i and j in X. That is, the relations of any member of a class of the partition are a subset of those of the central representative for the class. If a partition of nodes into blocks satisfies the central representatives condition, then the corresponding blockmodel constructed according to the zeroblock criterion is just the network of ties among the central representatives of the blocks.

Each of these generalizations of structural equivalence leads to a partitioning of network members into classes of individuals who may be said to be in the same position. The roles associated with the identified positions may be described by *role sets* in just the same way as White et al. (1976) suggest for a blockmodel. For each pair of classes or positions, we need to specify the conditions under which there is a link of some type from one class to another. In the case of an exact equivalence of one of the types described above, a link of type R_h is present whenever *any* individual in class i is linked to *any* individual in class j. For approximate equivalences, rules based on measures of the degree to which the requirements of the equivalence definition are satisfied may be devised (e.g., Pattison, 1988; also Borgatti et al., 1992).

Describing Role Sets in a Blockmodel

For each of the notions of social position that has been described, the resulting blockmodel summarizes the social positions that have been identified. As White et al. (1976) argued for blockmodels built from the definition of structural equivalence, the *role set* of a block (i.e., the relations of the block with other blocks) helps to characterize the social role associated with a position.

Faust and Wasserman (1992) have summarized the attempts that have been made to describe the possible forms of the role set of a block. These attempts are of three main kinds. First, in the blockmodel for a single relation, blocks can be distinguished according to the degree to which they *express* ties to other blocks, the degree to which they are the *recipients* of ties from other blocks, and the degree to which their expressed ties are directed *internally* (Burt, 1976; Marsden, 1989). As Marsden noted, the eight-class typology that results from these classifications is the most general one that characterizes the social role of a block in a single relation without referring to possible variations in the *pattern* of interblock ties (i.e., without allowing for heterogeneity in interblock relations).

Second, blockmodels for a single relation possessing just two blocks can be classified exhaustively (Faust & Wasserman, 1992; Lorrain, 1975; White et al., 1976) and likely interpretations of the different forms can be advanced. These interpretations tend to distinguish social roles according to levels of social cohesion, centrality, hierarchy, patterns of deference, and so on.

Third, commonly occurring structural forms can be identified and described in relation to a theory of structural positions and particular relation types (e.g., Breiger, 1979). Examples of such structural forms for a blockmodel for a single relation include those suggesting hierarchical distinctions, differentiation into center and periphery, and the presence of cohesive subgroups. For multirelational blockmodels, models for structural form are often sought using the "global role structure" approach of Boorman and White (1976; also Pattison, 1993a). Examples of forms that have been identified include the balance model for positive and negative affect relations (Cartwright & Harary, 1956); its generalizations for mutual and asymmetric affective ties (e.g., Davis, 1979; Johnsen, 1985, 1986; Pattison, 1993a); and models making distinctions in the strength of interpersonal ties (Breiger & Pattison, 1978; Granovetter, 1973; Pattison, 1993a).

Indeed, network concepts usually applied to the description of structure in a single network may also prove useful in these attempts to characterize social role. Such concepts include cohesion (the extent to which a subgroup of individuals display mutual ties), centralization (the extent to which an individual or group of individuals enjoy a "central" location in a network, for instance, by being tied directly to many other nodes, by being "close" to many other nodes, and by forming a part of the shortest paths connecting other pairs of nodes), and patterns of connectivity (the extent to which an individual or group of individuals vary in their capacity to reach or be reached by network paths of different types). Methods for characterizing variations in centrality, cohesion, and reachability are described in Wasserman and Faust (1994).

Social Positions in Local Networks

Less attention has been directed to the problem of identifying persons with similar social positions in local network data, although many of the definitions of equivalence and algorithms for finding approximations may be readily adapted to this case, as Everett, Boyd, and Borgatti (1990) have demonstrated. The general problem may be characterized as that of determining whether the focal individuals or *egos* of two networks have similar positions, where the meaning of "similar position" is determined by some type of equivalence. We assume that relations of the same *types* R_h ($h = 1, 2, \ldots, p$) have been assessed in a collection of local networks of order d. Some of the possible notions of position are as follows:

(1) Structural equivalence. To determine whether two *egos* are structurally equivalent, we need to regard the nodes of the local networks as labeled (i.e., a node is labeled i in both local networks only if it represents the same individual). The *union* of the two local networks may be constructed on the union of the members in the two networks, with a link of type R_h from i to j only if there is such a link in either local network. (We assume that, if two persons k and l are members of both local networks, then the relations between them are in agreement in the two networks. Of course, in practice, whether this condition is met depends, in part, on the measurement procedure. If the condition is not met, then a modified procedure for assessing approximate structural equivalence is required.[2]) We can then assess the degree of structural equivalence between the two *egos* in this composite network just as in

the complete network case (for instance, using a covariance or distance measure that has been standardized or not; the properties of these different measures are discussed by Faust & Romney, 1985, and Burt, 1986; see, also, Wasserman & Faust, 1994).

(2) Automorphic equivalence. For the other types of equivalence described above, the local networks need not be regarded as labeled (except at the node corresponding to *ego*) because the definitions refer only to similar relations of *ego* with similar *types* of other individuals. The *ego*s of two local networks may be defined as automorphically equivalent if the local network of one *ego* may be labeled using the node labels of the other in such a way that the two local networks become identical. The one restriction on this labeling is that *ego* in the second local network must have the same label as *ego* in the first. Thus ego_1 and ego_2 are *automorphically equivalent* if there is a one-to-one mapping α from the set of nodes X in the local network of ego_1 to the set of nodes Y in the local network of ego_2 satisfying (a) $\alpha(1) = 1$, and (b) $R_h[\alpha(i),\alpha(j)] = R_h(i, j)$ for all relations R_h and for all individuals i and j. *Extended* automorphic equivalence may also be defined by first constructing local networks reduced by a series of automorphic equivalences; two *ego*s share the same *iterated* role if the *ego*s are automorphically equivalent in these reduced local networks.

(3) Role equivalence. The definition of role equivalence may be applied directly to the *ego*s of two local networks; indeed, the definition was devised to be applicable across different networks (Winship & Mandel, 1983). A study by Leung, Pattison, and Wales (1993) that makes use of this possibility is described later.

(4) Regular equivalence. A local network version of regular equivalence may be defined on the disjoint union of the local networks for two *ego*s (Everett et al., 1990). Suppose that the set of members of the two networks are denoted by X and Y, with X and Y regarded as disjoint (i.e., their members have different labels) even though some individuals may belong to both local networks. The disjoint union of the two local networks is then a set of relations R_h among the members of $X \cup Y$, with a link of type R_h from i to j in the union if there was such a link in either constituent network. The *ego*s of the local networks are then regularly equivalent if there is a regular equivalence relation on the union of the networks that places the two *ego*s in the same class. Approximate measures of the regular equivalence of the two *ego*s may also be directly constructed in the disjoint union.

Algebraic Characterizations of Social Role

All of the above characterizations of social role rely on comparisons among the collections of relations that one individual has with another, that is, on some kinds of comparison among role relations. An approach adopting a more abstract characterization of the pattern of relationships held by an individual in a network has been proposed by Mandel (1978, 1983; also Breiger & Pattison, 1986; Pattison, 1989, 1993a; Pattison & Wasserman, 1993; Wu, 1983). It involves the construction of an algebra to represent relationships among relations in the local network vicinity of an individual. The algebra may be defined for individuals in complete networks as well as for the focal individual *ego* in a local network. In fact, we may observe that a complete network among a collection of individuals gives rise to a local network for each individual as *ego* in turn. The construction below is described for a local network.

The algebra is constructed from comparisons among paths in the network that have *ego* as their source. (The *source* of the path $T_1T_2 \ldots T_k$ in which $T_h(i_{h-1}, i_h) = 1$ for each $h = 1, 2, \ldots, k - 1$ is the node i_0, while i_k is a *target*.) For each path label $T_1T_2 \ldots T_k$, it is possible to identify the subset of local network members who are the target for such a path having *ego* as its source. The subset can be represented in the form of a binary vector termed a *relation vector* and denoted by $ego*T_1T_2 \ldots T_k$; the vector has entries $ego*T_1T_2 \ldots T_k(j) = 1$ if j is a target for a path $T_1T_2 \ldots T_k$ from *ego*, and 0 otherwise. For instance, in the network presented in Table 4.1, the relation vector $ego*P = [1\ 0\ 0\ 0\ 1\ 0]$, whereas $ego*PP = [1\ 1\ 0\ 0\ 1\ 1\ 0]$.

The relation vectors may be compared to determine whether a path of one type in a local network implies the presence of another type of path. In the local network of Table 4.1, for instance, paths of type P having *ego* as their source occur only if a path of type PP is also present. Relations such as this give rise to a partial ordering relation between pairs of paths A and B:

$$A \leq B \quad \text{if} \quad ego*A(j) \leq ego*B(j), \quad \text{for all } j,$$

where $ego*A(j) \leq ego*B(j)$ if *ego* is connected to j by either (a) paths of both types A and B, (b) a path of type B and not A, or (c) paths of neither type A nor type B. For instance, $P < PP$ in the local network of Table 4.1. If $ego*A(j) = ego*B(j)$, for all j, then we may write $A = B$;

in this case, the paths A and B link *ego* to exactly the same set of individuals in the local network.

In any local network, there are an infinite number of potential path labels, although only a finite number of these give rise to distinct relation vectors. It is possible to represent the orderings among all possible relation vectors using two finite tables (e.g., Pattison, 1993a). The orderings among relation vectors recorded in these two tables define the *local role algebra Q* of the local network. Mandel (1983) argued that the local role algebra provides an abstract characterization of the patterns and regularities in relational ties associated with an individual's social position in the local network. It can therefore be used to define a characterization of the individual's social *role*.

It follows from this claim that two individuals have the same social role if their local role algebras are identical. More generally, we can compare the social roles of two individuals by comparing the orderings among relation vectors in their local role algebras. The comparison may be performed either numerically (Breiger & Pattison, 1986; Mandel, 1983) or algebraically (Breiger & Pattison, 1986; Pattison, 1989, 1993a). Algebraic comparisons rely on the *nesting relation* for local role algebras. If Q_1 and Q_2 are two local role algebras defined on the same set $\{R_1, R_2, \ldots, R_p\}$ of relation labels, then Q_1 is *nested* in Q_2 if, whenever $A \le B$ in Q_2, then $A \le B$ in Q_1. Thus Q_1 is nested in Q_2 if any ordering relation that holds in Q_2 also holds in Q_1. The *joint role algebra JRA*(Q_1, Q_2) of Q_1 and Q_2 is the greatest role algebra that is nested in both Q_1 and Q_2, whereas the *common role algebra CRA*(Q_1, Q_2) of Q_1 and Q_2 is the least role algebra in which both Q_1 and Q_2 are nested. The joint role algebra is the greatest role algebra containing all of the orderings present in either Q_1 or Q_2, while the common role algebra is the least role algebra whose orderings are present in *both* Q_1 and Q_2. Indeed, the common role algebra constructed from the local role algebras of all of the nodes in a complete network is equivalent to the algebraic construction that has been proposed to characterize structure in complete networks (Boorman & White, 1976; Mandel, 1983; Pattison, 1993a).

Mandel (1983) also considered the problem of a *match* between the implicit characterization of role associated with a blockmodel for a network and the more direct characterization of role by a local role algebra. In a complete network, two individuals are regarded as playing the same social role if they are assigned to the same social position, that is, to the same *block* in a blockmodel for the network (where the blockmodel may be constructed using any of the definitions of equivalence reviewed above). Mandel (1983) argued that the two characterizations of role are *consistent* if the local role algebra for the block to which a person is assigned is nested in the local role algebra of the local network having the individual as *ego*. That is, each individual assigned to the same block should possess the features of social role described by the local role algebra of the block, although, in addition, an individual may possess some distinctive aspects of role.

The relational and algebraic approaches to the characterization of social role have both been demonstrated to be useful and, indeed, are linked in many ways (e.g., Mandel, 1983; Pattison, 1993a). For example, it can be shown that any regular (and hence, structural, automorphic or extended automorphic) equivalence in a complete or local network satisfies Mandel's criterion for consistency (Pattison, 1993b). Thus the mathematical basis of the various approaches that have been taken to describe social "locale" is relatively well understood. A major distinction among the approaches lies in the degree of "abstractness" with which they characterize social locale (also Faust, 1988). *Concrete* definitions, such as those based on structural equivalence, refer to the similarity of relations with the *same* other individuals, whereas the *abstract* definitions, such as automorphic, local role, or regular equivalence, refer to the similarity of relations with *similar* other individuals. Roles may be characterized in terms of the relations between a person's position and other positions (i.e., in terms of the role set of a block in a blockmodel) or they may be characterized more explicitly by the *structure* of relations in the vicinity of a position or individual, that is, in terms of a local role algebra. Thus developments in social network analysis offer a useful battery of concepts and methods for characterizing an individual's social context. I argue below that these developments offer an important methodological contribution to models of social cognition that pay attention to the social context in which it occurs.

Cognition and Social Context

We turn now to a consideration of the arguments that have been made about the nature of links between cognition and its social context. It is possible to distinguish at least three types of proposals about the ways in which cognition may be related to its social context. The first suggests that an individual's locale may be related to cognition because it plays a part in determining the specific *information* to which the individual is exposed. Thus individuals in different social locations may receive different information and participate in different social events and so they may come to construct knowledge differently. The second argument is that locale is related to characteristic *patterns of social interaction*. These patterns of interaction are likely to be associated with particular expectations about future social events and so may lead to certain types of cognitive "bias." The third, potentially more complex, argument is that an individual's social locale frames social cognitions because cognitive processes may directly involve the individual's *perceptions* of his or her social locale.

Information Bias

As noted earlier, the first argument is simply that relations in social networks serve as channels for the flow of social processes, and especially for the transmission of information. As a result, a person's location in a social network determines, at least in part, the information that that person receives and so, quite possibly, the cognitions that use such information. Thus the argument places particular emphasis on the extent to which an individual or group of individuals are in a position to receive information and so on their connectedness to other parts of a network. This type of argument is proposed, for example, as a part of Carley's (1986a, 1986b, 1989a, 1989b) model of the relationship between cognitive structure and social structure. It has also been used to explain the different rates of uptake of technical innovations (e.g., Rice, Grant, Schmitz, & Torobin, 1990). D. D. Brewer (1992) has also investigated a claim of this kind in an analysis of data from Galaskiewicz's (1985) study of charitable nonprofit organizations. Brewer argued that, if cultural knowledge is transmitted by communications among individuals possessing social ties, then persons in positions in a network where information flow is most focused should possess the greatest cultural knowledge. As a consequence, individuals in the most *central* network positions should have the greatest knowledge. In support of this hypothesis, Brewer found a moderate correlation between the centrality of an individual's position and the individual's cultural knowledge (assessed in his analysis by the number of officers of charitable nonprofit organizations who were recognized).

Position as Interaction History

The second argument concerning the relationship between social context and cognition is based on the proposition that a particular social locale may be associated with certain regular patterns of social interaction. The regularity of these patterns of interaction may lead an individual to develop distinctive expectations about future interactions and so to display certain cognitive "biases." In this view, a social locale carries a social "history," representing the collected influence of past social events on the construal of future ones. The argument is also incorporated in Carley's (1986a, 1986b) model and is exemplified, as well, by the work of Freeman and Romney (1987).

Carley's "constructuralist" view of knowledge acquisition is that individuals' cognitive structures, their propensity to interact with other individuals, the social structures they form, and the social consensus to which they give rise, are all being continuously constructed in a reflexive and recursive fashion as individuals interact with those around them (Carley, 1986a). Carley constructed an explicit model for the interaction between social structures (modeled as networks of social relations) and cognitive structures (represented by semantic models of human knowledge). Carley argues that social interaction is a "driving force" behind knowledge acquisition. When two individuals interact, they are likely to communicate facts (a *fact* is seen as a pair of concepts and a relation between them). The fact communicated *by* an individual depends clearly on the knowledge base of the communicating individual; further, a fact can be *accepted* as a communication by a second individual only if it shares concepts with at least one fact already present in the knowledge base of the receiving individual. Thus knowledge acquisition is dependent on social interactions as well as on individuals' current knowledge bases.

A number of consequences follow from Carley's model. These include the propositions that social interaction promotes knowledge acquisition, that shared social position leads to shared knowledge, and that the level of social interaction in a group of individuals determines the level of their shared knowledge. Carley illustrated her model with data from an empirical study of the relationship between the social structure of a group of MIT undergraduates and their cognitions about the concept "tutor." Interactions among students were recorded and used to construct blockmodels for the student group based on the structural equivalence definition. Students were also interviewed about the concept of "tutor" and the interviews were coded as knowledge bases. Using a set of procedures termed *frame technology*, Carley (1986b) was able to confirm the predictions of the model. For instance, individuals in the same block of the blockmodel demonstrated greater consensus than individuals in different blocks. Despite the difficulty of evaluating a model of such complexity, the results lend some illustrative support to the nature of the proposed mechanisms for the link between social locale and the acquisition of social knowledge.

Freeman and Romney's proposals (1987; also, Freeman, Romney, & Freeman, 1987) addressed the debate in the social networks literature initiated by Bernard, Killworth, and Sailer (e.g., Bernard, Killworth, Kronenfeld, & Sailer, 1984) over the accuracy of individuals' reports of social interactions. Bernard and his colleagues had demonstrated that there was substantial disagreement between records of social interactions in a fixed period of time and participants' *reports* of those interactions. Freeman et al. (1987) argued that the discrepancies could be explained, in part, by appealing to cognitive biases reflecting longer-term patterns of social interactions. They also provided a simple demonstration in support of their argument, using data on individuals' reports of attendance at a weekly colloquium series. Both false positive and false negative responses were more likely when there was a discrepancy between the long-term attendance data and attendance at the target meeting, and errors were biased in the direction of the long-term record.

Some studies have investigated individual differences in "accuracy" data of these types and have produced evidence in favor of systematic variations in accuracy according to social position. Romney and Faust (1982), for instance, have found support for the notion that similar social positions are associated with similar social perceptions. Specifically, they demonstrated that, in a network of participants in a graduate education program, the more people interacted with each other, the more they made similar judgments about the communication patterns of others and the more they shared accurate knowledge of those patterns.

Another investigation of the correlates of individuals' accuracy was conducted by Romney and Weller (1984), who demonstrated that an informant's accuracy about patterns of communication in a group was related to his or her *reliability* (namely, the correlation of the informant's responses with the group aggregate). In accounting for the finding, they informally introduced the basic propositions of *cultural consensus theory*,[3] namely, that (a) there exists an objective set of "facts" pertaining to some phenomenon under investigation (such as the pattern of interactions in a group), (b) individuals vary in the extent to which they know the facts, (c) the knowledge of an individual about the phenomenon of interest is independent of the knowledge of every other individual, and (d) the correlation of knowledge between any two individuals is a function of the extent to which each has knowledge of the "truth." These propositions lead to the expectation that the accuracy of an individual is related to his or her reliability and that more reliable individuals will have higher correlations among themselves than less reliable individuals. Romney and Weller confirmed these expectations in three of the four data sets that they analyzed. Boster, Johnson, and Weller (1987) have also examined the relationship between an individual's consensual knowledge about social proximities and his or her social position in a study of the members of an office of a university vice chancellor. They argued that their data also fit the cultural consensus model (Romney, Weller, & Batchelder, 1986) and showed that, whereas an individual's accuracy was related to his or her status in the organization, individuals' agreement about social proximities in the office was unrelated to their judged similarities.

It is interesting to note that these studies exhibit some differences in their findings about the relationship between agreement among individuals on social phenomena and the similarity of their social positions. Romney and Faust (1982) found that agreement was related to levels of social interaction, as did Romney and Weller (1984), although the latter authors argued that "reliability" was a stronger predictor of accuracy than interaction levels. Boster et al. (1987) found that the level of an individual's consensual knowledge was related to the status of the individual's formal position in the organization (Boster et al., 1987) and that agreement was not stronger for individuals who were seen as more similar in position (although there was some evidence for greater agreement among high-status individuals than among other office members).

The nature of the relationship between social position and consensual knowledge or accuracy is, as yet, not well understood. The cultural consensus model places strong constraints on its possible form and, in some types of network, there may be a conflict between the requirements of the consensus model and the argument for the role of social context that was introduced earlier. In assuming that the correlation between individuals' knowledge depends only on the extent to which each knows the truth (i.e., in assuming that the knowledge of one individual is independent of the knowledge of another), the cultural consensus model proposes that all local variations in knowledge associated with social positions may be explained by local variations in reliability. It may be argued that the validity of the latter proposition is likely to depend on the way in which social positions are related to one another, that is, on the *structure* of the network. If the network possesses a core-periphery structure or some type of hierarchical structure, then the arguments that have been reviewed for a relationship between social position and social cognition are likely to make similar predictions to the cultural consensus theory. If, on the other hand, the network displays a division into two or more factions or some other more complex structure, then the assumptions of cultural consensus theory are likely to break down (indeed, the model may be used to demonstrate the lack of consensus, as Romney, Batchelder, & Weller, 1987, have shown). Thus it would clearly be useful to explore more systematically the role of network structure in the relationship between consensual knowledge and social position.

In a somewhat different domain of study, Leung et al. (1993) investigated the proposition that the semantics of lexical items, such as "friend," are influenced by the social context of their use. They examined individuals' variations in meaning ascribed to the term *friend* among grade-10 high school students. They showed that, although there was substantial agreement in the characteristics of "friendship," subtle variations in the reported attributes of friendship could be discerned. In particular, ratings of the qualities of friendship and of characteristics of an ideal friend varied according to social positions determined from a network analysis of reported positive and negative affective ties. The social positions were identified in two stages. In the first stage, blockmodels for each of five class groups were constructed using the structural equivalence definition. In the second, Winship and Mandel's (1983) role-equivalence definition was used to identify sets of blocks from the class blockmodels having a similar social position and so to construct a "superblockmodel" describing relations between the "superblocks" thus identified. (The latter blockmodel is presented in Table 4.1.) Leung et al. demonstrated that individuals in superblocks 4, 2, and 6 saw "friendship" in a more positive light, with friendship characterized by the possession of many positive attributes (faithful, likes your company, funny, talkative, open, thoughtful, and so on). Individuals in superblocks 1 and 5, on the other hand, had less positive views of friendship. It can be seen from Table 4.1 that these two groups of blocks are distinguished by their social roles and, in particular, by the negative affective ties that they receive from other blocks. (Blocks 1 and 5 are the recipients of more negative affective ties than the other blocks, whereas blocks 2 and 4 receive fewest negative ties.) Thus there is some evidence for variation in the meaning ascribed to the abstract quality of "friendship" as a function of the social context in which the ascription is made.

In addition to these demonstrations of such effects in naturalistic settings, effects associated with the adoption of a social role on cognition have also been found in laboratory settings (e.g., see the review in Levine et al., 1993).

Structural Balance and Related Models

The third argument in support of a relationship between social cognition and its social context is based on the observation that a person's cognitions occur within a context of appraisals of the situations of others in the social environment. Thus, it is argued, a person's social position may be related in systematic ways to her perceptions of the cognitions of other individuals around her. Early arguments of this type were the so-called *consistency theories* (e.g., Fiske & Taylor, 1990) of which Heider's (1946, 1958) theory of "balance" is an example. Heider put forward the view that "unbalanced" states (i.e., those in which the affective relations among three entities comprise one negative relation and two positive relations, or three negative relations) would create a force toward action or cognitive reorganization. For instance, if person *a* likes person *b*, and *c* is an important entity (e.g., issue or third person), then there is a tendency for *a*'s attitude toward *c* to agree with that which *a* perceives *b* to hold toward *c*.

A number of models for patterns of affective relations among triples of individuals have been put forward as applications and/or generalizations of Heider's (1958) basic hypothesis. These variations include extensions of balance to relations among two or more individuals (rather than to perceived relations on the part of a single individual) and modifications to the assumptions about which states are likely to lead to cognitive reorganization (e.g., Cartwright & Harary, 1956; Davis, 1979; Holland & Leinhardt, 1971; Johnsen, 1985). Most recently, Johnsen (1986) has analyzed the various "microprocesses" by which sentiment structures might be generated. His analysis dealt with combinations of four basic processes that may link friendship (i.e., social relations) and agreement (i.e., cognitions). The four processes are as follows: (a) Those who agree on others tend to be mutual friends; (b) those who agree on others tend to have some friendship; (c) those who have some friendship tend to agree on others; and (d) mutual friends tend to agree on others. Each of these processes has a complement; for instance, the complement of the first process is that those who are not mutual friends tend to disagree on others. Each process also determines a set of triadic relations among individuals that are forbidden, in the sense of being in violation of the microprocess in equilibrium. Johnsen examined the conjunctions and disjunctions of all these processes and the associated sets of forbidden triads. He showed that empirically derived models for affective ties are accounted for substantially by the processes in which friendship induces agreement (or, equivalently, disagreement induces nonfriendship). His analysis provides a description of the way in which social network structure and social cognition may come to be mutually constrained.

Other arguments about the ways in which the social proximity of individuals comes to influence their social cognitions have also been made. Burt (1987), for instance, contrasted the position that social *cohesion* leads to shared views and behavior with the claim that individuals in similar social locations (i.e., who are *structurally equivalent*) come to make similar judgments. As Marsden and Friedkin (1993, also this volume) have observed, there are a variety of processes that can be advanced to underlie these claims, including information exchange, influence, and social comparison and these various processes may arise in the context of relations of communication, affect, authority, and even competition. These processes can also be described in relation to the three main arguments that have been outlined for the link between social cognition and social locale. Most commonly, arguments for the role of social cohesion have seen strong affective ties as the basis for influence, with communication (e.g., Galaskiewicz & Burt, 1991) or the resolution of conflict or inconsistency (e.g., Marsden & Friedkin, 1993) as the underlying mechanism. Proponents of the *structural equivalence* position, on the other hand, see "symbolic" communication among individuals in similar social positions (Galaskiewicz & Burt, 1991) as the key to social influence. For instance, Burt (1987) proposed that individuals in the same social positions in communication networks will "use each other as a frame of reference for subjective judgments and so make similar judgments even if they have no direct communication with each other." Indeed, because individuals in similar social locations may, in some circumstances, stand in a competitive relationship, there may be no positive affective relation underlying this form of influence.

It is clear, though, that individuals who are approximately structurally equivalent are likely to be similar in many respects, so that it is difficult to disentangle the possible mechanisms underlying their shared agreement. Thus individuals in similar social positions are likely to receive similar information from other network members; they are likely to have experienced similar patterns of interaction in the past and so to have developed similar expectations and biases; and they are also likely to develop similar perceptions about their social contexts. Thus all of the arguments linking social cognition to its network location would predict greater agreement, in general, for individuals who are in similar social positions than for individuals who are merely strongly tied. Perhaps not surprising, direct comparisons between *cohesion* and *structural equivalence* as correlates of behavioral or cognitive agreement have favored *structural equivalence* as the stronger one (e.g., Burt, 1987; Burt & Doreian, 1982; Galaskiewicz & Burt, 1991).

Krackhardt and Porter (1986) have extended Burt's (1982) proposals about the relationship between structural equivalence and social influence by arguing that individuals are influenced by those persons perceived to be in a similar, but not necessarily identical, social position to themselves, that is, by individuals who are perceived to be regularly equivalent to themselves. They suggested that the behavior of these persons will be more salient for the individual, although the way in which it influences an individual's cognitions may vary from one situation to another.

Erickson (1988) has also argued that attitudes are made, maintained, or modified primarily through interpersonal processes. She noted that there have been a number of attempts to predict the extent of attitude agreement among people as a function of their relationships and structural locations. Social comparison theory (e.g., Suls & Miller, 1977), for example, asserts that people prefer to compare themselves with others who are similar in salient respects. Social identity theory (e.g., Turner & Oakes, 1989) also asserts that individuals' cognitions are influenced by those around them, with influence strongest from individuals who are seen as sharing the same "social identity" and especially for those whose views are seen as prototypical of those of the "in-group."

Erickson (1988) argued that views such as these imply a relationship between social ties and cognitive phenomena such as attitude agreement. Thus the frequency, multiplexity, strength, and symmetry of dyadic relations would predict greater agreement (as well as the individual attributes that are usually studied). Beyond the dyadic level, denser cliques should have greater attitude similarity (and the relevant clique idea is density rather than reachability); and structurally equivalent people should have more similar attitudes because they "tend to interact with the same actors in the same way" (Burt, 1978).

The proposals that have been outlined emphasize different aspects of similarity in network position as relevant to the process of social influence and, as yet, there is insufficient theoretical elaboration or empirical evidence to address their distinctions. There is agreement, though, on the more basic claim that standard theories about person attitude formation and decision-making processes should be embedded in a network context and should attend to relevant attributes of an individual's social locale. It is also clear that the descriptions of social locale that have been reviewed permit the relationship between these attributes and social cognition to be explored in some detail.

The Content of Social Cognition

When the social context or social locale is itself seen as the subject of social cognition, the methods of social network analysis should be particularly helpful. Krackhardt (1987) argued that it was important to develop cognitive models for the *perception* of social relations in a network and introduced the concept of a *cognitive social structure* for a system of relationships among a set of individuals. The structure comprises the set of multiple networks perceived by *each* member of the network and so can be seen as a collection of relations $T = \{T_{ih}\}$, where $T_{ih}(k, l) = 1$ if person i reports a link of type h from person k to person l, and $T_{ih}(k, l) = 0$, otherwise. Krackhardt observed that such structures are needed to assess cognitive models for network relations, and he has used data of this type to assess models of the relations between perceptions of the social environment and other individual behaviors and characteristics, such as leaving a job or reputational power (e.g., Krackhardt, 1990; Krackhardt & Kilduff, 1990; Krackhardt & Porter, 1985, 1986).

Freeman, Freeman, and Michaelson (1988) have also examined individuals' *perceptions* of social structures, and they showed in a study of windsurfers at a Californian beach that the combined perceptions of the participant windsurfers matched very well the observations of interaction and spatial separation on the beach made by a team of observers. Michaelson and Contractor (1992) also identified relationships between the perceived similarity of pairs of individuals in a college class and various types of positional similarity (structural equivalence, automorphic equivalence, and regular equivalence). They found some evidence for the importance of positional similarity assessed by measures of the regular equivalence of individuals in the network.

Prospects for Research

We have reviewed above three types of argument that have been made about the nature of links between social cognition and the context in which it occurs. It should be noted that these arguments are not in opposition; rather, they can be seen as relating to different stages of a broadly conceived account of cognition. This account simply allows that cognition depends (a) on the information that reaches a person at a given point in time, (b) on previous information and events to which the person has been exposed, and (c) on relevant relationships in the immediate social environment. Nevertheless, it is possible that the different types of arguments may be associated most closely with distinctive aspects of individuals' positions in networks.

The first two arguments may be summarized as suggesting that, because network ties serve as channels for communication, the information that individuals receive and the knowledge that they construct depend on network location. Thus, from the perspective of these arguments, aspects of network structure that characterize important features of communication patterns are likely to be related to variations in social cognition. Persons with identical patterns of communication are those who have identical relations with others, that is, those who are structurally equivalent. Hence, for arguments of these first two types, positions defined by structural equivalence provide an appropriate means of characterizing social context. Further, the most relevant features of these positions are those that have implications for communication patterns, such as the extent to which individuals occupying these positions receive and send ties to other positions and the extent to which their position occupies a central location. These latter features are described by the role set of the position and are reflected also by aspects of its local algebra. In some cases it may also be helpful to characterize the communication structure of the network by constructing a blockmodel according to the central representative's condition. Such a blockmodel summarizes the network by assigning each individual to a block containing a *central representative*, that is, an individual whose ties include those of all other block members. Relations among the central representatives define relations in the corresponding blockmodel and summarize communication patterns in the network.

The third kind of argument pays more attention to the *pattern* of relational ties in an individual's local social environment. In particular, it emphasizes the salience of persons who are seen as "socially similar" to oneself. From the network perspective, individuals who are socially similar are those who possess similar patterns of social ties—that is, those who are equivalent in the more abstract sense described by the relations of automorphic, local role, and regular equivalence. In addition, individuals with similar local role algebras may also be seen as having similar patterns of social relations. Because regular equivalence satisfies Mandel's condition for consistency (that the local role algebra of a position defined by a regular equivalence block is nested in the local role algebra of each of its members), these two approaches to defining similarity lead to essentially similar descriptions of similarity of network location.

Empirical studies conducted to date have mostly concentrated on establishing that shared social positions in a complete network are, indeed, associated with shared cognitions. It is now possible, though, to further refine questions about the relationship between social cognition and its social locale. For instance, we may ask what *aspects* of similarity in social position are associated with cognition at various stages, that is, what features of *social role* are implicated in the description of the relationship between social cognition and its context? Such questions call for further theoretical articulation of models for social cognition as well as for further empirical investigation. In relation to both of these requirements, though, it may be noted that the description of social role in terms of a local role algebra may be especially helpful, because local role algebras provide an explicit rather than implicit representation of social role. These representations may be compared across individuals to produce detailed accounts of both the similarities and the differences in individuals' social contexts. They should therefore provide much greater specificity in determining the conditions under which social cognition is related to its social context. These representations also permit the study of the relationship between social cognition and its context to be conducted in local as well as complete networks. Studies of local networks are much easier to accommodate within standard social science research designs, and the availability of appropriate methods for describing social positions and roles in local networks should permit much greater freedom in the exploration of the role of context in a variety of social settings.

Thus, in summary, methodological advances in social network analysis provide a collection of theoretically salient descriptions of social context. Already it has been shown in the studies that have been reviewed that these descriptions lead to testable, and often supportable, hypotheses about the links between aspects of social context and social cognition. Many questions remain, and many will be further sharpened only after additional empirical investigation; it is clear, though, that these recent developments in network analysis offer a useful contribution to the investigation of the role of social context in social cognition.[4]

Notes

1. The work described in this chapter deals with the contribution of social network analysis to the study of social cognition. I have not described the potential contributions to more general models of cognition, although it can be argued that the methods of social network analysis provide useful tools for the analysis of networks arising in cognitive psychology, just as models for proximity data have done (e.g., Shoben & Ross, 1987).

2. For instance, the evidence for the presence of a link between a pair of individuals may be combined across two local networks, leading to a quantitative assessment of each link in the network that is the union of the two networks.

3. A formalization of cultural consensus theory has been offered by Romney, Weller, and Batchelder (1986; also, Batchelder & Romney, 1988).

4. A question that has not been addressed in this chapter is the means by which contextual information can be used in statistical models for aspects of social cognition. The studies described in the chapter illustrate some of the possibilities, such as (a) deriving measures that describe context at an individual level and (b) examining relationships between the positional similarity of pairs of individuals and their levels of shared knowledge or agreement (e.g., using the Quadratic Assignment procedure; Hubert, 1987). Models that combine features of these two schemes may also be useful; see, for example, Doreian (1989) and Marsden and Friedkin (this volume).

References

Anderson, C. J., Wasserman, S., & Faust, K. (1992). Building stochastic blockmodels. *Social Networks, 14*, 137-161.

Arabie, P., Boorman, S., & Levitt, P. (1978). Constructing blockmodels: How and why. *Journal of Mathematical Psychology, 17*, 21-63.

Arabie, P., Hubert, L. J., & Schleutermann, S. (1990). Blockmodels from the Bond Energy approach. *Social Networks, 12*, 99-126.

Batagelj, V., Doreian, P., & Ferligoj, A. (1992). An optimizational approach to regular equivalence. *Social Networks, 14*, 121-135.

Batagelj, V., Ferligoj, A., & Doreian, P. (1992). Direct and indirect methods for structural equivalence. *Social Networks, 14*, 63-90.

Batchelder, W. H. (1989). Inferring meaningful global network properties from individual actor's measurement scales. In L. C. Freeman, D. R. White, & A. K. Romney (Eds.), *Research methods in social network analysis* (pp. 89-134). Fairfax, VA: George Mason University Press.

Batchelder, W. H., & Romney, A. K. (1988). Test theory without an answer key. *Psychometrika, 53*, 71-92.

Bernard, H. R., Killworth, P. D., Kronenfeld, D., & Sailer, L. (1984). The problem of informant accuracy: The validity of retrospective data. *Annual Review of Anthropology, 13*, 495-517.

Boorman, S., & White, H. C. (1976). Social structure from multiple networks: II. Role structures. *American Journal of Sociology, 81*, 1384-1446.

Borgatti, S. P., Boyd, J. P., & Everett, M. G. (1989). Iterated roles: Mathematics and application. *Social Networks, 11*, 159-172.

Borgatti, S. P., & Everett, M. G. (1988). The class of all regular equivalences: Algebraic structure and computation. *Social Networks, 11*, 65-88.

Borgatti, S. P., Everett, M. G., & Freeman, L. C. (1992). *UCINET IV*. Columbia, SC: Analytic Technologies.

Boster, J. S., Johnson, J. C., & Weller, S. C. (1987). Social position, and shared knowledge: Actors' perceptions of status, role and social structure. *Social Networks, 9*, 375-387.

Breiger, R. L. (1979). Toward an operational theory of community elite structures. *Quality and Quantity, 13*, 21-57.

Breiger, R. L., Boorman, S. A., & Arabie, P. (1975). An algorithm for clustering relational data with applications to social network analysis. *Journal of Mathematical Psychology, 12*, 328-382.

Breiger, R. L., & Pattison, P. E. (1978). The joint role structure in two communities' elites. *Sociological Methods and Research, 7*, 213-226.

Breiger, R. L., & Pattison, P. E. (1986). Cumulated social roles: The duality of persons and their algebras. *Social Networks, 8*, 215-256.

Brewer, D. D. (1992). A note on the relationship between centrality and cultural knowledge in a professional network. *Connections, 15*, 21-28.

Brewer, M. B. (1988). A dual process model of impression formation. In T. K. Srull & R. S. Wyer, Jr. (Eds.), *Advances in social cognition: Vol. 1. A dual process model of impression formation* (pp. 1-36). Hillsdale, NJ: Lawrence Erlbaum.

Burt, R. S. (1976). Positions in networks. *Social Forces, 55*, 93-122.

Burt, R. S. (1978). Cohesion versus structural equivalence as a basis for network subgroups. *Sociological Methods and Research, 7*, 189-212.

Burt, R. S. (1982). *Toward a theory of structural action*. New York: Academic Press.

Burt, R. S. (1986). A cautionary note. *Social Networks, 8*, 205-211.

Burt, R. S. (1987). Social contagion and innovation: Cohesion versus structural equivalence. *American Journal of Sociology, 92*, 1287-1335.

Burt, R. S. (1990). Detecting role equivalence. *Social Networks, 12*, 83-91.

Burt, R. S., & Doreian, P. (1982). Testing a structural model of perception: Conformity and deviance with respect to journal norms in elite sociological methodology. *Quality and Quantity, 16*, 109-150.

Carley, K. M. (1986a). Knowledge acquisition as a social phenomenon. *Instructional Science, 14*, 381-438.

Carley, K. M. (1986b). An approach for relating social structure to cognitive structure. *Journal of Mathematical Sociology, 12*, 137-189.

Carley, K. M. (1989a). Structural constraints on communication: The diffusion of the Homomorphic Signal Analysis technique through scientific fields. *Journal of Mathematical Sociology.*

Carley, K. M. (1989b). The value of cognitive foundations for dynamic social theory. *Journal of Mathematical Sociology, 14*, 171-208.

Cartwright, D., & Harary, F. (1956). Structural balance: A generalization of Heider's theory. *Psychological Review, 63*, 277-293.

Davis, J. A. (1979). The Davis/Holland/Leinhardt studies: An overview. In P. W. Holland & S. Leinhardt (Eds.), *Perspectives on social network research* (pp. 51-62). New York: Academic Press.

Doreian, P. (1988). Equivalences in a social network. *Journal of Mathematical Sociology, 13*, 243-282.

Doreian, P. (1989). Models of network effects on social actors. In L. C. Freeman, D. R. White, & A. K. Romney (Eds.), *Research methods in social network analysis* (pp. 295-317). Fairfax, VA: George Mason University Press.

Erickson, B. (1988). The relational basis of attitudes. In B. Wellman & S. D. Berkowitz (Eds.), *Social structures: A network approach* (pp. 99-121). New York: Cambridge University Press.

Everett, M. G. (1985). Role similarity and complexity in social networks. *Social Networks, 7*, 353-359.

Everett, M. G., & Borgatti, S. P. (1988). Calculating role similarities: An algorithm that helps to determine the orbits of a graph. *Social Networks, 10*, 77-91.

Everett, M. G., Boyd, J. P., & Borgatti, S. P. (1990). Ego-centered and local roles: A graph-theoretic approach. *Journal of Mathematical Sociology, 15*, 163-172.

Faust, K. (1988). Comparison of methods for positional analysis: Structural and general equivalences. *Social Networks, 10*, 313-341.

Faust, K., & Romney, A. K. (1985). Does STRUCTURE find structure? A critique of Burt's use of distance as a measure of structural equivalence. *Social Networks, 7*, 77-103.

Faust, K., & Wasserman, S. (1992). Blockmodels: Interpretation and evaluation. *Social Networks, 14*, 5-61.

Fienberg, S. E., & Wasserman, S. (1981). Categorical data analysis of single sociometric relations. In S. Leinhardt (Ed.), *Sociological methodology 1981* (pp. 156-192). San Francisco: Jossey-Bass.

Fiske, S. T., & Taylor, S. E. (1990). *Social cognition* (2nd ed.). New York: McGraw-Hill.

Freeman, L. C., Freeman, S. C., & Michaelson, A. (1988). On human social intelligence. *Journal of Social and Biological Structures, 11*, 415-425.

Freeman, L. C., & Romney, A. K. (1987). Words, deeds and social structure: A preliminary study of the reliability of informants. *Human Organization, 46*, 330-334.

Freeman, L. C., Romney, A. K., & Freeman, S. C. (1987). Cognitive structure and informant accuracy. *American Anthropologist, 89*, 310-325.

Galaskiewicz, J. (1985). *Social organization of an urban grants economy.* New York: Academic Press.

Galaskiewicz, J., & Burt, R. S. (1991). Interorganization contagion in corporate philanthropy. *Administrative Science Quarterly, 36,* 88-105.

Granovetter, M. (1973). The strength of weak ties. *American Journal of Sociology, 78,* 1360-1380.

Heider, F. (1946). Attitudes and cognitive organization. *Journal of Psychology, 21,* 107-112.

Heider, F. (1958). *The psychology of interpersonal relations.* New York: John Wiley.

Holland, P. W., Laskey, K. B., & Leinhardt, S. (1983). Stochastic blockmodels: Some first steps. *Social Networks, 5,* 109-137.

Holland, P. W., & Leinhardt, S. (1971). Transitivity in structural models of small groups. *Comparative Group Studies, 2,* 107-124.

Hubert, L. J. (1987). *Assignment methods in combinatorial data analysis.* New York: Marcel Dekker.

Johnsen, E. C. (1985). Network macrostructure models for the Davis-Leinhardt set of empirical sociomatrices. *Social Networks, 7,* 203-224.

Johnsen, E. C. (1986). Structure and process: Agreement models for friendship formation. *Social Networks, 8,* 257-306.

Kim, K. H., & Roush, F. W. (1984). Group relationships and homomorphisms of Boolean matrix semigroups. *Journal of Mathematical Psychology, 17,* 236-246.

Krackhardt, D. (1987). Cognitive social structures. *Social Networks, 9,* 109-134.

Krackhardt, D. (1990). Assessing the political landscape: Structure, cognition and power in organizations. *Administrative Quarterly, 35,* 342-369.

Krackhardt, D., & Kilduff, M. (1990). Friendship patterns and culture: The control of organisational diversity. *American Anthropologist, 92,* 142-154.

Krackhardt, D., & Porter, L. W. (1985). When friends leave: A structural analysis of the relationship between turnover and stayers' attitudes. *Administrative Science Quarterly, 30,* 242-261.

Krackhardt, D., & Porter, L. W. (1986). The snowball effect: Turnover embedded in communication networks. *Journal of Applied Psychology, 71,* 50-55.

Leung, S., Pattison, P. E., & Wales, R. J. (1993). *The semantics of "friend."* Unpublished manuscript, University of Melbourne, Department of Psychology.

Levine, J. M., Resnick, L. B., & Higgins, E. T. (1993). Social foundations of cognition. *Annual Review of Psychology, 44,* 586-612.

Lorrain, F. P. (1975). *Reseaux sociaux et classifications sociales.* Paris: Hermann.

Lorrain, F. P., & White, H. C. (1971). Structural equivalence of individuals in social networks. *Journal of Mathematical Sociology, 1,* 49-80.

Mandel, M. (1978). *Roles and networks: A local approach.* Unpublished B.A. honours thesis, Harvard University, Department of Applied Mathematics.

Mandel, M. (1983). Local roles and social networks. *American Sociological Review, 48,* 376-386.

Marsden, P. V. (1989). Methods for the characterization of role structures in network analysis. In L. C. Freeman, D. R. White, & A. K. Romney (Eds.), *Research methods in social network analysis* (pp. 489-525). Fairfax, VA: George Mason University Press.

Marsden, P. V. (1990). Network data and measurement. *Annual Review of Sociology, 16,* 435-463.

Marsden, P. V., & Friedkin, N. E. (1993). Network studies of social influence. *Sociological Methods and Research, 22*, 125-149.

Michaelson, A., & Contractor, N. (1992). Structural position and perceived similarity. *Social Psychology Quarterly, 55*, 300-310.

Morgan, D. L., & Schwalbe, M. L. (1990). Mind and self in society: Linking social structure and social cognition. *Social Psychology Quarterly, 53*, 148-164.

Nadel, S. F. (1957). *The theory of social structure.* Melbourne: Melbourne University Press.

Pattison, P. E. (1980). *An algebraic analysis for multiple social networks.* Unpublished doctoral dissertation, University of Melbourne, Department of Psychology.

Pattison, P. E. (1982). The analysis of semigroups of multirelational systems. *Journal of Mathematical Psychology, 25*, 87-118.

Pattison, P. E. (1988). Network models: Some comments on papers in this special issue. *Social Networks, 10*, 383-411.

Pattison, P. E. (1989). Mathematical models for local social networks. In J. A. Keats, R. Taft, R. A. Heath, & S. H. Lovibond (Eds.), *Mathematical and theoretical systems* (pp. 139-149). Amsterdam: North Holland.

Pattison, P. E. (1993a). *Algebraic models for social networks.* New York: Cambridge University Press.

Pattison, P. E. (1993b). *Algebras in local networks.* Unpublished manuscript, University of Melbourne, Department of Psychology.

Pattison, P. E., & Wasserman, S. (1993). *Algebraic models for local social networks based on statistical methods.* Unpublished manuscript.

Rice, R. E., Grant, A. E., Schmitz, J., & Torobin, J. (1990). Individual and network influences on the adoption and perceived outcomes of electronic messaging. *Social Networks, 12*, 27-55.

Romney, A. K., Batchelder, W. H., & Weller, S. C. (1987). Recent applications of cultural consensus theory. *American Behavioral Scientist, 31*, 163-177.

Romney, A. K., & Faust, K. (1982). Predicting the structure of a communications network from recalled data. *Social Networks, 4*, 285-304.

Romney, A. K., & Weller, S. C. (1984). Predicting informant accuracy from patterns of recall among individuals. *Social Networks, 6*, 59-77.

Romney, A. K., Weller, S. C., & Batchelder, W. H. (1986). Culture as consensus: A theory of culture and informant accuracy. *American Anthropologist, 88*, 313-338.

Schneider, D. J. (1991). Social cognition. *Annual Review of Psychology, 42*, 527-561.

Shoben, E. J., & Ross, B. H. (1987). Structure and process in cognitive psychology using multidimensional scaling and related techniques. In R. R. Ronning, J. A. Glover, J. C. Conoley, & J. C. Witt (Eds.), *The influence of cognitive psychology on testing* (pp. 229-266). Hillsdale, NJ: Lawrence Erlbaum.

Suls, J. M., & Miller, R. L. (Eds.). (1977). *Social comparison processes.* New York: Hemisphere.

Turner, J. C., & Oakes, P. (1989). Self-categorization theory and social influence. In P. B. Paulus (Ed.), *Psychology of group influence* (2nd ed., pp. 233-275). Hillsdale, NJ: Lawrence Erlbaum.

Wasserman, S., & Anderson, C. J. (1987). Stochastic *a posteriori* blockmodels: Construction and assessment. *Social Networks, 9*, 1-36.

Wasserman, S., & Faust, K. (1994). *Social network analysis: Methods and applications.* New York: Cambridge University Press.

White, D. R., & Reitz, K. P. (1989). Rethinking the role concept: Homomorphisms on social networks. In L. C. Freeman, D. R. White, & A. K. Romney (Eds.), *Research methods in social network analysis* (pp. 429-488). Fairfax, VA: George Mason University Press.

White, H. C., Boorman, S. A., & Breiger, R. L. (1976). Social structure from multiple networks: I. Blockmodels of roles and positions. *American Journal of Sociology, 81*, 730-780.

Winship, C. (1988). Thoughts about roles and relations: An old document revisited. *Social Networks, 10*, 209-231.

Winship, C., & Mandel, M. (1983). Roles and positions: A critique and extension of the blockmodelling approach. In S. Leinhardt (Ed.), *Sociological methodology 1983-1984* (pp. 314-344). San Francisco: Jossey-Bass.

Wu, L. L. (1983). Local blockmodel algebras for analysing social networks. In S. Leinhardt (Ed.), *Sociological methodology 1983-1984* (pp. 272-313). San Francisco: Jossey-Bass.

PART II

Anthropology and Communication

5

Anthropological Contributions to the Study of Social Networks

A Review

JEFFREY C. JOHNSON

There are certain important branches of science, each of which deals with certain class or kinds of structures, the aim being to discover the characteristics of all structures of that kind. So atomic physics deals with the structure of atoms, chemistry with the structure of molecules, crystallography and colloidal chemistry with the structure of crystals and colloids, and anatomy and physiology with the structure of organisms. There is, therefore, I suggest, place for a branch of natural science which will have for its task the discovery of the general characteristics of those social structures of which the component units are human beings.

A. R. Radcliffe-Brown,
Structure and Function
in Primitive Society (1952, p. 190)

AUTHOR'S NOTE: I would like to thank Amy Whitcher for her help in searching the dark corridors of the library. Thanks to Kay Evans for her patience and tolerance in the course of producing this review. Russ Bernard, Kim Romney, and Stanley Wasserman provided helpful comments on earlier drafts of this manuscript. I would also like to thank Doug White for making me aware of and sending me some important literature for inclusion in this review. However, I alone remain responsible for any omissions or errors. If I forgot someone, let me apologize in advance.

Much has happened in the 40 years since Radcliffe-Brown wrote these words that might resemble his anticipated "branch of natural science" dedicated to the examination of the kinds of structures in which humans are involved. Although certainly not a discipline in the strictest sense, "social network analysis" or "structural analysis" (as referred to by some in sociology, and not to be confused with structuralism in anthropology) has evolved over this period and has some of the elements of Radcliffe-Brown's "branch" of science. The early concern for social structure by social anthropologists and Barnes's formalization of a social network, which up until that time had largely been used as a metaphorical convention, have led to the development of an "integrated scientific specialty" resembling what Kuhn would call normal science (Hummon & Carley, in press, p. 1). This review explores two questions: First, what roles have social and cultural anthropologists played in the development of this scientific specialty? Second, how have social network studies contributed to the advancement of anthropological knowledge?

To provide some continuity, this review will pick up from Mitchell's 1974 review of social networks in the *Annual Review of Anthropology*. As Mitchell did, we will continue the controversial discussion of whether there is something uniquely identifiable as social network theory, and it will be shown how the American tradition of cognitive anthropology has, since 1974, become an important influence in the developing paradigm called social networks.

In concluding his review, Mitchell left the reader with the clear impression that much remained to be done concerning the implementation of propositions from mathematical graph theory for the study of social networks (see also Barnes, 1969). In addition, he identified other analytical procedures (other than graph theory) that are "needed to handle the sort of problems that anthropological studies using social networks seem to involve" (Mitchell, 1974, p. 297). One such method, which he called "functorial mapping," had only begun to be recognized as important for analyzing structural problems in the study of social networks. It was, of course, the ideas of blockmodeling and structural equivalence introduced in the now classic article by Lorrain and White (1971). Referring to these "new" analytical procedures, Mitchell (1974) pointed out that the "data concerning all the links in a social network relating to some event or series of events in which the analyst is interested will have to be recorded in greater detail and more systematically than has customarily been done" (p. 297).

Twenty years later there are, indeed, more detailed and systematic methods available for collecting and analyzing social network data. But much has not changed or, depending on one's perspective, has moved away from rigor. The concept of social networks is used widely in anthropology as a metaphor (e.g., O'Connor, 1990). Walsh and Simonelli (1986), for example, see scientific rigor as a hindrance, impractical and unnecessary for anthropological research on social networks. In this view the most "promising" work treats networks and related processes as a "given" (Walsh & Simonelli, 1986, p. 46). These authors, for example, describe the "function" of support networks among migrants using the concept as a "heuristic" device (p. 50). In a sense, viewing networks as a given relegates network explanations to the same circularity as many cultural explanations.

Bax (1979) attacks social network analysis, claiming that the "antithetical thinking" inherent in this approach is the result of an almost exclusive preoccupation with the further refinement and development of analytical techniques.[1] Criticisms like these reflect strong sentiment among many anthropologists regarding what they see as the limits of the scientific method. This review recognizes the existence of such work but will focus exclusively on studies of social networks by anthropologists who are identified with scientifically based analytical approaches.

Anthropology and the Question of Network Theory

Mitchell (1974) described how the "compact institutional analysis characteristic of the structural approach" that focused on small-scale societies seemed less suited for the study of humans in more complex settings. These inadequacies led to the modification of ideas concerning roles and to the development of transaction theories, action theories, and social exchange approaches (Whitten & Wolfe, 1974). In turn, work in these areas stimulated the need for network concepts and a network approach more generally.

At the time of Mitchell's review, social anthropologists who were influential in the development and use of social network analysis felt strongly that there was really no such thing as network theory per se. Barnes (1972) viewed the idea of social networks as an "orienting statement" and argued that a theory of social networks may never exist. Bott saw social networks as a basic idea that could be used in many "frames of reference." Kapferer (1973) recognized no network theory but saw the network approach as simply a method for data collection and analysis. Kapferer and Wolfe (1970), and Whitten and Wolfe (1974) all proposed that exchange theory, action theory, or role theory were all suited for an adequate explanation of network phenomena. Mitchell's (1974) own view on the existence of network theory was much more upbeat:

> My own view on the subject is that the debate is more about words than reality. There is no network theory in the sense of "basic assumptions together with a set of derived propositions which are interlinked and capable of being tested" (Kapferer, 1973, p. 84). But I suspect there are few theories in social anthropology of this kind at all. That propositions may be derived from a consideration of the characteristics of social networks is, I think, evident. (p. 283)

Mitchell has been vindicated.[2] Since 1974 there have been many changes and advances in the area of social network analysis. Developments in the application of graph theory (e.g., Barnes & Harary, 1983), algebraic approaches (e.g., Borgatti & Everett, 1989), stochastic models (e.g., Anderson, Wasserman, & Faust, 1992), and blockmodels (Faust & Wasserman, 1992) and related ideas on equivalence to social phenomena provide evidence that network or structural theory is emerging (see Wellman, 1988, for a discussion). In fact, 5 years before Mitchell's landmark article (and apparently unknown to Mitchell), Boyd (1969) articulated a set of algebraic problems in the study of kinship structure. Boyd's work would, in time, contribute much to social network analysis. In sociology, and paralleling the work of Boyd, sociologists were developing the structural framework for the study of social networks, and network computer programs were being written that would help overcome analytical barriers. Finally, Mitchell could not have anticipated the eventual influence of cognitive anthropology on what has come to be known as social network analysis.

Analytical Versus Metaphorical

The hierarchical graph in Figure 5.1 represents one possible avenue for organizing the range and types of network approaches used in anthropology, and this review will use this organizational convention where appropriate. Aside from the first major bifurcation between the formal/analytical and metaphorical use of social networks, a distinction is made between the study of whole networks and ego networks. Within "whole networks" there is a division among studies of relations, studies

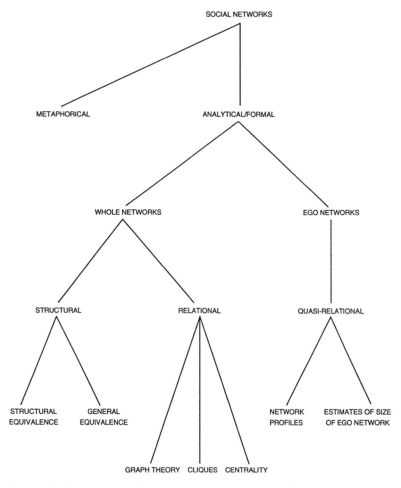

Figure 5.1. Organization of Types of Network Approaches Used in Anthropology

of structures, and statistical approaches to the study of networks. Although all "whole networks" can be represented in matrix form, and the relational or structural analysis of these matrices can lead to similar conclusions, there may be conditions where this will not be the case. In addition, some difference lies on whether a measure is determined on the basis of the internal structure of a matrix or simply on its marginals (e.g., network activity versus structural equivalence; see Johnson, Poteat,

& Ironsmith, 1991, for a discussion of this). More important, the structural ideas are more in line with the ideas of Nadel (1957) and Goodenough (1969) concerning status and role (Reitz & White, 1989). With regard to the structural approach, i and j can occupy the same position (e.g., play the same role, such as manager) without having any actual ties to one another or ties to any common others but having ties to the same "types" of others (e.g., general equivalence). The relational approach, as described here, depends directly on the nature of the actual linkages between i and j in terms of such things as clique membership (i.e., cliques represent areas of intense interaction in a network). A review of this line of reasoning can be found in Burt (1983) or Doreian (1989). Ego networks, on the other hand, can be viewed as quasi-relational (a series of ego networks for unrelated egos) and involve different data collection procedures (e.g., random sampling) and theoretical assumptions and explore different aspects of social networks. Finally, there are statistical approaches to the study of networks (for a review of work in this vein, see Wasserman & Faust, 1994).

Social Versus Cultural Anthropology

It is evident that social anthropology was instrumental in the development of what we now know as social network analysis. Although Radcliffe-Brown viewed social structure as a network of social relations, it was such people as John Barnes, J. Clyde Mitchell, Bruce Kapferer, Elizabeth Bott, and Jeremy Boissevain, to name a few, who, dissatisfied with the traditional rigidity and limitations of traditional structural-functionalism in studies of complex systems, began to explore how actual ties, as opposed to institutional structure, influenced behavior. Still, it cannot be denied that these researchers' earlier work was influenced by their structural-functional roots, in which norm consensus and normative behavior was "achieved" (Mitchell, 1974, p. 285). A good example of this is Epstein's (1969b) study of gossip in which network structure was the independent variable while the dependent variable was norm development.

The theoretical training and orientation of these early network scholars limited the application of some concepts in anthropology such as culture, particularly as popularized in American anthropology. To many social anthropologists, the notion of culture was irrelevant or, even to some, problematic. As Radcliffe-Brown notes (1952):

While I have defined social anthropology as the study of human society, there are some who define it as the study of culture. It might perhaps be thought that this difference of definition is of minor importance. Actually it leads to two different kinds of study, between which it is hardly possible to obtain agreement in the formulations of problems. (p. 189)

Some scholars saw little difference between social anthropology and sociology, claiming that social anthropology was not a branch of cultural or general anthropology as asserted by some (Murdock, 1951) "but rather a kind of sociology" (Watson, 1984, p. 353). Further, some may have claimed the existence of deep hostilities between British social anthropologists and North American "cultural anthropologists" (Watson, 1984). For example, Murdock (1951) saw social anthropology as "simply that branch of cultural anthropology that deals with interpersonal relationships" (p. 471). This did not sit well with some social anthropologists, particularly in light of the belief of many that the concept of culture lacked utility and was conceptually ambiguous (Watson, 1984).

The polemics of this debate aside, it is clearly the case that these differences in perception limited the importance, application, and concern for social network concepts in cultural anthropology prior to the 1970s, the period in which "social network analysis" was so heavily influenced by social anthropologists. In the 1960s and, particularly the 1970s, within cultural anthropology both ethnoscience and cognitive anthropology came into being, although it was primarily an American movement. Based on the early writings of Goodenough, for example, and pioneered by such people as Charles Frake, Mary Black, Duane Metzger, Volney Stefflre, A. Kimball Romney, and Roy D'Andrade, work in this area involved the search for a better understanding of culture as a more clearly defined concept that was manifested in research involving the systematic investigation of folk classification and belief systems. In addition, people began to explore the relationship between culture and cognition and began to look for human cognitive universals. Cognitive anthropologists were interested in learning, the classification or coding of knowledge or symbolic information and individual decision making. For a review of this area in these early years, see Durbin (1974).

The study of culture was seen as somewhat analogous to the study of language. As Honigmann (1976) saw it:

The cognitivist program was largely written by Americans who also favored the newly coined word "emic," taken from "phonemic" and contrasting with "etic" (from "phonetic") to label their standpoint. British social anthropologists who emphasized norms, while cognitively inclined, were not emicists; they did not in the manner of a linguist discovering phonemes look for criteria implicitly or explicitly recognized by the actors themselves.

There could not be room for a fully emic point of view in a tradition, as one writer put it, "since it was generally believed that natives are assumed to have only a partial and inaccurate view of the types of social relationships making up their social system, and to be capable of analyzing the processes by which the system operates." (p. 252)

Social anthropologists did not ignore what the cognitivists saw as constituting culture (e.g., shared beliefs). Social anthropologists were just not interested in eliciting and measuring individual perception and cognition (i.e., the emic perspective). To some extent, one group was interested in the interaction between language, meaning, and behavior (e.g., behavior in an approach to a cognitive task), while the other was more interested in behavior, in which norms were seen to play an important role (as etically derived).

It should be pointed out that Noble (1973), in her essay on social networks as a conceptual framework in family analysis, questions whether there should not be more attention paid to individual action and motivation as psychologists were seen to do. She even recognizes Chomsky's focus on cognitive processes as opposed to patterns of overt behavior. In addition, Jongmans (1973), in the same edited volume, used the idea of "structural balance" for looking at perceptions of obligation. This was largely a social psychological way of viewing the problem (Heider, 1946).

This is not to say that some British social anthropologists, however, were not interested in individual-based explanations for behavior. Following in the tradition of Bronishaw Malinowski and Raymond Firth, such scholars as Edmond R. Leach and, in particular, Fredrick Barth viewed individuals as making choices that would ultimately benefit them in terms of rewards, such as prestige and the accumulation of valued resources. Structure in this case is a product of the interactions involved in acquiring those benefits. Although these ideas were not cognitive in the sense of the "natives' point of view," there was a focus on individual action and choice and the approach came to be known as transactional analysis. Foster (1978) recognizes the importance of this emphasis on individual action and, more important, points to an interesting linkage between these British scholars and the American cognitive anthropologists:

> Perhaps the best-known development of these ideas in the British tradition is Frederick Barth's (1966) method of transactional analysis. In the United States, the development of individual-oriented research was closely tied to a body of work variously called cognitive anthropology, ethnoscience, the new ethnography, ethnosemantics, componential analysis, and just plain formal analysis. (p. 248)

These important developments were critical in the cross-fertilization between cognitive anthropology and social network analysis. First, cognitive anthropologists were generally much more formally oriented than were other anthropologists. Analytical techniques for exploring and modeling the relationships among items and attributes in a semantic domain (multidimensional scaling, cluster analysis, and so on) could be readily transferred to the study of patterning in social relations. Second, many cognitive anthropologists were engaged in enterprises in which social structure, most often kinship, was a primary focus. This included how social structure or organization influenced decisions for postmarital residence (Quinn, 1975) or studies focusing on formal cognitive models of kinship (Romney, 1965). Third, prompted by Pelto and Pelto (1975), some cognitive anthropologists began to reject the traditional view of culture sharing as invariant and began to examine systematically intracultural variation. Some students of intracultural variation saw social structure as an important influence on that variation (Boster, 1985). Finally, the study of intracultural variation was aided by a formalization of the concept of culture. The cultural consensus model developed by Romney, Weller, and Batchelder (1986) starts from the idea that culture is consensus and provides formal guidelines for determining that which is cultural (that is, shared). The cultural consensus model addresses ambiguities associated with competing definitions of culture (Kroeber & Kluckholm, 1952) and offers a replicable method for exploring cultural knowledge and its variation.

Most of the cognitive anthropologists in the late 1960s and early 1970s were interested more in the structure of semantic domains, including kinship, than in the relationship between social structure and cognition. One notable exception was Volney Stefflre, who lectured extensively on the important interrelationship between what he called "heads" (individual cognition) and social organization. Unfortunately, Stefflre's ideas were not widely published and are only now reaching a wider audience. Simply, he viewed interaction in networks as a key to the development of shared meanings, expectations, linguistic behavior, and general consensus (Stefflre, 1986).

This idea of interaction spheres having an influence on cognition is certainly not new. Festinger, Chachter, and Bak (1950) conceptualized how social structure mediated the influence of network members on one another's attitudes. But this kind of social psychological thinking contrasts sharply with the network approaches of the social anthropological pioneers and has led to other studies of the relation between activity and perception in groups (Boster, Johnson, & Weller, 1987; Romney & Weller, 1984) and to studies of the relation between social interaction and intracultural variation (Johnson & Boster, 1990).

What has this historical difference in approach between cultural and social anthropology got to do with developments in social network analysis, particularly as they relate to anthropology? In a recent sociology of science study, Hummon and Carley (in press) identify six main path structures of citation in the journal *Social Networks*. Three of these paths have definite influence from anthropologists working on sets of specific theoretical and methodological issues in the study of social networks. Two of these paths have a clear cognitive influence, while the third relates to problems in the study of roles. The following sections examine these and other developments in terms of theory, models, and method and, more important, in terms of the exchange of knowledge and ideas between anthropology and social network analysis. In sum, one might make the following observation: In a sense, social psychology is to sociology as cognitive anthropology is to social anthropology.

Cognition and Networks

A debate—largely conducted by anthropologists and, in its most heated period, spanning 12 years—surfaced when two scholars challenged what seemed to be a rather accepted belief that the self-reports of informants concerning, for example, "who did you interact with most today?" were accurate proxies for actual behavior. Killworth and Bernard (1976a), in the initial contribution to a series of articles, made the first of several compelling arguments that began to cast doubt on the correspondence between the self-report of informants, or cognitive data, and actual observations of their behavior. A series of studies followed (Bernard & Killworth, 1977; Bernard, Killworth, & Sailer, 1980, 1982; Bernard, Killworth, Sailer, & Kronenfeld, 1984; Killworth & Bernard, 1979-1980; referred to here as BKS), producing several data sets that, as analyzed by the authors, seemed to point to little overlap between informants' reports and behavioral observations of network interactions.

These findings did not go unchallenged. A number of scholars reanalyzed the BKS data sets or conducted original research to specifically address this question. Romney and Faust (1983), for example, in a reanalysis of the BKS tech data (data on members of an office), showed that the accuracy of an informant depended on the extent to which he or she interacted with other members of the group. Those informants who interacted more frequently with group members reported more accurately on group behavior. In addition, the higher the judged similarity of two actors of the communication patterns of others, the more they tended to interact with each other. Romney and Weller (1984), in a reanalysis of all four BKS data sets, found that informant accuracy is even more a function of informant reliability or the correlation of each informant's response to the group aggregate. Hammer (1985), in investigating the correspondence between behavioral and cognitive data, used two of the BKS data sets and data from a donut shop (Hammer, Polgar, & Salzinger, 1969) and found such discrepancies to be systematic and to reflect aspects of an informant's observed and interactive relations.

In some original research on the question of the correspondence between behavioral and cognitive data, Freeman and Romney (1987) and Freeman, Romney, and Freeman (1987) explored factors affecting individual recall. They showed that, although informants may not be very accurate in their reports on who was present at a particular event, the reports are influenced by long-term patterns of participation and do accurately reflect the *usual* and *regular behaviors* of group or event participants (i.e., regular attendees).

Johnson and Miller (1986) compared three measures of social structure in a fish camp in Alaska (Johnson & Miller, 1983), one cognitive and two behavioral. They found that the correspondence between behavioral and cognitive data was dependent on the generalizability of the cognitive measures used. In this case, unconstrained judged similarity data of the perceived similarity among fishermen correlated higher with the two behavioral measures than the behavioral measures did with each other.

This debate, and the series of studies that inspired it, shed light not only on the issue of the reliability of cognitive network data, it also sparked interest in a whole range of matters concerning cognition and social structure. These include such concerns as the relationship between one's position in a network and perception of the structure of the group or simply knowledge of the group. This work also stimulated interest in how network position and subgroup membership affect factors in human cognition more generally.

Freeman, Freeman, and Michaelson (1988) further explored the question of accuracy by studying the ability of individual group members to define subgroup structure as compared against a behavioral standard. They found that the aggregate perception of subgroup structure corresponded very well with the subgroup structure determined by the observation of actual behavior. This was not unlike Bernard et al.'s (1982) finding that at the global level (aggregate) there was a much higher correspondence between recall and behavior. But this line of inquiry did not assess the accuracy of an individual informant nor did it explain precisely how informants were defining subgroup membership.

In a subsequent reanalysis of the data from their 1988 article, Freeman, Freeman, and Michaelson (1989) explored the accuracy of individual informants and the cognitive models used to determine subgroupings. Possible cognitive models of subgroup structure were tested against four models discussed by Sailer and Gaulin (1984), which conceptualized alternative ways individual observers might make sense of the patterns of social interaction of fellow group members. Freeman et al. (1989) found that individuals can indeed report accurately on the observable interaction patterns of *other* group members and that the four models all provided adequate alternative approximations as to how people might cognitively define observed subgroups. A definitive answer as to the precise models employed by humans in defining subgroup membership on the basis of observed interactions, however, could not be determined. These studies also have implications for ethnographic research and reliance on key informants in that members of communities, as studied here, all seemed to have a good deal of knowledge of group structure.

This concern for informant recall and the models people use to cognitively define and organize human groups is related to the question of how individuals store their social networks in their heads. Killworth and Bernard (1982), in keeping with their interest in both cognitive and behavioral network data, applied the idea of a "mental map" to investigate how world maps can be drawn from people's cognitive understanding of their own social networks. Similar to some of their small world experiments, they asked informants to name an individual who might happen to know any one of 100 foreign targets. Based on informant responses, they produced a similarity index between all pairs of the 100 targets, and subjected the subsequent similarity matrix to multidimensional scaling. The aggregated "mental map" of informants loosely resembled a Mercator projection of the world. From an anthropological standpoint, this study is important in that it "opens the way to a systematic, cross-cultural study of how people store their complex social networks in their minds" (Killworth & Bernard, 1982, p. 308). This work is related to a series of other studies by these authors discussed in another section.

Although not specifically termed a network study, Boster in a series of articles (1985, 1986) found that deviations from a shared cultural model of Aguaruna Jivaro manioc identification was patterned according to the sexual division of labor, individual expertise, and, more important, membership in kin and residential groups. Subsequent work extended this to include the influences of exchange relations. This (in combination with the findings of Romney and Weller, Romney and Faust, and Freeman, Romney and Freemen) stimulated Boster, Johnson, and Weller (1987) to explore the relationship between variation of knowledge among individuals and the social relations and positions of those individuals. Cognitive (e.g., pile sort, triads) and network data (e.g., work relations, advice relations) were both collected from employees in a university administrative office. Applying the cultural consensus model, they found that consensus about the similarities of office actors and the structural position of these actors influences their approach to the consensus. However, the expectation that two individuals who are judged as similar will themselves agree with each other was not confirmed. Those individuals who agree with each other are not necessarily those who are judged similar by other informants. Michaelson and Contractor (1992) extended this idea to explore how structural position influenced perceived similarity. In a study of students in a communication class, they found that the perceived similarity of other classmates corresponded better with general equivalence models than with structural equivalence models, suggesting perceived similarity may be more a function of the roles actors play rather than just simply their patterns of interaction.

Krackhardt (1987) has contributed significantly to this line of inquiry by studying actors' perception of the structure of the entire group network, as opposed to simply asking each informant to report on his or her own network ties. Krackhardt argues that data of this type are uniquely appropriate for investigating (a) the symmetry between an actor's perception of his or her network position and that position as perceived by other network actors, (b) the effects of network position on the individual perception of structure, and (c) the effects of network position on agreement with others on network structure (see also Krackhardt & Kilduff, 1990).

If network position and degree of activity in a network influence informant accuracy and knowledge of the group, will position, group membership, or activity influence knowledge or cognition concerning other domains of interest? Johnson and Boster (1990; also discussed in Johnson, 1990) examined the relationship between perception of similarity of different kinds of meat and meat products found at the grocery store and membership in upper- and lower-middle-class networks. Based on a snowball sample through a town in Missouri, they partitioned the network on the basis of on "which side of the tracks" one resided. In comparing these two subgroups, one upper middle class and one lower middle class, the approach to the cognitive task (i.e., unconstrained judged similarity of fresh and processed meats) varied as a function of subgroup membership. The upper-middle-class subgroup sorted on the basis of degree of processing while the lower-middle-class group sorted on the basis of type of meat irrespective of processing (e.g., canned, fresh, frozen versus beef, poultry, fish, pork). In addition, both groups differed on the frequency with which they ate meals with others in their network. The upper-middle-class subgroup ate meals much more often with one another than did members of the lower-middle-class subgroup (i.e., dinner parties, lunch at the country club). Many of the social activities of the lower-middle-class subgroup centered on the church. In addition to the importance in accounting for differences in approach to a cognitive task on the basis of subgroup membership, this study has important implications for understanding differences in "taste" as a function of social class (Bourdieu, 1984).

In some related research, this emphasis on the individual behavior or action of individuals has also been stressed by Foster and Seidman (1989) and they developed a set of procedures that, as they put it, "are adapted from a body of research in cognitive anthropology" (p. 52). These authors examined networks and individual action, applying it in their research on kinship and on brand congruence within friendship networks on a college campus (Reingen, Foster, Brown, & Seidman,

1984). They found that clique membership had a significant effect on brand choice.

Similar to Foster and Seidman's focus on individual action is the idea of innovation adoption as influenced by the structural characteristics of a network. In a test of Burt's (1983) proposition that two structurally equivalent actors will adopt an innovation at about the same time, Johnson (1986) examined the diffusion of two innovations through the same network of commercial fishermen. He found that Burt's model accounted for the adoption process under the proviso that the definition of structural equivalence or "perceived social similarity" varies as a function of information availability. When available information about an innovation was low, it was in the best interest of individuals to share it only with socially close others, thus maintaining a competitive advantage. In a similar study, Johnson and Orbach (1990a) showed how structural equivalence influenced the individual decisions of commercial fishermen to migrate in the course of their yearly fishing activities. The theoretical importance of these studies is the linkage between perceived social similarity, as determined by the patterns of social relations, and individual choice.

Truex (1981) studied informants' cognition on kinship relations so as to produce a "hypothetical" model of recruitment in mobilizations for the accomplishment of various tasks. What is important about this study is its attempt to consider not just simply the semantic aspects of kinship, the focus of most cognitive anthropologists, but the dynamic potential of kin relations for providing resources and different forms of aid. He found three levels of the normative expectations of kin with highest expectations for closest kin or direct lineals and lowest expectations for distant consanguines and affines. This focus on the role aspects within kinship systems is unusual and follows to some extent in the role elicitation work of Goodenough (1969) and Boyd, Haehl, and Sailer (1971). Unfortunately, this important work has gone largely uncited. It is to the work on networks and kinship that we now turn and, as we shall see, the treatment of roles in the network analysis of kinship has also been rarely addressed.

Kinship and Networks

Aside from ethnography, there is probably no other area of study that has been more associated with anthropology than kinship. In addition, the thinking of early structural scholars, although not very methodologically sophisticated, did follow a kind of network logic (Foster & Seidman, 1979). Yet, with only a few exceptions, network concepts, methods, and approaches were used little in the study of kinship. A good example of this is presented by Foster and Seidman (1979) in their reexamination of Fortes's study of kinship among the Tallensi (Fortes, 1940, 1945, 1949). It is, of course, unrealistic to expect that Fortes, or any of the other kinship scholars of that time period, would have taken a formal network approach when the formalization of a social network itself in anthropology had yet to be developed. Ironically, by the time more formal social network concepts (e.g., density) and approaches (e.g., graph theory) had begun to be more widely accepted and understood, kinship as a focus of study had become unfashionable (Barnes, 1980). Furthermore, it was the very people who contributed to making the study of social networks a legitimate enterprise in anthropology (i.e., social anthropologists studying more urban complex societies) that rejected the importance of more traditional institutional constraints on behavior such as kinship.[3] Social networks, particularly in urban settings, were seen as the solution to the problems inherent in the static structural-functional approach of which kinship was an integral part. In addition, and as noted by Truex (1981), cognitive anthropologists began to study kinship not in the network sense of accounting for actual kinship relations but, instead, through examining the semantic structure of kinship domains.

These, however, were not the only limiting factors in bringing together networks ideas and kinship in a more widespread manner. There was little communication among, or even awareness of, several important scholars during the 1960s and early 1970s who were interested in understanding kinship from a decidedly structural or network point of view. The two most striking examples concern the work of White (1963), a sociologist, and Boyd (1969), an anthropologist, both of whom had considerable mathematical training. Each was working on problems in kinship from an algebraic perspective, while others were applying graph theory. These two approaches addressed different conceptual problems in the study of kinship. This is illustrated by Sailer's (1978) discussion of the difference between cliques (as formalized using graph theory) and the blockmodel:

> Cliques, however, are not to be confused with roles. Here is an example of the difference. One would expect the cliques in a kin network to be entities

such as families, clans, lineages, etc. The roles of interest in a kin network, though, are kin-types, e.g., father and son. Families are certainly interesting structures in their own right, but they are not roles. Rather, they are nodes in a higher order relation. Clusters and cliques, as structures, correspond to such concepts as the family or clan. The mathematical structure that corresponds to the role, such as father or boss, is the "block." A "blockmodel" is a set of such blocks and the relationships between them. The cluster concept is still relevant, however. A "block" can be defined as a set of actors clustered together by virtue of their structural equivalence. (p. 75)

Although there is a relationship between positional or "block" methods and clique-finding algorithms, the two generally are used in solving fundamentally different theoretical problems in the study of kinship. Graph-theoretic and related clique approaches have been the most commonly used techniques to date. Most notable among the kinship analyses employing these approaches are Jackson (1976), Hage (1979), Hage and Harary (1983), and Foster and Seidman (1979, 1989).

In a series of articles, Foster and Seidman (1979, 1989; Seidman & Foster, 1978) attempt to solve a nagging problem in defining subgraphs that will have general applications in the study of kinship. Recognizing that the definition of a clique as a maximally complete subgraph was theoretically, conceptually, and empirically too restrictive, they searched for a definition that was more sociologically interpretable, particularly with regards to kinship (e.g., lineages and clans). Their solution was the k-plex, which can be defined as a graph where each node or actor is adjacent to all but $k - 1$ other nodes or actors. Thus a 1-plex is a maximally complete subgraph (maximal in the sense that adding any additional ties would violate the definition of clique under these constraints). Using this clique-finding procedure, they applied it to Fortes's Tallensi analysis as an example (Foster & Seidman, 1979). Claiming that Fortes's thinking was basically graph theoretic, they proposed "to substitute some of the content of graph theory for the 'logic of kinship' as the calculus of structural analysis" (p. 336). Central to their analysis was the idea of basic structures, which was a subgraph that can be defined on the basis of some inherent properties without reference to a "particular representative" (p. 337). These basic structures are often found to be isomorphic with portions or subsets of graphs and "when such subsets are sociologically interpretable, we call them basic structural units (BSUs)" (p. 339). BSUs are the foundation of their analysis and have interesting properties in that they can represent global, as well as local, structures. Thus a large, complex network of local BSUs (person cliques) can be reduced to reveal simpler global structure (cliques of cliques).

Given that Fortes's original analysis was for the entire Tallensi society (35,000 people), the approach advocated by Foster and Seidman has implications for both macro- and microproblems. In addition, they found that the k-plex concept was useful in formalizing Fortes's notion of a clan as a network of lineages and in addressing the idea of "guy ropes," a set of structural conditions that maintain balance and stability.

In a series of other examples, Hage (1976a, 1976b, 1979) and Hage and Harary (1982a, 1983) explore how graph-theoretic notions of structural balance, rank, signed relations, and transitivity again provide a formal characterization for kinship systems described by other anthropologists. One example is Hage and Harary's (1983) reinterpretation of Silerbauer's work on kinship among the Bushmen of the Kalahari using coloring to partition the categories of respect and disrespect. In addition, balance theory characterized patterns of joking relations well in that one should only joke with a joking partner of his joking partner, avoid the avoidance partner of his joking partner, and not joke with the avoidance partner of a joking partner. In another example, they reexamine Whitten's study of marriage among the Canelos Quichua of eastern Ecuador. Here they show how "intransitive cyclical structures can provide real as well as imaginary solutions to problems of status asymmetry" (Hage & Harary, 1983, p. 73) by illustrating graphically how to produce a structural escape from the indebtedness of a man to his wife's brother. Hage and Harary's 1983 book gives numerous other examples of the applicability of graph theory to the study of kinship systems.

But what of the other role-based approach to the study of kinship? Boyd's 1969 article on kinship algebras was important at the time in terms of representing a new and promising algebraic framework for the study of kinship relations as networks. There appears to be little subsequent work by others following this line of inquiry, at least in terms of kinship analysis. Although clearly anthropological in its importance, the article was published in the *Journal of Mathematical Psychology* and has received only a few citations in anthropology. However, the article did inspire others in profound ways. This is from the Acknowledgments in Lorrain and White's (1971) classic article on blockmodels:

> The determinant stimulus that led us to the ideas set forth in the present paper came from Boyd's 1966 dissertation (the core of which was subsequently

published—Boyd 1969), where the decisive step was made, introducing and exemplifying a particular type of reduction of a network. (p. 49)

This is not to say that Boyd abandoned this line of reasoning (e.g., Boyd et al., 1971) but that subsequent work built upon his original ideas without necessarily any concern for the study of kinship per se (see Boyd, 1979-1980, 1989, 1991, 1992). Schweizer (1988) has more recently applied these ideas in his use of structural and regular equivalence to study ties among Javanese households. In this case, the structure of network links is partitioned by three equivalence methods into subsets based on kinship roles, generatorial status, religious activity, and economic exchange, all partitions that would be difficult to discern with the use of traditional kinship representation and analysis. In pursuit of improved methods for graphically representing kinship systems, White and Jorian (1992) have recently presented the idea of P graph analysis. This method has the potential to solve many of the problems inherent in graphically representing complex kinship networks and will facilitate the empirical testing of theoretical kinship models of both a network and an algebraic form.

In concluding this section, we look to a 1980 article by J. A. Barnes, in which he anticipated future directions in the study of kinship. He did see network analysis as playing an important role in the future of kinship analysis but also saw that much needed to be done in terms of implementation and integration (Barnes, 1980). In the 13 years since Barnes's article, this is still largely the case. Much of the work reviewed in this section has itself been largely ignored, at least as far as kinship research is concerned. Whereas Foster and Seidman's development of the k-plex as a clique-finding algorithm and their subsequent development of a computer program to do k-plex analysis has been recognized (primarily by sociologists), its application in the study of kinship never really developed.[4] Similarly, Hage and Harary's work has been acknowledged more for the application of graph-theoretic ideas in areas other than kinship (analysis of myth, social networks more generally). Further, it is difficult to determine how the more recent contributions of White and Jorian (1992) and Schweizer (1988) will be used in future work on kinship.

Given the unpopularity of pure kinship analysis and the continuing disappearance of "traditional" societies worldwide, it may be more realistic to view kinship as just one of many elements in a network model. Plattner (1978), for example, shows how the socioeconomic structure of two occupations in a Mexican town corresponds with the structure of kin relations. In another Mexican example, Thomas (1978) examines the relationship between kinship involvement (based on a kind of centrality) and the accumulation of wealth. In sum, the importance of kinship cannot be denied, but the reality of external constraints (e.g., increased industrialization) will necessarily limit the preeminence of pure kinship analysis in anthropology in the future.

Ethnography and Networks

There is no doubt that networks were an important element in the earlier work of social anthropologists in urban settings (Epstein, Mitchell, and so on), but it was more than the complexity of urban life that led these researchers to rely on these concepts so centrally in their work. Had they been survey researchers, it is doubtful that the notion of a social network would have had such a prominent place in their studies. Because they were ethnographers, engaged in the web of everyday life, an understanding of social networks was critical for obtaining the latest gossip, seeking information on hard-to-see events (e.g., rituals, drug use), and establishing friendships that would ultimately lead to the development of key informant relationships. It was the ethnographic context itself that, explicitly or implicitly, made understanding networks of relations so important. Wolfe (1978) too saw a contrast between survey research and the natural linkage between networks and ethnography:

> Ethnographic experience, in contrast, makes deliberate use of all connections possible, as a matter of course, to get entree and develop rapport. Whether she or he intends to or not, the anthropologist must learn a great deal about the network of relations of her or his informants. (p. 57)

Aside from the more intuitive conceptual use of the idea of networks, there are three fundamental problems in conducting ethnography that have been explicitly addressed through the use of social network concepts and analytical techniques. First, there is a problem in discovering and observing the activities of hard-to-find populations or subpopulations. Partridge used a snowball technique (although he did not call it that) to move through a Colombian community to more accurately characterize cannabis use (see Kimball & Partridge, 1979). Second, ethnographic research can be complex in that it involves a variety of settings including work, leisure, home, and church. Sanjek (1978) describes how the network-serial method, first described by Epstein (1969a), can be used to gain a sample of settings in which informants provide self-reports of their network activities (i.e., ego-centered networks). Finally, the question of sampling and representativeness in ethnographic research was important even before Mead (1953) expressed the need to be concerned about validity and the "proper specification of the informant" (p. 646) lest ad hoc selection lead to bias. Lex and Wolfe's (1967) concerns were specifically expressed in network terms when they stated: "So varied is the total network that one ethnographer's sampling must always be in doubt" (p. 2).

These issues are addressed by Werner and Schoepfle (1987) in their discussion of a "networking" sample (p. 189) and in more detail by Johnson (1990) in his discussion of snowball sampling and informant selection. To Werner and Schoepfle, the proper selection of consultants (similar to key informants) is dependent on the proper identification of the range of social groups across a system of actors. Consultants would be recruited from the range of such groups and would be experts or specialists "on some aspect of daily life" (Werner & Schoepfle, 1987, p. 189).

Johnson (1990) provides several examples of the use of snowball sampling, different measures of centrality, and network partitioning in selecting informants. He sees the use of these techniques as a means for producing a "theoretically" representative sample of informants. In one example, a snowball sample through a community of commercial fishermen yields a binary matrix that is partitioned into subgroups on the basis of structural equivalence (i.e., similarity in patterns of relations). Displaying the network of relations with the use of correspondence analysis, subgroups (as determined by cluster analysis) are encompassed by circles, and directed links between subgroups are shown. Informants are selected on the basis of membership in each of the subgroups and on the basis of betweenness centrality as manifested in linkages between subgroups. Thus information can be obtained on the activities, or other important information, concerning the subgroups in a systematically determined fashion. Also, key informants located in strategic places (e.g., as determined by centrality or betweenness) provide the ethnographer with more efficient and valid means for accessing a variety of kinds of data.[5]

Network analysis has also played an important part in the validation of ethnographic observation, interpretation, and explanation through triangulation. For example, Mitchell (1989) reanalyzed Kapferer's (1972) data on networks in a tailor shop using blockmodeling, clustering, and betweenness measures. Kapferer's original partitioning of the network into clusters, although based largely on what Mitchell saw as "personal judgement," was supported in this reanalysis. While Mitchell labeled Kapferer's analysis "personal judgement," it can be seen as judgment guided by a sound ethnographic understanding of the research context. Morrill (1991) provides a good recent example of the beneficial mix of ethnographic and formal network methods in the study of conflict management among corporate executives. Reitz (1988) was also concerned with correspondence between formal methods for partitioning networks into subgroups (i.e., operationalizes the idea of a group) and the ethnographic interpretation of such subgroups. Finally, and probably more important, formal social network analysis in combination with the richness of ethnographic description and analysis can significantly enhance both the validity and the readability of a given work. The study by Bernard and Killworth (1973) on the social structure aboard a research vessel is a wonderful early example of how the joint use of these approaches can make for a better overall research enterprise.

Urban Social Networks

Considering the historical importance of urban research on the development of network concepts and methods, we will briefly examine a sample of some of the more recent work in this tradition. In a 1978 special issue of *Urban Anthropology*, a number of anthropologists explore the importance of social networks in everyday urban life. Included was work on the urban elderly by Sokolovsky and Cohen (1978) that is similar to the Sokolovsky, Cohen, Berger, and Geiger work (1978) on the personal networks of ex-mental patients. Kapferer (1978) argues for a redefinition of the concept of marginality and cautions that the concept should only be applied in specific urban situations. Foster and Seidman (1982) defined urban structures on the bases of a collection of overlapping cliques. Finally, Weisner (1978) examined the nature of rural-urban ties and urban migration, finding that rural-urban networks were highly interconnected and that these linkages were three-dimensional, involving clan affiliations, social status, and residence.

Mitchell (1987) conducted a study of the personal networks of 10 urban homeless women in exploring the concepts of strong and weak ties. This work corroborates other research in finding that strong ties among the women are primarily linkages involving emotional support or aid. Johnson and Orbach (1990b) examined how the process of urbanization (i.e., institution of zoning) and migration into a once rural area has led to the "gentrification" of commercial fishing that was clearly evident in the patterning of social relations (i.e., structural equivalence). They show how these patterns have definite political implications in terms of both the institution and the enforcement of zoning regulations. Finally, Greenbaum and Greenbaum (1985), using a personal network approach, examined how residential proximity and ethnicity influence the morphology and character of ego networks (e.g., ethnic composition, number of relations). Counter to expectations, they found that length of residence tended to restrict the proximity of relations and that variation in ethnic composition had little effect on the structure of personal networks.

Ego Networks

Research examining the characteristics of an ego's network has historically been the most commonly used approach in the study of social networks. This goes back to the earlier work of Bott, Kapferer, and other social anthropologists engaged in the study of urban complex social systems. The initial popularity of this approach, as opposed to the study of whole networks, is understandable given the limited number of analytical and computational tools (e.g., network analysis programs and large, fast computers) available at the time and the boundary specification problem inherent in the study of complex urban populations. In addition, the study of ego networks fits well into the ethnographic tradition of using key informants and participant observation. With the advent of greater computing power and the development of techniques for the study of whole networks, studies of ego networks have become relatively less common, but no less important. Aside from urban research, the primary focus of ego-centered approaches falls into two primary areas of research. The first concerns the relationship between social support, as determined by the characteristics of an ego's network, and health or well-being or some other dependent variable (for a more general in-depth review of this area, see Walker, Wasserman, & Wellman, this volume). The second general area has focused on the characterization of ego networks within a population in terms of such things as size: Who do people know and how do they know them? An understanding of these characteristics can provide for interesting cross-cultural comparisons and aid in revealing the global aspects of networks.

Bernard and Killworth and several of Bernard's students have produced a large body of work investigating the global character of networks and estimations of the size of an individual's personal network. Much of this earlier work focused on the small world problem (Killworth & Bernard, 1979) in which Killworth and Bernard model the decision making of intermediaries in a small world experiment in terms of a Markov process. In a related study, Killworth and Bernard (1978) perform what they call a reverse small world experiment, where they try to estimate both the number and the kinds of people known to an informant. This particular experiment is important because it provided a basic method for investigating the size and character of an informant's network. The development of this technique allowed these researchers to investigate a series of questions concerning the size of people's networks and variation in size as a function of individual attributes, social group membership (e.g., upper class), or membership in a culture. It is this concern for variation in the characteristics of personal networks within and between cultures that is of particular interest to anthropologists, and these researchers have paved the way for investigations of this type.

Driven by the questions first posed by the small world experiment (Poole & Kochen, 1978) and in pursuit of answers to questions posed in earlier research (Killworth & Bernard, 1979), Bernard, Killworth, and McCarty (1982) conducted an experimental investigation of 50 informants to examine who people know and why. Each of the 50 informants was allowed to ask any question concerning 50 target persons. Once informants felt they had enough information, they provided acquaintances from their own networks who might know, or at least serve as a first step in finding, the target. Location, occupation, age, and sex accounted for 50% of questions ever asked about targets. In another related study, Killworth, Bernard, and McCarty (1984) examined ways to measure patterns of acquaintanceship using the reverse small world methodology.

These studies provided the foundation for investigations into intra- and cross-cultural variation in the size and characteristics of personal networks. Bernard et al. (1988) "look for the rules that govern who people know and how they know each other" (p. 155). They are concerned with finding those rules that are culture-independent and any variation that might be due to measurement problems. They carry on in their experimental tradition in the study of social structure in three distinct cultures: Mormons in Utah, Paiutes in Arizona, and Ponapeans in Micronesia and include a comparison with a Gainesville, Florida, sample. In the first of a series of findings, it was apparent that Ponapeans and Paiutes made significantly more choices than both the Mormons and the Gainesville informants. They speculate this could be due to the effects of size and complexity of a network on recall. They go on to show the differential importance of occupation, sex, location, and the perceived similarity of targets in making choices.

In the above experiment, Bernard et al. (1988) question their findings on the basis of measurement problems (i.e., differential response to their test). Spawned by a comparison of data obtained from the network component of the General Social Survey and the Reverse Small World procedure (Bernard, Shelley, & Killworth, 1987), Bernard et al. (1990) more recently attempted to answer this question, as well as others, through a comparison of four methods for studying personal networks. The comparison consists of a method for eliciting intimates described by Burt (1984), a social support inventory used by McCallister and Fischer (1983), the Reverse Small World instrument described above, and a global network method developed by Poole (Poole & Kochen, 1978) and improved by Freeman and Thompson (1989). The sample of informants included a group from Jacksonville, Florida, and one from Mexico City. In comparing the two groups, they found that the Jacksonville informants reported more network members than the Mexico City informants independent of the method employed. In addition, they replicated aspects of former studies. Killworth, Johnsen, Bernard, Shelley, and McCarty (1990) attempted to more closely estimate the size of informants' networks for both the Jacksonville, Florida, and the Mexico City samples. Discussing both the difficulties and the potential sources of error in making estimates of this type, they estimated network size for the Jacksonville respondents to be $1,700 \pm 400$ and for Mexico City about 600.

In a study related to both reverse small world methodology and more recent work by the authors on estimation of hard-to-count populations

(Bernard, Johnsen, Killworth, & Robinson, 1989), Shelley, Bernard, and Killworth (1990) tried to operationalize the strength of network ties. Strength in this context is a function of the amount of time it took both to send and to receive messages from other members of their network. Perceived closeness was found to relate to the speed with which messages are transmitted and received. In addition, relatives transmitted faster than friends or acquaintances, and women faster than men. Finally, McCarty (1992) interviewed 47 informants in depth so as to discover the nature of perceived cliques among 60 alters that ego "knows." This approach allowed for an understanding of the factors underlying perceived clique membership within ego-centered networks.

Although we have included this body of work in the ego-network section, it could just as well have been included under cognition. This work also contributes to our understanding of a variety of intracultural and cross-cultural constraints on human recall and how and what people know and remember about the social networks of which they are a part.

We now turn briefly to some related research that follows in the urban tradition of Mitchell and Barnes but deals specifically with health and gerontological issues. Hurd, Pattison, and Llamas (1981) and Muriel Hammer (1963, 1981, 1983) are examples of both early and later work that has recognized the link between networks and health.[6] Most of these studies have explored the linkage between the characteristics of personal or ego networks (e.g., amount of social support) and health and well-being, both physical and mental. Sokolovsky et al. (1978) collected data on the personal networks of ex-mental patients in a Manhattan single room occupancy hotel. Their analysis shows that schizophrenics with smaller, less connected networks were at higher risk for rehospitalization. In a study on the impact of relocation of the urban elderly into single room occupancy hotels, Eckert (1983) found that both mental and physical impacts of the move on the elderly were mediated by the morphological and functional characteristics of the elderly's personal networks. Extending this line of inquiry to the rural elderly, Van Willigen (1989) showed how the rural elderly trade larger networks postretirement for more social involvement and are therefore not socially isolated. McClain (1987) examined how personal networks influence decisions concerning choosing home or hospital birth. In this case networks played a more significant role among mothers choosing home birth. Finally, Shelley (1992) demonstrated how the personal networks of patients with end stage renal disease affect health outcomes. In comparing the networks of hemodialysis and peritoneal dialysis patients, she uncovered the relationship among network density, depression, health, and network size.

Whole Networks

This section provides a brief summary of some of the methodological, theoretical, and substantive work by anthropologists studying whole networks. We begin with a short description of developments in positional or structural analysis originating with the pioneering work of Boyd (1969). Since Boyd's elaboration of a homomorphic reduction and Lorrain and White's subsequent refinements and extensions, the idea of clustering on the basis of position as opposed to interactive intensity (cohesion) has benefited from the work of Sailer (1978) and, more recently, John Boyd, Martin Everett, Steve Borgatti, Katherine Faust, Doug White, and Carl Reitz, to name a few anthropologists or individuals with at least some anthropological sympathies. Much of this work has focused on resolving a number of technical issues but has been limited in terms of substantive applications (aside from Sampson's monastery data). As a result, we concentrate on the contributions of anthropologists to this ongoing technical work, particularly in terms of the relation between various models and theoretical and conceptual work in the social sciences.

The sociological importance of social positions and corresponding roles has been described earlier in our discussion of kinship. There are a variety of mathematical models (e.g., structural equivalence, automorphic equivalence, regular equivalence) that fit with the different conceptualizations of position and role found in the literature. Faust (1988), however, makes an important distinction between structural equivalence and general equivalence. In structural equivalence, the extent to which individuals occupy similar positions depends on the extent to which they share the same relations to the same others. On the other hand, in general equivalence the extent to which individuals occupy similar positions depends on the extent to which they share relations with the same "types" of others independent of whether they are the "same" others. General equivalence was alluded to by Sailer (1978) and formalized by White and Reitz (1983) in the development of regular equivalence. Since then Everett and Borgatti and others have further refined the mathematics behind the idea of general equivalence. For a review of these see, for example, Everett (1985), Pattison (1988), and Borgatti and Everett (1989).[7]

Social anthropologists originally were attracted to the idea of a social network so as to escape the static nature of structural-functionalism. However, networks are still primarily treated in a cross-sectional manner in which the dynamic qualities of social networks, although given much lip service, are largely ignored. An early exception to this is Bernard and Killworth's (1973) study of conflict aboard an oceangoing research vessel. Although this work was mentioned earlier as a good example of the mix between ethnography and formal network methods, we can also view this piece as initiating important ideas about the formation and stability of group structure over time. They elaborate and formalize how the ability of humans to communicate effectively puts limits on the size of human groups at various levels. More important, they hypothesized that the structure of a closed group forms quickly (within 2 weeks) and stays relatively stable over time. These ideas were further refined and formalized in a subsequent paper by Killworth and Bernard (1976b) relating group formation and stability to the idea of dissonance.

This earlier research on the dynamics of group formation has influenced the work of Boster and Johnson (1992) and Johnson, Boster, and Palinkas (1991) in their studies of the winter-over crews at the South Pole station. One aspect of this research focuses on how quickly group structure forms and the stability of the structure during the winter-over isolation. Knowledge of these processes has implications, for example, for the production of improved procedures for composing groups for extreme environments (e.g., space stations). Romney, Borgatti, and Nakao (1989) have, in an application of three-way correspondence analysis, also shown the tendency for group structure to form quickly and stay stable over time. Others too have explored the dynamics of small groups, or groups more generally, in research on information flow, conflict and group fissioning (Zachary, 1977), the emergence of virtual groups (Stephenson, 1990), the formation of coalitions in an office (Thurman, 1979-1980), power struggles in a Chinese community (Schweizer, 1991), and a study of the social connections of three networks over time (Hammer, 1980).

Roles in groups are also dynamic and may emerge and disappear depending on the needs of the group. The emergence of roles and the performance of small groups in isolation is discussed by Johnson and Finney (1986). Johnson and Miller (1983) describe the dynamics of role emergence in their study of a commercial fish camp in Alaska. In this case, group structure allowed for the emergence of the role of "court-jester" during a stressful period (a strike) producing a positive, humorous reference point that led to better group cohesion.

A number of methods for the study of whole networks have been developed by anthropologists. These methods are particularly suited for investigating anthropological problems in fieldwork settings. Killworth and Bernard (1974) describe a clique-finding technique (CATIJ) that is based on the use of a card-sorting data collection procedure. This procedure allowed for both individual and aggregate cognitive pictures of a research ship's social structure, and its development was influenced by Bernard's earlier training in cognitive anthropology.[8] Sorting procedures of this type are well suited for field situations (Johnson, 1990) and have been used in other network studies (Boster et al., 1987; Johnson & Miller, 1983) that are centrally concerned with both individual and aggregate cognition. White and McCann (1988) describe the use of entailment analysis in the study of the eighteenth-century chemical revolution. As they put it, the technique "detects tendencies toward set-subset relationships among binary variables" (p. 381). The method has been applied not only to network analysis but in cross-cultural research (Burton, Brudner, & White, 1977) and in the study of cognition (Boster & Johnson, 1989). Similarly, Dow, Burton, White, and Reitz (1984), in attacking Galton's Problem in cross-cultural research, apply the idea of network autocorrelation and show how it is equally applicable in the study of social networks (Dow, Burton, & White, 1982).

Finally, in a series of articles (Hage & Harary, 1982b; Hage, Harary, & James, 1986) and culminating in a book (Hage & Harary, 1991), Hage and Harary apply graph theory to problems in exchange, power, and mediation among Oceanic peoples. These authors provide a comprehensive demonstration of the applicability of graph theory for modeling trade and transport networks (e.g., Kula ring) and other exchange relations (e.g., marriage exchange). They also relate these models to power, hierarchy, intimacy, stratification, and other factors important to Oceanic ethnology.

Summary and Conclusion

Before answering the two questions originally posed concerning the give-and-take between anthropology and social network analysis, it is instructive to review some of the findings of Hummon and Carley (in press) in their study on citation and normal science in social network research. In a 1988 survey of social network researchers, they found that three of the top five scholars perceived to have been most influential in the "social network" community prior to 1970 were anthropologists. By 1988 only one of the top ten scholars perceived to be prominent was an anthropologist (eighth position). These earlier anthropological scholars were, as one might imagine, social anthropologists and included Mitchell, Bott, and Barnes, all scholars who were pioneers in formalizing the concept of a social network. However, sociology came to dominate all but two of the top ten positions by 1988. The only anthropologist in this list, H. Russell Bernard, had written extensively in the area of social networks. More important, Bernard, although early concerned with network theory, had been instrumental in initiating and researching the "cognitive" controversy on the validity of retrospective network data and became most noted for this line of inquiry.

This dominance of sociologists by the 1980s is not surprising as evidenced by the informal citation analyses of some of the articles reviewed here. First, citations by anthropologists of the earlier social anthropological works had begun to subside by the mid-1970s and had become but a trickle by the 1980s. Second, the earlier work of Boyd, although mostly ignored in mainstream anthropology, had fostered a significant amount of important work in social network analysis conducted and cited primarily by sociologists. Third, even some of the promising work on networks and kinship analysis by Foster and Seidman was recognized more by sociologists than anthropologists, mostly for their development of the k-plex and the computer program SONET rather than for any contribution to the study of kinship. Fourth, the graph-theoretic work of Hage and Harary, if used by anthropologists at all, has been employed mostly in solving non-social network problems. Finally, it is primarily in the areas of cognition and social networks and role analysis that a critical mass of anthropologists are citing one another's work and this is generally within the confines of the journal *Social Networks*.

In summarizing the contributions made by anthropologists to the study of social networks, some things become strikingly clear. A number of anthropologists have contributed much to the study of social networks in the area of role analysis, substantive applications of and theoretical developments in graph theory, network data collection and analytical techniques, the representation and analysis of kinship networks, and cognition and social networks. With few exceptions, however, these anthropological contributions have been largely ignored by mainstream anthropology. One can speculate as to why. It may be that at this point in time anthropologists are no longer interested in the study of social structure (see Whitten, 1984).[9] Or it could be that philosophical divisions in the discipline have led many to avoid and ignore the formal, scientific contributions of anthropologists engaged in social network analysis (see Romney, 1989, for a general discussion of this problem). Whatever the reason, it is clear that anthropologists have contributed much to the study of social networks and will in the future continue to contribute to that "branch of natural science" whose task is "the discovery of the general characteristics of those social structures of which the component units are human beings" (Radcliffe-Brown, 1952, p. 190).

Notes

1. In all fairness to Bax, the once promising area of small group research was stifled by a split between researchers concerned with the mathematical aspects of small groups and those concerned with pure form (Johnson & Finney, 1986). The possibility of this occurring in social network analysis is real, but there is strong evidence suggesting that the "formalists" and "substantivists," so to speak, are still talking. In anthropology, for example, there have been successful collaborations between mathematicians and fieldworkers including Bernard and Killworth, Foster and Seidman, and Hage and Harary, to name a few. It is expected that these kinds of collaborations will continue into the future.

2. Like Mitchell and similar to Romney (1989), Killworth et al. (1984), and Bernard and Killworth (1976), this problem should be viewed in terms of models, measurement, and determining what is independent and dependent.

3. Even as recently as 1985, network-oriented researchers have stated the need to "move beyond kinship studies" in anthropological work on contemporary complex societies (Schweizer, 1985, p. 179).

4. This problem of lack of citation has been acknowledged as a general problem in anthropology by Romney (1989) and Johnson (1991).

5. Johnson, Boster, and Holbert (1989) simulated snowball samples to discover potential errors in estimating centrality. This was important in that it provided a basis for understanding the potential bias in selecting key informants on the basis of centrality measures.

6. Boissevain (1973) also recognized the potential impact of network structure on such things as mental health.

7. Steve Borgatti, an Irvine graduate, was the author of ANTRHOPAC, an important computer package used primarily by cognitive anthropologists. He is also a principal author of the new version of UCINET, one of the most comprehensive network computer packages now available. In support of the argument on the link between cognitive

anthropology and social network analysis, both packages have a high degree of overlap in analytical methods.

8. The development of CATIJ was a direct result of Bernard's interaction in graduate school with Kenneth Hale and Duane Metzger during his earlier training in cognition and linguistics (Bernard, personal communication).

9. In the introduction to a 1984 *American Ethnologist* special issue on social structure and social relations, which did not contain a "formal" network article, Whitten (1984) made the following observation in terms of a call for papers on this special issue: "Some of the comments made to the editor and associate editors subsequent to the call for papers are worth mentioning as they reflect, perhaps, collective perceptions held by many other cultural anthropologists from various vantage points within the United States: 'Issues of social structure are now dead'; 'The study of social structure is no longer at the cutting edge of cultural anthropology'; 'Nobody really does that kind of thing anymore.' " (p. 637).

References

Anderson, C. J., Wasserman, S., & Faust, K. (1992). Building stochastic blockmodels. *Social Networks, 14,* 137-161.

Barnes, J. A. (1969). Graph theory and social networks: A technical comment on connectedness and connectivity. *Sociology, 3*(2), 215-242.

Barnes, J. (1980). Kinship studies: Some impressions of the current state of play. *Man, 15,* 293-303.

Barnes, J. A., & Harary, F. (1983). Graph theory in network analysis. *Social Networks, 5,* 235-244.

Bax, M. (1979). Figuration analysis: A better perspective for networker; with an illustration from Ireland. *Anthropological Quarterly, 51,* 221-230.

Bernard, H. R., Johnsen, E. C., Killworth, P. D., Shelley, G. A., McCarty, C., & Robinson, S. (1990). Comparing four different methods for measuring personal social networks. *Social Networks, 12,* 179-215.

Bernard, H. R., Johnsen, E. C., Killworth, P. D., & Robinson, S. (1989). Estimating the size of an average personal network and of an event subpopulation. In M. Kochen (Ed.), *The small world* (pp. 159-175). Norwood, NJ: Ablex.

Bernard, H. R., & Killworth, P. D. (1973). On the social structure of an ocean-going research vessel and other important things. *Social Science Research, 2,* 145-184.

Bernard, H. R., & Killworth, P. D. (1976). Deterministic models of social networks. In P. Holland & S. Leinherdt (Eds.), *Social networks: Surveys, advances, and commentaries.* New York: Academic Press.

Bernard, H. R., & Killworth, P. D. (1977). Informant accuracy in social network data II. *Human Communications Research, 4,* 3-18.

Bernard, H. R., Killworth, P. D., Evans, M. J., McCarty, C., & Shelly, G. A. (1988). Studying social relations cross-culturally. *Ethnology, 27,* 155-179.

Bernard, H. R., Killworth, P. D., & McCarty, C. (1982). Index: An informant-defined experiment in social structure. *Social Forces, 61,* 99-133.

Bernard, H. R., Killworth, P. D., & Sailer, L. (1980). Informant accuracy in social network data IV: A comparison of clique-level structure in behavioral and cognitive network data. *Social Networks, 2,* 191-218.

Bernard, H. R., Killworth, P. D., & Sailer, L. (1982). Informant accuracy in social network data V: An experimental attempt to predict actual communication from recall data. *Social Science Research, 11*, 30-66.

Bernard, H. R., Killworth, P., Sailer, L., & Kronenfeld, D. (1984). On the validity of retrospective data. *Annual Review of Anthropology, 13*, 495-517.

Bernard, H. R., Shelley, G. A., & Killworth, P. D. (1987). How much of a network does the GSS and RSW dredge up? *Social Networks, 9*, 49-61.

Boissevain, J. (1973). An exploration of two first order zones. In J. Boissevain & J. C. Mitchell (Eds.), *Network analysis: Studies in human interaction* (pp. 125-150). The Hague, the Netherlands: Mouton.

Borgatti, S. P., & Everett, M. G. (1989). The class of all regular equivalences: Algebraic structure and computation. *Social Networks, 11*, 65-88.

Boster, J. S. (1985). Selection for perceptual distinctiveness: Evidence from Aguaruna Jivaro varieties of Manihot esculenta. *Economic Botany, 39*(3), 310-325.

Boster, J. S. (1986). Exchange of varieties and information between Aguaruna manioc cultivators. *American Anthropologist, 88*(2), 429-436.

Boster, J. S., & Johnson, J. C. (1989). Form or function: A comparison of expert and novice judgement of similarity among fish. *American Anthropologist, 91*(4), 866-889.

Boster, J. S., & Johnson, J. C. (1992, February). *Network structure and roles in isolated groups.* Paper presented at the 12th annual International Sunbelt Social Network Conference, San Diego, CA.

Boster, J. S., Johnson, J. C., & Weller, S. (1987). Social position and shared knowledge: Actors' perception of status, role, and social structure. *Social Networks, 9*, 375-387.

Bourdieu, P. (1984). *Distinction: A social critique of the judgement of taste.* Cambridge, MA: Harvard University Press.

Boyd, J. P. (1969). The algebra of group kinship. *Journal of Mathematical Psychology, 6*, 139-167.

Boyd, J. P. (1979-1980). The universal semigroup of relations. *Social Networks, 2*, 91-117.

Boyd, J. P. (1989). Social semigroups and green relations. In L. C. Freeman, D. R. White, & A. K. Romney (Eds.), *Research methods in social network analysis* (pp. 215-254). Fairfax, VA: George Mason University Press.

Boyd, J. P. (1991). *Social semigroups: A unified theory of scaling and blockmodelling as applied to social networks.* Fairfax, VA: George Mason University Press.

Boyd, J. P. (1992). Relational homomorphisms. *Social Networks, 14*, 163-186.

Boyd, J. P., Haehl, J. H., & Sailer, L. (1971). Kinship systems and inverse semigroups. *Journal of Mathematical Sociology, 2*, 37-61.

Burt, R. S. (1983). *Toward a structural theory of action.* New York: Academic Press.

Burt, R. (1984). Network items and the general social survey. *Social Networks, 6*, 293-339.

Burton, M., Brudner, L., & White, D. (1977). A model of the sexual division of labor. *American Ethnologist, 4*, 227-251.

Doreian, P. D. (1989). Models of network effects on social actors. In L. C. Freeman, D. R. White, & A. K. Romney (Eds.), *Research methods in social network analysis* (pp. 295-317). Fairfax, VA: George Mason University Press.

Dow, M. M., Burton, M. L., & White, D. R. (1982). Network autocorrelation: A simulation study of a foundational problem in regression and survey research. *Social Networks, 4*, 169-200.

Dow, M. M., Burton, M. L., White, D. R., & Reitz, K. P. (1984). Galton's problems as network autocorrelation. *American Ethnologist, 11*(4), 754-770.

Durbin, M. (1974). Cognitive anthropology. In J. J. Honigmann (Ed.), *Handbook of social and cultural anthropology* (pp. 447-478). Chicago: Rand McNally.

Eckert, J. K. (1983). Dislocation and relocation of the urban elderly: Social networks as mediators of relocation stress. *Human Organization, 42*, 39-45.

Epstein, A. L. (1969a). The network and urban social organization. In J. C. Mitchell (Ed.), *Social networks in urban situations* (pp. 77-116). Manchester: Manchester University Press.

Epstein, A. L. (1969b). Gossip, norms, and social network. In J. C. Mitchell (Ed.), *Social networks in urban situations* (pp. 117-127). Manchester: Manchester University Press.

Everett, M. G. (1985). Role similarity and complexity in social networks. *Social Networks, 7*, 353-359.

Faust, K. (1988). Comparison of methods of positional analysis: Structural and general equivalences. *Social Networks, 10*, 313-341.

Faust, K., & Wasserman, S. (1992). Blockmodels: Interpretation and evaluation. *Social Networks, 14*, 5-61.

Festinger, L., Chachter, S., & Bak, K. (1950). *Social pressures in informal groups.* Stanford, CA: Stanford University Press.

Fortes, M. (1940). The political system of the Tallensi of the Northern Territories of the Gold Coast. In M. Fortes & E. E. Evans-Pritchard (Eds.), *African political systems.* London: Oxford University Press.

Fortes, M. (1945). *The dynamics of clanship among the Tallensi.* London: Oxford University Press.

Fortes, M. (1949). *The web of kinship among the Tallensi.* London: Oxford University Press.

Foster, B. L. (1978). Formal network studies and the anthropological perspective. *Social Networks, 1*, 241-255.

Foster, B. L., & Seidman, S. B. (1979). Network structure and the kinship perspective. *American Ethnologist, 8*, 329-355.

Foster, B. L., & Seidman, S. B. (1982). Urban structures derived from collection of overlapping subsets. *Urban Anthropology, 11*, 177-192.

Foster, B. L., & Seidman, S. B. (1989). A formal unification of anthropological kinship and social methods. In L. C. Freeman, D. R. White, & A. K. Romney (Eds.), *Research methods in social network analysis* (pp. 41-59). Fairfax, VA: George Mason University Press.

Freeman, L. C., Freeman, S. C., & Michaelson, A. G. (1988). On human social intelligence. *Journal of Social and Biological Structure, 11*, 415-425.

Freeman, L. C., Freeman, S. C., & Michaelson, A. (1989). How humans see social groups: A test of the Sailer-Gaulin models. *Journal of Quantitative Anthropology, 1*(3), 229-238.

Freeman, L. C., & Romney, A. K. (1987). Words, deeds and social structure. *Human Organization.*

Freeman, L. C., Romney, A. K., & Freeman, S. C. (1987). Cognitive structure and informant accuracy. *American Anthropologist, 89*, 310-325.

Freeman, L. C., & Thompson, C. R. (1989). Estimating acquaintanceship volume. In M. Kochen (Ed.), *The small world* (pp. 147-158). Norwood, NJ: Ablex.

Goodenough, W. H. (1969). Rethinking "status" and "role." In S. Tyler (Ed.), *Cognitive anthropology* (pp. 311-330). New York: Holt, Rinehart & Winston.

Greenbaum, S. D., & Greenbaum, P. E. (1985). The ecology of social networks in four urban neighborhoods. *Social Networks, 7*, 47-76.

Hage, P. (1976a). Structural balance and clustering in Bushmen kinship relations. *Behavioral Science, 21*, 36-37.

Hage, P. (1976b). The atom of kinship as a directed graph. *Man* (n.s.), *11*, 558-568.

Hage, P. (1979). Graph theory as a structural model in cultural anthropology. *Annual Review of Anthropology, 8*, 115-136.

Hage, P., & Harary, F. (1982a). On reciprocity in kinship relations. *Cambridge Anthropology, 9*, 39-43.

Hage, P., & Harary, F. (1982b). Mediation and power in Melanesia. *Oceania, 52*, 124-135.

Hage, P., & Harary, F. (1983). *Structural models in anthropology*. London: Cambridge University Press.

Hage, P., & Harary, F. (1991). *Exchange in Oceania: A graph theoretic analysis*. New York: Clarendon.

Hage, P., Harary, F., & James, B. (1986). Wealth and hierarchy in the Kula ring. *American Anthropologist, 88*, 108-115.

Hammer, M. (1963). Influence of small social networks as factors on mental health admission. *Human Organization, 22*, 243-251.

Hammer, M. (1980). Predictability of social connections over time. *Social Networks, 2*, 165-180.

Hammer, M. (1981, January). *Impact of social networks on health and disease*. Paper presented at the annual meeting of the AAAS.

Hammer, M. (1983). "Core" and "extended" social networks in relation to health and illness. *Social Science and Medicine, 17*(7), 405-422.

Hammer, M. (1985). Implications of behavioral and cognitive reciprocity in social network data. *Social Networks, 7*, 189-201.

Hammer, M., Polgar, S. K., & Salzinger, K. (1969). Speeds predictability and social contact patterns in an informal group. *Human Organization, 28*, 235-242.

Heider, F. (1946). Attitudes and cognitive organization. *Journal of Psychology, 21*, 107-112.

Honigmann, J. J. (1976). *The development of anthropological ideas*. Homewood, IL: Dorsey.

Hummon, N. P., & Carley, K. (in press). Social networks vs. normal science. *Social Networks*.

Hurd, G. A., Pattison, E. M., & Llamas, R. (1981). Models of social network intervention. *International Journal of Family Therapy, 3*, 246-257.

Jackson, J. E. (1976). Vaupe's marriage: A network system in the northwest Amazon. In C. A. Smith (Ed.), *Regional analysis II social systems* (pp. 65-93). New York: Academic Press.

Johnson, J. C. (1986). Social networks and innovation adoption: A look at Burt's use of structural equivalence. *Social Networks, 8*, 343-364.

Johnson, J. C. (1990). *Selecting ethnographic informants*. Newbury Park, CA: Sage.

Johnson, J. C. (1991, March). *The future of the tool: Are we destined to be lost in the land of the giants?* Paper presented at the annual SFAA Conference, 50th Anniversary Invited Symposium, Charleston, SC.

Johnson, J. C., & Boster, J. S. (1990, February). *Of pigs, cows, chickens, and shrimp: Community structure and cognitive variation.* Paper presented at the 10th Annual International Sunbelt Social Network Conference, San Diego, CA.

Johnson, J. C., Boster, J. S., & Holbert, D. (1989). Estimating relational attributes from snowball samples through simulation. *Social Networks, 11*, 135-158.

Johnson, J. C., Boster, J. S., & Palinkas, L. (1991). *Social structure, agreement, and conflict in groups in extreme and isolated environments.* Proposal to the National Science Foundation, Washington, DC.

Johnson, J. C., & Finney, B. R. (1986). Structural approaches to the study of groups in space: A look at two analogs. *Journal of Social Behavior and Personality, 1*(3), 325-347.

Johnson, J. C., & Miller, M. L. (1983). Deviant social positions in small groups: The relation between role and individual. *Social Networks, 5*, 51-69.

Johnson, J. C., & Miller, M. (1986). Behavioral and cognitive data: A note on the multiplexity of network subgroups. *Social Networks, 8*, 65-77.

Johnson, J. C., & Orbach, M. K. (1990a). Migratory fishermen: A case study in interjurisdictional natural resource management. *Ocean and Shoreline Management, 13*, 231-252.

Johnson, J. C., & Orbach, M. K. (1990b). A fishery in transition: The impact of urbanization on Florida's spiny lobster fishery. *City and Society, 4*, 88-104.

Johnson, J. C., Poteat, G. M., & Ironsmith, M. (1991). Structural vs. marginal effects: A note on the importance of structure in determining sociometric status. *Journal of Social Behavior and Personality, 6*, 489-508.

Jongmans, D. C. (1973). Politics on the village level. In J. Boissevain & J. C. Mitchell (Eds.), *Network analysis: Studies in human interaction* (pp. 167-218). The Hague, the Netherlands: Mouton.

Kapferer, B. (1972). *Strategy and transaction in an African factory.* Manchester: Manchester University Press.

Kapferer, B. (1973). Social network and conjugal role in urban Zambia: Toward a reformulation of the Bott hypothesis. In J. Boissevain & J. C. Mitchell (Eds.), *Network analysis: Studies in human interaction* (pp. 83-110). The Hague, the Netherlands: Mouton.

Kapferer, B. (1978). Structural marginality and the urban social order. *Urban Anthropology, 5*(2), 287-320.

Killworth, P. D., & Bernard, H. R. (1974). CATIJ: A new sociometric and its application to a prison living unit. *Human Organization, 33*, 335-350.

Killworth, P. D., & Bernard, H. R. (1976a). Informant accuracy in social network data. *Human Organization, 35*, 269-286.

Killworth, P. D., & Bernard, H. R. (1976b). A model of human group dynamics. *Social Science Research, 5*, 173-224.

Killworth, P. D., & Bernard, H. R. (1978). The reversal small-world experiment. *Social Networks, 1*, 159-192.

Killworth, P. D., & Bernard, H. R. (1979). A pseudomodel of the small world problem. *Social Forces, 58*, 477-505.

Killworth, P. D., & Bernard, H. R. (1979-1980). Informant accuracy in social network data, III: A comparison of triadic structures in behavior and cognitive data. *Social Networks, 2*, 19-46.

Killworth, P. D., & Bernard, H. R. (1982). A technique for comparing mental maps. *Social Networks, 3*(4), 307-312.

Killworth, P. D., Bernard, H. R., & McCarty, C. (1984). Measuring patterns of acquaintanceship. *Current Anthropology, 25*, 381-397.

Killworth, P. D., Johnsen, E. C., Bernard, H. R., Shelley, G. A., & McCarty, C. (1990). Estimating the size of personal networks. *Social Networks, 12*, 289-312.

Kimball, S. T., & Partridge, W. L. (1979). *The craft of community study: Fieldwork dialogue.* Gainesville: University Presses of Florida.

Krackhardt, D. (1987). Cognitive social structures. *Social Networks, 9*, 109-134.

Krackhardt, D., & Kilduff, M. (1990). Friendship patterns and culture: The control of organizational diversity. *American Anthropologist, 92*, 142-154.

Kroeber, A. L., & Kluckholm, C. (1952). *Culture: A critical review of concepts and definitions.* Cambridge: Peabody Museum.

Lex, B. W., & Wolfe, A. W. (1967). *The effects of first contacts by researchers in urban fieldwork.* Paper presented at the Central States Anthropological Society Meetings, Chicago.

Lorrain, F., & White, H. C. (1971). Structural equivalence of individuals in social networks. *Journal of Mathematical Sociology, 1*, 49-80.

McCallister, L., & Fischer, C. (1983). A procedure for surveying personal networks. In R. Burt & J. Minor (Eds.), *Applied network analysis.* Beverly Hills, CA: Sage.

McCarty, C. (1992). *Perceived clique definition in ego-centered networks.* Unpublished doctoral dissertation, University of Florida, Gainesville.

McClain, C. S. (1987). Some social network differences between women choosing home and hospital birth. *Human Organization, 46*, 146-152.

Mead, M. (1953). National character. In A. L. Kroeber (Ed.), *Anthropology today* (pp. 642-667). Chicago: University of Chicago Press.

Michaelson, A., & Contractor, N. S. (1992). Structural position and perceived similarity. *Social Psychology Quarterly, 55*(3), 300-310.

Mitchell, J. C. (1974). Social networks. *Annual Review of Anthropology, 3*, 279-299.

Mitchell, J. C. (1987). The components of strong ties among homeless women. *Social Networks, 9*, 37-47.

Mitchell, J. C. (1989). Algorithms and network analysis: A test of some analytical procedures on Kapferer's tailor shop material. In L. C. Freeman, D. R. White, & A. K. Romney (Eds.), *Research methods in social network analysis* (pp. 319-365). Fairfax, VA: George Mason University Press.

Morrill, C. (1991). The customs of conflict management among corporate executives. *American Anthropologist, 93*, 871-893.

Murdock, G. P. (1951). British social anthropology. *American Anthropologist, 53*, 465-473.

Nadel, S. F. (1957). *The theory of social structure.* London: Cohen and West.

Noble, M. (1973). Social network: Its use as a conceptual framework in family analysis. In J. Boissevain & J. C. Mitchell (Eds.), *Network analysis: Studies in human interaction* (pp. 3-14). The Hague, the Netherlands: Mouton.

O'Connor, M. I. (1990). Women's networks and the social needs of Mexican immigrants. *Urban Anthropology, 19*, 81-92.

Pattison, P. E. (1988). Network models: Some comments on papers in this special issue. *Social Networks, 10*, 383-411.

Pelto, P. J., & Pelto, G. H. (1975). *Anthropological research: The structure of inquiry.* Cambridge: Cambridge University Press.

Plattner, S. M. (1978). Occupation and kinship in a developing society. *Human Organization, 37,* 77-83.

Poole, I. de S., & Kochen, M. (1978). Contacts and influence. *Social Networks, 1,* 5-51.

Quinn, N. (1975). Decision models of social structure. *American Ethnologist, 2,* 19-45.

Radcliffe-Brown, A. R. (1952). *Structure and function in primitive society.* New York: Free Press.

Reingen, P. H., Foster, B. L., Brown, J. J., & Seidman, S. B. (1984). Brancongruence in interpersonal relations: A social network analysis. *Journal of Consumer Research, 11,* 771-783.

Reitz, K. P. (1988). Social groups in a monastery. *Social Networks, 10,* 343-357.

Reitz, K. P., & White, D. R. (1989). Rethinking the role concept: Homomorphisms on social networks. In L. C. Freeman, D. R. White, & A. K. Romney (Eds.), *Research methods in social network analysis* (pp. 429-488). Fairfax, VA: George Mason University Press.

Romney, A. K. (1965). Kalmuk Mongol and the classification of lineal kinship terminologies. *American Anthropologist, 67,* 127-141.

Romney, A. K. (1989). Quantitative models, science, and cumulative knowledge. *Journal of Quantitative Anthropology, 1*(1-2), 153-224.

Romney, A. K., Borgatti, S. P., & Nakao, K. (1989, February). *Three-way correspondence analysis: The Newcomb and Nordlie data.* Paper presented at the Sunbelt IX Social Network Conference, Tampa, FL.

Romney, A. K., & Faust, K. (1983). Predicting the structure of a communications network from recalled data. *Social Networks, 4,* 285-304.

Romney, A. K., & Weller, S. C. (1984). Predicting informant accuracy from patterns of recall among individuals. *Social Networks, 4,* 59-77.

Romney, A. K., Weller, S. C., & Batchelder, W. H. (1986). Culture as consensus: A theory of culture and informant accuracy. *American Anthropologist, 88,* 313-338.

Sailer, L. D. (1978). Structural equivalence: Meaning and definition, computation and application. *Social Networks, 1,* 73-90.

Sailer, L., & Gaulin, S. (1984). Proximity, sociability, and observation: The definition of social groups. *American Anthropologist, 86,* 91-98.

Sanjek, R. (1978). A network method and its uses in urban ethnography. *Human Organization, 37,* 257-268.

Schweizer, T. (1985). Soziale schichtung in kolonialen Java. *Anthropos, 80,* 153-183.

Schweizer, T. (1988). Detecting positions in networks: A formal analysis of loose social structure in rural Java. *American Anthropologist, 90,* 944-953.

Schweizer, T. (1991). The power struggle in a Chinese community, 1950-1980: A social network analysis of the duality of actors and events. *Journal of Quantitative Anthropology, 3*(1), 19-44.

Seidman, S. B., & Foster, B. L. (1978). A note on the potential for genuine cross-fertilization between anthropology and mathematics. *Social Networks, 1,* 65-72.

Shelley, G. A. (1992). *The social networks of people with end state renal disease: Comparing hemodialysis and peritoneal dialysis patients.* Unpublished doctoral dissertation, University of Florida, Department of Anthropology.

Shelley, G. A., Bernard, H. R., & Killworth, P. D. (1990). Information flow in social networks. *Journal of Quantitative Anthropology, 2,* 201-225.

Sokolovsky, J., & Cohen, C. (1978). The cultural meaning of personal networks for the inner-city elderly. *Urban Anthropology, 5*(2), 323-342.

Sokolovsky, J., Cohen, C., Berger, D., & Geiger, J. (1978). Personal networks of ex-mental patients in a Manhattan SRO hotel. *Human Organization, 37,* 5-15.

Stefflre, V. J. (1986). *Developing and implementing marketing strategies.* New York: Praeger.

Stephenson, K. (1990). The emergence of virtual groups. *Ethnology, 29,* 279-296.

Thomas, J. S. (1978). Kinship and wealth in a Maya community. *Human Organization, 37,* 24-28.

Thurman, B. (1979-1980). In the office: Networks and coalitions. *Social Networks, 2,* 47-63.

Truex, G. F. (1981). Kinship and network: A cognitive model of interaction. *Social Networks, 3,* 53-70.

Van Willigen, J. (1989). *Gettin' some age on me: Social organization of older people in rural American community.* Lexington: University Press of Kentucky.

Walsh, A. C., & Simonelli, J. (1986). Migrant women in the oil field: The functions of social networks. *Human Organization, 45,* 43-52.

Wasserman, S., & Faust, K. (1994). *Social network analysis: Methods and applications.* New York: Cambridge University Press.

Watson, G. (1984). The social construction of boundaries between social and cultural anthropology in Britain and North America. *Journal of Anthropological Research, 40,* 351-366.

Weisner, T. S. (1978). The structure of sociality: Urban migration and urban-rural ties in Kenya. *Urban Anthropology, 5,* 199-223.

Wellman, B. (1988). Structural analysis: From method and metaphor to theory and substance. In B. Wellman & S. D. Berkowitz (Eds.), *Social structures: A network approach* (pp. 19-61). Cambridge: Cambridge University Press.

Werner, O., & Schoepfle, G. M. (1987). *Systematic fieldwork* (2 vols.). Newbury Park, CA: Sage.

White, D. R., & Jorian, P. (1992). Representing and computing kinship: A new approach. *Current Anthropology, 33*(4), 454-463.

White, D. R., & McCann, H. G. (1988). Cites and fights: Material entailment analysis of the eighteenth-century chemical revolution. In B. Wellman & S. D. Berkowitz (Eds.), *Social structures: A network approach* (pp. 380-400). Cambridge: Cambridge University Press.

White, D. R., & Reitz, K. P. (1983). Graph and semigroup homomorphisms on networks of relations. *Social Networks, 5,* 193-234.

White, H. C. (1963). *Anatomy of kinship.* Englewood Cliffs, NJ: Prentice-Hall.

Whitten, N. (1984). Introduction. *American Ethnologist, 11*(4), 635-641.

Whitten, N., & Wolfe, A. (1974). Network analysis. In J. Honigmann (Ed.), *Handbook of social and cultural anthropology* (pp. 717-746). Chicago: Rand McNally.

Wolfe, A. (1970). On structural comparisons of networks. *Canada Review of Sociology and Anthropology, 7*(4), 226-244.

Wolfe, A. W. (1978). The rise of network thinking in anthropology. *Social Networks, 1,* 53-64.

Zachary, W. W. (1977). An information flow model for conflict and fission in small groups. *Journal of Anthropological Research, 33,* 452-473.

6

Primate Social Networks

DONALD STONE SADE
MALCOLM M. DOW

Alloprimate Social Networks

Groups of alloprimates (the other primates: nonhuman primates) are ideal subjects for the study of social interaction and the application of the methods of social network analysis. Social relations among alloprimates are complex enough to be interesting but lack the symbolic complexities of human social intercourse. A fairly complete record of social interactions can be obtained under good conditions of observation on a group of monkeys or apes. In contrast, studies on human social networks are generally based on highly abstracted measures of social relations. It has been possible occasionally to observe a single group of monkeys consistently for many years (e.g., Sade, Chepko-Sade, Schneider, Roberts, & Richtsmeier, 1985). Thus the detailed dynamics of social organization can be studied over a significant portion of the life span of the species. Curiously, the formal methods of social network analysis have not been widely employed by behavioral primatologists. Perhaps the easy access to computing power made possible by the personal computer will make these methods more attractive to students of the alloprimates. The studies reviewed below indicate the value of formal network methods to the analysis of alloprimate society. In addition, students of human social networks may see opportunities for comparative investigations of social processes unencumbered by cultural tradition.

Brief History of Studies of Alloprimate Social Organization

The earliest studies of social organization of alloprimates were conducted in the 1930s by the psychologist C. R. Carpenter on gibbons in Thailand, howler monkeys on Barro Colorado, Panama, and the colony of rhesus monkeys that he established on Cayo Santiago, Puerto Rico (republished in Carpenter, 1964). Carpenter's work emphasized what he considered species-typical patterns of interaction between and among age/sex classes: infants, juveniles, and adult males and females. Although little in the way of social network analysis emerged from Carpenter's work, one might see his studies as the first to formally measure social roles within alloprimate groups.

No studies were conducted on alloprimate societies again until after World War II. Then a number of investigators from several countries initiated studies of groups of alloprimates of several species (see Altmann, 1967, for a good entry into the early literature). Although much of the work on alloprimate social behavior was qualitative, several of the early studies were quantitative. These emphasized the interactions that were observed between identified individuals. Still, even sociograms based on quantitative data, the most elementary treatment of social networks, were used in only a few studies of alloprimate social organization.

Sociograms

Kummer (1968) used simple sociograms to represent the interactional patterns observed within several small social units of Hamadryas baboons. The incidence and orientation of a number of social signals between individually identified baboons were combined in his sociograms. These clearly showed the adult-male focal nature of this species and, as cross-sectional samples of one-male units in different stages of development, showed the unique social ontogeny of the Hamadryas baboon.

Sade (1965) tabulated each observed incidence of grooming between rhesus monkeys in a free-ranging group in the Cayo Santiago, Puerto Rico, colony. He used sociograms to illustrate the changing patterns in the grooming network over a 3-year period in one family. He also showed for the social group as a whole that grooming was much more frequent between members of the same genealogy than between unrelated individuals. This study confirmed the earlier, qualitative findings of Japanese primatologists (Imanishi & Altmann, 1965) that kinship relations strongly influenced interactional relations. Sade (1966) also studied the ontogeny of social relations in a cohort of rhesus monkeys over several years. He used the relative frequency of grooming, play, and close spatial relations to construct sociograms that illustrated the development of social companionship for each individual in the cohort. Soczka (1974) described the structure of a group of seven juvenile crab-eating macaques. Grooming, play, and body contact were analyzed separately. These behaviors were also combined into a single, affiliative network by finding the union of the respective 1/0 interaction matrices. The structure for each network and for the combined networks were displayed as sociograms in which individuals were ordered according to whether their frequency of interaction was significantly greater or less than the group mean.

Clark (1985) studied a nocturnal species, Galago crassicaudatus, usually considered "solitary" because individuals disperse while foraging. Clark, however, kept records of social interactions among 23 marked individuals. Sociograms show that an affiliative social network linked individuals of all age/sex classes.

Hanby (1980) compared the social structure of six captive groups of rhesus macaques using sociograms representing various degrees of spatial proximity. Although the groups were fairly small (9-18 monkeys), the complexity of the sociograms makes visual comparison difficult. This paper reaches the limit of usefulness for social analysis of the visual display of relatively unreduced data.

Cliques and Clusters

Several attempts to identify interactional subgroups within larger social units have been made. The n-clique structure of the grooming networks in a group of rhesus monkeys was found by an algorithm based on Luce (1950) and on Ross and Harary (1952), for $n = \{1, 2, 3\}$ (Sade, 1972). This confirmed the results of a centrality analysis (discussed below) that males were less homogeneous in their position in the grooming network than were females. Kaplan and Zucker (1980), using the same algorithm as Sade (1972), showed the n-clique structure, for $n = \{1, 2, 3\}$, in the grooming network of a group of 19 patas monkeys. Low- and high-ranking individuals tended to form separate cliques. A sociogram based on the cliqual composition of the grooming network clearly shows the social structure of this group of monkeys.

Chepko-Sade, Reitz, and Sade (1989) performed a hierarchical cluster analysis (Reitz, 1982) on the grooming network of a prefission group of rhesus monkeys in a retrospective study. Criteria of both "leadership" and "closeness" were included in the analysis. The results revealed that many of the lines of fission within the group along which a complete division occurred during the following year (Chepko-Sade & Sade, 1979) were already detectable in the grooming network.

Chimpanzees offer a special opportunity for applying network methods to the analysis of social organization. These animals live in dispersed populations in which small subgroups may be out of contact with others for days at a time. Nishida and Hiraiwa-Hasegawa (1987) performed a hierarchical cluster analysis on association patterns in a population of chimpanzees in the Mahale Mountains, Tanzania, and showed that a single social network united the 30 animals in the population in spite of the dispersed foraging ecology of the species.

Chapais (1983) mapped the spatial proximity network in a group of rhesus monkeys using a maximum spanning tree algorithm to show the subclusters of male-female orientations during the nonmating season. Two high-ranking males and a high-ranking female were central in this analysis.

Dow and de Waal (1989) developed a set of assignment procedures (Hubert, 1987) to evaluate subgroups within a larger social network, once the subgroups have been identified by a clustering procedure or by a priori biological criteria such as genealogical relationship. The procedures provide measures of compactness (the degree to which interaction concentrates within the subgroup), isolation (the degree to which subgroups are distinct from other subgroups), and the degree to which interactional flow within, out of, or into subgroups dominates. Randomization procedures permit statistical evaluation of each measure.

All of these methods should be more widely and routinely applied by primate behaviorists, who still rely heavily on qualitative assessment or simple frequency counts to describe social structure.

One qualitative study, however, shows the value of social network thinking for theory in studies of alloprimate behavior. Although largely qualitative because of a generally inadequate literature, Maryanski's (1987) review of social organization of the African great apes suggests that weak ties play a unifying role in wild populations, in both the chimpanzee and the gorilla, as well as in humans. This contrasts with the usual view that these three, closely related species show major divergences in social organization due to divergent ecological adaptations.

This study should stir field primatologists to greater efforts to collect quantitative records of social interaction in these species.

Centrality

Statuses of individuals within alloprimate social groups usually have been measured on only two dimensions: rank in the dominance hierarchy and some estimate of the degree to which an individual is central or peripheral in the social group.

Sade (1972) described the relation between the grooming and the agonistic networks ("dominance hierarchy") among rhesus monkeys in a correlational analysis. Both the agonistic and the grooming networks were expressed as interaction matrices. The "dominance" matrix, showing the frequency and direction of wins and losses in agonistic interactions, was reordered to minimize values below the main diagonal. In the case of dyads within which no interactions were observed, transitivity was assumed, so that an ordinal rank could be assigned to each individual. Because the network approached a "linear dominance hierarchy," each monkey was assigned an ordinal "dominance" rank. The grooming network was also expressed as an interaction matrix in which the frequency and direction of grooming interactions within each dyad were tabulated. This matrix was then censored to a 1/0 matrix by dividing each cell by its row marginal and converting to 1 or 0 according to whether or not it equaled or exceeded a prechosen proportion. An index of centrality was calculated for each individual from the 1/0 matrix. This was the sum of the inward directed 1-, 2-, and nonredundant 3-paths. The redundant 3-paths were removed using the method of Ross and Harary (1952). This may have been the first attempt to measure the characteristics of a social network, beyond frequency of interaction, in an alloprimate. The results were that dominance rank and centrality were correlated for females, but not for males.

The relation between centrality in the grooming network and rank in the agonistic network for males was investigated further in a later paper (Sade, Altmann, Loy, Hausfater, & Breuggeman, 1988). A group of rhesus monkeys was studied longitudinally for 3 years. This period was divided into shorter intervals by various criteria. Agonistic rank and grooming centrality were found by the same methods as in the earlier paper (Sade, 1972). The size and membership of the social group changed somewhat over the 3-year period due to normal demographic events, and the intensity of observation varied somewhat. Therefore the centrality indices were normalized by a randomization procedure to make them comparable across intervals. This study showed that dominance rank and centrality for males were not tightly coupled. Rather, their dynamic relationship suggested a considerable complexity in the psychology of social status in alloprimates.

In a later paper Sade (1989) calculated centrality as the sum of inward directed n-paths in the grooming network for a group of 16 rhesus monkeys using a simple counting algorithm that computed paths of length $n = \{1, 2, \ldots 15\}$. The coefficient of variation for centrality across individuals increased from $n = 1$ to $n = 3$, then remained relatively constant, increasing again for path lengths of $n > 10$. The very large number of inward directed paths of the longer lengths caused Sade to wonder if there were an optimal path length for indicating social status.

Centrality in the grooming network in a group of gelada monkeys during two different time periods was described by Stephenson and Zelen (1989) using a procedure based on matrix inversion that summarized the information in all paths linking the animals in the group. These authors use the resulting centrality indices to interpret changes in the group structure following experimental changes in group membership. Although this procedure is mathematically elegant, it is not at all clear how the results are to be referred back to the behavior of the baboons. This is likely to be a pervasive problem in adapting methods from human sociology to studies of alloprimate behavior. Several other definitions of centrality, such as "betweenness" and "closeness," are available (reviewed in Freeman, 1979) but seem to have little applicability to alloprimate social networks. In an alloprimate group, no information (such as messages or memos) passes from one individual through a second and on to a third. Therefore concepts such as "betweenness" or "closeness" are moot when applied to the alloprimates. This is not to say that there are not cascades of events that may be transmitted through the network. An example is redirected aggression passing "down" the dominance hierarchy.

Agonistic Dominance

The "dominance hierarchy," or preferably the "agonistic network" (Knox & Sade, 1991), has been the most studied of all the social networks within alloprimate or other animal groups. A complete review would be impossible here, but several studies deserve special mention in the present context. Since Schjelderup-Ebbe (1922) discovered linear dominance hierarchies in chickens, similar social structures have been found in many species of vertebrates. The dominance-subordination relation is generally indicated when attacks by one individual are responded to with displays of defeat by the victim. It has naturally been assumed that the winner in such a contest is somehow physically and perhaps genetically superior to the loser. However, examination of the network properties of agonism have cast doubt on this assumption. Landau (1951) and Chase (1974) showed that, for individual differences to be the source of hierarchies as linear as actually observed, either physical characteristics would have to show much higher variance in natural populations than is usually the case or relatively small differences in physical characteristics would have to constrain the probability of winning or losing an agonistic interaction to an unreasonably high degree. Iverson and Sade (1990) argued that models of stochastic transitivity were more appropriate for empirically observed agonistic networks than were the usual models that assume strict transitivity and connectedness of agonistic relations. These latter authors also showed that the strongest model of stochastic transitivity, Equality, accounted satisfactorily for several empirically observed agonistic networks in several species, including baboons and rhesus monkeys. Equality means the probability of one animal beating another in a contest across all dyads, irrespective of the distance between the two individuals in the network. This implies that the hierarchy does not order individuals on basis of differences in ability.

These theoretical studies make quite puzzling the fact that linear or near-linear dominance hierarchies are frequently observed. Chase (1982) reasoned that the way in which hierarchies form might explain why near-transitive networks are so often observed without any requirement that individuals be ordered according to a scale of merit. Chase (1982) discovered that, of the four possible sequences of formation of dyadic dominance relations within each possible triad of individuals in the hierarchy, two—double dominance (DD) and double subordination (SS)—would automatically guarantee a linear hierarchy if followed within every triad. Observations of the establishment of dominance relations within triads in an experimental flock of chickens showed that most did follow the two sequences, DD and SS, that guaranteed a linear hierarchy. Mendoza and Barchas (1983) repeated Chase's experiments, but in rhesus monkeys, and also found that most sequences of formation of dominance relations within triads conformed to DD or SS, guaranteeing a near-linear hierarchy for the group as a whole.

Do these findings imply that the "dominance hierarchy" does not exist as any real biological structure but only as an intellectual construct in the mind of the human investigator? Altmann (1981) argued exactly this point, and in fact his reasoning challenges the reality of any emergent organization above the level of the dyadic relation. However, Altmann also suggested that, if the monkeys themselves could be shown to have a mental or cognitive (not necessarily conscious) recognition of the hierarchy or a portion of it, then the hierarchy might be properly said to exist. He suggested an experiment on dominance hierarchy formation that could reveal whether a monkey could possess the social concept of a dominance hierarchy or at least whether it could recognize social relations not directly resulting from it own interactions: Let two monkeys establish the dominance-subordination relation while a third, hidden monkey observes. Then let the dominant of the pair interact with the monkey that observed him beat the other. If the third monkeys in a series of experiments become subordinate to the initial dominants more often than chance would predict, then a social concept would be implied. In fact, the experiments of Mendoza and Barchas (1983) designed to test Chase's model of hierarchy formation come close to the requirements of Altmann's experiment.

Although most studies of social interaction among alloprimates have emphasized dyadic interactions, there are a few other attempts to describe "tripartite" relations, all of which imply some degree of social concept on the part of the interacting individuals (reviewed in Hinde, 1983, pp. 152-153). Most examples show that the usual pattern of agonistic interaction with a dyad is altered by the interference (Kaplan, 1977) or even mere presence of a third individual.

Several other studies have also suggested that alloprimates may recognize social relations between other individuals. Breuggeman (1973) noted that free-ranging rhesus monkeys sometimes pick up an infant other than their own and search for and deliver it to the infant's own mother. Dasser (1988), displaying photographs of interacting monkeys in an ingenious experiment, revealed that monkeys have an abstract concept of the mother-infant relation. De Waal (1982) found many indications that chimpanzees not only recognize social relations among other individuals in their society but also use this knowledge to manipulate social interaction to achieve personal and reproductive ends. Walters

(1980) argued that maturing baboons must have a concept of the dominance hierarchy and target their interactions so as to achieve an appropriate adult status. Further review of the cognitive abilities of the alloprimates would lead away from the topic of this chapter (but see Essock-Vitale & Seyfarth, 1987; Sade, 1991). Yet this area of research is an exciting new approach to the study of alloprimate social networks. One wonders whether someday studies on alloprimates equivalent to those on humans that combine social network analysis with projective techniques from social psychology and psychiatry (Omark, Strayer, & Freedman, 1980) might be possible.

If the dominance hierarchy is a real structure in alloprimate societies then difference in rank should associate with other variables of social interaction. De Waal (1991) argued that rank distance was a feature of central importance in the social organization of rhesus monkeys. He tested five hypotheses on the effects of rank distance on social interaction of several kinds and showed that rank distance correlated significantly with several behaviors. He was able to partial out the effects of kinship, a confounding variable in several previous studies, on these correlations. His major finding that monkeys are attracted to others of similar rank independent of kinship is an important contribution to our understanding of the nature of the social bond in this species.

Even closely related species of monkeys may differ in the typical characteristics of the agonistic network. Thierry (1986) compared the agonistic networks within one group each of three species of macaques: the rhesus, Java, and Tonkena. She compared symmetry in aggression, behaviors that occurred subsequent to aggression, the intensity of aggression, and reconciliation following aggression and found significant differences in the patterning of each between species. This work is perhaps the best example of objective, cross-specific comparison of social organization in alloprimates.

Knox and Sade (1991) reversed the usual direction of analysis in a unique study of the agonistic network in emperor tamarins. They used the network characteristics of each component of display to identify the degree to which each of 24 components indicated threat or submission. Reasoning that the chief network characteristic of an agonistic display was the asymmetry of interaction within the dyad, they developed an assignment procedure (Hubert, 1987) that compared this feature for each component simultaneously with the most extreme component of threat and the most extreme component of submission. The result was a ranking of all components from extreme threat to extreme submission.

Components that were not significantly similar to either end of the spectrum were considered to be nonagonistic.

Social Roles and Social Structure

As previously mentioned, Carpenter's (1964) pioneering work introduced simple measures of roles into studies of primate societies. Roles were seen as arising from persistent interaction patterns among individuals based on such factors as age, sex, and dominance. Recording these activity patterns and specifying how the corresponding social roles interrelate is the core problem in developing a theory of primate (or human) social structure. As Carpenter emphasized, such description and specification is also central to the larger problem of drawing interpopulation and interspecific comparisons of social structure.

The study by Pearl and Schulman (1983) is by far the most ambitious formal study of role relations within primate groups. Drawing upon a variety of mathematical modeling techniques in network analysis, Pearl and Schulman attempt to uncover and then compare the "surface structure" of two primate societies. This latter concept is one of the levels in Hinde's (1983) elaborate but poorly operationalized theory of animal social organization. Pearl and Schulman describe "surface" social structure in terms of the interaction and superposition of multiple networks of relations. Whereas most earlier primate sociometric studies were limited to the analysis of single relationships, that is, single $N \times N$ interaction matrices, they overcome this methodological limitation by employing "blockmodels" (Boorman & White, 1976; White, Boorman, & Breiger, 1976) of multiple social networks to operationalize role interlock and the related concept of surface social structure.

Pearl and Schulman apply the blockmodel approach (using the CONCOR algorithm) to six interaction matrices collected on all individuals in two distinct social groups of rhesus monkeys. Data on grooming, play, threats, fear grimacing, mating, and nearest-neighbor networks were obtained for a group of 110 provisioned rhesus monkeys on Cayo Santiago, Puerto Rico, and a group of 25 wild rhesus monkeys in northeastern Pakistan. Successive application of CONCOR to the six stacked matrices yielded a 5-block partition of the Pakistan population and a 12-block partition of the Cayo Santiago population. Within the Pakistan population, similarly ranked adults appear to occupy similar positions, though juveniles are grouped according to sex. The Cayo

Santiago population, on the other hand, reveals many blocks split along genealogical lines, even though no genetic relatedness network was included. Examination of the reduced blockmodel zero-one image matrices, however, reveals many similarities in role relations across the two populations: Grooming and mating are primarily adult behaviors; play is primarily a juvenile behavior; and fear grimace and threat are conspicuously lower and upper triangular matrices, respectively.

Within the approach to blockmodeling adopted by Pearl and Schulman, "role interlock" is generated from combinations of the previously obtained binary image matrices. At this second level of analysis, the goal is not identification of persistent patterns of relations among individuals, that is, roles, but identification of patterns among the social relations themselves. Here, sets of unique combinations of the initial blockmodel image matrices ("generators") are collected into role tables that display the nature of role interlock between role relations. Comparison of role structures across two populations is then based on the "joint homomorphic reduction" of pairs of corresponding role tables, one from each population, which yields a measure of distance between the two tables. Pearl and Schulman calculate the distances between 14 different pairs of role tables generated by combinations of corresponding positive and negative ties within each population. The very low distances produced suggest that the way the various role relations interlock is similar in the two populations. Further evidence of this similarity in overall social structure is suggested by a multidimensional scaling of the distances. Clustering by similarity of image matrices (generators) rather than social group (Cayo Santiago versus Pakistan) also strongly implies a common structure.

In their classic paper introducing blockmodeling methods, White et al. (1976) make the following observation:

> Observation of troops and packs of primates and other vertebrates is beginning to result in systematic reports of network ties among individual animals. . . . If we were to find blockmodels fitting such data, they would suggest to us that these ties are of strength (durability, intensity) comparable to strong ties among humans and that individuality is as pronounced among animals as among people. (p. 774)

The Pearl and Schulman paper demonstrates quite clearly that blockmodels do indeed fit primate data, and it also suggests that further applications of this general approach are likely to prove valuable in the search for cross-species and cross-population generalizations. Especially interesting in this regard is the suggestion by White et al. concerning the individuality expressed by primates in social groups. In fact, the more recently developed "local role" blockmodeling approaches (Brieger & Pattison, 1986; Wu, 1984) provide representations of social structure from an individualistic perspective rather than the global perspective of classical White et al. blockmodeling, as employed by Pearl and Schulman. Local role blockmodels reveal how occupants of particular positions or blocks view role interlock within the social structure, and these perspectives on role sets can also be formally compared across populations or species. It seems likely that these local role approaches will soon be usefully applied in primate network research.

Conclusions

Quantitative network studies of alloprimate social structure are relatively recent. They have largely made use of methods developed for describing human social networks. As the above brief review of this type of research demonstrates, formal algebraic and quantitative network methods have much to offer behavioral primatologists in their search for broad generalizations about the social architecture of animal societies. Formal methods also offer an unambiguous language for comparing social networks of humans with those of the other primates, an essential ingredient for a truly comparative science of society.

References

Altmann, S. A. (1967). *Social communication among primates.* Chicago: University of Chicago Press.

Altmann, S. A. (1981). Dominance relationships: The Cheshire cat's grin? *Behavioral and Brain Sciences, 4,* 430-431.

Boorman, S. A., & White, H. C. (1976). Social structure from multiple networks II: Role structures. *American Journal of Sociology, 81,* 1384-1446.

Breuggeman, J. A. (1973). Parental care in a group of free-ranging rhesus monkeys (Macaca mulatta). *Folia Primatologica, 20,* 178-210.

Brieger, R., & Pattison, P. (1986). Cumulated social roles: The duality of persons and their algebras. *Social Networks, 8,* 215-256.

Carpenter, C. R. (1964). *Naturalistic behavior of nonhuman primates.* University Park: Pennsylvania State University Press.

Chapais, B. (1983). Structure of the birth season relationship among adult male and female rhesus monkeys. In R. A. Hinde (Ed.), *Primate social relationships: An integrated approach* (pp. 200-208). Sunderland, MA: Sinauer Associates.

Chase, I. D. (1974). Models of hierarchy formation in animal societies. *Behavioral Science, 19,* 374-382.

Chase, I. D. (1982). Dynamics of hierarchy formation: The sequential development of dominance relationships. *Behaviour, 80,* 218-240.

Chepko-Sade, B. D., Reitz, K. P., & Sade, D. S. (1989). Sociometrics of Macaca mulatta IV. Network analysis of social structure of a pre-fission group. *Social Networks, 11,* 293-314.

Chepko-Sade, B. D., & Sade, D. S. (1979). Patterns of group splitting within matrilineal kinship groups: A study of social group structure in Macaca mulatta (Cercopithecidae: Primates). *Behavioral Ecology and Sociobiology, 5,* 67-86.

Clark, A. B. (1985). Sociality in a nocturnal "solitary" prosimian: Galago crassicaudatus. *International Journal of Primatology, 6,* 581-600.

Dasser, V. (1988). A social concept in Java monkeys. *Animal Behaviour, 36,* 225-230.

de Waal, F. B. M. (1982). *Chimpanzee politics: Power and sex among apes.* New York: Harper.

de Waal, F. B. M. (1991). Rank distance as a central feature of rhesus monkey social organization: A sociometric analysis. *Animal Behaviour, 41,* 383-395.

Dow, M. M., & de Waal, F. B. M. (1989). Assignment methods for the analysis of network subgroup interactions. *Social Networks, 11,* 237-255.

Essock-Vitale, S., & Seyfarth, R. M. (1987). Intelligence and social cognition. In B. B. Smuts, D. L. Cheney, R. M. Seyfarth, R. W. Wrangham, & T. T. Struhsaker (Eds.), *Primate societies* (pp. 452-461). Chicago: University of Chicago Press.

Freeman, L. C. (1979). Centrality in social networks: Conceptual clarification. *Social Networks, 1,* 215-239.

Hanby, J. P. (1980). Relationships in six groups of rhesus monkeys I. Networks. *American Journal of Physical Anthropology, 52,* 549-564.

Hinde, R. A. (Ed.). (1983). *Primate social relationships: An integrated approach.* Sunderland, MA: Sinauer Associates.

Hubert, L. J. (1987). *Assignment methods in combinatorial data analysis.* New York: Marcel Dekker.

Imanishi, K., & Altmann, S. A. (Eds.). (1965). *Japanese monkeys.* Alberta, Canada: University of Alberta.

Iverson, G. J., & Sade, D. S. (1990). Statistical issues in the analysis of dominance hierarchies in animal societies. *Journal of Quantitative Anthropology, 2,* 61-83.

Kaplan, J. R. (1977). Patterns of fight interference in free-ranging rhesus monkeys. *American Journal of Physical Anthropology, 47,* 279-287.

Kaplan, J. R., & Zucker, E. (1980). Social organization in a group of free-ranging patas monkeys. *Folia Primatologica, 34,* 196-213.

Knox, K. L., & Sade, D. S. (1991). Social behavior of the emperor tamarin in captivity: Components of agonistic display and the agonistic network. *International Journal of Primatology, 12*(5), 439-480.

Kummer, H. (1968). *Social organization of Hamadryas baboons.* Chicago: University of Chicago Press.

Landau, H. G. (1951). On dominance relations and the structure of animal societies. I: Effect of inherent characteristics. *Bulletin of Mathematical Biophysics, 13,* 1-19.

Luce, R. D. (1950). Connectivity and generalized cliques in sociometric group structure. *Psychometrika, 15,* 169-190.

Maryanski, A. (1987). Gorilla and chimpanzee social networks: Is there strength in weak ties? *Social Networks, 9,* 191-215.

Mendoza, S. P., & Barchas, P. R. (1983). Behavioral processes leading to linear status hierarchies following group formation in rhesus monkeys. *Journal of Human Evolution, 12,* 185-192.

Nishida, T., & Hiraiwa-Hasegawa, M. (1987). Chimpanzees and bonobos: Cooperative relationships among males. In B. B. Smuts, D. L. Cheney, R. M. Seyfarth, R. W. Wrangham, & T. T. Struhsaker (Eds.), *Primate societies* (pp. 165-177). Chicago: University of Chicago Press.

Omark, D. R., Strayer, F. F., & Freedman, D. G. (Eds.). (1980). *Dominance relations: An ethological view of human conflict and social interaction.* New York: Garland.

Pearl, M. C., & Schulman, S. R. (1983). Techniques for the analysis of social structure in animal societies. *Advances in the Study of Behavior, 13,* 107-146.

Reitz, K. P. (1982). *Social groups: A network approach.* Unpublished doctoral dissertation, University of California, Irvine.

Ross, I. C., & Harary, F. (1952). On the determination of redundancies in sociometric chains. *Psychometrika, 15,* 195-208.

Sade, D. S. (1965). Some aspects of parent-offspring relations in a group of rhesus monkeys, with a discussion of grooming. *American Journal of Physical Anthropology, 23,* 1-17.

Sade, D. S. (1966). *Ontogeny of social relations in a group of free-ranging rhesus monkeys (Macaca mulatta).* Unpublished doctoral dissertation, University of California, Berkeley.

Sade, D. S. (1972). Sociometrics of Macaca mulatta. I. Linkages and cliques in grooming matrices. *Folia Primatologica, 18,* 196-223.

Sade, D. S. (1989). Sociometrics of Macaca mulatta III: *n*-Path centrality in grooming networks. *Social Networks, 11,* 273-292.

Sade, D. S. (1991). Kinship. In J. D. Loy & C. B. Peters (Eds.), *Understanding behavior* (pp. 229-241). New York: Oxford University Press.

Sade, D. S., Altmann, M., Loy, J., Hausfater, G., & Breuggeman, J. A. (1988). Sociometrics of Macaca mulatta: II. Decoupling centrality and dominance in rhesus monkey social networks. *American Journal of Physical Anthropology, 77,* 409-425.

Sade, D. S., Chepko-Sade, B. D., Schneider, J. M., Roberts, S. S., & Richtsmeier, J. T. (1985). *Basic demographic observations on free-ranging rhesus monkeys.* New Haven, CT: Human Relations Area Files.

Schjelderup-Ebbe, T. (1922). Beitrage zur Sozialpsychologie des Haushuhns. *Zeitschrift für Psychologie, 88,* 225-252.

Soczka, L. (1974). Ethologie sociale et socimetrie: Analyse de la structure d'un groupe de singes crabiers (Macaca fascicularus = irus) en captivité. *Behaviour, 50,* 254-269.

Stephenson, K., & Zelen, M. (1989). Rethinking centrality: Methods and examples. *Social Networks, 11,* 1-38.

Thierry, B. (1986). A comparative study of aggression and response to aggression in three species of macaque. In J. G. Else & P. C. Lee (Eds.), *Primate ontogeny, cognition and social behaviour* (pp. 307-313). Cambridge: Cambridge University Press.

Walters, J. (1980). Interventions and the development of dominance relationships in female monkeys. *Folia Primatologica, 34,* 61-89.

White, H. C., Boorman, S. A., & Breiger, N. L. (1976). Social structure from multiple networks I: Blockmodels of roles and positions. *American Journal of Sociology, 81,* 730-780.

Wu, L. (1984). *Local blockmodel algebras for social network analysis: Sociological methodology 1983/84.* San Francisco: Jossey-Bass.

7

Network Analysis and Computer-Mediated Communication Systems

RONALD E. RICE

Computer-Mediated Communication Systems: Constraints and Interaction

Networks, as a theoretical perspective, analytical construct, methodological approach, and pragmatic concern, have been important to a wide variety of communication research concerns, including small groups (Shaw, 1978), R&D collaboration (Allen, 1977), organizational communication (Tushman, 1977), organizational structure and relations (Aldrich & Whetten, 1981; Tichy, 1981), and numerous other topics such as diffusion of innovations and national development (Rogers & Kincaid, 1981). The breadth and depth of network-oriented research in the communication sciences is too vast to even outline in a single chapter. Rather, this chapter limits its focus to one specific, but new and growing area of interest: the adoption, uses, and implications of computer-mediated communication (CMC) systems.

AUTHOR'S NOTE: Portions of the section "Aspects of Computer-Monitored Data" are adapted from Rice (1990a). I thank Stan Wasserman and Julie Billingsley for their helpful comments on an earlier draft of this chapter. The manuscript of this chapter was provided in 1991.

CMC systems bring together capabilities of both computers and telecommunication networks to facilitate the creating, structuring, processing, storing, retrieving, and exchanging of (perhaps multimedia) content among multiple users. CMC systems include electronic mail, computer conferencing, computer bulletin boards, facsimile, teletex and videotex, voice messaging, group decision support systems, and related media such as desktop videoconferencing and other "groupware" (see, among others, Galegher, Kraut, & Egido, 1990; Hiltz & Turoff, 1978; Johansen, Vallee, & Spangler, 1979; Kerr & Hiltz, 1982; Kiesler, 1986; Licklider & Vezza, 1978; Rice, 1980, 1987b; Rice & Associates, 1984; Vallee, 1984).

Designers, implementors, managers, and users of CMC systems may program the computer to structure communication processes (such as polling on-line groups or prioritizing and summarizing incoming content to reduce overload). CMC systems can reduce or alter some of the temporal, physical, and social constraints on communication. For example, at the place and time preferred, a user can send messages or documents and apply the computer's processing capabilities to create, store, format, and distribute; and a receiver may scan, read, print, forward, copy, edit, or delete the content. Other potential changes associated with CMC systems are consequences of the capabilities of telecommunication networks to connect diverse, often unacquainted users in different locations. For example, users can expand their networks by seeking out and sending messages to other individuals whom they may not know personally (such as through distribution lists or bulletin boards).

Because of the combination of computers and transmission networks, CMC systems have attributes that reduce some constraints, and impose others, on human and organizational communication (see Rice, 1987b). Potential changes in communication may reinforce traditional network patterns but may also foster new kinds of interaction, data, and processes, perhaps institutionalizing new organizational structures or changing the nature of interpersonal relations (Huber, 1984, 1990). Thus, because CMC systems are physical networks, they can be used to structure communication flow and content and they facilitate communication among networks of users, and because network analysis can raise our awareness of the multidirectionality of influence, network analysis is a theoretically and practically appropriate method for the study of the adoption, uses, and implications of CMC systems.

A Network Approach

This review emphasizes how network analysis approaches, data, and methods have been used to help answer ongoing research questions about CMC systems. The following review focuses on only a few central distinctions in CMC research that uses network analysis methods: (a) structurational phase, (b) time period, (c) unit of analysis, (d) conceptualization of structure, and (e) aspects of computer-monitored data. Table 7.1 describes the empirical studies reviewed here according to these five distinctions.

Structurational Phase

Primary among the distinctions that may be useful is the theoretical orientation toward the role of CMC systems. The simplest theoretical concern is often called the "technological imperative"—that is, does the CMC system "cause" certain outcomes? However, continual meta-theoretical as well as practical concerns about how social and organizational change comes about have led not only to investigations of many different components of "technology" and "outcomes" but also to new questions about the primacy of technology as a causative agent, questions about the assumptions underlying studies of computing in general, and questions about whether causality can even be a defensible focus of research on human behavior (Burell & Morgan, 1979; Kling, 1980). Thus any review of research on CMC systems in general, but in particular those that take a network perspective, must apply some simultaneously simplifying but also clarifying framework to identify these different underlying theoretical orientations (Rice, 1992).

Contractor and Eisenberg (1990) have attempted to integrate Giddens's (1984) structurational theory and Burt's structural theory of action (1982) to develop a useful initial framework for applying a network perspective to the study of CMC systems. Social and organizational networks not only constrain and influence how individuals adopt and use technologies such as CMC systems to accomplish goals, but the very appropriation of such systems, with their own objective and perceived constraints and capabilities, in turn constrains, influences, and perhaps changes individuals' goals, actions, and social relations. Orlikowski (1992) has more generally developed this approach to help understand the diversity of uses and consequences associated with organizational

Table 7.1   Categorization of Empirical Studies of Networks and CMC Systems

Authors	Phase	Data	Time	Unit	Structure
Anderson & Jay (1985)	A/U	M	C	N	P
Anderson, Jay, Anderson, & Schweer (1987)	A/U	M	C	N	P
Anderson, Jay, & Hackman (1983)	A/U	M	L	N	P
Aydin & Rice (1991)	U	—	C	N	R/P
Bernard, Killworth, & Sailer (1982)	U	I	L	E	R
Bikson & Eveland (1990)	U/I	M	L	N	R
Bizot, Smith, & Hill (1991)	U/I	M	L	N	R
Black, Levin, Mehan, & Quinn (1983)	U	M	L	N	R
Burkhardt (1991)	I	—	L	N	R
Burkhardt & Brass (1990)	A/U/I	—	L	E/N	R/P
Corman (1990)	U	I	L	E	R
Danowski (1982)	U/I	I	L	N	R
Danowski (1988)	U	M	L	N	R
Danowski & Edison-Swift (1985)	U/I	M	L	N	R
Davis, Bagozzi, & Warshaw (1989)	U	—	C	E	R
Dykman (1986)	U	—	C	E	R
Eveland & Bikson (1987)	U/I	M	L	N	R
Eveland & Bikson (1988)	U/I	M	L	N	R
Feldman (1987)	U/I	M	C	E	R
Finholt, Sproull, & Kiesler (1990)	U/I	M	L	N	R
Finn (1987)	U/I	I	L	N	R
Foster & Flynn (1984)	U/I	—	L	E	R
Freeman (1980)	U/I	—	L	E	R
Freeman (1984)	U/I	—	L	N	R
Fulk (1993)	A/U	—	L	E	R
Gurbaxani (1990)	A	M	L	N	R
Gutek (1982)	U/I	M	L	E	R
Harasim (1987)	U/I	M	L	E	R
Hart & Rice (1988)	I	—	L	N	R/P
Hartman et al. (1991)	U/I	M	L	E	R
Hayne, Rice, & Licker (1994)	I	I	L	E/N	R
Hepworth (1989)	U/I	M	L	N	R
Higgins, McClean, & Conrath (1985)	U	M	C	E	—
Hiltz (1982)	U	I	L	E	R
Hiltz (1984)	A/U/I	M	L	E	R

informational systems. She argues that communication technologies present both opportunities for and limits to human choice, organizational design, and technology development and use. Thus we can identify three phases in which social networks and CMC systems may

Table 7.1 continued

Authors	Phase	Data	Time	Unit	Structure
Hiltz (1986)	U/I	M	L	E	R
Hiltz & Turoff (1978)	U/I	M	L	E	R
Holmes (1986)	U/I	M	L	N	R
Johansen, Vallee, & Spangler (1979)	U	M	L	N	R
Kerr & Hiltz (1982)	A	M	L	E	R
Kiesler, Siegel, & McGuire (1984)	U	I	L	E	R
Kiesler & Sproull (1986)	U	I	C	—	—
Killworth & Bernard (1976)	U	M	C	N	R
Leduc (1979)	U/I	—	L	E	R
MacGregor, Lee, & Safayeni (1991)	U/I	—	C	N	R
Markus (1990a)	U	M	L	E	R
McKenney, Doherty, & Sviokla (1986)	U/I	M	L	N	P
Newell & Clark (1990)	A	—	C	E	R
O'Keefe, Kernaghan, & Rubenstein (1975)	A/U	—	L	E	R
Papa (1990)	U/I	—	L	N	R
Pava (1983)	U/I	—	L	N	R
Quinn, Mehan, Levin, & Black (1983)	U/I	M	L	N	R
Rice (1982)	U/I	M	L	N	R/P
Rice (in press)	U/I	M	L	E/N	R/P
Rice & Aydin (1991)	I	—	C	N	R/P
Rice & Barnett (1985)	U/I	M	L	N	R/P
Rice & Danowski (1993)	U	M	C	N	R
Rice, Grant, Schmitz, & Torobin (1990)	A/I	—	L	N	R
Rice & Love (1987)	U	M	L	N	R
Rice & Shook (1990)	U	M	C	N	R
Robey, Vavarek, & Saunders (1990)	U/I	M	L	N	P
Safayeni, MacGregor, & Lee (1987)	I	—	C	E	R
Schaefermeyer & Sewell (1988)	U	I	C	E	R
Schmitz & Fulk (1991)	U	—	C	E	R
Sherblom (1988)	U	M	C	E	R
Walker (1985)	U/I	—	C	N	P

NOTE: Phase: *A* = adoption, *U* = use, *I* = institutionalization; data: *M* = monitored data, *I* = initiated data; time: *C* = cross-sectional, *L* = longitudinal; unit: *E* = ego network, *N* = full network; structure: *R* = relational, *P* = positional. Some publications include several studies; the listings reflect the most complex of the categories of any of the studies in that publication.

influence each other: (a) adoption, (b) use, and (c) institutionalization (or, as Rice, 1987b proposed, input, conversion, and output).

Within each phase, designers, researchers, theorists, implementors, and users may be interested in different variables and relationships as well as different conceptions of the role of CMC systems, as, for example, outcomes of social processes, ongoing social processes, or influences on other social processes. Within the first phase, studies may be concerned with how variables such as potential adopters' network position, the social system's critical mass, or social information processing influence the adoption and use of CMC networks. Within the second phase, studies may be interested in how usage reflects communication constraints, the distribution, form, and content relations of usage, and the extent to which CMC networks complement ongoing (organizational) networks. Within the third phase, studies may focus on whether, and how, CMC networks influence outcomes, such as intra- or interorganizational networks, including scientific communication networks.

The fundamental point of this framework is that CMC systems are not independent, objective, asocial "technologies" that cause outcomes, but are products of, become embedded in, and reinstitutionalize ongoing social processes. Because few studies make explicit which of these assumptions underlie their analyses, it seems useful to organize such studies according to these three general structurational phases.

Time Period

Because the rationale for most CMC studies is to understand the adoption, implementation, or impacts of such systems in specific (typically organizational) contexts, longitudinal research designs would seem to be required. However, the bulk of CMC studies still use cross-sectional data, whether collected at one time period, or aggregated into one time period, due to constrained data collection, incomplete organizational access, inadequate conceptualization, or insufficient methodological training.

Unit of Analysis

The majority of network-oriented CMC studies collect and analyze data at the level of individual respondents (or "ego networks"). This perspective may be as simple as using estimates or actual counts of how many others or what categories of others one communicates with as individual-level variables. The crucial distinction here is that neither the raw data nor the summary indices are based on a link-list or matrix of interactions; the analysis is still focused solely on the individual's personal network and cannot represent systemwide influences or structures. Alternatively, a study may take the perspective of the full network (such as all the members of a group or organizational unit or all the users of a CMC system). Typically such studies use responses to a questionnaire roster or computer-monitored who-to-whom message data. The analysis may proceed at the group level as well as use individual-level network indices.

Conceptualization of Structure

In the *relational* or *cohesion* view, the basis of structure is the extent to which actors interact directly and indirectly as they process resources and information (Rogers & Kincaid, 1981). The relational network model thus conceptualizes a "clique" as those who interact more with each other than with others, forming highly cohesive or dense subsets. In the *positional* view, individuals occupy the same "position," or are equivalent, to the extent that they interact with the same, or similar, others, thus having similar roles or sets of obligations, status, and expectations (Burt, 1980; Lorrain & White, 1971). These positions are defined by the pattern of relationships, both present and absent, relative to all others in the social system (perhaps across multiple network relations). These two conceptualizations are quite general, and a wide variety of measures, levels of analysis, and network algorithms are associated with each (Rice & Richards, 1985), and these may be used in conjunction with other standard descriptive, bivariate, and multivariate analytical techniques. While there are many terms and varieties of relational and positional groupings, the following discussions will refer to relational groupings as "cliques" and positional groupings as "positions," unless more specific terms are appropriate. The term *group*, or *grouping*, will be used as the general term indicating some set of actors, whether a clique or a position. The majority of CMC network studies to date apply the relational perspective, largely because of the inherent preference communication researchers have for operationalizing interaction as direct relationships and groups as cliques of dense interactions. However, more fundamentally, it is difficult to argue that conceptualizations of groupings of CMC users that include nonlinkage to others are of primary concern to the study of CMC contexts. Indeed, as Rice (1987a) argues, electronic networks may be substantially different than material-based networks precisely because of the ephemerality of the social space. One of the particularly intriguing aspects of CMC systems is the ability to reduce precisely such status and gender cues (Rice, 1984), usually communicated by nonverbal cues (appearance, gender, race, age, office furnishings, and so on) that reinforce or establish roles, social differentiation, and thus network structure in the first place. Thus some of the underlying concerns to positional advocates—differences of social status and rank, and a closed social system with limited material resources—seem, so far, less relevant to an understanding of the flow of messages through a CMC system.

Aspects of Computer-Monitored Communication Data

Sources

An intriguing aspect of studying CMC systems is that they can be more or less unobtrusive components of the research design (Webb, Campbell, Schwartz, & Sechrest, 1966). The system may be programmed to *monitor* and collect, unobtrusively, communication usage or network data. A more obtrusive and reactive use of CMC systems is to *initiate* user activities or system structures that would not otherwise have occurred, collected by the computer for immediate feedback or later analysis, such as on-line questionnaires (Harasim, 1987; Hiltz, 1979; Schaefermeyer & Sewell, 1988) or on-line controlled experiments investigating effects of CMC in small groups (Finn, 1987; Hiltz, 1982; Hiltz & Turoff, 1978; Kiesler, Siegel, & McGuire, 1984; Rice, 1984).

Kinds

There are at least four categories of kinds of CMC data possible—extent of sampling, measures of usage, measure of network flow, and content.

A CMC system's computer can be programmed to monitor a *census* or requested *samples* of usage. Samples may consist of selected users, time frames, sets of commands, or content (such as message headers with specific topics, or the full text of the messages). CMC network studies have analyzed censuses of interactions within one or more selected time frames (Danowski & Edison-Swift, 1985; Eveland & Bikson, 1987; Rice & Love, 1987; Robey, Vavarek, & Saunders, 1990) or from the entire time series of network data since the initiation of the system (Rice, 1982).

The computer supporting a CMC system may be programmed to collect various measures of *usage*, such as the number of times a user "logs on" to a system, the duration of sessions, specific messaging functions used (such as initiating a new message or replying to someone else's message, copying or forwarding a message to someone else, sending a message to a distribution list), various sequences of commands, errors made, the time of certain interactions, or the percentage of day spent using the system (see Rice & Borgman, 1983; and Rice, 1990a, for reviews).

Network flow data collected by a CMC system are typically limited only by the number of users, the accuracy of accounting records, and memory limitations in the network analysis program. The raw data are links (indicators of messages) identified by the account number of the sender and receiver, length, initiation date, and, in some systems, the receipt date. Such data may be aggregated across categories of users, across specific individuals across time, and so on.

Analyses of full-text message *content* and network flows (whether collected in electronic form or printed transcripts) may be combined in a variety of ways to illuminate how users' social structure both provides a context for meaning and is affected by the content exchanged within that structure. Message headers (such as the "Subject:" field) or the computer-monitored transcripts, if stored in computer-readable form, may be automatically content-analyzed by computer programs (Weber, 1984). Analysis of *content networks* considers the number of similar words that co-occur in a given unit (such as an on-line message or a message-response pair) as a measure of the strength of the relationship between concepts. The weighted relationships between concepts can be network-analyzed to detect patterns of meaning communicated via the system over time (Danowski, 1982, 1988), such as through scaling and clustering the distances among the concepts, identifying equivalent positions of meanings, or describing links within and across concept cliques. Or, content networks of responses to open-ended survey questions or focus group comments can be compared with the respondents' level or type of system usage (Rice & Danowski, 1993). *Content-network comparison* analyzes the relationships of the content of messages exchanged by users to the network of message flows among the users (Danowski & Edison-Swift, 1985). *Content-network mapping* analyzes the content communicated by system users according to its distribution among their cliques or positions (Rice & Love, 1987; Robey et al., 1990).

Accuracy and Validity

When self-reported relationships from each of two individuals disagree, it is typically impossible to disentangle measurement error (due to problems of recall, biased responses, questionnaire wording, and so on) from "true" asymmetries in the relation. However, computer-monitored network data represent the "true" (that is, accurately measure the behavioral component of) CMC messaging, so hypotheses involving reciprocity, asymmetry, transitivity, and so on can be explicitly separated and tested.

Such aspects of computer-monitored CMC data are significant in light of ongoing questions about self-report communication and network data. Self-reported measures of a wide range of behaviors—including responses to network questions about the number and intensity of linkages with other individuals—often disagree with comparable measures of observed (possibly "actual") behavior (Bernard, Killworth, Kronenfeld, & Sailer, 1984). Self-reported amount of system usage and interactions are not highly correlated with comparable computer-monitored measures (Bizot, Smith, & Hill, 1991; Killworth & Bernard, 1976; Rice & Shook, 1988), even when respondents are surveyed on-line within minutes of actual system use (Bernard, Killworth, & Sailer, 1982). For example, diary data significantly understate recorded frequency of communication as monitored by a PBX system (Higgins, McClean, & Conrath, 1985). Bikson and Eveland (1990) found that up to 24% of their sample reported use or nonuse of the CMC system that was discrepant with computer-monitored records.

Thus computer-monitored usage and network data are potentially more *accurate* than corresponding self-report data. However, monitored system usage or network data may represent a different aspect of human communication than does perceived usage, so they are not necessarily more *valid*. Results from several studies support this interpretation. Different demographic and information need variables differentially predict monitored usage versus self-report usage (Rice & Shook, 1988). The two data sources differentially predict perceived system benefits (see Rice, 1990a). Computerized but voluntary questionnaires tend to have similar response rates but higher response variance than written questionnaires (Sproull, 1986), produce less socially desirable responses to closed-ended questions and more disclosing responses to open-ended questions, exhibit greater completion rates and fewer item completion mistakes (Kiesler & Sproull, 1986), and attract a different subsample than equally accessible written questionnaires (Kiesler & Sproull, 1986; Newsted, 1985). However, Corman (1990) found that computer-initiated collection of network data (via an on-line programmed unstructured Q-sort) had a somewhat higher test-retest reliability and more frequent imbalances and asymmetries than did self-report network data.

Indeed, there is no fundamental reason to expect actual CMC usage averaged over a considerable period to be highly correlated with the reported percentage of time spent using the system in an average workday or week (typical measures). Computer-monitored measures of numbers of messages sent or received, unless weighted by message length or importance of the content, are treated equally, yet much interpersonal communication is insignificant, routine, and less memorable, while in other cases a single sentence can be very memorable and have significant consequences. CMC data also only reflect CMC interactions; if one sends a message by CMC but receives a response by telephone, the CMC data may indicate that the initial message was never reciprocated. Thus CMC data strip away contextual and content-related cues, perhaps removing some of the underlying salience of communication events.

Computer-monitored usage and network data should be considered, then, as one addition to a broader, triangulation approach to understanding communication networks using a variety of channels, rather than as a superior replacement for self-report measures (Williams, Rice, & Rogers, 1988).

Privacy and Ethics

There are potential problems of privacy and ethics in collecting and analyzing data about users' communication behavior. Knowledge of the people with whom a respondent communicates may be a major invasion of privacy, because one's network can reveal patterns of information use and associations with specific other individuals or groups. In studies of communication technology networks that are explicitly experimental, public, or government sponsored, users typically sign consent forms or voluntarily share their communication (Rice, 1982). Other studies solve the problem by randomly reassigning identification codes to the data, so that the merged questionnaire and system data cannot be attributed to specific individuals, or by using only summary measures (Eveland & Bikson, 1987; Rice, Hughes, & Love, 1989). In private organizations, unfortunately, there are usually no human subjects review boards to scrutinize the use and collection of computer-monitored data.

Phase I: Networks and Adoption of CMC Systems

Does Network Position Affect Adoption and Use?

Before a system is available for adoption or use, of course, it must be designed, developed, and implemented in the adopting organization. Only a few studies of this aspect of the adoption phase take a network perspective. Walker (1985) combined nearly a score of network measures to show how network position predicted cognition about software development practices, and used multidimensional scaling to describe how office location corresponded with project team interaction. Pava (1983) used sociograms of project role relationships to show how informal coalitions dynamically develop around topics of contention and should be identified and used in managing the development and implementation process. Newell and Clark (1990), using simple self-reports of organization ego networks, found that British inventory and control system manufacturers were less innovative than comparable U.S. manufacturers, partially due to less communication and interaction with external organizations, conferences, and associations.

Most network-oriented implementation studies, however, focus on the individual users' adoption and use stages, generally analyzing the influence of clique density or position occupancy.

O'Keefe, Kernaghan, and Rubenstein (1975) showed that greater internal cohesion within cliques of hospital researchers and clinicians positively influenced use of a medical information system during a 6-month period. Papa (1990) emphasized the importance of network factors as sources of information and role models whereby employees may learn how to increase their performance using an insurance information query system. He concluded that one's self-reported network diversity, size, and amount of interaction (collected every day for 5 weeks after introduction of the system) all positively influenced work performance increases as well as the learning curve with which an employee reached a 10% higher performance level, once presystem performance was controlled for.

Anderson and Jay (1985) used blockmodeling to determine whether one's position in a set of 24 physicians' self-reported referral, consultation, discussion, and on-call coverage networks affected the extent to which physicians used (as measured by the system) a computer-based hospital information system (HIS). Membership in the four resulting positions (especially positions that were most central and multiplex) was positively associated with both adoption and use of the HIS, independent of physicians' background and practice characteristics. Anderson, Jay, and Hackman (1983) regressed variables on the three dimensions produced by a smallest-space analysis of the same combined matrices, and found that the dimensions were best predicted by, respectively, high usage of the system, involvement in medical education, and involvement in professional activities. In a similar study, Anderson, Jay, Anderson, and Schweer (1987) predicted computer-monitored HIS usage based upon 30 physicians' membership in structurally equivalent positions in the consultation network. Six positions emerged and were differentiated by physicians' prominence, number of residents, and the lag between the hospital adoption and the physician's first use. Social influence, as measured by the "normative values" of relationally close others (Burt, 1982), predicted time of adoption, use of system, attitude toward the system, and time since the organization adopted.

Does Critical Mass Influence Adoption and Use?

Markus (1990a), Rice (1982), and others have theorized that the value of any particular CMC system rises, and thus the relative cost of adoption decreases, as a "critical mass" of individuals begins to use the system. Because interaction among users provides the basis for this critical mass, associated propositions are most appropriately tested using network data. Rice, Grant, Schmitz, and Torobin (1990), using data from a small government agency, found that the single best predictor of an individual's adoption of an electronic messaging system 9 months after implementation was the individual's self-reported connectedness (relational out-degrees of the ego's network) in the office communication network before implementation. At the industrial level of analysis, Gurbaxani (1990) used critical mass theory to develop a logistic model that nearly perfectly fit the over-time (1981-1988) adoption by U.S. universities of BITNET (a major academic CMC network; see also Schaefermeyer & Sewell, 1988).

Does Social Information Processing Affect CMC Use and Attitudes?

The social information processing model, developed in reaction to the failure of individual attributes or objective task measures to sufficiently explain reactions to job designs, brought theories of social influence to the organizational setting (Salancik & Pfeffer, 1978). Recent followers of this theory argue that individual perceptions of ambiguous phenomena such as a new organizational CMC system are likely to be influenced by the opinions, information, and behaviors of salient others (Fulk, Steinfield, & Schmitz, 1990). Individual-level social information processing for each respondent may be operationalized as the result of first multiplying each other's attitude toward the system with the frequency of communication with the respondent, and then averaging that result over all the respondent's communicants. Group-level social information processing may be operationalized as simply the group's average attitude toward the system or, more generally, membership in different cliques or positions (Rice, 1993).

Empirical results are, so far, mixed. Rice and Aydin (1991) compared the influence of relationally proximate and structurally equivalent sources of social information processing at both the individual and the group levels of analysis. They found a weak individual-level positive influence on one's attitude toward a hospital information system only from those with whom one communicates directly, and a weak group-level negative influence from the mean of one's position, implying that social information based on direct communication produces some convergence in attitudes but that social information that includes others with whom one may have no communication as a member of one's position may lead to discrepant attitudes. Schmitz and Fulk (1991) showed that the attitudes of a respondent's supervisor and the five closest communication partners positively influenced the respondent's attitude toward a CMC system. Further, self-reported usage of the system by these significant others also predicted the respondent's self-reported usage. Using the same data, Fulk (1993) used measures from both emergent groupings (a respondent's five named others) and formal groupings (a respondent's coworkers) to show that social influences on respondents' technology-related attitudes and behavior were greater, and involved both internalization and compliance, when the respondents were highly attracted to their work groups.

But other studies fail to find a social information processing effect. Davis, Bagozzi, and Warshaw (1989) found that MBA students' attitudes toward a software package were not influenced by subjective peer norms. And Dykman (1986) found no influence of manager's use of a CMC system or availability of important communicating others on the relationship between respondents' system use and perceived satisfaction with the system. In a study of a small government office (Rice et al., 1990), clique membership was identified by a relational network program and overlaid onto a multidimensional scaling of the raw frequency matrix. This visual portrayal clearly showed that adoption was pervasive in two cliques, but not in the third clique or among isolates. This indicated preliminary support for a group-level social information processing explanation of adoption. However, neither this group-level effect, nor individual-level social information processing, was a significant influence once critical mass was controlled for.

In addition to critical mass, another alternative explanation to the group-level effect of social information processing is that membership in different social worlds brings with it shared socialization processes and professional norms, and it is these that influence group members' attitudes toward an information system. Aydin and Rice (1991) conducted blockmodeling analysis on individuals' self-reported network relations that had been grouped into five hospital occupations (such as physicians and administrators). Mean attitudes did differ across these positions, generally ordered according to increasing distance from the administrators' position as portrayed on a multidimensional scaling of the positional relations. However, as only the physicians talked more to themselves than to any other position, the occupational membership effect could not be attributed to relationally based social information processing.

Summary

Network analysis perspectives, methods, and measures have helped us understand how social structure constrains and shapes actions of designer, implementors, innovators, and users of CMC systems. Greater clique density or centrality, and common clique or positional membership, seems to facilitate social constructions of reality and shared resources, leading to similar adoption and usage patterns. Critical mass appears to be an important influence on adoption and evaluation of CMC systems. And using network measures to test social information processing theory indicates that use of a CMC system and attitudes toward it by relationally proximate others has a slight effect on individual's attitudes and use. Yet results so far are mixed; we still need to test for other structural explanations, such as critical mass and professional identification. By bringing to bear measures and constructs of social structure, we can begin to see how simple notions of either autonomous technology or autonomous individuals are incomplete.

Phase II: Use of CMC System Networks

Are Communication Constraints Associated With CMC Usage Networks?

Several studies have analyzed the ability of CMC systems to overcome the communication constraint of physical distance as a prime explanation of network flows (Feldman, 1987; Rice, 1987b). Properties of the users' context, such as physical proximity, may be tested for their influence on usage levels or CMC network relations. For example, in a study of two ad hoc task forces, Bikson and Eveland (1990) found that, while members of one task force without a CMC system exhibited a high (negative, as expected) association between a spatial distance network and their self-reported communication network, the task force with a CMC system exhibited generally little relationship, indicating that their use of the system removed the distance constraint. Users in a study by Bizot et al. (1991) sent 22% of their (computer-monitored) messages to others within the same work group, 19% within the same section, 20% within the same division, and 17% across divisions. However, employees of R&D organizations in a study by Eveland and Bikson (1987) sent 45% of all their (computer-monitored) messages to others in the immediate location, with declining percentages as the distance between the sender and received increased. Feldman (1987) found that CMC can facilitate the sharing of new information through organizational weak ties because it reduces the costs of signaling one's interests and of finding other people with similar interests. Markus (1990a) developed a detailed theoretical argument about what kinds of resources and interests are needed to develop the necessary critical mass to support such widespread usage. These results indicate that, while the ability to cross major organizational and geographic boundaries is a motivation for system use, task interdependency may be a greater motivation, while access and cost issues also play influential roles.

Do On-Line Groups Show More Equal Participation and Reciprocity?

Text-based CMC systems may reduce the amount of social presence or information richness (nonverbal communication, social cues, equivocal information, or perception of the other user's "closeness") (Daft & Lengel, 1986; Short, Williams, & Christie, 1976) and other cues (such as nonverbal, organizational, physical proximity, and status) in the content of the communication, thus limiting the applicability of CMC systems for more socioemotional communication activities. However, the reduction of these nonverbal and social cues may improve the equality of participation and access by those otherwise constrained in interpersonal communication (such as employees with lower organizational status, who have speech difficulties, or who are members of minority groups) (Rice, 1984). Simple cross-tabulation of on-line interactions among individuals generally indicates that, although asymmetry and differential participation still exist, participation is more equal than in face-to-face groups (Johansen et al., 1979).

In some instances, CMC systems can reinforce rather than reduce status differences. For example, while Robey et al. (1990) found some integration of occupational roles over time in an analysis of a semester's worth of (computer-monitored) content and network transcripts from an on-line course for medical professionals, they did find strong patterns of asymmetric relationships that mirrored professional status hierarchies. Tests of hypothesized cross-categorical relationships indicated that physicians sent more messages to nurses than vice versa, while most teachers and physicians occupied a unique structural equivalence position because they received messages similarly from all others.

Harasim (1987), Hartman et al. (1991), Hiltz (1986), and Quinn, Mehan, Levin, and Black (1983) found, based on computer transcripts and system records, that on-line courses can foster more equal discussion relations among students than do traditional classrooms. Based on self-reported ego-network data in one study, teachers also communicated more with less able students in on-line course sections, and the less able students themselves communicated more with other students, than in comparable face-to-face courses (Hartman et al., 1991). Further, student-student interactions in the on-line class at the end of the semester were not associated with interactions reported early in the semester, while they were for the traditional sections, indicating that the CMC system helped develop new interaction patterns.

Another implication of the reduction of status and other cues is that the content of the information and the level of reciprocity among users may become predominant criteria for the development and maintenance of communication roles, rather than more obvious social factors such as organizational hierarchy, material resources, or ability to dominate a meeting. Rice (1982) tested various log-linear models (proposed by Marsden, 1981) of the within- and across-group computer-monitored messaging among 800 users in 10 groups over 24 monthly time periods and found that a model of "strict reciprocity" (different pairs of groups communicate reciprocally, while within-group preferences are similar across groups) became the best-fitting model after the first 4 months or so. As predicted, groups that occupied positions that could not sustain above-average sending (transmitters) or above-average receiving (receivers) or both (carriers)—primarily task-oriented groups that were necessarily focused on within-group communication—quickly became isolates within the system.

Are Discourse Networks Different in CMC?

The ability to capture the content of CMC messaging allows for analyses of differences in network patterns and in how and what they communicate.

Several studies have examined the propositions of social presence and information richness theories noted above. Rice and Love (1987) analyzed the network flows and content from 6 weeks' worth of transcripts printed out from a public computer bulletin board used by physicians and nurses. First, clique members and isolates were identified. Then their messages were categorized into socioemotional or task-oriented content by means of Bales's Interaction Process Analysis (Bales, 1950). Users who sent more messages sent more overall socioemotional content, but there were few differences in socioemotional content of messages sent by clique members as compared with those sent by isolates. Thus, even if CMC systems *do* suppress socioemotional content (although the study also found that about 30% of the content was, indeed, socioemotional in nature), such content is not always necessary to maintain on-line groups. Finholt, Sproull, and Kiesler (1990) found that, based on a longitudinal study using observational, self-report, and computer-monitored data from seven ad hoc programming task groups, CMC communication involved more discussion of scheduling, task assignment, and socioemotional topics, while face-to-face communication involved more consensus building and problem solving. Robey et al. (1990) showed that content of messages exchanged over a computer conference was significantly related to users' occupational status relations. For example, higher status users (physicians) sent more opinions, information, and requests for opinions to those lower in status (nurses). Bizot et al. (1991) reported that over 90% of the (computer-monitored) messages sent in an organizational CMC were clearly related to the business of the organization, reflecting a strong administration policy against social uses of the system (perhaps based on some narrow sense of "productivity" criteria for using new organizational media). Note that this is a clear instance of explicit institutionalization by a formal organizational policy rather than "caused" by the characteristics of the technology.

Removing the constraint of linear sequencing of communications inherent in most traditional communication interactions may also give rise to new forms and problems of communication. Quinn et al. (1983) showed that relationships among content categories in on-line class discussions were less linear. That is, comments did not necessarily follow in sequential response to a single prior comment (such as a teacher's question) but rather often referred to prior comments in a different order than they were sent or to multiple prior comments by other students. Further, they involved more even distribution of procedural discussions than in face-to-face classrooms. Black, Levin, Mehan, and Quinn (1983), Quinn et al. (1983), and Holmes (1986) have analyzed content networks in the form of "multiple threads of conversation" revealed in the computer-monitored transcripts of CMC portions of university courses. Here, the "node" is the comment or message, and the relationships are the references among the posted messages. These relationships are displayed graphically and analyzed much like transcripts of spoken conversations by conversation analysts or linguists. Multiple threads occur because CMC comments may be responses to an item added several entries ago but just recently read by the particular respondent, a response to multiple previous topics, or conditional comments that reduce the effect of having to wait for a response to a particular question before being able to provide some information or make a decision. Such threads are quite unlike the sequential response relationships in face-to-face or written communication. They may be conceptualized as multiplex, nonhierarchical content links. Black et al. (1983) conclude that "the structure of discourse is not fixed, but rather the product of participant interaction and properties of the medium through which dialog is pursued" (p. 75).

Finally, network analysis of comments about a CMC system may provide insights not available through traditional content analysis, which can provide frequency counts of various themes but cannot reveal patterns of word associations. Rice and Danowski (1993), for example, showed that the set of people who used a voice mail system more for messaging (processing communications across individuals and groups) than for answering (traditional store-and-forward of messages when someone does not answer their telephone) used somewhat different clusters of words (such as "improve communication," "access others on the system," and "group distribution").

Does CMC Complement Organizational Networks?

Eveland and Bikson (1987) analyzed patterns of 69,000 computer-monitored messages sent among 800 users in an R&D organization over a period of nearly 2 years. They took a relational, group-level approach to answering the question of whether the system supported project-related communication. Analyses of 100 samples from users showed that there were no differences in usage levels across departments, programs, or professional categories. Three quarters of the messages crossed departmental boundaries, indicating high cooperation among research disciplines within broad organizational functions, while only 40% of the messages crossed specific research project boundaries. The communication structures within and across research projects were generally not clustered, as were departmental network relations, according to smallest-space analysis of the message flows. Thus using electronic mail allowed individuals in different departments to work collaboratively on R&D projects. Bizot et al. (1991) found similar results. They collected 3 days' worth of messaging (on a commercial integrated messaging and document system, PROFS) and asked each respondent to answer a questionnaire and to comment on the messaging log in an anonymous manner. In this traditionally hierarchical R&D organization, 83% of all messages were sent within a division, and 93% of messages were sent to a recipient either one job type above or below the sender, indicating little circumventing of the traditional organizational structure.

In a different approach to this question, Rice and Shook (1990) used the quadratic assignment procedure (Hubert & Schultz, 1976) to show that the network of status relationships among job levels was associated with the patterns of use of different communication media by respondents in four organizations. While, in each organization, pattern of attendance in meetings was the best predictor of job level, in one organization the second best predictor was use of its CMC system. Thus, clearly, CMC usage can complement preexisting organizational structure.

But this does not mean simply mirroring prior communication networks. Rice (1994) found that initially the network of email communications among members of an R&D organization were strongly correlated with work and social networks, but, over time, it diverged from those as well as from formal mentor-intern relations. Gutek (1982) developed a unique research design to identify influences of an integrated information/communication system on attitudes and interactions of a single secretary-manager dyad, using multiple surveys and observations over 20 months during preimplementation, stable (computer-monitored) usage, and after removal of the system. Attitudes were most positive during the stable use phase, but the system had little impact on secretary-managerial interactions or the reasons for those interactions.

Some studies have related performance both to use of email networks and to the extent to which those networks complement other organizational networks. Finholt et al. (1990) used simple cross-tabulations of computer-monitored messaging among groups of student programmers using a CMC over four time periods. They found that high-performing groups exchanged greater-than-expected individual messages with other high-performing groups and sent greater-than-expected broadcast messages to all groups. Further, messaging between managers and nonmanagers was greater than expected. The authors interpreted these patterns as supporting spoke and hublike functional CMC patterns in the groups, which lead to higher performance. Rice's (1994) study of mentors and interns in an R&D organization showed that, while simple amount of messaging, or even email network centrality, were not much associated with evaluations of the interns' performance several months later, general work communication and the interns' location within the email network were negatively associated with performance! Rice suggested that overparticipation in early email cliques narrows interns' research focus, encourages the clustering of low performers, and limits interns from associating with wider organizational networks, such as with other mentors.

These results may be less likely to hold for groups with no prior history or that are not embedded in organizational structures, and when other communication channels are not constrained. For example, Markus (1990b) studied four field-study groups that had access to CMC systems as well as participating in weekly face-to-face meetings, showing that level and type of usage varied considerably within and across groups. CMC network data as well as observations and self-reports showed that social contexts help explain CMC communication structures—including one group using the system primarily so that two antagonistic members would not have to meet face-to-face!

Summary

An important technological characteristic of CMC systems is that they can overcome spatial and temporal constraints. Yet CMC communication patterns in ongoing organizations continue to reflect some of the physical distance relationships, which probably reflect task and resource interdependencies. Another important characteristic is reduced social and nonverbal cues, which theoretically can reduce status differences and domination based on appearance, oral skills, and so on. This is often reflected in more equal participation, more reciprocal communication, and less sequential or linear comments, although CMC systems may still be used to reinforce salient status differences. Further, the reduced social cues do not seem to prevent communication of socioemotional content, and CMC groups do not necessarily exchange more of such content than do CMC isolates. CMC may be used to overcome traditional organizational boundary constraints (such as departments, manager/subordinate relations, headquarters/branch separation), especially in project-related activities and collaborative work. Yet CMC may also reflect an organization's traditional hierarchy if organizational policy demands this.

Phase III: CMC Systems and Institutionalization of Networks

Does Critical Mass Affect CMC Use and Outcomes?

In accord with Markus's (1990a) propositions, Rice et al. (1990) found that the best predictor of some communication-related outcomes was the extent to which an individual communicated with others who had also adopted the system, after implementation of the system, even when social information processing variables were controlled for. That is, "critical mass" seems a theoretically and empirically important construct, in which ongoing network structures influence individuals' CMC usage networks.

Does CMC Change Intraorganizational Networks and Structure?

Organizational structure is central to a wide variety of concerns of organizational communication theorists, such as employee innovativeness, R&D unit performance, and organizational effectiveness in the face of changing environments. Traditionally, studies of the effects of computer systems on organizational structure measured structure as differentiation, task scope, centralization, hierarchy, formalization, and so on (James & Jones, 1976), but rarely from a network perspective. Robey (1981), for example, found no changes in formal structure in five of eight organizations that had implemented information systems, and reinforcement in the other three, and proposed elsewhere (1977) that such changes are more dependent on the organization's task environment than on technology. Wigand (1985) summarized government statistics showing relatively high levels of unemployment among managers and administrators in the early 1980s, and recounted organizational instances of "flattening of the hierarchy," both evidence of the ability of information and CMC systems to gather, distribute, and monitor organizational information and provide end users with direct access to it. However, only recently have studies applied network analysis to the enduring question of the effect of systems on organizational structure.

Eveland and Bikson (1987) found little evidence of changes in the departmental or project communication clusters over the 18-month period of study, indicating that the electronic mail system supported, but did not alter, the *intra*organizational structure of the R&D organization. Another longitudinal study also found that (self-reported) CMC usage networks may develop to complement preexisting task and social network positions (McKenney, Doherty, & Sviokla, 1986). Safayeni, MacGregor, and Lee (1987) provided evidence, based on self-reported and cross-sectional ego-network and dyadic data, that use of the system led to more task-dependent connections where each member of the dyad felt he or she could influence the other's job, to more positive views of others as sources of influence on performance, and to a more flexible organizational network where social relations were the basis of adjusting task dependencies rather than formal procedures. In a later analysis of these data, MacGregor, Lee, and Safayeni (1991) did not find an effect of the CMC system on organizational communication patterns between organizational units compared with functions where the system was not implemented. However, inspection of simple cross-unit interaction tables indicated that frictions and conflict among functions increased, partially due to a poorly designed system implemented for the lower level employees that led to asymmetric messaging among some of the units. Sherblom (1988) studied 157 messages involving one middle-level manager. His content analysis showed that messages sent upward in the hierarchy were more restricted in function (mostly involving exchange of information); functional categories were more evenly distributed among peer messages; and subordinates were more likely to "sign" their mail than were superiors, indicating that "an electronic paralanguage reflects, reinforces and recontextualizes the organizational structural hierarchy" (p. 50). Such studies lead to the inference that there may be subtle, but not extensive, changes in preexisting organizational networks due to CMC use.

However, other studies find considerable evidence for changes in organizational networks, especially for novel situations or new groups, as the actors institutionalize the altered relationships due to new organizational technologies. Danowski and Edison-Swift (1985) analyzed monitored CMC system usage and content data before, during, and after an administrative crisis experienced by a number of offices in a statewide county extension service, using a relational approach to group-level networks. Relational analysis of the words in the CMC messages showed that crises galvanized the interorganizational network into shared but temporary concern. The structure of the content networks was influenced by the introduction of new communication messages, sent in the prior month, relating to the budgetary source of the crisis. Relational network patterns among users seemed to be more robust, adaptive, or enduring than relationships among communication content during the crisis. Indeed, the issue of how CMC and information systems may facilitate crisis management has only recently received much attention (Rice, 1990b).

Feldman (1987) argued that, because the asynchronous nature of CMC makes it unnecessary for people to communicate at the same time, and because the development of distribution lists makes it easy to define groups of people with common interests and then signal one's own interests and share information with all members of that group simultaneously, the costs of interacting through weak ties are greatly reduced. Her study of the content of messages sent to or from 96 users indicated that 60% of the messages would not have been sent without the CMC system. This percentage is higher for people who did not know one another, who did not communicate other than by CMC, who were spatially or organizationally distant, and who used distribution lists. Feldman also argues that such weak tie messages aid in organizational socialization, shared interpretations, and solving problems.

Burkhardt and Brass (1990) explored the notion of institutionalization using a longitudinal relational approach, analyzing both ego and system networks. They found that, over time, employees in general, but early adopters in particular, increased their power and relational network centrality as they used a new nutrient data analysis and dissemination system. Because individuals' initial power (as rated by other members of the network) and network centrality had no influence on level of adoption, the authors concluded that the system did not reinforce, but changed, preexisting structure and power differences. Multidimensional scaling of the self-reported interaction networks reinforced these results, showing that the network became more centralized overall, but adopters became even more central. Finally, structural equivalence among the actors was significantly correlated with their relative adoption times only at the fourth and final time period, indicating that adoption similarity influenced structural similarity. That is, individuals adjusted their patterns of interaction to learn from those adept at using the new technology. Burkhardt (1991) extended this analysis by investigating the extent to which the new system altered social dynamics, which in turn provided opportunities for the users to create shared interpretations of the system, thus reinstitutionalizing the social structure. Results showed that two relational matrices—(a) path distances based upon the self-reported binary relations among network members and (b) self-reported interactions with powerful others—were associated with a computer efficacy similarity matrix, especially for those with *high* values on a self-monitoring scale. The matrix of users' structural equivalence was also associated with both (a) a matrix of similarity of users' attitudes toward the computer and (b) a matrix of similarity of computer use, especially for those with *low* values on the self-monitoring scale. Thus those who were less aware of their own behaviors and attitudes apparently were more influenced by the usage and attitudes of structurally equivalent others.

Eveland and Bikson (1988) and Bikson and Eveland (1990) found strong evidence that CMC systems can influence the development and maintenance of both task and social networks among groups that had not interacted before as opposed to ongoing organizational groups. They provided CMC access to one of two task forces consisting of randomly assigned retirees and soon-to-retire employees. The supported task force exhibited fluctuating leadership patterns over three time periods, greater communication in all channels, greater connectedness in (self-reported) network structure, less centralization over time, more multiplex subcommittee relations and thus less clustering according to task force subgroups, continued (computer-monitored) on-line communication after the report was completed, and considerable (computer-monitored) messaging across the task subgroups. Foster and Flynn (1984) also found evidence of changes in organizational form, roles, and relationships in one company that implemented a computing and communication system. While they used a narrative case study rather than network methods, their results indicated that the system facilitated both social and task contacts, a shift from primarily vertical to lateral communications, the development of a less structured on-line structure that complemented the formal, protocol-driven hierarchy, and an increase in shared responsibilities for overall task completion. Leduc (1979) found a similar shift from vertical superior-subordinate interactions to more interconnection among and across roles after the implementation of a CMC system.

Finally, the implementation of CMC networks raises the possibility of institutionalizing perceived, rather than actual, networks. Hayne, Rice, and Licker (1994) analyzed the use of anonymous commenting in a group support system (GSS) by seven work groups from four organizations to see if participants could identify the authors of the anonymous comments. They found that participants were willing and able to make attributions but that those attributions were extremely inaccurate. Lower inaccuracy was associated in two of the seven groups with greater total prior communication, greater prior network betweenness centrality, and greater prior pairwise communication. These results suggest that the use of GSS anonymity features does not mean than users are not making attributions and, worse, that these attributions are probably inaccurate, creating biases and false evaluations that cannot be countered by the other participants. Such processes could institutionalize new, but unfounded, organizational network relations and assessments.

Does CMC Influence Scientific Communication Networks?

Because communication across institutional and geographic boundaries, and within and across disciplines, is crucial to the development of science, some attention has been focused on the extent of use of CMC systems by, and their influence on, scientific communities. Lievrouw and Carley (1991) and Newell and Sproull (1982) argue that, in spite of disciplinary, economic, and cultural constraints on this development, the traditional cycle of scientific communication (conceptualization, documentation, and popularization, with some feedback loops) may change, by increased collaboration, diffusion, and feedback through CMC networks, leading to an era of "telescience." Hiltz (1984), Hiltz and Turoff (1978), and Kerr and Hiltz (1982) have provided consistent evidence that such networks do increase in intensity, diversity, and the "stock" of ideas. Researchers who already knew more other researchers who are now on-line (a self-reported ego-network approach) were more likely to use the system more and perceive greater benefits. While this result is consistent with the critical mass studies, Hiltz interpreted this as implying the necessity for a culture of trust among possible scientific competitors.

Freeman (1980) has applied more sophisticated network methodology to this question. He tested the notion that the "backcloth" of social structure (based on network relations such as colleagues, fellow students, teacher-student pairs) is the basis for any "traffic" of communication interaction, including CMC usage. Using Q-analysis, he identified a variety of "backcloth" simplices (relations of relations), and then compared the self-reported "friend" network relations before, and 7 months after, using the nationwide computer conferencing system also studied by Hiltz (1984) and Rice (1982). The number of "friend" links and the number of dyads reporting "close friend" relations both increased. But one of these relations involved people who had never even met before, implying that use of the CMC system produced a small change in the social backcloth itself. In Freeman's 1984 study of the same set of researchers, he found that "strict awareness" relations based on a multiplex self-reported network among the CMC users were stable over three time periods but that 31% of the null awareness relations changed to symmetric relations between time two and time three. On the basis of these studies, he concludes that "the computer, it seems, can perhaps take the place of protracted face-to-face interaction and provide the sort of social structure out of which a scientific specialty can grow" (Freeman, 1984, p. 201).

Does CMC Change Interorganizational Networks and Structure?

New interorganizational networks may develop that have no prior material counterpart. Under these conditions, the basis of relationships may differ from that of material or face-to-face relations and may be particularly unstable under conditions of change by external factors. For example, interorganizational network relations changed in a longitudinal analysis of computer-monitored messaging behavior by approximately 800 members of 10 research groups using a nationwide computer conferencing system over a 24-month period, when new groups entered or left the system. Based upon the best-fitting log-linear model (the "strict reciprocity" model described in the section on "participation and reciprocity" above), and output from a noneuclidean metric multidimensional scaling program to model change in location over time, the entire system was found to recover its equilibrium after a few months of such "system shock" (Rice, 1982; Rice & Barnett, 1985).

One growing focus of organizational research is the development and management of interorganizational networks (Hepworth, 1989; Mulgan, 1991). The extension of one organization's boundaries through information networks is likely to affect both the initiating organization as well as the other organizations within a particular industry, such as through increased economies of scope, communication, and cross-organizational projects (Estrin, 1986). As Hart and Saunders (1991) note: "Networking technology bridges inter-organization units that share interdependent computing systems, and interacts with existing power structures to alter relations between organizations" (p. 6). Internally, such networks may lead to fragmentation of the information systems department, with attendant coordination problems and resulting changes in centralization. Externally, they may provide opportunities for oligopoly and price-setting, and decreased ease of entry of other organizations; consolidation, shrinkage, and process redistribution may also result as well as different forms of market segmentation and relationships among buyers, suppliers, rivals, and industry participants (Cash & Konsynski, 1985). These preliminary results and speculations seem ideally suited for testing with network analysis methods.

A wider conceptualization of such information system networks considers cross-industry networks resulting from the increasing convergence of software, computing, telecommunication, and information resources (Fombrun & Astley, 1982) as private computer networks "will allow firms to increase their span of control in geographical and market space, through more flexible technical and social divisions of labor" (Hepworth, 1989, p. 93). Hart and Rice (1988) tested resource dependency hypotheses on data measuring extent of relations (as measured by linkages varying from short-term leasing through permanent merger and acquisition) among these four industries, comparing videotex (a more complex service) versus teletext services during the 1980s. Clustering of the normalized form of these two matrices showed that, indeed, relations in the videotex industry involved more subclusters and involved more permanent linkages, as studied by permutation tests comparing hypothesized relations with empirical relations.

A still wider approach considers international information networks, which are changing the mechanisms of control by, relationships among, and nature of the economies of transnational corporations and nation-states. Mulgan (1991), for example, argues that such networks should be analyzed from the perspective of control, due to its "recognition of process and structure, and its recognition that effective power, influence and achievement depend on the ability to formulate strategies and understandings, on channels of command, feedback and surveillance" (p. 8). As Braman (1991) suggests, the growing "ephemeralization," or the "replacement of space and exchange of physical materials (weapons and barriers) with information flows for national security purposes," may lead to increased "confidence in each other's actions and feelings of security in the domestic and international environments." Hepworth (1989) argues that possible changes due to intra- and interorganizational computer networks are far more complex than centralization or decentralization, noting that firms may develop less bureaucratic but larger information work structures and smaller, separate production functions, with new structures such as electronic quasi-integration (shared computer communication infrastructure), electronic franchising (licensing of database services), internationalizing, electronic subcontracting, and information-based specialization. Relational and positional analyses over time of various material and information networks would be necessary to thoroughly test such intriguing propositions.

Summary

Simple technological imperative approaches are concerned primarily with the effects of CMC systems on users and organizations, such as organizational structure and relationships with other organizations. Not only have we seen that CMC systems are not simple causal agents but even that, in the institutionalization phase, CMC systems may be embedded in a variety of other influences. Even users' attitudes toward the outcomes of CMC systems may be influenced through critical mass and social information processing. Organizational network structures may or may not change along with implementation of CMC systems, but such change may be less likely within single organizations, especially if there is a long organizational history and if there is no explicit policy of using the system to alter structure. CMC systems may or may not reinforce prior power relations. Early adoption of a highly uncertain organizational phenomenon may increase one's value to other organizational members, but only if adoption is voluntary and access is equal. The evidence implies increases in lateral and some diagonal communication, although such systems can be used to reinforce managerial-subordinate relations. Change in structure seems more likely with interorganizational and cross-industrial computer networks, as a host of economic, political, and technological forces constrain and alter organizational relationships. Invisible colleges may be facilitated by the growth of academic CMC networks, leading to new and intense relationships that would not have occurred otherwise. In turn, researchers and others may design these systems to support computer conferences for their own specialties.

Conclusion

The ability of CMC systems to monitor, and even initiate, system usage provides more accurate, larger, and longitudinal data sets. Network-level analyses and methods are necessary to properly embed the individual in a wider set of structural relations, many of which are often unknown to the participants themselves. Both relational and positional analyses provide the ability to identify how membership or role occupancy supersedes individual-level attributes, though with different underlying conceptualizations about what constitutes structure and roles. CMC systems, because they facilitate human communication through computer-based telecommunication networks, may be practically and conceptually intertwined with group, organizational, social, and transnational structures. These structures affect the adoption of CMC systems, influence how network members use the system, and in turn may be altered—even reinstitutionalized—by users communicating through CMC systems. Prior research has provided some examples of how CMC research can use network perspectives, constructs, and methods to articulate, operationalize, and test theories about these processes.

References

Aldrich, H., & Whetten, D. (1981). Organization-sets, action-sets, and networks: Making the most of simplicity. In P. Nystrom & W. Starbuck (Eds.), *Handbook of organizational design* (pp. 385-407). New York: Oxford University Press.

Allen, T. (1977). *Managing the flow of technology.* Cambridge: MIT Press.

Anderson, J., & Jay, S. (1985). Computers and clinical judgment: The role of physician networks. *Social Science and Medicine, 20*(10), 969-979.

Anderson, J., Jay, S., Anderson, M., & Schweer, H. (1987, February). *The diffusion of computer applications in medical practice.* Paper presented at the Social Networks Conference, Florida.

Anderson, J., Jay, S., & Hackman, E. (1983). The role of physician networks in the diffusion of clinical applications of computers. *International Journal of Bio-Medical Computing, 14*, 195-202.

Aydin, C., & Rice, R. E. (1991). Social worlds, individual differences, and implementation: Predicting attitudes toward a medical information system. *Information and Management, 20*, 119-136.

Bales, R. F. (1950). *Interaction process analysis: A method for the study of small groups.* Cambridge, MA: Addison-Wesley.

Bernard, H., Killworth, P., Kronenfeld, D., & Sailer, L. (1984). The problem of informant accuracy: The validity of retrospective data. *Annual Review of Anthropology, 13*, 495-517.

Bernard, H. R., Killworth, P. D., & Sailer, L. (1982). Informant accuracy in social-network data V. An experimental attempt to predict actual communication from recall data. *Social Science Research, 11*, 30-66.

Bikson, T., & Eveland, J. D. (1990). The interplay of work group structures and computer support. In J. Galegher, R. Kraut, & C. Egido (Eds.), *Intellectual teamwork: Social and technological bases of cooperative work* (pp. 245-290). Hillsdale, NJ: Lawrence Erlbaum.

Bizot, E., Smith, N., & Hill, T. (1991). Use of electronic mail in a research and development organization. In J. Morell & M. Fleischer (Eds.), *Advances in the implementation and impact of computer systems* (Vol. 1, pp. 65-92). Greenwich, CT: JAI.

Black, S., Levin, J., Mehan, H., & Quinn, C. (1983). Real and non-real time interaction: Unraveling multiple threads of discourse. *Discourse Processes, 6*, 59-75.

Braman, S. (1991). Contradictions in brilliant eyes. *Gazette: The International Journal for Mass Communication, 47*(3), 177-194.

Burell, G., & Morgan, G. (1979). *Sociological paradigms and organizational analysis.* London: Heinemann.

Burkhardt, M. (1991). *Institutionalization following a technological change.* Unpublished paper, University of Pennsylvania, Wharton School, Philadelphia.

Burkhardt, M., & Brass, D. (1990). Changing patterns or patterns of change: The effects of a change in technology on social network structure and power. *Administrative Science Quarterly, 35*, 104-127.

Burt, R. S. (1980). Models of network structure. *Annual Review of Sociology, 6*, 79-141. (Palo Alto, CA: Annual Reviews)

Burt, R. S. (1982). *Toward a structural theory of action: Network models of social structure, perception, and action.* New York: Academic Press.

Cash, J., Jr., & Konsynski, B. (1985, March/April). IS redraws competitive boundaries. *Harvard Business Review*, pp. 134-142.

Contractor, N., & Eisenberg, E. (1990). Communication networks and new media in organizations. In J. Fulk & C. Steinfield (Eds.), *Organizations and communication technology* (pp. 143-172). Newbury Park, CA: Sage.

Corman, S. (1990). Computerized vs. pencil and paper collection of network data. *Social Networks, 12*(4), 375-384.

Daft, R. L., & Lengel, R. H. (1986). Organizational information requirements, media richness and structural design. *Management Science, 32,* 554-571.

Danowski, J. (1982). Computer-mediated communication: A network-based content analysis using a CBBS conference. In M. Burgoon (Ed.), *Communication yearbook* (Vol. 6, pp. 905-924). Beverly Hills, CA: Sage.

Danowski, J. (1988). Organizational infographics and automated auditing: Using computers to unobtrusively analyze communication. In G. Goldhaber & G. Barnett (Eds.), *Handbook of organizational communication* (pp. 385-434). Norwood, NJ: Ablex.

Danowski, J., & Edison-Swift, P. (1985). Crisis effects on intraorganizational, computer-based communication. *Communication Research, 12*(2), 251-270.

Davis, F., Bagozzi, R., & Warshaw, P. (1989). User acceptance of computer technology: A comparison of two theoretical models. *Management Science, 35,* 982-1003.

Dykman, C. (1986). *Electronic mail systems: An analysis of the use/satisfaction relationship.* Unpublished doctoral dissertation, University of Houston, Department of Information Science.

Estrin, D. (1986, October). The organizational consequences of interorganization computer networks. *ACM Conference Proceedings on Office Information Systems,* pp. 11-20.

Eveland, J. D., & Bikson, T. (1987). Evolving electronic communication networks: An empirical assessment. *Office: Technology and People, 3,* 103-128.

Eveland, J. D., & Bikson, T. (1988). Workgroup structures and computer support: A field experiment. *ACM Transactions on Office Information Systems, 6*(4), 354-379.

Feldman, M. (1987). Electronic mail and weak ties in organizations. *Office: Technology and People, 3,* 83-101.

Finholt, T., Sproull, L., & Kiesler, S. (1990). Communication and performance in ad hoc task groups. In J. Galegher, R. Kraut, & C. Egido (Eds.), *Intellectual teamwork: Social and technological bases of cooperative work* (pp. 291-325). Hillsdale, NJ: Lawrence Erlbaum.

Finn, T. A. (1987). Process and structure in computer-mediated group communication. In B. Ruben (Ed.), *Information and behavior* (Vol. 2). New Brunswick, NJ: Transaction.

Fombrun, C., & Astley, W. (1982). The telecommunications community: An institutional overview. *Journal of Communication, 32*(4), 56-68.

Foster, L., & Flynn, D. (1984, December). Management information technology: Its effects on organizational form and function. *MIS Quarterly*, pp. 229-236.

Freeman, L. (1980). Q-Analysis and the structure of friendship networks. *International Journal of Man-Machine Studies, 12*(3), 367-378.

Freeman, L. (1984). The impact of computer based communication on the social structure of an emerging scientific specialty. *Social Networks, 6*(3), 201-221.

Fulk, J. (1993). Social construction of communication technology. *Academy of Management Journal, 36*(5), 921-950.

Fulk, J., Steinfield, C. W., & Schmitz, J. (1990). A social information processing model of media use in organizations. In J. Fulk & C. Steinfield (Eds.), *Organizations and communication technology* (pp. 117-140). Newbury Park, CA: Sage.

Galegher, J., Kraut, R., & Egido, C. (Eds.). (1990). *Intellectual teamwork: Social and technological bases of cooperative work.* Hillsdale, NJ: Lawrence Erlbaum.

Giddens, A. (1984). *The constitution of society: Outline of the theory of structuration.* Cambridge, MA: Polity.

Gurbaxani, V. (1990). Diffusion in computing networks: The case of BITNET. *Communications of the ACM, 33*(12), 65-75.

Gutek, B. (1982). Effects of "office of the future" technology on users: Results of a longitudinal field study. In G. Mensch & R. J. Niehaus (Eds.), *Work, organizations and technological change* (pp. 191-212). New York: Plenum.

Harasim, L. (1987). Teaching and learning on-line: Issues in computer-mediated graduate courses. *Canadian Journal of Educational Communication, 16*(2), 117-135.

Hart, P., & Rice, R. E. (1988). Inter-industry relations in electronic news services. *Journal of the American Society for Information Science, 39*(4), 252-261.

Hart, P., & Saunders, C. (1991, August). *Elaborations on electronic data interchanges: Antecedents and consequences.* Paper presented at the Academy of Management Conference, Miami.

Hartman, K., Neuwirth, C., Kiesler, S., Sproull, L., Cochran, C., Palmquist, M., & Zubrow, D. (1991). Patterns of social interaction and learning to write. *Written Communication, 8*(1), 79-113.

Hayne, S., Rice, R. E., & Licker, P. (1994). Social cues and anonymous group interaction using group support systems. *Proceedings of the Twenty-Seventh Hawaiian International Conference of Systems Sciences, 4,* 73-81.

Hepworth, M. (1989). Computer networks in multilocational firms. In M. Hepworth, *Geography of the information economy* (chap. 4, pp. 93-128). London: Belhaven.

Higgins, C., McClean, R., & Conrath, D. (1985). The accuracy and biases of diary communication data. *Social Networks, 7*(2), 173-188.

Hiltz, S. R. (1979, Winter). Using computer conferencing to conduct opinion research. *Public Opinion Quarterly,* pp. 562-571.

Hiltz, S. R. (1982). Experiments and experiences with computerized conferencing. In R. Landau, J. Bair, & J. Siegman (Eds.), *Emerging office systems* (pp. 182-204). Norwood, NJ: Ablex.

Hiltz, S. R. (1984). *Online communities: A case study of the office of the future.* Norwood, NJ: Ablex.

Hiltz, S. R. (1986). The "virtual classroom": Using computer-mediated communication for university teaching. *Journal of Communication, 36*(2), 95-104.

Hiltz, S. R., & Turoff, M. (1978). *The network nation: Human communication via computer.* Reading, MA: Addison-Wesley.

Holmes, M. (1986). *A conversational analysis of computer-mediated discourse.* Minneapolis: University of Minnesota, Department of Speech Communication.

Huber, G. (1984). The nature and design of post-industrial organizations. *Management Science, 30*(8), 928-951.

Huber, G. (1990). A theory of the effects of advanced information technologies on organizational design, intelligence, and decision-making. *Academy of Management Review, 15*(1), 47-71.

Hubert, L., & Schultz, J. (1976). Quadratic assignment as a general data analysis strategy. *British Journal of Mathematical and Statistical Psychology, 29,* 190-241.

James, L., & Jones, A. (1976). Organizational structure: A review of structural dimensions and their conceptual relationships with individual attitudes and behavior. *Organizational Behavior and Human Performance, 16,* 74-113.

Johansen, R., Vallee, J., & Spangler, K. (1979). *Electronic meetings: Technical alternatives and social choices.* Reading, MA: Addison-Wesley.

Kerr, E., & Hiltz, S. R. (1982). *Computer-mediated communication systems.* New York: Academic Press.

Kiesler, S. (1986, January-February). The hidden messages in computer networks. *Harvard Business Review,* pp. 46-48, 52-54, 58, 60.

Kiesler, S., Siegel, J., & McGuire, T. (1984). Social psychological aspects of computer-mediated communication. *American Psychologist, 39*(10), 1123-1134.

Kiesler, S., & Sproull, L. (1986). Response effects in the electronic survey. *Public Opinion Quarterly, 50,* 402-413.

Killworth, P., & Bernard, H. R. (1976). Informant accuracy in social network data. *Human Organization, 35,* 269-286.

Kling, R. (1980). Social analyses of computing: Theoretical perspectives in recent empirical research. *Computing Surveys, 12*(1), 61-110.

Leduc, N. (1979, September). Communicating through computers. *Telecommunications Policy,* pp. 235-244.

Licklider, J. C. R., & Vezza, A. (1978). Applications of information networks. *Proceedings of the IEEE, 66*(11), 1330-1346.

Lievrouw, L., & Carley, K. (1991). Changing patterns of communication among scientists in an era of "Telescience." *Technology in Society, 12,* 457-477.

Lorrain, F., & White, H. (1971). Structural equivalence of individuals in social networks. *Journal of Mathematical Sociology, 1,* 49-80.

MacGregor, J., Lee, E., & Safayeni, F. (1991). *Some subtle effects of electronic mail on patterns of communication between different organization functions.* Unpublished paper, University of Victoria School of Business, British Columbia.

Markus, M. L. (1990a). Toward a critical mass theory of interactive media: Universal access, interdependence and diffusion. In J. Fulk & C. Steinfield (Eds.), *Organizations and communication technology* (pp. 194-218). Newbury Park, CA: Sage.

Markus, M. L. (1990b). Asynchronous technologies in small face-to-face groups. *Information, Technology and People, 6*(1), 29-48.

Marsden, P. (1981). Models and methods for characterizing the structural parameters of groups. *Social Networks, 3,* 1-27.

McKenney, J., Doherty, V., & Sviokla, J. (1986). *The impact of electronic networks on management communication: An information processing study* (Paper). Boston: Harvard Graduate School of Business.

Mulgan, G. (1991). *Communication and control: Networks and the new economies of communication.* New York: Guilford.

Newell, A., & Sproull, R. F. (1982). Computer networks: Prospects for scientists. *Science, 215*(12), 842-851.

Newell, S., & Clark, P. (1990). The importance of extra-organizational networks in the diffusion and appropriation of new technologies. *Knowledge: Creation, Diffusion, Utilization, 12*(2), 199-212.

Newsted, P. (1985). Paper versus online presentations of subjective questionnaires. *International Journal of Man-Machine Studies, 23*, 231-247.

O'Keefe, R., Kernaghan, J., & Rubenstein, A. (1975). Group cohesiveness: A factor in the adoption of innovations among scientific work groups. *Small Group Behavior, 6*(3), 282-292.

Orlikowski, W. (1992). The duality of technology: Rethinking the concept of technology in organizations. *Organization Science, 3*(3), 398-427.

Papa, M. J. (1990). Communication network patterns and employee performance with new technology. *Communication Research, 17*(3), 344-368.

Pava, C. (1983). *Managing new office technology.* New York: Free Press.

Quinn, C., Mehan, H., Levin, J., & Black, S. (1983). Real education in non-real time: The use of electronic message systems for instruction. *Instructional Science, 11*, 313-327.

Rice, R. E. (1980). Computer conferencing. In B. Dervin & M. Voigt (Eds.), *Progress in communication sciences* (Vol. 2, pp. 215-240). Norwood, NJ: Ablex.

Rice, R. E. (1982). Communication networking in computer conferencing systems: A longitudinal study of group roles and system structure. In M. Burgoon (Ed.), *Communication yearbook* (Vol. 6, pp. 925-944). Beverly Hills, CA: Sage.

Rice, R. E. (1984). Mediated group communication. In R. E. Rice & Associates, *The new media: Communication, research and technology* (pp. 129-154). Beverly Hills, CA: Sage.

Rice, R. E. (1987a). Communication technologies, human communication networks and social structure in the information society. In J. Schement & L. Lievrouw (Eds.), *Social aspects of the information society* (pp. 107-120). Norwood, NJ: Ablex.

Rice, R. E. (1987b). Computer-mediated communication and organizational innovation. *Journal of Communication, 37*(4), 65-94.

Rice, R. E. (1990a). Computer-mediated communication system network data: Theoretical concerns and empirical examples. *International Journal of Man-Machine Studies, 30*, 1-21.

Rice, R. E. (1990b). From adversity to diversity: Applications of communication technology to crisis management. In T. Housel (Ed.), *Advances in telecommunications management: Vol. 3. Information technology and crisis management* (pp. 91-112). New York: JAI.

Rice, R. E. (1992). Contexts of research on organizational computer-mediated communication: A recursive review. In M. Lea (Ed.), *Contexts of computer-mediated communication* (pp. 113-144). London: Harvester-Wheatsheaf.

Rice, R. E. (1993). Using network concepts to clarify sources and mechanisms of social influence. In W. Richards, Jr., & G. Barnett (Eds.), *Advances in communication network analysis* (pp. 43-52). Norwood, NJ: Ablex.

Rice, R. E. (1994). Relating electronic mail use and network structure to R&D work networks and performance. *Journal of Management Information Systems, 11*(1), 9-20.

Rice, R. E., & Aydin, C. (1991). Attitudes towards new organizational technology: Network proximity as a mechanism for social information processing. *Administrative Science Quarterly, 36*, 219-244.

Rice, R. E., & Barnett, G. (1985). Group communication networking in an information environment: Applying multidimensional scaling. In M. McLaughlin (Ed.), *Communication yearbook* (Vol. 9, pp. 315-326). Beverly Hills, CA: Sage.

Rice, R. E., & Borgman, C. (1983). The use of computer-monitored data in information science and communication research. *Journal of the American Society for Information Science, 34*(1), 4, 247-256.

Rice, R. E., & Danowski, J. (1993). Is it really just like a fancy answering machine? Comparing semantic networks of different types of voice mail users. *Journal of Business Communication, 30*(4), 369-397.

Rice, R. E., Grant, A., Schmitz, J., & Torobin, J. (1990). Individual and network influences on the adoption and perceived outcomes of electronic messaging. *Social Networks, 12*(1), 27-55.

Rice, R. E., Hughes, D., & Love, G. (1989). Usage and outcomes of electronic messaging at an R&D organization: Situational constraints, job level, and media awareness. *Office: Technology and People, 5*(2), 141-161.

Rice, R. E., & Love, G. (1987). Electronic emotion: Socioemotional content in a computer-mediated communication network. *Communication Research, 14*(1), 85-108.

Rice, R. E., & Richards, W., Jr. (1985). An overview of communication network analysis methods. In B. Dervin & M. Voigt (Eds.), *Progress in communication sciences* (Vol. 6, pp. 105-165). Norwood, NJ: Ablex.

Rice, R. E., & Shook, D. (1988). Access to, usage of, and outcomes from an electronic message system. *ACM Transactions on Office Information Systems, 6*(3), 255-276.

Rice, R. E., & Shook, D. (1990). Relationships of job categories and organizational levels to use of communication channels, including electronic mail: A meta-analysis and extension. *Journal of Management Studies, 27*(2), 195-229.

Rice, R. E., & Associates. (1984). *The new media: Communication, research and technology.* Beverly Hills, CA: Sage.

Robey, D. (1977). Computers and management structure: Some empirical findings re-examined. *Human Relations, 30,* 963-976.

Robey, D. (1981). Computer information systems and organization structure. *Communications of the ACM, 24*(10), 679-687.

Robey, D., Vavarek, K., & Saunders, C. (1990). *Social structure and electronic communication: A study of computer conferencing.* Unpublished paper, Florida International University, Department of Decision Sciences and Information Systems, Miami.

Rogers, E. M., & Kincaid, L. D. (1981). *Communication networks: A new paradigm for research.* New York: Free Press.

Safayeni, F., MacGregor, J., & Lee, E. (1987). Social and task-related impacts of office automation: An exploratory field study of a conceptual model of the office. *Human Systems Management, 7,* 103-114.

Salancik, G. R., & Pfeffer, J. (1978). A social information approach to job attitudes and task design. *Administrative Science Quarterly, 23,* 224-252.

Schaefermeyer, M., & Sewell, E. (1988). Communicating by electronic mail. *American Behavioral Scientist, 32*(2), 112-123.

Schmitz, J., & Fulk, J. (1991). Organizational colleagues, information richness and electronic mail: A test of the social influence model of technology use. *Communication Research, 18*(4), 487-523.

Shaw, M. E. (1978). Communication networks. In L. Berkowitz (Ed.), *Group processes* (pp. 313-349). New York: Academic Press.

Sherblom, J. (1988). Direction, function and signature in electronic mail. *Journal of Business Communication, 25,* 39-54.

Short, J., Williams, E., & Christie, B. (1976). *The social psychology of telecommunications*. London: Wiley.

Sproull, L. (1986). Using electronic mail for data collection in organization research. *Academy of Management Journal, 29*(1), 159-169.

Tichy, N. (1981). Networks in organizations. In P. Nystrom & W. Starbuck (Eds.), *Handbook of organizational design* (Vol. 2, pp. 225-249). New York: Oxford University Press.

Tushman, M. L. (1977). Special boundary roles in the innovation process. *Administrative Science Quarterly, 22*, 587-603.

Vallee, J. (1984). *Computer message systems*. New York: McGraw-Hill.

Walker, G. (1985). Network position and cognition in a computer software firm. *Administrative Science Quarterly, 30*, 103-130.

Webb, E., Campbell, D., Schwartz, R., & Sechrest, L. (1966). *Unobtrusive measures: Nonreactive research in the social sciences*. Chicago: Rand-McNally.

Weber, R. (1984). Computer-aided content analysis. *Qualitative Sociology, 7*(1-2), 126-147.

Wigand, R. T. (1985). Integrated communications and work efficiency: Impacts on organizational structure and power. *Information Services and Use, 5*, 241-258.

Williams, F., Rice, R., & Rogers, E. M. (1988). *Research methods and the new media*. New York: Free Press.

PART III

Politics and Organizations

8

Intraorganizational Networks

The Micro Side

DAVID KRACKHARDT
DANIEL J. BRASS

Thirteen years ago Tichy (1981) suggested that organizational research incorporate a network perspective. There has been a great deal of research on interorganizational networks, but to date relatively little has been done in the area of organizational behavior (OB) (House & Singh, 1987; Ilgen & Klein, 1989; O'Reilly, 1991; Staw, 1984). No doubt this is because macroresearch has been done primarily by sociologists while micro-OB is typically the domain of psychologists, who have been slower to adopt a network perspective in field studies. Our purpose is to outline some traditional micro-OB questions and suggest how network analysis has been used and can be used to enlighten and enliven answers to them.

As a departure point, we will use the five themes that O'Reilly (1991) found dominated the research agendas of micro-OB over the past decade: motivation, leadership, job design, turnover/absenteeism, and work attitudes. In addition, we will review one other area, power, which crosses the domains of micro- and macro-OB, often now called "meso" OB (Rosseau, 1985). To our knowledge, very little network analysis has been applied to the first three of these six areas. Therefore in these cases we will suggest how these areas could benefit by incorporating network theory. For the last three areas, we review the network literature as applied to them and suggest how this work may be expanded. We begin with the area of turnover and absenteeism, where some network research has revealed interesting findings.

Turnover and Absenteeism

Turnover and absenteeism are two distinct types of employee withdrawal, and they have separate causes and consequences (Mowday, Porter, & Steers, 1982). Despite researchers' call for considering them separately (Mobley, 1980), they are frequently discussed interchangeably under the same heading. But, from a networker's perspective, their distinctions become clear. First, we will discuss the emphasis that has been placed on turnover. Then we will suggest how network theory prompts us to change this emphasis and how absenteeism emerges with its own prediction.

Turnover has been the subject of study for many years (Mowday et al., 1982; Price, 1977). But, with few exceptions (e.g., Dalton & Tudor, 1979), the work has been dominated by a relatively narrow agenda: (a) assume turnover is detrimental to the organization and (b) treat turnover as a dependent variable. That is, the goal of this research, as O'Reilly (1991, p. 442) points out, has been to throw more and more independent and moderator variables into the already crowded models predicting turnover. Thus, he concludes, the most interesting developments in this literature have been methodological, demonstrating how survival and event history analysis can be used to deal with these data, which often do not conform to the underlying statistical assumptions in more traditional methods.

It is unlikely that turnover events are independent of one another (Krackhardt & Porter, 1986), a fact that draws into question the legitimacy of even the more sophisticated survival and event history models applauded by O'Reilly. Rather, as some people leave, the news of such events will likely influence others to consider leaving also. Moreover, there are likely to be social and attitudinal consequences for those who stay. Thus turnover could be a powerful independent variable, one that predicts both subsequent turnover events and consequences to those who remain.

Such effects are not uniformly distributed across all members of the organization. Not all members will be induced to reconsider their employment status because someone, somewhere, has left the organization. Not all stayers will be equally affected by the occasional departure of another employee. It is in this thorny part of the problem that network theory provides a rich perspective.

A pair of articles by Krackhardt and Porter (1985, 1986) based on what later became known as the "MacDonald's Restaurant Studies" (Rogers, 1987, p. 289) provide some direction. In one study, Krackhardt and Porter (1986) found that turnover occurred in clusters, calling it a "snowball effect." These clusters were significantly related to people's roles in the organization. These roles, in turn, were derived not from their position in the organizational chart but from their position in the advice network. Krackhardt and Porter suggested that, if people see others leave who are in a similar network position (role) as themselves, then this is particularly relevant information about the nature of their jobs and about alternatives to working at that particular organization. Thus people in similar positions are induced also to consider leaving, resulting in clusters of leavers within these informal role types.

Absenteeism, on the other hand, implies continued membership in the organization and leads to different network predictions. One critical element of absenteeism is that it can be thought of as emanating from a set of values, work attitudes, and norms about what is appropriate behavior in the organization (Steers & Rhodes, 1978). Norms are often communicated, negotiated, and enforced through friendship ties (Krackhardt & Kilduff, 1990). Thus, while turnover clusters might be related to role similarity, absenteeism would be more related to direct friendship ties. In contrast to the Krackhardt-Porter result, then, we suggest the absenteeism rates will be clustered in friendship groups.

In their second study, Krackhardt and Porter (1985) observed the effects of turnover on those who decided to remain. In this case, they looked at friends of those who left. Contrary to what one might expect, those who were friends of the leavers became significantly more satisfied and committed to the organization after their friends left than those who were not friends of the leavers. Krackhardt and Porter suggest a "rotten apple" theory to explain these results: People leave because they are unhappy with some aspect of the job (they dislike the supervisor, the work, and so on). Before they leave, they expend some energy complaining about the work. And to whom do they complain? Their friends. Thus, after these complainers leave, the surviving friends are relieved of the never-ending source of negative cues about the workplace, resulting in increasing satisfaction with the workplace.

Absenteeism, on the other hand, would have little in common with turnover in this model. Friends who are regularly absent due to disaffection return to depress their colleagues again. Thus we would expect that being a friend of those who are absent frequently would in no way improve one's workplace attitudes following absentee behavior. The work relating networks to turnover and absenteeism has begun. Rogers (1987, p. 289) referred to the network approach to turnover as a "turbocharger" in an area that had floundered recently. But there is much to do, both in extending this work to the area of absenteeism and in investigating further the relationship between turnover and informal structures.

Power

Although O'Reilly (1991) did not include the topic of power in his review of micro-OB, the concept is a central one in the field. A structural network perspective on power and influence has been the topic of much research. The finding that central network positions are associated with power has been reported in small, laboratory work groups (Shaw, 1964), interpersonal networks in organizations (Brass, 1984, 1985; Brass & Burkhardt, 1993; Burkhardt & Brass, 1990; Fombrun, 1983; Krackhardt, 1990; Tushman & Romanelli, 1983), organizational buying systems (Bristor, 1992; Ronchetto, Hutt, & Reingen, 1989), intergroup networks in organizations (Astley & Zajac, 1990; Hinings, Hickson, Pennings, & Schneck, 1974), interorganizational networks (Boje & Whetten, 1981; Galaskiewicz, 1979), professional communities (Breiger, 1976), and community elites (Laumann & Pappi, 1976).

Theoretically, actors in central network positions have greater access to, and potential control over, relevant resources, such as information in the case of a communication network. Actors who are able to control relevant resources, and thereby increase others' dependence on them, acquire power. In addition to increasing others' dependence on them, actors must also decrease their dependence on others. They must have access to relevant resources that is not controlled or mediated by others. Thus two measures of centrality, closeness (representing access) and betweenness (representing control) correspond to resource dependence notions (Brass, 1984, 1992). Both measures have been shown to contribute to the variance in reputational measures of power as well as promotions in organizations (Brass, 1984, 1985). In addition, simple degree centrality measures of the size of one's ego network have been associated with power (Brass & Burkhardt, 1992, 1993; Burkhardt & Brass, 1990).

As the above research indicates, there is a general agreement that centrality is related to power, and a variety of different measures of centrality have been used to establish the relationship. However, disagreement exists as to which measure best captures the concept. The three most commonly used graph-theory measures of centrality are degree, closeness, and betweenness (Freeman, 1979).

Although few studies have included more than one measure of centrality, all three measures have been shown to relate to power in different studies. Research including both the closeness and the betweenness measures of centrality (Brass, 1984, 1985) indicated that, while the two measures overlapped, both contributed unique variance in explaining promotions and perceptions of power. In a later reanalysis of this data (Brass & Burkhardt, 1992), the degree measure of centrality was included. Results showed that the degree measure explained as much variance as either the closeness or the betweenness measure. When controlling for degree, betweenness did not significantly increase the variance explained in reputational measures of power, while closeness slightly increased it. When controlling for either betweenness or closeness, the degree measure of centrality significantly increased the explained variance.

In addition to the measures of centrality, other issues revolving around social networks and power have been noted by Brass (1992). These include the direction of ties, the strength of ties, links, transaction content of the network, the unit of reference, and positively and negatively connected networks.

Direction of Ties

Knoke and Burt (1983) have emphasized the distinction between symmetric and asymmetric ties, arguing that being the object of the relation rather than the source is an indication of superordination. They refer to measures that distinguish between source and object as measures of prestige. The difference between symmetric measures of centrality and asymmetric measures of prestige may be the difference between leaders and followers. Although their analyses showed the symmetric centrality measures to be highly correlated with the asymmetric prestige measures, Knoke and Burt (1983) found that only the prestige measure predicted early adoption of a medical innovation. Similarly, Burkhardt and Brass (1990) found that all employees increased their closeness centrality (symmetric measure) following the introduction of new technology. However, the early adopters of the new technology increased their in-degree prestige and their power significantly more than the later adopters.

Transaction Content of Networks

Complex organizations contain a multitude of networks arising from a variety of relationships. As workers exchange inputs and outputs in an organizational work flow, the performance of the task, which continues the successful flow of work, may be a resource and potential source of power. Because the inputs and outputs for each task can be specified, it is possible to refine the degree and betweenness measures of centrality. Brass (1984) measured transaction alternatives by counting the number of alternative sources of inputs and the destinations for outputs for each task. Conversely, he also measured criticality, defined as the number of alternative paths through which the work may flow if the focal task position is removed. These two egocentric measures explained large amounts of variance in supervisors' and subordinates' perceptions of influence.

Just as the division of labor produces a horizontal work-flow network of task positions, it also produces a vertical network of task positions—the organization's hierarchy of authority. Although the hierarchy represents an easily obtainable network of relationships, it has seldom been used in this manner. Level in the hierarchy has been shown to be strongly related to perceptions of power in an organization (Brass & Burkhardt, 1993; Fombrun, 1983). However, Ibarra (1993) found that the informal structure (network centrality) was equally or more important than the formal structure (hierarchical rank) in predicting power as measured by involvement in technical and administrative innovations.

The communication network is typically described as an informal, emergent network, although many of the relationships shadow the prescribed work flow and hierarchy of authority. Centrality in the communication network has frequently been the focus of studies of power (Blau & Alba, 1982; Brass, 1984, 1985; Brass & Burkhardt, 1993; Burkhardt & Brass, 1990; Fombrun, 1983; Tushman & Romanelli, 1983). To the extent that information exchange is reflected in the advice network, betweenness centrality in the advice network has been related to power (Krackhardt, 1990).

Because almost all friends communicate with each other, Brass (1984, 1985) reported considerable overlap between communication and friendship measures of centrality, with both relating to influence. For example, Krackhardt (1990) found that betweenness centrality in the friendship network related to perceptions of power even when controlling for centrality in the advice network.

In his study of a unionization vote in an organization, Krackhardt (1992) found that employees tended to rely on trusted friends in making their decisions. Based on this and previous research (Krackhardt & Stern, 1988), Krackhardt proposed that friendship links are particularly important when employees experience uncertainty. However, Burkhardt and Brass (1990) found that, rather than relying on established friends, employees changed their communication patterns when faced with the uncertainty of a technological change. These seemingly conflicting results may be reconciled by considering the type of uncertainty faced in each situation. In the unionization vote (Krackhardt, 1990), employees had enough information but were uncertain about how to vote. When encountering the change in technology (Burkhardt & Brass, 1990), employees lacked information about the new technology and sought out new contacts so as to learn the system.

Although the transaction content of network connections may overlap (for example, friends and work-flow connections may provide advice), the importance of content has been emphasized by Ibarra in her studies of men's and women's networks (Ibarra, 1992, 1993). Ibarra found that homophily (tendency to form same-sex network relationships) had differential effects for men and women in terms of acquiring power. While men formed homophilous ties across multiple networks, women experienced dual networks: social support and friendship from other women and instrumental ties (advice and communication) to men. Women in this advertising firm were constrained in their choices because men occupied the most powerful positions (Ibarra, 1992).

Brass (1985) found similar results in his study of men's and women's networks and differential connections to the dominant coalition. Studying an interpersonal network of nonsupervisory employees, closeness to the dominant coalition in the organization was strongly related to power and promotions. The dominant coalition was identified by a cohesive subset analysis of the interaction patterns of the top executives in the company. Brass (1985) also found that men were more closely linked to the dominant coalition (composed of four men) and were perceived as more influential than women. Assuming that power positions in most organizations are dominated by men, women may be forced to forgo any preference for homophily in order to build connections with the dominant coalition. Thus the organizational context places constraints on preferences for homophily, especially for women and minorities (Ibarra, 1993).

Units of Reference

Individuals in organizations are embedded within work groups, work groups are embedded within departments, and departments are embedded within divisions or entire organizations. Thus determining the appropriate unit of reference, the boundaries of the appropriate network, can affect the relationship between network position and power. For example, in comparing centrality within a work group (employees with the same immediate supervisor), within a department (formal organizational designations), and within the entire organization, Brass and Burkhardt (1992) found that centrality (degree, closeness, and betweenness) within an employee's department explained the most unique variance in perceptions of power and subsequent promotions.

Theory and the choice of research questions may designate some units of reference as more appropriate than others. However, the possibility of multiple sources of power in organizations suggests that multiple units of reference may be an appropriate strategy for both employees and researchers. Additionally, research has found that membership in departments is related to individual power (Blau & Alba, 1982; Brass, 1984; Ibarra, 1992, 1993). This raises the possibility that departmental centrality may interact with individual centrality within departments to further explain perceptions of power.

Cognitive Maps

In other applications of social networks, Krackhardt (1990) found that the accuracy of individual cognitive maps of the social network in an organization was related to perceptions of influence. That is, power was related to the degree to which an individual's perception of the interaction network matched the "actual" social network. In a case analysis, Krackhardt (1992) also demonstrated how a lack of knowledge of the social networks in a firm prevented a union from successfully organizing employees.

Coalitions

The relation between networks and coalitions in organizations has also been the focus of several authors (Bacharach & Lawler, 1980; Murnighan & Brass, 1991; Stevenson, Pearce, & Porter, 1985; Thurman, 1979). Murnighan and Brass (1991) demonstrated how coalitions are formed one actor at a time, and require the founder to have an extensive ego network of weak ties. Thurman (1979) described how leveling countercoalitions are formed through existing social network ties.

Work Attitudes

As O'Reilly has noted, work-related attitudes are the subject of numerous publications in micro-OB. Work-related attitudes, such as job satisfaction, are affective evaluations about aspects of one's work environment (O'Reilly, 1991, p. 435). Just as similar people prefer to interact, theory and research have also noted that those who interact become more similar (Carley, 1991; Kaufer & Carley, 1993). Employees may adopt similar attitudes to those with whom they interact or those who occupy similar positions in the social network. Thus most social network studies have focused on attitude similarity.

Erickson (1988) provides the theory and research concerning the "relational basis of attitudes." She argues that people are not born with their attitudes, nor do they develop them in isolation. Attitude formation and change occur primarily through social interaction. As people attempt to make sense of reality, they compare their own perceptions with those of others—in particular, similar others. For example, Kilduff (1990) found that MBA students made decisions similar to their perceived friends regarding job interviews with organizations.

Following Erickson (1988), Rice and Aydin (1991) investigated the effects of relational, positional, and spatial proximity on attitude similarity. They found that employees' attitudes about new technology were similar to attitudes of those with whom employees communicated frequently and their immediate supervisors. However, one interesting finding was that estimates of others' attitudes were not correlated with others' actual (reported) attitudes. Two explanations are possible for this finding. One is social projection—individuals project their own attitudes onto others. Rice and Aydin (1991) found a positive relationship between an individual's attitudes and that individual's estimate of others' attitudes. The second explanation is the possibility that employees politely agree with expressed opinions, even if those opinions are counter to their own true feelings.

In another study, Rentsch (1990) found that members of an accounting firm who interacted with each other had similar interpretations of organizational events and that these meanings differed qualitatively across different interaction groups. Krackhardt and Kilduff (1990) found that friends had similar perceptions of others in the organization, even when controlling for demographic and positional similarities. Danowski (1980) got mixed results on the relationship between connectivity and attitude uniformity. Innovation groups displayed homogeneity in attitudes, but production groups did not.

Burkhardt (1991) found attitude similarity among structurally equivalent actors, and Walker (1985) found that structurally equivalent individuals had similar cognitive judgments of means-ends relationships regarding product success. Galaskiewicz and Burt (1991) found similar evaluations of nonprofit organizations among structurally equivalent contributions officers, and structural equivalence explained these contagion effects better than a relational cohesion approach. Structural equivalence does not hinge on direct interaction/communication among actors. Rather, the similarity in attitudes stems from actors occupying similar positions, or roles, in the network. According to Burt (1982), actors cognitively compare their own attitudes and behaviors with those of others occupying similar roles rather than being influenced by direct communications from others in dissimilar roles.

Taking a slightly different approach, Dean and Brass (1985) argued that highly central employees, by virtue of their greater number of links, would be exposed to more diversity of opinion than peripheral employees. They found that central employees' attitudes about job characteristics were more similar to observable reality as measured by the perceptions of an outside observer. They argued that increased social interaction leads to a convergence of perceptions similar to observable reality.

Although the above evidence suggests that employees who interact or who occupy similar positions in the network will have similar attitudes, a great many questions about the effects of social influence on attitudes remain (see also the following section on job design). Attitude formation is obviously a complex process requiring further research.

Job Satisfaction

Perhaps the most frequently researched attitude in organizational studies is job satisfaction (O'Reilly, 1991). Despite the attention to job satisfaction in the small group laboratory network studies of the 1950s (see Shaw, 1964, for a review), there have been surprisingly few social network studies addressing job satisfaction in organizations. The early laboratory studies found that central actors were more satisfied than peripheral actors in these small (typically five-person) groups. In one of the few organizational studies, Roberts and O'Reilly (1979) found that relative isolates (zero or one link) in the communication network were less satisfied than participants (two or more links).

However, Brass (1981) found no relationship between centrality (closeness) in the work flow of work groups or departments and employee satisfaction. Centrality within the entire organization's work flow was negatively related to satisfaction in this sample of nonsupervisory employees. Brass (1981) suggested that this latter finding may be due to the routine jobs associated with the core technology of the organization. He found that job characteristics mediated the relationship between work-flow network measures and job satisfaction. Similarly, Ibarra and Andrews (1993) found that centrality in advice and friendship networks was related to perceptions of autonomy. Moch (1980) also found that integration in the work network (two or more links) was associated with job characteristics and internal motivation. However, isolates with high growth needs reported high job involvement.

In a recent study of 47 managers in an entrepreneurial firm, Kilduff and Krackhardt (1993) found a negative relationship between centrality (betweenness) in the friendship network and job satisfaction. However, they also found that managers whose cognitive maps of the social networks were more schema-consistent were more satisfied and committed. *Schema consistency* referred to the tendency to perceive friendship ties as reciprocated (symmetric) and transitive. Combining these findings, Kilduff and Krackhardt (1993) argued that mediating the relationships between actors (betweenness centrality) who are not themselves friends may create conflicting expectations and stress.

Following this line of reasoning, it is also possible that multiplex relationships may create similar sources of stress and thereby limit job satisfaction. Failure to maintain one relationship may result in the loss of the other. Thus an employee may feel "forced" to agree to the work-related demands of a friend in order to maintain the friendship.

Although further research is needed, these limited results suggest that there may be an optimum degree of centrality in social network that is neither too little nor too great regarding satisfaction. Isolation is probably negatively related to satisfaction, while a high degree of centrality, or multiplexity, may lead to conflicting expectations, communication overload, and stress.

Job Design

The area of job design generated some of the most intellectually interesting and promising research of the past decade (Hackman & Oldham, 1980). In its primary form, the job design literature argued that manipulating key characteristics of work (skill variety, task identity, task significance, autonomy, and task feedback) would substantially affect job attitudes and performance. The major challenge to this model came from Salancik and Pfeffer's (1978) work on social information processing (SIP). They argued that the five job dimensions were not solely objective but instead were the result of subjective judgments made by employees. These judgments, in turn, they argue, were heavily influenced by social cues. Support for this perspective has been reasonably strong (e.g., Griffin, 1983).

A curious paradox emerges, however, if we take the SIP model seriously. What makes the SIP model interesting is that two people, both exposed to the same job, could evaluate it differently because of the different social cues that they are exposed to. For example, in an organizational setting, we might find one group (call them the Optimists) of workers who all like the way a particular job is structured and another group (the Pessimists) who all dislike the same job. Now, suppose one person from each group bumps into the other at the lunch line, and they start discussing their jobs. They are exchanging social cues. The optimist is now contaminated with a small number of pessimist cues, and vice versa. According to the model, each should move slightly in the direction of the other. As they return to their groups, some small amount of this contagion rubs off on their fellow workers, who are left slightly less adamant in their positions. Over time, as they encounter each other in committee meetings or at the local bar, they slowly move toward each other in their evaluations. Eventually, they meet in the undistinguishable middle, both groups feeling lukewarm about the job.

It has been argued that the diameter of the United States is, with all but certainty, six or less (Pool & Kochen, 1978). That means, if we count the number of weak ties it takes for one person to "reach" another in the intractable social network among all people in this country, the largest number of ties that separates any two people is six. Certainly, then, the number of links one must have to travel through for any one person in the far reaches of an organization to get to another person is less than that. From this, we conclude that no two groups within an organization are totally isolated from one another. Thus the entropic process described by the simple version of SIP must lead to an equilibrium wherein everyone eventually agrees on the characteristics of the job. The fact that everyone does not agree on such job evaluations was what prompted researchers to explore the SIP model in the first place. Therefore for the SIP model to make such a long-run equilibrium prediction is problematic.

In the real world, we do not observe unanimity in these judgments. We could explain this discrepancy by claiming the SIP model is wrong or by claiming that it is at least partially wrong, or we could modify the SIP model, using a network perspective, so that it does not make such obviously wrong predictions. We will draw from Krackhardt's (1993) network model of endogenous preferences to illustrate how the SIP model might be enhanced to avoid this problem. We will retain the fundamental assumption about people influencing each other as they interact. However, by adding an interesting second assumption about such an influence process, we avoid the entopic result.

Assumption 1: Principle of interaction. The degree of influence person j has on person i's evaluation of a set of job characteristics as they pertain to a particular job is proportional to the amount of time i and j spend interacting with each other. This assumption is consistent with the formulation as Salancik and Pfeffer (1978) originally proposed it.

Assumption 2: Principle of reflected exclusivity. The degree of influence person j has on person i's evaluation of a set of job characteristics as they pertain to a particular job is inversely proportional to the amount of time person j spends with all others (including self).

We can formalize this process into a matrix of influence patterns (Krackhardt, 1993). What is interesting in this model is that the structure of interactions *totally determines* the equilibrium of the distribution of evaluations of the jobs. This model extends the SIP model by formally describing the process by which people differentially influence each other in their evaluations. The original SIP model only suggests that social cues of various types will influence people's judgments. This network model predicts how much every person will be influenced and what the individual's evaluation will be, relative to all the other individual evaluations.

Leadership

There is no more resilient theme in organizational behavior than the cry for better understanding of leadership (see Bass, 1990, for a comprehensive review). Almost all of the research, however, has looked at the set of followers as an undifferentiated group, whom the leader tries to influence as a whole in some way. A fresh break with this tradition has been offered by Graen and his colleagues with the introduction of the "leader-member exchange" (LMX) model (Graen, 1976; Graen, Liden, & Hoel, 1982; Graen, Novak, & Sommerkamp, 1982). In this model, leaders are seen as establishing different relationships with their subordinates, resulting in different outcomes for the in-group (those with a strong relationship with the leader) and the out-group (those with a weaker relationship with the leader).

We believe that Graen's work has offered a fresh perspective on the leadership literature by focusing on different relationships that enhance certain outcomes. We would like to extend this idea of relationship to argue that a leader must look beyond simply the relationships between herself and her followers; she must also take into account the relationships among those followers (see Fernandez, 1991).

Being strongly connected to subordinates has two functions for a leader. Following the Graen line of reasoning, such relationships can enhance the leader's influence and persuasive powers with those to whom she is connected. These people are more likely to view the leader positively and cooperate with requests or commands handed down from the leader.

The second possible function is that connections provide for information flow from followers to their leader. It is important for a leader to keep in touch with followers, to know how they are doing, to uncover problems or even counterproductive norms that might be emerging in the group. A leader is dependent on her contacts for the availability and veracity of such information.

Also, it is probably unreasonable and even inadvisable for a leader to be strongly connected to everyone in his group. To do so may require too much of his time without sufficient payoff (Krackhardt, 1994). But to be isolated from his group would be equally ill-advised. Instead, the middle ground, one consistent with the LMX literature, is probably best: Leaders should develop strong relations with some but not all his subordinates. The natural question emerging from this discussion is this: With which of the followers should the leader connect? From the network theorist's point of view, the answer depends on the informal structure in the group.

There are two principles that one should pay attention to if one is choosing among subordinates to develop strong relationships with. First, if there is heterogeneity in the centrality scores among the followers, it is most efficient to be connected to the most central players. The central players tend to be more powerful (Brass, 1984, 1992) and also tend to have access to more relevant information that could be passed back to the leader (Krackhardt, 1990).

Second, if the group is divided into cohesive subsets, it is important that the leader have strong connections to at least one member of each subgroup. To concentrate the leader's connections within one cohesive subset is disadvantageous for two reasons. First, many connections to members of the same subset, who are connected to each other, will be redundant (Granovetter, 1973). The leader will not be getting new and different information from each of her time-consuming links. Second, because groups whose members have connections to the leader are more likely to cooperate with the leader, leaving a cohesive subset without such connections reduces the leader's leverage over that group. By spreading ties out among the various cohesive subsets, the leader is maximizing his ability to mobilize all his followers and minimizing the chances that a disenfranchised group will resist or rebel.

Motivation

There are several prominent theories of motivation. Many of these parallel a rational, almost economist's model of human cognition. For example, expectancy-valence theory (Porter & Lawler, 1968; Vroom, 1964) suggests that people are motivated to choose a course of action that maximizes the probability of a valued outcome. The theory accepts as exogenous (unexplained) how these values that are attributed to outcomes come about. Network theory would suggest that such values are at least in part determined through a social process. By interacting with others, these value judgments are influenced in predictable ways (e.g., Erickson, 1988).

We will focus here on the role motivation plays on Stacy Adams's (1965) equity theory. In his formulation of the equity model, a Person evaluates whether the ratio of his or her inputs (efforts, investments, contributions, and so on) to outcomes (rewards, benefits, satisfactions, and so on) is equal to the ratio of inputs to outcomes of some Other or Others. If these ratios are unequal, Adams claims Person will be motivated by the inequity to seek some means for reestablishing equilibrium by making the two ratios equal. Person has at her disposal the several options to return to equity: She could change her inputs or outcomes; she could change her perception of these, without changing their objective states; finally, Adams claims that she could change her choice of Other as a comparison base.

Most of the research in equity theory has focused on identifying and measuring the set of inputs and outcomes that are valued and relevant to Person. More recently, a few studies (e.g., Kulik & Ambrose, 1992; Oldham & Kulik, 1986a, 1986b) have heeded Goodman's (1977) admonition that "little attention has been given to the types of referents people select" (p. 108). Equity theory as posed by Adams provides little guidance as to who the Other might be. The identity of the Other is often assumed to be a given, just as the existence of values is assumed to be given in the aforementioned motivation theories.

One possible model is that Persons choose their referent Others on a set of attributes or criteria (Goodman, 1974, 1977). But, if one takes equity theory seriously, and we posit that Persons are free to choose their comparative Others, we then run into a paradox: Why don't Persons choose Others who will balance the equation and reduce the inequity immediately? And, by extension, why would inequity ever exist?

But we know from field studies that inequity is experienced by organizational employees (Oldham & Kulik, 1986b). We conclude, then, that people are involuntarily brought to compare themselves with Others (for reasons not clearly explained by equity theory itself) who yield uncomfortable inequities. Here is where network theory and the social forces inherent therein are useful. We propose that the choice of comparison Others is constrained by the network of relations that Person and Others are embedded in. We suggest this can happen through two different mechanisms: through direct comparison with Others one is tied to and through the indirect effects of role comparisons in the network.

Direct Effects of Network Ties

At the most obvious level, it is reasonable to propose that people with whom Person has frequent and strong ties (Granovetter, 1973) are likely to be comparative Others. The reasons for this are obvious. People with whom one has frequent contact are likely to provide direct information about their efforts, experiences, rewards, and opportunities (see the sections on job design and work attitudes). Faced with such undeniable confirmation of Others' inputs and outcomes, it is difficult to exclude them in one's equity calculations.

Another, more subtle force operates here also. Persons who interact frequently tend to become similar in their attitudes and beliefs (Carley, 1986, p. 160). As Festinger (1954, p. 120) proposed in his early work, people compare themselves with Others who are similar on some set of attributes. Thus, not only do direct ties provide concrete information for comparative purposes, they reinforce those comparisons by inducing similarity between Person and those Others.

Indirect Effects of Network Ties:
Structurally Equivalent Roles

A close look at the predecessors to equity theory provides some guidance of this quest for the elusive Other. As stated earlier, Festinger stressed similarity as a basis for choosing comparative Others, and that interaction leads to similarity. However, similarity can also occur without direct interaction. In a discussion of the concept of relative deprivation, Merton and Kitt (1950) separate out comparisons between those who directly interact and those who merely share certain statuses. They claim that

> some similarity in status attributes between the individual and the reference group must be perceived or imagined, in order for the comparison to occur at all. Once this minimal similarity obtains, other similarities and differences pertinent to the situation will provide the context for shaping evaluations. (p. 61)

Clearly, similarity is a common theme in these theoretical claims. But similarity on what dimensions? An answer for this is provided by role theory (Nadel, 1957).

The roles inferred from relationships are called "structurally equivalent" roles (Lorrain & White, 1971). Two individuals are structurally equivalent (occupy the same role) to the extent that they share the same relationships with the same set of other people. Returning now to our motivation theory, we would argue that people who occupy structurally equivalent roles, despite their job titles, will see each other as comparable Others for purposes of determining equity. Conversely, those who have similar job titles but do not occupy structurally equivalent roles will not see each other as comparable Others for purposes of determining equity.

The Role of Cognitive Social Structures

Thus far, we have ignored one important part of Adams's (1965) theory. As he has emphasized, what is critical is how Person defines or perceives the situation, not some objective reality (or how the researcher defines it). In the current context, this translates to which Others the focal Person perceives as occupying the same role. The importance of this difference was underscored by Burt (1982, chap. 5), who found that adjusting the structural similarities between actors in a network to more closely correspond to perceptions of similarities improved his predictions.

Krackhardt (1987) developed Burt's argument further, suggesting that, to truly assess the effect of perceived structural equivalence, one should assess the individual's perception of the network in which she is embedded and then calculate structural equivalence among actors based on these perceptions. Krackhardt refers to a set of such perceptions as "cognitive social structures." Krackhardt (1987) argues that such cognitive maps often better represent what network theorists are trying to capture in their models. His argument is directly applicable to equity theory, where Adams's work is perceptually anchored. We suggest that the predictive power of the structural equivalence and direct ties are enhanced if we use Person's map of the social structure rather than "objective" behavioral relations.

Conclusion

We have outlined how network analysis could enhance the research agendas of those scholars exploring six different areas within the micro side of organizational behavior. Three of these areas—turnover, attitudes, and especially power—have already incorporated network theory and methods. Three of the areas—motivation, leadership, and job design—have to date remained largely untouched by network analysis. In all cases, we have argued that the network paradigm has the potential to add at a minimum a different perspective to these age-old problems and perhaps could function as the "turbocharger" that Rogers envisioned for all of our work.

O'Reilly, in his 1991 review, noted the recent increase in OB research that has paid more attention to context. This realization has led to more cross-level work, generally incorporating more macro-level constructs (such as demography) into micro-level research. As this trend continues, we expect network analysis to take an even more prominent place in the repertoire of OB explanations of organizational phenomena.

References

Adams, J. S. (1965). Inequity in social change. In L. Berkowitz (Ed.), *Advances in experimental social psychology* (pp. 267-300). New York: Academic Press.

Astley, W. G., & Zajac, E. J. (1990). Beyond dyadic exchange: Functional interdependence and sub-unit power. *Organization Studies, 11*(4), 481-501.

Bacharach, S. B., & Lawler, E. J. (1980). *Power and politics in organizations.* San Francisco: Jossey-Bass.

Bass, B. M. (1990). *Bass & Stogdill's handbook of leadership: Theory, research, and managerial applications* (3rd ed.). New York: Free Press.

Blau, J. R., & Alba, R. D. (1982). Empowering nets of participation. *Administrative Science Quarterly, 27,* 363-379.

Boje, D. M., & Whetten, D. A. (1981). Effects of organizational strategies and contextual constraints on centrality and attributions of influence in interorganizational networks. *Administrative Science Quarterly, 26,* 378-395.

Brass, D. J. (1981). Structural relationships, job characteristics, and worker satisfaction and performance. *Administrative Science Quarterly, 26,* 331-348.

Brass, D. J. (1984). Being in the right place: A structural analysis of individual influence in an organization. *Administrative Science Quarterly, 29,* 519-539.

Brass, D. J. (1985). Men's and women's networks: A study of interaction patterns and influence in an organization. *Academy of Management Journal, 28,* 327-343.

Brass, D. J. (1992). Power in organizations: A social network perspective. In G. Moore & J. A. White (Eds.), *Research in politics and society* (pp. 295-323). Greenwich, CT: JAI.

Brass, D. J., & Burkhardt, M. E. (1992). Centrality and power in organizations. In N. Nohria & R. Eccles (Eds.), *Networks and organizations: Structure, form, and action* (pp. 191-215). Boston: Harvard Business School Press.

Brass, D. J., & Burkhardt, M. E. (1993). Potential power and power use: An investigation of structure and behavior. *Academy of Management Journal, 36,* 441-470.

Breiger, R. L. (1976). Career attributes and network structure: A blockmodel study of biomedical research specialty. *American Sociological Review, 41*, 117-135.

Bristor, J. M. (1992). Influence strategies in organizational buying: The importance of connections to the right people in the right places. *Journal of Business-to-Business Marketing, 1*, 63-98.

Burkhardt, M. E. (1991). *Institutionalization of technical change* (Working paper). Philadelphia: University of Pennsylvania, Wharton School.

Burkhardt, M. E., & Brass, D. J. (1990). Changing patterns or patterns of change: The effect of a change in technology on social network structure and power. *Administrative Science Quarterly, 35*, 104-127.

Burt, R. S. (1982). *Toward a structural theory of action*. New York: Academic Press.

Carley, K. M. (1986). An approach for relating social structure to cognitive structure. *Journal of Mathematical Sociology, 12*(2), 137-189.

Carley, K. M. (1991). A theory of group stability. *American Sociological Review, 56*, 331-354.

Dalton, D. R., & Tudor, W. D. (1979). Turnover turned over: An expanded and positive perspective. *Academy of Management Review, 4*, 225-236.

Danowski, J. A. (1980). Group attitude uniformity and connectivity of organizational communication networks for production, innovation, and maintenance content. *Human Communication Research, 6*, 299-308.

Dean, J. W., & Brass, D. J. (1985). Social interaction and the perception of job characteristics in an organization. *Human Relations, 38*, 571-582.

Erickson, B. H. (1988). The relational basis of attitudes. In B. Wellman & S. D. Berkowitz (Eds.), *Social structures: A network approach* (pp. 99-121). Cambridge: Cambridge University Press.

Fernandez, R. M. (1991). Structural bases of leadership in intraorganizational networks. *Social Psychology Quarterly, 54*(1), 36-53.

Festinger, L. (1954). A theory of social comparison processes. *Human Relations, 7*, 117-140.

Fombrun, C. J. (1983). Attributions of power across a social network. *Human Relations, 36*, 493-508.

Freeman, L. C. (1979). Centrality in social networks: Conceptual clarification. *Social Networks, 1*, 215-239.

Galaskiewicz, J. (1979). *Exchange networks and community politics*. Beverly Hills, CA: Sage.

Galaskiewicz, J., & Burt, R. S. (1991). Interorganizational contagion in corporate philanthropy. *Administrative Science Quarterly, 36*, 88-105.

Goodman, P. S. (1974). An examination of the referents used in evaluation of pay. *Organizational Behavior and Human Performance, 12*, 170-195.

Goodman, P. S. (1977). Social comparison processes in organizations. In G. Salancik & B. Staw (Eds.), *New directions in organizational behavior*. Chicago: St. Clair.

Graen, G. (1976). Role making processes within complex organizations. In M. D. Dunnette (Ed.), *Handbook of industrial and organizational psychology*. Chicago: Rand McNally.

Graen, G. B., Liden, R. C., & Hoel, W. (1982). Role of leadership in the employee withdrawal process. *Journal of Applied Psychology, 67*, 868-872.

Graen, G. B., Novak, M., & Sommerkamp, P. (1982). The effects of leadership-member exchange and O.B. design on productivity and satisfaction: Testing a dual attachment model. *Organizational Behavior and Human Performance, 30*, 109-131.

Granovetter, M. (1973). The strength of weak ties. *American Journal of Sociology, 78,* 1360-1380.

Griffin, R. W. (1983). Objective and social sources of information in task redesign: A field experiment. *Administrative Science Quarterly, 28,* 184-200.

Hackman, J. R., & Oldham, G. R. (1980). *Work redesign.* Reading, MA: Addison-Wesley.

Hinings, C. R., Hickson, D. J., Pennings, J. M., & Schneck, R. E. (1974). Structural conditions of intraorganizational power. *Administrative Science Quarterly, 19,* 22-44.

House, R. J., & Singh, J. (1987). Organizational behavior: Some new directions for I/O psychology. *Annual Review of Psychology, 38,* 669-718.

Ibarra, H. (1992). Homophily and differential returns: Sex differences in network structure and access in an advertising firm. *Administrative Science Quarterly, 37,* 422-447.

Ibarra, H. (1993). Personal networks of women and minorities in management: A conceptual framework. *Academy of Management Review, 18,* 56-87.

Ibarra, H., & Andrews, S. B. (1993). Power, social influence and sense-making: Effects of network centrality and proximity on employee perceptions. *Administrative Science Quarterly, 38,* 277-303.

Ilgen, D. R., & Klein, H. S. (1989). Organizational behavior. *Annual Review of Psychology, 40,* 327-351.

Kaufer, D. S., & Carley, K. (1993). *Communication at a distance: The influence of print on a socio-cultural organization and change.* Hillsdale, NJ: LEA Publishers.

Kilduff, M. (1990). The interpersonal structure of decision making: A social comparison approach to organizational choice. *Organizational Behavior and Human Decision Processes, 47,* 270-288.

Kilduff, M., & Krackhardt, D. (1993). *Schemas at work: Making sense of organizational relationships.* Unpublished manuscript.

Knoke, D., & Burt, R. S. (1983). Prominence. In R. S. Burt & M. J. Miner (Eds.), *Applied network analysis: A methodological introduction* (pp. 195-222). Beverly Hills, CA: Sage.

Krackhardt, D. (1987). Cognitive social structures. *Social Network, 9,* 109-134.

Krackhardt, D. (1990). Assessing the political landscape: Structure, cognition, and power in organizations. *Administrative Science Quarterly, 35,* 342-369.

Krackhardt, D. (1992). The strength of strong ties: The importance of philos. In N. Nohria & R. Eccles (Eds.), *Networks and organizations: Structure, form, and action* (pp. 216-239). Boston: Harvard Business School Press.

Krackhardt, D. (1993, March 12-14). *Endogenous preference: A structural approach.* Paper presented at the Conference on Non-rational Elements of Organizational Decision Making, Cornell University, School of Industrial and Labor Relations.

Krackhardt, D. (1994). Constraints on the interactive organization as an ideal type. In C. Heckscher & A. Donnellan (Eds.), *The post-bureaucratic organization* (pp. 89-111). Thousand Oaks, CA: Sage.

Krackhardt, D., & Kilduff, M. (1990). Friendship patterns and culture: The control of organizational diversity. *American Anthropologist, 92,* 142-154.

Krackhardt, D., & Porter, L. W. (1985). When friends leave: A structural analysis of the relationship between turnover and stayer's attitudes. *Administrative Science Quarterly, 30,* 242-261.

Krackhardt, D., & Porter, L. W. (1986). The snowball effect: Turnover embedded in communication networks. *Journal of Applied Psychology, 71,* 50-55.

Krackhardt, D., & Stern, R. N. (1988). Informal networks and organizational crises: An experimental simulation. *Social Psychology Quarterly, 51,* 123-140.

Kulik, C. T., & Ambrose, M. L. (1992). Personal and situational determinants of referent choice. *Academy of Management Review, 17,* 221-237.

Laumann, E. O., & Pappi, F. U. (1976). *Networks of collective action: A perspective on community influence systems.* New York: Academic Press.

Lorrain, F., & White, H. C. (1971). Structural equivalence of individuals in social networks. *Journal of Mathematical Sociology, 1,* 49-80.

Merton, R. K., & Kitt, A. S. (1950). Contributions to the theory of reference group behavior. In P. F. Lazarsfeld & R. K. Merton (Eds.), *Studies in the scope and method of "The American Soldier"* (pp. 40-104). New York: Free Press.

Mobley, W. H. (1980, August). *Some unanswered questions in turnover and withdrawal research.* Paper presented at the 40th annual meeting of the Academy of Management, Detroit, MI.

Moch, M. K. (1980). Job involvement, internal motivation, and employees' integration into networks of work relationships. *Organizational Behavior and Human Performance, 25,* 15-31.

Mowday, R. T., Porter, L. W., & Steers, R. M. (1982). *Employee-organizational linkages: The psychology of commitment, turnover and absenteeism.* New York: Academic Press.

Murnighan, J. K., & Brass, D. J. (1991). Intraorganizational coalitions. In B. Sheppard, R. Lewicki, & M. Bazerman (Eds.), *Research on negotiations in organizations* (pp. 283-307). Greenwich, CT: JAI.

Nadel, S. F. (1957). *The theory of social structure.* London: Cohen and West.

Oldham, G. R., & Kulik, C. T. (1986a). Relations between job facet comparisons and employee reaction. *Organizational Behavior and Human Decision Processes, 38,* 28-47.

Oldham, G. R., & Kulik, C. T. (1986b). Relations between situational factors and the comparative referents used by employees. *Academy of Management Journal, 29,* 599-608.

O'Reilly, C. A., III. (1991). Organizational behavior: Where we've been, where we're going. *Annual Review of Psychology, 42,* 427-458.

Pool, I. de S., & Kochen, M. (1978). Contacts and influence. *Social Networks, 1,* 5-51.

Porter, L. W., & Lawler, E. E. (1968). *Managerial attitudes and performance.* Homewood, IL: Irwin-Dorsey.

Price, J. L. (1977). *The study of turnover.* Ames: Iowa State University Press.

Rentsch, J. R. (1990). Climate and culture: Interaction and qualitative differences in organizational meanings. *Journal of Applied Psychology, 75,* 668-681.

Rice, R. E., & Aydin, C. (1991). Attitudes toward new organizational technology: Network proximity as a mechanism for social information processing. *Administrative Science Quarterly, 9*(4), 219-244.

Roberts, K. H., & O'Reilly, C. A., III. (1979). Some correlates of communication roles in organizations. *Academy of Management Journal, 22,* 42-57.

Rogers, E. M. (1987). Progress, problems and prospects for network research: Investigating relationships in the age of electronic communication technologies. *Social Networks, 9*(4), 285.

Ronchetto, J. R., Hutt, M. D., & Reingen, P. (1989). Embedded influence patterns in organizational buying systems. *Journal of Marketing, 53,* 51-62.

Rousseau, D. M. (1985). Issues of level in organizational research: Multi-level and cross-level perspectives. In L. L. Cummings & B. M. Staw (Eds.), *Research in organizational behavior* (Vol. 1, pp. 1-37). Greenwich, CT: JAI.

Salancik, G. R., & Pfeffer, J. (1978). A social information processing approach to job attitudes and task design. *Administrative Science Quarterly, 23*, 224-253.

Shaw, M. E. (1964). Communication networks. In L. Berkowitz (Ed.), *Advances in experimental social psychology* (pp. 111-147). New York: Academic Press.

Staw, B. M. (1984). Organizational behavior: A review and reformation of the field's outcome variables. *Annual Review of Psychology, 35*, 627-666.

Steers, R. M., & Rhodes, S. R. (1978). Major influences on employee attendance: A process model. *Journal of Applied Psychology, 63*, 391-407.

Stevenson, W. B., Pearce, J. L., & Porter, L. (1985). The concept of coalition in organization theory and research. *Academy of Management Review, 10*, 256-268.

Thurman, B. (1979). In the office: Networks and coalitions. *Social Networks, 2*, 47-63.

Tichy, N. M. (1981). Networks in organizations. In W. H. Starbuck & P. C. Nystrom (Eds.), *Handbook of organizational design: Remodeling organizations and their environments* (Vol. 2, pp. 225-249). New York: Oxford University Press.

Tushman, M. L., & Romanelli, E. (1983). Uncertainty, social location and influence in decision making: A sociometric analysis. *Management Science, 29*, 12-23.

Vroom, B. H. (1964). *Work and motivation.* New York: McGraw-Hill.

Walker, G. (1985). Network position and cognition in a computer firm. *Administrative Science Quarterly, 30*, 103-130.

9

Networks of Interorganizational Relations

MARK S. MIZRUCHI
JOSEPH GALASKIEWICZ

For decades, a closed-system framework dominated organizational analysis. Although some works, such as Selznick's (1949) study of the Tennessee Valley Authority, had focused on organizational environments, it was only in the 1970s that the environment began to play a major role in organizational research. As attention shifted to the environment, researchers focused more on interorganizational relations. At the same time, network analysis was emerging from the small groups lab and being applied to real life settings. Because of its focus on the relations among social actors, network analysis was seen by many organizational researchers in the 1970s as a logical way to study relations among organizations (Aldrich & Whetten, 1981; Evan, 1978; Paulson, 1985; Van de Ven, Emmett, & Koenig, 1975). We argue that network analysis has contributed greatly to both interorganizational analysis and organizational theory in general. We focus on three approaches to the study of interorganizational relations: the resource dependence, social class, and institutional perspectives. Although we recognize the value and richness of network studies using qualitative methods (for example, Eccles & Crane,

AUTHORS' NOTE: Research for this chapter was supported by a National Science Foundation Presidential Young Investigator Award (SES-8858669 and SES-9196148) to Mizruchi and a National Science Foundation Research Grant (SES-8887258) to Galaskiewicz. Please address correspondence to Mark S. Mizruchi, Department of Sociology, University of Michigan, Ann Arbor, MI 48109-1382.

1988; Powell, 1990; Stern, 1979), we shall restrict ourselves to applications employing quantitative techniques.

Theoretical Background

The Resource Dependence Framework

Although it has roots in Selznick's work as well as in Emerson (1962), Blau (1964), and Thompson (1967; also Katz & Kahn, 1966; Levine & White, 1961; Litwak & Hylton, 1961), the resource dependence model received its first interorganizational treatment in a collection of articles edited by Zald (1970) and its most comprehensive treatment in Pfeffer and Salancik (1978). The basic principle of the resource dependence model is that organizations operate in turbulent and uncertain environments, over which they attempt to gain control. Because critical resources are often controlled by other organizations, organizations must find ways to ensure a smooth and predictable flow of resources from other organizations. One strategy is to co-opt the source of the dependence; another is to use one's ties to leverage resources from the other organization; a third is to make alter dependent on ego (Cook, 1977). Once an interorganizational strategy has been pursued, a network of relations is created that may constrain actors' subsequent behavior. Although most of the early studies employed the individual organization as the unit of analysis, later resource dependence theorists conceptualized the organization/environment interface in interorganizational network terms (Benson, 1975; Boje & Whetten, 1981; Rogers, 1974; Stern, 1979).

The Social Class Framework

Concurrently with the rise of the resource dependence framework, social class theorists were developing an alternative analysis of the corporation in American society. Influenced by the work of C. Wright Mills (1956), these theorists argued that the linkages among dominant corporate actors had social as well as economic roots. The linkages between corporations or among firms, foundations, universities, country clubs, policymaking groups, and government agencies were viewed as having more to do with ensuring the continued dominance of upper-class/capitalist interests than with helping to meet the resource needs of organizational actors.

This perspective was first articulated by Domhoff (1967) and Zeitlin (1974; see also Sonquist & Koenig, 1975; Useem, 1984). These theorists were most interested in the linkages across institutional sectors. Other class theorists were more interested in the social organization of the economy. Studies of the disproportionate power of banks (Mintz & Schwartz, 1985), the role of family holdings and interest groups (Scott, 1979, 1987), and the influence of class-based networks on corporate behavior (Ratcliff, 1980) dominated the literature in the 1980s.

The Institutional Framework

Organizations do not have free rein to pursue resources but must behave in accordance with the laws and traditions of their societies. As cultural systems become more complex and the power of the state and dominant subcultures permeates the boundaries of the organization, decision makers are forced to adapt accordingly, even if doing so runs contrary to their resource needs or the interests of the top management team.

DiMaggio and Powell's (1983) article was the first within the institutional framework to focus explicitly on interorganizational fields as networks (see also Carroll, Goldstein, & Gyenes, 1988). The network among individuals in different organizations was identified as an important element in explaining how organizations come to look alike and behave similarly. Studies taking off from DiMaggio and Powell's statement include Galaskiewicz (1985a; Galaskiewicz & Burt, 1991; Galaskiewicz & Wasserman, 1989) and Fligstein (1990).[1]

Discussion

Despite their differences, there is considerable overlap among these three perspectives. One could argue that networks between corporations and cultural, educational, and government agencies are efforts to influence the social definitions under which organizations operate, a position consistent with both the institutional and the social class models. Studies of political interest groups (Clawson & Neustadtl, 1989; Laumann & Knoke, 1987; Mizruchi, 1989), traditionally identified with the resource dependence or social class perspectives, could be viewed within the institutional framework as examples of how organizations seek to co-opt political actors who represent generalized belief systems.

Much of the social welfare literature on interorganizational relations could be classified into either the resource dependence or the institutional frameworks. In his study of employment service agencies, for example, Aldrich (1976) found that an important predictor of interorganizational resource transactions was the presence of a government mandate to interact (see also Hall, Clark, Giordano, Johnson, & Van-Roekel, 1977). Warren, Rose, and Bergunder (1974) found that an important component of interorganizational coordination was the "institutionalized thought structure" shared by administrative staff in different organizations. And Galaskiewicz and Shatin (1981) found that human service organizations were more likely to cooperate if their administrators had similar cultural and religious heritages, especially if operating in turbulent environments.

Finally, within the massive literature on interlocking directorates, work by Mintz and Schwartz (1985), Mizruchi (1982), and Roy and Bonacich (1988) borrows from both the resource dependence and the social class perspectives, as does the more recent work on corporate behavior by Ornstein (1984), Palmer, Friedland, and Singh (1986), and Mizruchi (1989, 1992). Although we try to keep the three theoretical frameworks distinct in the review that follows, in reality, much of the research in this field defies easy categorization.

Global Network Structures

Researchers have used both relational and positional methods to describe the global structure of networks. Relational techniques focus on direct ties between actors and often identify densely connected cliques of organizations using graph-theoretic techniques. A widely used algorithm developed by Alba (1973), for example, was based on the identification of "maximal complete subgraphs," or groups in which each actor is tied to every other actor (see also Mokken, 1979). Positional techniques focus on ties to third parties and identify actors that are "structurally equivalent," that is, have identical relations with other members of the group (Lorrain & White, 1971). One popular structural equivalence implementation, based on discrete distance, is blockmodeling, developed by White, Boorman, and Breiger (1976); another is a clustering approach based on continuous distances, employed by Burt (1982).

Relational Techniques for the
Study of Global Structures

The classic study by Sweezy (1953), in which the American business community was found to be organized into a series of interest groups dominated by a major family or financial institution, provided the impetus for network analyses of interlocking directorates. In one of the first of such studies, Levine (1972) employed multidimensional scaling to produce a spherical mapping of the relations among 70 large U.S. nonfinancial firms and 14 large financial institutions. Levine found that the firms were organized into a series of geographically based clusters centered on financial institutions. Sonquist and Koenig (1975) employed graph theory to analyze the interlocks among 797 large U.S. firms. Using the algorithm developed by Alba (1973), they identified 32 cliques of varying size and density, most of which were, as in Levine's study, regionally based with a bank in the center. A pioneering study by Dooley (1969) found geographically based cliques using a similar technique. Fennema and Schijf (1979) and DiDonato, Glasberg, Mintz, and Schwartz (1988) provide comprehensive reviews of this early work on interlocks.

Researchers using relational techniques have also studied organizational fields at the community level. Using smallest space analysis, Laumann and Pappi (1976) looked at the overlapping memberships among 65 organizations. They found that highly specialized organizations tended to occupy the periphery of the network, with more integrative organizations in the center. In a related study, Galaskiewicz (1979) focused on the flows of money, information, and support among 73 organizations in a midsized American community. Galaskiewicz found considerable clustering by functional areas, with coordinating organizations again in the center of the networks. In a similar study, Rogers (1974) found homogeneous clusters of agricultural, social welfare, and environmental organizations. These studies suggested that differentiation was based primarily on activity or functional area, with similar organizations at a shorter social distance from one another.

Positional Techniques for the
Study of Global Structures

Researchers have also employed positional approaches to study the global structure of networks. Breiger, Boorman, and Arabie (1975) reproduced Levine's findings, using blockmodels to identify clusters of firms. Allen (1978) factor-analyzed the interlock matrix among 250 large U.S. corporations in both 1935 and 1970. He also found a structure of geographically based groups, often led by a financial institution. He argued that, because the groups in 1970 were less discrete than those in 1935, the corporate elite structure had become more diffuse. Positional techniques have also been used at the community level. Knoke and Rogers (1979) constructed blockmodels of a network of 159 public and private agencies in 16 Iowa counties. In contrast to the research described above, they found little homogeneity within blocks and considerable diversity in the relations among blocks. However, in a principal components analysis designed to identify structurally equivalent actors, Galaskiewicz and Krohn (1984) found that clusters in two communities were composed of organizations having similar activities. They also found a distinct hierarchical ordering among positions, with organizations in the most dominant positions having reputations for being more influential in community affairs. Finally, Knoke and Wood's (1981) and Knoke's (1983) analyses of networks of money, information, and support of 32 and 70 social influence organizations, respectively, also produced homogeneous clusters based on the groups' activities.

Despite the apparent differences between relational and positional clustering techniques, they have consistently yielded similar results. In studies of interlocking directorates, both techniques have identified geographically based clusters, with banks among the most central firms. Allen (1982) compared his factor-analysis results with those based on a hierarchical cluster analysis and found striking similarities between the two. In community studies based on a variety of interorganizational relations, both techniques grouped together organizations of similar types. One reason for the convergence between the two approaches is that members of maximal complete subgraphs automatically share a certain number of ties in common (the other members of the subgroup). This increases the likelihood that they will be structurally equivalent in terms of the larger network (Mizruchi, 1984). Burt (1982) argued that relational clustering techniques could be viewed as a subset of positional techniques. Some authors dispute this claim, however (Wasserman & Faust, 1994).

Global analyses of interorganizational networks have provided detailed and provocative descriptions of the structure and differentiation within networks. They have failed to provide systematic evidence on the origins or behavioral consequences of these structures, however. We shall address these issues in the following sections.

The Emergence of Interorganizational Networks

Laumann, Galaskiewicz, and Marsden (1978) criticized the literature on interorganizational relations for ignoring the factors that lead to the creation of global networks. Several studies have taken on this challenge, however (Oliver, 1990; Schermerhorn, 1975; Van de Ven, 1976). In this section, we examine (a) the effect of organizations' positions in the economy on the formation of interfirm ties and (b) the effect of ties between individuals in different organizations on the formation of cooperative relations at the interorganizational level.

Position in the Economy and Interfirm Ties

Several studies hypothesized that firms with high levels of dependence on external financing would be more likely to have representatives of financial institutions on their boards. The findings of these studies have been equivocal, however. Analyses by Dooley (1969), Pfeffer (1972), Pfeffer and Salancik (1978), Mizruchi and Stearns (1988), and Lang and Lockhart (1990) supported this contention. But Allen (1974) failed to find support, and Pennings (1980) found mixed levels of support, depending on the measure of capital dependence.

Burt (1983) showed that one could predict interlocks at the level of the establishment by examining the structure of economic transactions at the industry level. An industry has high "structural autonomy," according to Burt, to the extent that its own concentration is high and the concentration of the industries with which it transacts business is low. Burt showed that an industry's structural autonomy is positively associated with its profitability (see Ziegler, 1984, for a similar study of Germany). He argued further that establishments in industry A will attempt to co-opt representatives of establishments in industries that exert market constraint on A's profits. Burt's findings indicate a positive association between constraint and director interlocks between firms in different industries.

Burt's findings on profitability and concentration echo those produced by industrial organization economists (Scherer, 1980) and resource dependence theorists (Pfeffer & Salancik, 1978). The unique aspect of Burt's model is the explicit attempt to conceptualize interindustry transactions as a social structure. An industry's ability to provide a resource on which other industries are dependent (that is, its centrality in interindustry transaction networks), and its own social structure (its level of concentration), are the bases for its profitability. Similarly, industries that are constrained are compelled to co-opt those upon whom they are dependent.

As noted earlier, researchers in the social class tradition have argued that interlocks are based more on social class ties than on organizational resource needs. Based on this suggestion, a novel test of the resource dependence model was proffered by Koenig, Gogel, and Sonquist (1979), Ornstein (1980), and Palmer (1983): If interlocks between firms reflect ongoing business relations, then ties that are accidentally broken (through death or retirement) should be replaced. These studies indicated, however, that the vast majority of accidentally broken ties were not replaced. This suggested to some that the resource dependence model of interlocking was inadequate.

These claims were moderated in subsequent studies, however. Ornstein (1984) and Palmer et al. (1986) refocused their attention onto the determinants of the reconstitution that did exist. Stearns and Mizruchi (1986), meanwhile, argued that the resource dependence model would not necessarily suggest that most broken ties would be reconstituted. For one thing, some firms will replace a broken tie by establishing a new interlock with a different firm in the same industry, creating what Stearns and Mizruchi call a functional, as opposed to a direct, reconstitution. Moreover, a tie may not be reconstituted when broken, but it may still, at one time, have been indicative of a dependence relation between firms. Nor does failure to reconstitute a tie guarantee that the newly established interlock will not reflect a resource dependence relation. In recent years, most researchers have emphasized the compatibility of the resource dependence and class models (see Mizruchi, 1989; Ornstein, 1984, p. 230; Palmer et al., 1986), although occasional debates still take place (see Pfeffer, 1987; Soref & Zeitlin, 1987).[2]

Networks Among Persons and Cooperative Interorganizational Relations

Granovetter (1985) argued that organizational decision makers use their social networks to overcome the uncertainty and distrust that often plague market exchanges. In this respect, social networks are a means of reducing transaction costs. This can be seen as a trade-off: Enter the marketplace and incur the costs of verifying the credibility of prospective partners and/or hammering out detailed contracts, or enter into business relations with firms and people one already knows and trusts (or who have honorable reputations) and hope that the savings in transaction costs will offset the higher price that one may pay for goods and services.

In a study of firms' relations with investment banks, Baker (1987b) showed how preexisting ties between companies and the interpersonal ties of company employees influence subsequent cooperative relations. Baker's financial officers also reported that their firms often used nonmarket ties (such as family, business and professional, and college and professional school ties) to reduce uncertainty and ensure satisfactory performance when assembling the financing for a deal. This latter finding again suggests that existing social networks influence subsequent interorganizational relations.

Much of the new work on intercorporate relations outside of North America has attempted to account for the character of global network structures. Scott (1987), for example, showed that the different forms of interfirm relations in Britain, France, and Germany can be traced to their three distinct paths of historical development: (a) the "entrepreneurial" system in Britain, in which development was generated by small, family-owned firms; (b) the "holding" system in France, characterized by a series of interest groups centered on specific family or financial interests; and (c) the "hegemonic" system in Germany, based on alliances of large banks and commercial firms, by means of shared loan consortia, stockholding, and director interlocks (see also Stokman, Ziegler, & Scott, 1985). Much of the new institutional research on interfirm structures in East Asia attempts to account for variations in network structures (see, for example, Gerlach, 1992, and Hamilton, Orru, & Biggart, 1987; see Scott, 1991, for a review of this literature).

Effects of Network Position on Organizational Behavior and Strategy

Once interorganizational networks are in place, they influence subsequent organizational behavior and strategy. We believe that the consequences of network ties remain the key issue in demonstrating the value of network analysis. Research has focused on the effects of interorganizational network structures on four outcomes: organizational power, performance, strategic decision making, and noneconomic activities such as philanthropy and political contributions.

Network Determinants of Power

Interorganizational network analyses have repeatedly demonstrated a correlation between centrality and power. Both Laumann and Pappi (1976) and Galaskiewicz (1979) found that, the more central the organization, the greater its reputation for influence in community affairs or in a functional area (see also Boje & Whetten, 1981; Knoke, 1983; Miller, 1980; Perrucci & Lewis, 1989). As Galaskiewicz (1979) noted, it was not the level of resources per se that determined an organization's power but "the set of resources that actors [could] mobilize through their existing set of social relationships" (p. 151).

The way in which network centrality is measured can influence one's substantive conclusions. Moving beyond measures based on the raw number of ties, Bonacich (1972) adapted an eigenvector measure that took into account the centrality of those with whom one was tied, and Freeman (1979) presented a measure based on actors' "betweenness." More recent modifications include those by Mizruchi, Mariolis, Schwartz, and Mintz (1986), Bonacich (1987), Stephenson and Zelen (1989), Tam (1989), and Friedkin (1991).

Mizruchi and Bunting (1981), for example, examined a network of 166 large firms in 1904 using four measures, including three variants of the Bonacich eigenvector measure. As they moved from the least to the most sophisticated of the four measures, the centrality of firms in the network shifted sharply. Mintz and Schwartz (1985) distinguished between "hubs" (units tied to many less central units) and "bridges" (units tied to a few highly central units). And Mizruchi et al. (1986) introduced the distinction between "reflected" and "derived" centrality, the quantitative analogues to hub and bridge centrality. In a study of major American railroad companies between 1886 and 1905, Bonacich and Roy (1986) examined the relations between centrality (using Bonacich's measure) and power. Using financial control over other railroads as their indicator of power, they found that centrality in the entire network was a poor predictor of power but that centrality within one's interest group (identified by a latent class analysis) was a strong predictor. This suggested that centrality will be a poor predictor of power if the network is highly fragmented, as was the system they studied. Although numerous studies have found positive associations between centrality and power, then, these findings must be interpreted with care. The effects may depend on the way centrality is measured.

Network Determinants of Organizational Performance

If interlocking is a successful method of co-optation, then ceteris paribus, heavily interlocked firms should be more profitable than less interlocked firms. Studies of the effect of interlocking on profitability have been inconclusive, however. Burt (1983) found that, once market constraint among industries was controlled, the effect of interlocking on profits was nearly zero. Pennings (1980), employing a variety of indicators of both interlocking and profitability, found similarly inconclusive results. On the other hand, using the concept of enterprise groups, or groups of firms tied together through ownership and directorate ties (Berkowitz, Carrington, Kotowitz, & Waverman, 1979), Carrington (1981) found a positive association between interlocking and profitability. And Meeusen and Cuyvers (1985) found a positive association between interlocks with banks and profitability in Belgium and the Netherlands (although they also found a negative relation between interlocks with financial holding companies and profitability).

One problem with the interlock-profits link is that heavily interlocked firms are often those that are in financial difficulty (Dooley, 1969; Meeusen & Cuyvers, 1985, p. 63; Mizruchi & Stearns, 1988; also Boeker & Goodstein, 1991, on hospitals). Mintz and Schwartz (1985) suggest that representatives of a firm's banks often take seats on a firm's board during financial crises. This suggestion was supported in interviews with bankers conducted by Richardson (1987). The possibility that interlocks can be indicative of financial distress as well as strength suggested the possibility of a curvilinear relation between interlocking and profitability. Bunting (1976) proposed an inverted U-shaped model of the interlocking-profitability relation. The results of his analysis of 167 large U.S. firms in seven different years between 1904 and 1974 provide support for the model. Richardson (1987) applied a cross-lagged panel model to data on 200 large Canadian firms to examine the simultaneous effects of interlocks on profitability and vice versa. His findings confirm those of Dooley (1969) and Mizruchi and Stearns (1988), that interlocking is a result of low or declining profits. Richardson found no support for the view that interlocking improved subsequent profitability, however. It appears that interlocking directorates have little impact upon profits among U.S. firms. Interlocks may, however, have a positive impact on profits in nations in which the division of labor among financial institutions differs from that in the United States, such as Canada, Belgium, and the Netherlands. Perhaps alternative types of interorganizational relations, such as joint ventures, equity sharing, or long-term contracts between suppliers and customers have a more consistent impact on performance, but this has yet to be demonstrated empirically.

Network Determinants of Corporate Strategies

Researchers within the resource dependence, social class, and institutional models have had a long-standing interest in organizational behavior and corporate strategy. If networks bind and constrain, as well as provide opportunities for interaction, as suggested by Granovetter (1985), then an organization's network position should influence its behavior and strategies.

Indeed, researchers have discovered several ways by which networks influence strategies. Ratcliff (1980), for example, showed that banks embedded in local networks of interlocking directorates, and whose directors were members of prominent social clubs in St. Louis, were more likely to engage in lending to corporations and less likely to engage in mortgage lending than banks that were peripheral in these networks. Palmer, Friedland, Jennings, and Powers (1987) found that firms that were owned and controlled by either family coalitions or banks were less likely to employ the multidivisional form than firms that were management controlled. In a study of the use of "greenmail," the private repurchase of company stock, Kosnik (1987) found that firms that resisted greenmail had more outside directors and more directors who represented firms with which the focal firm had transactions than did firms that paid greenmail. Studies by Cochran, Wood, and Jones (1987), Singh and Harianto (1989), and Wade, O'Reilly, and Chandratat (1990) found that the proportion of outside directors on a firm's board was positively associated with the existence of "golden parachute" policies for the firm's top executives. Davis (1991), in a study of the adoption by firms of takeover defenses (known as "poison pills"), found that firms were more likely to adopt poison pills when they shared directors with firms that had already adopted. Baysinger,

Kosnik, and Turk (1991) found a negative association between the proportion of outside board members and firms' research and development expenditures. And Goodstein and Boeker (1991) found an association between changes in corporate governance (including board structure) and changes in strategies relating to service delivery among hospitals.

Research has also shown that networks influence the ways in which organizations secure resources. Stearns and Mizruchi (1993) showed that the type of financial institution represented on a nonfinancial firm's board is associated with the type of financing the firm employs. Firms with insurance company officers on their boards, for example, were more likely to employ long-term debt, the form in which insurance companies specialize. Firms with commercial bankers on their boards were more likely to employ short-term debt.

A familiar prescription in the strategy literature is that firms diversify their portfolios to minimize dependence on any one source. In a study of the relations between 18 agencies and their United Fund in 66 cities, Pfeffer and Leong (1977) found, as predicted by the resource dependence model, that the relation between outside funds raised and allocations from the United Fund was larger for agencies that were less dependent upon the Fund and on whom the Fund was more dependent (see Provan, Beyer, & Kruytbosch, 1980). In a study of firms' use of investment banks, Baker (1990) found that firms with relatively low levels of debt and without high dependence on a single investment bank were more likely to establish relations with many investment banks. This improved their ability to manage their transactions.

Network Determinants of
Participation in Noneconomic Activity

As noted above, proponents of the social class model have suggested that interlocking directorates reflect the presence of a dominant class that exercises power in the cultural, social, and political arenas. The first attempts to assess this argument focused on individuals who sat on multiple corporate boards. Useem (1979) and Ratcliff, Gallagher, and Ratcliff (1979) found that interlocked directors were disproportionately involved in leadership positions in cultural, philanthropic, and policy-making organizations (see also Moore, 1979). Ogliastri and Davila (1987) have identified a similar pattern in Colombia. Taira and Wada (1987) provide a fascinating discussion of the career life-cycle patterns of Japanese elites. Noting that elites generally begin their careers in government positions and then move to positions in private industry, Taira and Wada suggest that this places enormous pressure on government to be subservient to business. These studies, however, focused on the role of individuals in organizations rather than on organizations per se.

Social networks can also be important in the corporate funding of nonprofit organizations. Galaskiewicz (1985a, 1985b) found that firms whose executives were enmeshed in the social networks of the Minneapolis-St. Paul philanthropic elite gave more money to charity than did more peripheral firms. Galaskiewicz and Wasserman (1989) showed that companies gave more money to specific charitable organizations if those organizations were previously funded by firms whose CEO or giving officer was socially tied to the donor's CEO or giving officer. Given the reluctance of firms to give away profits, peer pressure was an important factor in stimulating charitable contributions. In deciding to whom to contribute, it made more sense to rely on the "good word" and "good deeds" of those one knew and trusted than to try to verify the credibility of the nonprofit on one's own.

Mizruchi (1989, 1992) has shown that networks can affect firms' political behavior. Based on a model derived from the resource dependence and social class models, Mizruchi found that market constraint between firms was positively associated with the similarity of firms' political contribution patterns. In addition, firms that had indirect interlocks through banks and insurance companies (and thus were more structurally equivalent) were more likely to contribute to the same candidates than were firms that were tied to one another. One possible reason for this finding is that structurally equivalent actors are in contact with a large number of similar sources of influence. Alternatively, actors that are in similar structural positions may, as a result of competition, strive to emulate one another, as suggested by Burt (1987).

Analysts have also attempted to link network position with economic and political power. Wallace, Griffin, and Rubin (1989), borrowing from Perrone (1984), argued that the power of labor across industries was a function of workers' ability to disrupt the operation of the economy, which was viewed as a function of the industry's centrality in the network of interindustry transactions. As expected, they found that workers in central industries had higher wages than workers in peripheral industries.

Jacobs (1988) argued that the political power of business should vary as a function of its level of social organization. Employing a longitudinal design, he operationalized business power in terms of corporate tax rates, based on the assumption that powerful groups will pay lower taxes. The social organization of business was operationalized in terms of the concentration of assets among the largest 100 U.S. manufacturing firms. Consistent with his prediction, Jacobs found that corporate tax rates declined as concentration increased. Along a similar line, Mizruchi (1992, chap. 8) has shown that industries with high levels of concentration and whose largest members contribute to the same political candidates are more likely to be successful in securing the passage of relevant legislation in Congress.[3]

Discussion

Despite the extensive research showing that networks have consequences for organizational behavior, only recently have sociologists begun to examine the role that networks play in the formation and operation of markets. White (1981, 1988; Leifer & White, 1987) has suggested that producers in a market select appropriate niches based on the volume-revenue curves of the other members of one's industry. Thus a firm's relation to other producers in its industry, rather than information about demand for its product, becomes the determinant of the firm's production and price schedule. Berkowitz (1988) and Friedmann (1988) have provided important reconceptualizations of markets at the interfirm and international levels, respectively. In his recent work on "structural holes," Burt (1992) notes that strategically located firms can restrict the flow of information in markets. And Baker (1984) has shown that, on the floor of the Chicago stock exchange, the size, density, and fragmentation of various communication networks affect the volatility of prices.[4]

Other topics that would benefit from further applications of network analysis include sponsorship events, joint ventures, public-private partnerships, and other short-term cooperative efforts between organizations (Faulkner & Anderson, 1987). The literature on governmental and nonprofit organizations is replete with studies that show that network ties are crucial in overcoming interorganizational collective action problems (see Rogers & Whetten, 1982; Turk, 1977).

Conclusion

Network analysis has had a growing impact on the field of interorganizational relations, contributing to research within the resource dependence, social class, and institutional models. This approach has allowed us to understand the ways in which organizational decision making is embedded in social structures, at both the interpersonal and the interorganizational levels. Administrators and executives are enmeshed in an elaborate network of social relations both within and across organizations. Whether they are viewed as benefits or obstacles, these networks influence the choices and strategies that organizational decision makers pursue.

The network perspective has also allowed analysts to predict how organizations will behave in response to power-dependence relations. Extensive research has demonstrated that organizations will seek to co-opt the sources of external threats (Burt, 1983; Pfeffer & Salancik, 1978). The network approach has enabled us to identify and operationalize the sources of these threats. Centrality within a network of resource transactions gives actors an edge in bargaining, for example. Many, if not most, studies within the resource dependence tradition now take into account an organization's network centrality as well as its structural position.

Network analysis has also made contributions to both institutional theory and the social class model. It has informed the study of mimetic behavior among firms (DiMaggio & Powell, 1983) and has enabled researchers to specify precisely how contagion takes place—whether through direct contact among agents (Galaskiewicz & Wasserman, 1989) or through contact with the same, or similar, third parties (Galaskiewicz & Burt, 1991; Mizruchi, 1992). And it has enabled researchers to demonstrate the economic and political consequences of social relations among firms (Clawson & Neustadtl, 1989; Mizruchi, 1992; Ratcliff, 1980).

Network analysis has begun to infiltrate the population ecology model as well. This link was first suggested by Aldrich (1982) and McPherson (1983). DiMaggio (1986) argued that the population ecology concept of a "niche" can be operationalized as a group of structurally equivalent organizations. Burt (1992) has developed this idea in his recent work on market niches. And Miner, Amburgey, and Stearns (1990), in a study of Finnish newspapers over a 200-year period, have shown that network ties can affect the likelihood of survival among firms and thus influence an industry's long-run population dynamics.

The study of interorganizational relations has benefited greatly from network analysis, but much remains to be done. Although a dialogue has developed between network analysis and the transaction cost model (Aldrich, 1982; Burt, 1983, pp. 72-74; Granovetter, 1985; Powell, 1990), we have found no studies that test whether social relations across organizational boundaries effect make-or-buy decisions (such as those studied by Walker & Poppo, 1991). We would expect this effect to exist given the importance of uncertainty and the potential for opportunism in such situations. In the coming years, we envision a more careful mapping of interfirm joint ventures and equity arrangements (Powell, 1990), a more careful analysis of network position and corporate performance, more work on the use of interpersonal networks to gain access to capital and other scarce resources, and more sophisticated efforts to describe market structures.

Notes

1. Baker (1987a) has described the definition of money as the nature of transactions between sectors of the financial community and the institutions that are in positions to determine this definition. Fombrun and Shanley (1990), based on a *Fortune* survey of corporate executives, found that firms' reputations for quality and their financial conditions were associated with their conformity to socially defined norms such as charitable contributions.

2. In an important study of broken ties in the Netherlands, Stokman, Van der Knoop, and Wasseur (1988) argued that the nature of executive career patterns and the limited pool from which directors are recruited play a major role in the extent of reconstitution. Their study adds an additional dimension to resource dependence and social class models of interlocks. See Zajac (1988) for a related argument.

3. See Knoke (1993) for a thorough review of work on interorganizational influence networks and power.

4. In a survey of investors, Shiller and Pound (1989) found that decisions to purchase stock were influenced by word-of-mouth communication.

References

Alba, R. (1973). A graph theoretic definition of a sociometric clique. *Journal of Mathematical Sociology, 3*, 113-126.

Aldrich, H. E. (1976). Resource dependence and interorganizational relations: Relations between local employment service offices and social service sector organizations. *Administration and Society, 7,* 419-454.

Aldrich, H. E. (1982). The origins and persistence of social networks: A comment. In P. V. Marsden & N. Lin (Eds.), *Social structure and network analysis* (pp. 281-293). Beverly Hills, CA: Sage.

Aldrich, H. E., & Whetten, D. A. (1981). Organization sets, action sets and networks: Making the most of simplicity. In P. C. Nystrom & W. H. Starbuck (Eds.), *Handbook of organizational design* (pp. 385-408). New York: Oxford University Press.

Allen, M. P. (1974). The structure of interorganizational elite cooptation: Interlocking corporate directorates. *American Sociological Review, 39,* 393-406.

Allen, M. P. (1978). Economic interest groups and the corporate elite structure. *Social Science Quarterly, 58,* 597-615.

Allen, M. P. (1982). The identification of interlock groups in large corporate networks: Convergent validation using divergent techniques. *Social Networks, 4,* 349-366.

Baker, W. E. (1984). The social structure of a national securities market. *American Journal of Sociology, 89,* 775-811.

Baker, W. E. (1987a). What is money? A social structural interpretation. In M. S. Mizruchi & M. Schwartz (Eds.), *Intercorporate relations* (pp. 109-144). New York: Cambridge University Press.

Baker, W. E. (1987b, September). *Do corporations do business with the bankers on their boards? The consequences of investment bankers as directors.* Paper presented at the Nags Head Conference on Corporate Interlocks, Kill Devil Hills, NC.

Baker, W. E. (1990). Market networks and corporate behavior. *American Journal of Sociology, 96,* 589-625.

Baysinger, B. D., Kosnik, R. D., & Turk, T. A. (1991). Effects of board and ownership structure on corporate R&D strategy. *Academy of Management Journal, 34,* 205-214.

Benson, J. K. (1975). The interorganizational network as a political economy. *Administrative Science Quarterly, 20,* 229-249.

Berkowitz, S. D. (1988). Markets and market-areas: Some preliminary formulations. In B. Wellman & S. D. Berkowitz (Eds.), *Social structures: A network approach* (pp. 261-303). New York: Cambridge University Press.

Berkowitz, S. D., Carrington, P., Kotowitz, Y., & Waverman, L. (1979). The determination of enterprise groupings through combined ownership and directorship ties. *Social Networks, 1,* 391-413.

Blau, P. M. (1964). *Exchange and power in social life.* New York: Wiley.

Boeker, W., & Goodstein, J. (1991). Organizational performance and adaptation: Effects of environment and performance on changes in board composition. *Academy of Management Journal, 34,* 805-826.

Boje, D. M., & Whetten, D. A. (1981). Effects of organizational strategies and constraints on centrality and attributions of influence in interorganizational networks. *Administrative Science Quarterly, 26,* 378-395.

Bonacich, P. (1972). Technique for analyzing overlapping memberships. In H. Costner (Ed.), *Sociological Methodology* (pp. 176-185). San Francisco: Jossey-Bass.

Bonacich, P. (1987). Power and centrality: A family of measures. *American Journal of Sociology, 92,* 1170-1182.

Bonacich, P., & Roy, W. G. (1986). Centrality, dominance and interorganizational power in a network structure: Interlocking directorates among American railroads, 1886-1905. *Journal of Mathematical Sociology, 12*, 127-135.

Breiger, R. L., Boorman, S. A., & Arabie, P. (1975). An algorithm for clustering relational data with applications to social network analysis and comparison with multidimensional scaling. *Journal of Mathematical Psychology, 12*, 328-383.

Bunting, D. (1976). Corporate interlocking: Part III—Interlocks and return on investment. *Directors and Boards, 1*, 4-11.

Burt, R. S. (1982). *Toward a structural theory of action.* New York: Academic Press.

Burt, R. S. (1983). *Corporate profits and cooptation.* New York: Academic Press.

Burt, R. S. (1987). Social contagion and innovation: Cohesion versus structural equivalence. *American Journal of Sociology, 92*, 1287-1335.

Burt, R. S. (1992). *Structural holes: The social structure of competition.* Cambridge, MA: Harvard University Press.

Carrington, P. J. (1981). *Horizontal co-optation through corporate interlocks.* Unpublished doctoral dissertation, University of Toronto, Department of Sociology.

Carroll, G. R., Goldstein, J., & Gyenes, A. (1988). Organizations and the state: Effects of the institutional environment on agriculture cooperatives in Hungary. *Administrative Science Quarterly, 33*, 233-256.

Clawson, D., & Neustadtl, A. (1989). Interlocks, PACs, and corporate conservatism. *American Journal of Sociology, 94*, 749-773.

Cochran, P. L., Wood, R. A., & Jones, T. B. (1985). The composition of boards of directors and incidence of golden parachutes. *Academy of Management Journal, 28*, 664-671.

Cook, K. S. (1977). Exchange and power in networks of interorganizational relations. *Sociological Quarterly, 18*, 62-82.

Davis, G. F. (1991). Agents without principles? The spread of the poison pill through the intercorporate network. *Administrative Science Quarterly, 36*, 583-613.

DiDonato, D., Glasberg, D. S., Mintz, B., & Schwartz, M. (1988). Theories of corporate interlocks: A social history. *Research in the Sociology of Organizations, 6*, 135-157.

DiMaggio, P. J. (1986). Structural analysis of organizational fields: A blockmodel approach. In B. M. Staw & L. L. Cummings (Eds.), *Research in organizational behavior* (pp. 335-370). Westport, CT: JAI.

DiMaggio, P. J., & Powell, W. W. (1983). The iron cage revisited: Institutional isomorphism and collective rationality in organizational fields. *American Sociological Review, 82*, 147-160.

Domhoff, G. W. (1967). *Who rules America?* Englewood Cliffs, NJ: Prentice-Hall.

Dooley, P. C. (1969). The interlocking directorate. *American Economic Review, 59*, 314-323.

Eccles, R. G., & Crane, D. B. (1988). *Doing deals: Investment banks at work.* Boston: Harvard Business School Press.

Emerson, R. (1962). Power-dependence relations. *American Sociological Review, 27*, 31-41.

Evan, W. M. (1978). *Interorganizational relations.* Philadelphia: University of Pennsylvania Press.

Faulkner, R. R., & Anderson, A. B. (1987). Short-term projects and emergent careers: Evidence from Hollywood. *American Journal of Sociology, 92*, 879-909.

Fennema, M., & Schijf, H. (1979). Analyzing interlocking directorates: Theory and method. *Social Networks, 1*, 297-332.

Fligstein, N. (1990). *The transformation of corporate control*. Cambridge, MA: Harvard University Press.

Fombrun, C., & Shanley, M. (1990). What's in a name? Reputation building and corporate strategy. *Academy of Management Journal, 33*, 233-258.

Freeman, L. C. (1979). Centrality in social networks: Conceptual clarification. *Social Networks, 1*, 215-239.

Friedkin, N. E. (1991). Theoretical foundations for centrality measures. *American Journal of Sociology, 96*, 1478-1504.

Friedmann, H. (1988). Form and substance in the analysis of the world economy. In B. Wellman & S. D. Berkowitz (Eds.), *Social structures: A network approach* (pp. 304-325). New York: Cambridge University Press.

Galaskiewicz, J. (1979). *Exchange networks and community politics*. Beverly Hills, CA: Sage.

Galaskiewicz, J. (1985a). Professional networks and the institutionalization of the single mind set. *American Sociological Review, 50*, 639-658.

Galaskiewicz, J. (1985b). *Social organization of an urban grants economy*. Orlando, FL: Academic Press.

Galaskiewicz, J., & Burt, R. S. (1991). Interorganization contagion in corporate philanthropy. *Administrative Science Quarterly, 36*, 88-105.

Galaskiewicz, J., & Krohn, K. (1984). Positions, roles and dependencies in a community interorganization system. *Sociological Quarterly, 25*, 527-550.

Galaskiewicz, J., & Shatin, D. (1981). Leadership and networking among neighborhood human service organizations. *Administrative Science Quarterly, 26*, 434-448.

Galaskiewicz, J., & Wasserman, S. (1989). Mimetic processes within an interorganizational field: An empirical test. *Administrative Science Quarterly, 34*, 454-479.

Gerlach, M. (1992). *Alliance capitalism*. Berkeley: University of California Press.

Goodstein, J., & Boeker, W. (1991). Turbulence at the top: A new perspective on governance structure changes and strategic change. *Academy of Management Journal, 34*, 306-330.

Granovetter, M. (1985). Economic action and social structure: The problem of embeddedness. *American Journal of Sociology, 91*, 481-510.

Hall, R., Clark, J., Giordano, P., Johnson, P., & VanRoekel, M. (1977). Patterns of interorganizational relationships. *Administrative Science Quarterly, 22*, 457-474.

Hamilton, G. G., Orru, M., & Biggart, N. W. (1987). Enterprise groups in East Asia: An organizational analysis. *Shoken Kaizai, 161*, 78-106.

Jacobs, D. (1988). Corporate economic power and the state: A longitudinal assessment of two explanations. *American Journal of Sociology, 93*, 852-881.

Katz, D., & Kahn, R. L. (1966). *The social psychology of organizations*. New York: Wiley.

Knoke, D. (1983). Organization sponsorship and influence reputation of social influence associations. *Social Forces, 61*, 1065-1087.

Knoke, D. (1993). Networks of elite structure and decision making. *Sociological Methods and Research, 22*, 23-45.

Knoke, D., & Rogers, D. L. (1979). A blockmodel analysis of interorganizational networks. *Sociology and Social Research, 64*, 28-52.

Knoke, D., & Wood, J. R. (1981). *Organized for action*. New Brunswick, NJ: Rutgers University Press.

Koenig, T., Gogel, R., & Sonquist, J. (1979). Models of the significance of interlocking corporate directorates. *American Journal of Economics and Sociology, 38*, 173-186.

Kosnik, R. D. (1987). Greenmail: A study of board performance in corporate governance. *Administrative Science Quarterly, 32*, 163-185.

Lang, J. R., & Lockhart, D. E. (1990). Increased environmental uncertainty and changes in board linkage patterns. *Academy of Management Journal, 33*, 106-128.

Laumann, E. O., Galaskiewicz, J., & Marsden, P. V. (1978). Community structure as interorganizational linkages. *Annual Review of Sociology, 4*, 455-484.

Laumann, E. O., & Knoke, D. (1987). *The organizational state.* Madison: University of Wisconsin Press.

Laumann, E. O., & Pappi, F. U. (1976). *Networks of collective action.* New York: Academic Press.

Leifer, E. M., & White, H. C. (1987). A structural approach to markets. In M. S. Mizruchi & M. Schwartz (Eds.), *Intercorporate relations* (pp. 85-108). New York: Cambridge University Press.

Levine, J. H. (1972). The sphere of influence. *American Sociological Review, 37*, 14-27.

Levine, S., & White, P. (1961). Exchange as a conceptual framework for the study of interorganizational relationships. *Administrative Science Quarterly, 5*, 583-601.

Litwak, E., & Hylton, L. F. (1961). Interorganizational analysis: A hypothesis of coordinating agencies. *Administrative Science Quarterly, 6*, 395-421.

Lorrain, F., & White, H. C. (1971). Structural equivalence of individuals in social networks. *Journal of Mathematical Sociology, 1*, 49-80.

McPherson, M. (1983). An ecology of affiliation. *American Sociological Review, 48*, 519-532.

Meeusen, W., & Cuyvers, L. (1985). The interaction between interlocking directorships and the economic behaviour of companies. In F. N. Stokman, R. Ziegler, & J. Scott (Eds.), *Networks of corporate power* (pp. 45-72). Cambridge: Polity.

Miller, J. (1980). Access to interorganizational networks as a professional resource. *American Sociological Review, 45*, 479-496.

Mills, C. W. (1956). *The power elite.* New York: Oxford University Press.

Miner, A. S., Amburgey, T. L., & Stearns, T. M. (1990). Interorganizational linkages and population dynamics: Buffering and transformational shields. *Administrative Science Quarterly, 35*, 689-713.

Mintz, B., & Schwartz, M. (1985). *The power structure of American business.* Chicago: University of Chicago Press.

Mizruchi, M. S. (1982). *The American corporate network, 1904-1974.* Beverly Hills, CA: Sage.

Mizruchi, M. S. (1984). Interlock groups, cliques, or interest groups? Comment on Allen. *Social Networks, 6*, 193-199.

Mizruchi, M. S. (1989). Similarity of political behavior among large American corporations. *American Journal of Sociology, 95*, 401-424.

Mizruchi, M. S. (1992). *The structure of corporate political action.* Cambridge, MA: Harvard University Press.

Mizruchi, M. S., & Bunting, D. (1981). Influence in corporate networks: An examination of four measures. *Administrative Science Quarterly, 26*, 475-489.

Mizruchi, M. S., Mariolis, P., Schwartz, M., & Mintz, B. (1986). Techniques for disaggregating centrality scores in social networks. In N. B. Tuma (Ed.), *Sociological Methodology* (pp. 26-48). Washington: American Sociological Association.

Mizruchi, M. S., & Stearns, L. B. (1988). A longitudinal study of the formation of interlocking directorates. *Administrative Science Quarterly, 33*, 194-210.

Mokken, R. (1979). Cliques, clubs, and clans. *Quality and Quantity, 13*, 161-173.

Moore, G. (1979). The structure of a national elite network. *American Sociological Review, 44*, 673-692.

Ogliastri, E., & Davila, C. (1987). The articulation of power and business structures: A study of Colombia. In M. S. Mizruchi & M. Schwartz (Eds.), *Intercorporate relations* (pp. 233-263). New York: Cambridge University Press.

Oliver, C. (1990). Determinants of interorganizational relationships: Integration and future directions. *Academy of Management Review, 15*, 241-265.

Ornstein, M. D. (1980). Assessing the meaning of corporate interlocks: Canadian evidence. *Social Science Research, 9*, 287-306.

Ornstein, M. D. (1984). Interlocking directorates in Canada: Intercorporate or class alliance? *Administrative Science Quarterly, 29*, 210-231.

Palmer, D. (1983). Broken ties: Interlocking directorates and intercorporate coordination. *Administrative Science Quarterly, 28*, 40-55.

Palmer, D., Friedland, R., Jennings, P. D., & Powers, M. E. (1987). The economics and politics of structure: The multidivisional form and the large U.S. corporation. *Administrative Science Quarterly, 32*, 25-48.

Palmer, D., Friedland, R., & Singh, J. V. (1986). The ties that bind: Organizational and class bases of stability in a corporate interlock network. *American Sociological Review, 51*, 781-796.

Paulson, S. K. (1985). A paradigm for the analysis of interorganizational networks. *Social Networks, 7*, 105-126.

Pennings, J. M. (1980). *Interlocking directorates*. San Francisco: Jossey-Bass.

Perrone, L. (1984). Positional power, strikes, and wages. *American Sociological Review, 49*, 412-421.

Perrucci, R., & Lewis, B. L. (1989). Interorganizational relations and community influence structure: A replication and extension. *Sociological Quarterly, 30*, 205-223.

Pfeffer, J. (1972). Size and composition of corporate boards of directors: The organization and its environment. *Administrative Science Quarterly, 17*, 218-228.

Pfeffer, J. (1987). A resource dependence perspective on intercorporate relations. In M. S. Mizruchi & M. Schwartz (Eds.), *Intercorporate relations* (pp. 25-55). New York: Cambridge University Press.

Pfeffer, J., & Leong, A. (1977). Resource allocations in United Funds: Examination of power and dependence. *Social Forces, 55*, 775-790.

Pfeffer, J., & Salancik, G. R. (1978). *The external control of organizations*. New York: Harper & Row.

Powell, W. W. (1990). Neither market nor hierarchy: Network forms of organization. In L. L. Cummings & B. Staw (Eds.), *Research in organizational behavior* (pp. 295-336). Greenwich, CT: JAI.

Provan, K., Beyer, J. M., & Kruytbosch, C. (1980). Environmental linkages and power in resource-dependence relations between organizations. *Administrative Science Quarterly, 25*, 200-225.

Ratcliff, R. E. (1980). Banks and corporate lending: An analysis of the impact of the internal structure of the capitalist class on the lending behavior of banks. *American Sociological Review, 45*, 553-570.

Ratcliff, R. E., Gallagher, M. E., & Ratcliff, K. S. (1979). The civic involvement of bankers: An analysis of the influence of economic power and social prominence in the command of civic policy positions. *Social Problems, 26*, 298-313.

Richardson, R. J. (1987). Directorship interlocks and corporate profitability. *Administrative Science Quarterly, 32*, 367-386.

Rogers, D. O. (1974). Sociometric analysis of interorganizational relations: Application of theory and measurement. *Rural Sociology, 39*, 487-503.

Rogers, D. O., & Whetten, D. A. (1982). *Interorganizational coordination.* Ames: Iowa State University Press.

Roy, W. G., & Bonacich, P. (1988). Interlocking directorates and communities of interest among American railroad companies, 1905. *American Sociological Review, 53*, 368-379.

Scherer, F. M. (1980). *Industrial market structure and economic performance.* Chicago: Rand McNally.

Schermerhorn, J. R., Jr. (1975). Determinants of interorganizational cooperation. *Academy of Management Journal, 18*, 846-856.

Scott, J. (1979). *Corporations, classes, and capitalism.* London: Hutchinson.

Scott, J. (1987). Intercorporate structures in western Europe: A comparative historical analysis. In M. S. Mizruchi & M. Schwartz (Eds.), *Intercorporate relations* (pp. 208-232). New York: Cambridge University Press.

Scott, J. (1991). Networks of corporate power. *Annual Review of Sociology, 17*, 181-203.

Selznick, P. (1949). *TVA and the grass roots.* New York: Harper & Row.

Shiller, R. J., & Pound, J. (1989). Survey evidence on diffusion of interest and information among investors. *Journal of Economic Behavior and Organization, 12*, 47-66.

Singh, H., & Harianto, F. (1989). Management-board relationships, takeover risk, and the adoption of golden parachutes. *Academy of Management Journal, 32*, 7-24.

Sonquist, J. A., & Koenig, T. (1975). Interlocking directorates in the top U.S. corporations: A graph theory approach. *Insurgent Sociologist, 5*, 196-229.

Soref, M., & Zeitlin, M. (1987). Finance capital and the internal structure of the capitalist class in the United States. In M. S. Mizruchi & M. Schwartz (Eds.), *Intercorporate relations* (pp. 56-84). New York: Cambridge University Press.

Stearns, L. B., & Mizruchi, M. S. (1986). Broken-tie reconstitution and the functions of interorganizational interlocks: A re-examination. *Administrative Science Quarterly, 31*, 522-538.

Stearns, L. B., & Mizruchi, M. S. (1993). Board composition and corporate financing: The impact of financial institution representation on type of borrowing. *Academy of Management Journal, 36*, 603-618.

Stephenson, K., & Zelen, M. (1989). Rethinking centrality: Methods and examples. *Social Networks, 11*, 1-37.

Stern, R. (1979). The development of an interorganizational control network. *Administrative Science Quarterly, 24*, 242-266.

Stokman, F. N., Van der Knoop, J., & Wasseur, F. W. (1988). Interlocks in the Netherlands: Stability and careers in the period 1960-1980. *Social Networks, 10*, 183-208.

Stokman, F. N., Ziegler, R., & Scott, J. (Eds.). (1985). *Networks of corporate power.* Cambridge, MA: Polity.

Sweezy, P. M. (1953). Interest groups in the American economy. In P. M. Sweezy (Ed.), *The present as history.* New York: Monthly Review Press.

Taira, K., & Wada, T. (1987). Business-government relations in modern Japan: A Todai-Yakkai-Zaikai complex? In M. S. Mizruchi & M. Schwartz (Eds.), *Intercorporate relations* (pp. 264-297). New York: Cambridge University Press.

Network marketing entails distribution of products and services through a network of independent businesspeople, who in turn either take care of the distribution themselves or recruit others to do so. The canonical examples are Tupperware (Miller, 1991) and the pyramidal Amway structure. The formal hierarchical structure characteristic of such sales networks as Amway's is probably atypical of social networks in general, but this approach to marketing is now being promoted by lecturers in the marketing profession and adopted by a variety of firms in diverse industries. Consider, for example, the Network Marketing Store, a chain of brokerage firms allowing persons interested in sales and distribution to shop for suitable manufacturers. The founder of the "Store" optimistically hopes to open 1,000 such outlets (each with an upper limit of 2,000 members) by the year 2001 (Miller, 1991).

MCI's 1992 "Friends and Family" campaign offers discount calls to residential customers when dialing a telephone number from a list prespecified by the customer, who in turn must furnish MCI with the names and other information about the "targets" on the list. The latter are then contacted by MCI's sales force in an attempt to induce them to enroll in the discount plan. Advertising by competitors of MCI has depicted this effort as both an invasion of privacy and an imposition by one friend or family member upon another.

As the two cases illustrate, social networks can and have provided the foundation for effective marketing strategies. The challenges facing both marketing strategists and marketing scientists are, however, to move beyond the anecdotal cases to a better understanding of the potential the field of social networks can offer to such questions as these:

1. Which types of social networks can be used as a basis for marketing strategy?
2. How do we identify and measure social networks?
3. How do we mobilize and manage social networks?
4. Which marketing decisions can benefit from the social network concepts and methods?

The purpose of this chapter is to address these four questions.

A Taxonomy of Social Networks in Marketing

Social networks in marketing can be classified along a number of attributes, including the level of formalism, whether the network is centered on a marketing-related task, the behavior and nature of relationships among the members of the social networks, the degree to which the transaction is recurring, the degree to which the buyers and sellers are organized, and so on. But, in this chapter, we focus on two key aspects: (a) whether the social network is a network of consumers or a corporate network of employees and stakeholders other than consumers and (b) whether the network is under the control of the firm, as in the case of MCI, which initiated its Friends and Family Program. Figure 10.1 illustrates the resulting taxonomy of four types of social networks in marketing.

The four types of social networks have the following characteristics:

(1) Consumer networks under the control of (or initiated by) the firm. Tupperware parties and pyramid schemes have well-established marketing practices that rely heavily on the power of social networks. A more recent innovative creation of social networks for marketing purposes is MCI's Friends and Family program.

The creation of social networks for marketing purposes is not limited to consumer markets and is quite popular in industrial markets as well, especially through the creation and use of user and referral networks. The latter are an extremely important part of the industrial selling process. In addition, as firms seek to become more marketing oriented, they focus on establishing multiple relationships between members of their organization and those of client organizations.

(2) Consumer networks not under the control of the firm. In contrast to the social networks in the first group, which are created by the firm for its own marketing program, the social networks of this category exist independently of the firm's own efforts and are not under its control. Networks in this category include buying centers, the social networks created by those engaged in word-of-mouth communication as part of any diffusion of innovation process, affinity groups that have been the target of many credit card companies, direct marketing buying club efforts, and the growing number of networks of users of electronic bulletin boards.

Organizational buying behavior includes all activities of organizational members as they define a buying situation and identify, evaluate, and choose among alternative brands and suppliers. The *buying center* includes all members of the organization who are involved in that

		The Members of the Network	
		Consumers	Stakeholders Other Than Consumers
Control	Under the control of the firm	∘ MCI Friends and Family ∘ Tupperware party ∘ Pyramid schemes ∘ Referral networks ∘ User groups	∘ Cross-functional teams ∘ Quality circles
	Not under the control of the firm	∘ Buying centers ∘ Word-of-mouth communication ∘ Affinity groups ∘ Buying groups ∘ Users of electronic bulletin boards	∘ Network organization ∘ Strategic alliances (joint ventures, comarketing and copromotion arrangements, and so on) ∘ Outsourcing ∘ Integrating the voice of the customer with R&D ∘ Supplier relations ∘ Interorganizational negotiations ∘ Interlocking board membership

Figure 10.1. A Taxonomy of Social Networks in Marketing

process. The roles involved are those of user, influencer, decider, buyer, and gatekeeper (who controls the flow of information into the buying center). Its members are motivated by a complex interaction of individual and organizational goals, and their relationships with one another involve all the complexities of interpersonal interactions (Webster & Wind, 1972, p. 14).

The emphasis upon the *buying center* (a term first introduced by Robinson, Faris, & Wind, 1967) represents an advance from the days when marketing programs, sales efforts, and marketing research in this area focused almost exclusively on an individual purchasing agent or manager (see Johnston's highly useful review, 1981, p. 78).

Buying centers can be extended to families; but, despite the rich literature on family buying behavior, we know of no social network studies of family purchasing behavior (see Ferber, 1977; Wind, 1976, p. 56, 1978b, p. 75).

(3) Stakeholders' (other than consumers') networks under the control of the firm. The 1980s and 1990s began witnessing increased disenchantment with the traditional organizational structure and processes as well as increased corporate efforts to reinvent, reorganize, and rethink the corporations (see, for example, Wind, Holland, & West, 1993; Wind & West, 1991). Many of these efforts included a shift from the traditional hierarchical, bureaucratic organization to a flatter, cross-functional, and group-empowered organization. As such, empowered cross-functional teams become the building blocks of the organization. Such teams, whether formal product/market units, market units, or product units or less formal task forces, are all based on a task-oriented network having both formal and informal relationships among its members.

In fact, the organization is increasingly viewed as a network of smaller networks (teams). Although the firm has final control over its quality circle or other cross-functional teams because the firm empowers them, the control is not via traditional authority lines but through the creation of a shared vision and culture. Internal cross-disciplinary teams that are marketing driven and social networks based are becoming an important part of the organizational architecture, as firms broaden their views of marketing to include internal marketing and marketing to all stakeholders and not only to consumers (Wind et al., 1993). Also, becoming marketing oriented requires that each individual and team has both internal as well as external customers.

(4) Stakeholders' (other than consumers') networks not under the control of the firm. To help achieve short- and long-term corporate objectives and prepare to become a successful twenty-first-century enterprise, firms are increasingly reinventing themselves as *network organizations* (Perrow, 1992; Wilson & Dobrzynski, 1986; Wind & West, 1991). Companies are adopting the concept of the hollow corporation (Wilson & Dobrzynski, 1986), which suggests that, through strategic alliance and outsourcing, the firm can obtain many of the functions it requires without having to perform all of them internally, and there is increased interest in the management of the organization as well as the management of a network of organizations.

The enormous growth in strategic alliances clearly demonstrates the increased importance of managing a network of organizations. This observation encompasses all domains of business operations: from research and development (R&D) through manufacturing to marketing, promotion, and distribution and the extreme increase in outsourcing. Other forces that shift the organization toward becoming a network organization include the need to manage the relationships with key stakeholders, the focus on becoming customer driven, and the pursuit of quality. All these forces have led to the development of processes for incorporating the voice of the customer within R&D and other vital activities of the firm as well as building long-term relationships with suppliers and other key stakeholders.

The recent focus on corporate governance includes broadening the representation on boards of key constituencies and the inclusion of members with broader expertise. Thus broadening the traditional role of the board and its interlocking directors enhances it as one of the important networks that link the organization with other external bodies (see Mizruchi & Galaskiewicz, 1993).

All these forces highlight the importance of managing a network of organizations, having effective interorganizational negotiation capabilities, and the development of effective long-term interorganizational relationships with the key stakeholders of the firm.

Identifying and Measuring Social Networks

As with all segments, social networks can be either measured and identified directly through research or created through the "self-selection" process by members of the segment. Although MCI's Friends and Family Program was geared toward the latter approach, most other uses of social networks in marketing require a research effort (by either marketing research or the firm's sales force) to identify the members of a social network and measure/assess their relationships (see Wasserman & Faust, 1994, chap. 2, for a general discussion of the problems involved). Many of the advances in this area of identifying and measuring social networks in marketing have been in the context of buying center research.

Approaches to Identifying Buying Center Members

There have been three key approaches to the identification of buying center members:

(a) Using and relying on a key informant *as the representative of the buying center to identify the other members of the buying center.* In most

cases, the key informant has been a purchasing manager. In recent years, both researchers and salespeople have occasionally focused on two or more informants to allow for better calibration of the results.

(b) Using knowledge of the buying process and buying situation to determine who, conceptually, are the likely members of the buying center. Thus, in a "new task" situation involving the purchase of components for the development of a new product, the buying center would typically include key members of the R&D, operations, purchasing, and marketing departments. In a straight rebuy situation, the purchasing agent may be viewed as the only relevant member of the buying center, and so on.

(c) Exhaustive snowball sampling to define the constituency of buying centers. This laborious procedure, which has been used, for example, by Johnston and Bonoma (1981) and by Moriarty and Bateson (1982), begins with having a single individual name as many people involved in the buying process as can be recalled. Each of them is asked in turn the same question. The procedure is continued until no new names are found. Moriarty and Bateson (1982, p. 182) noted that such sampling is extremely expensive and "financially impractical for most empirical studies."

Relevant Data

Given (a) the consensus that organizational buying involves a number of individuals acting as a group and/or subgroups and (b) the availability of a number of approaches for identifying relevant members of the "buying center," the obvious next question is (c) which types of data to collect and how to analyze and portray them.

Lilien and Wong (1984) used nonsociometric data on patterns of involvement in the buying decisions for 16 product categories in the metalworking industry. The authors then used a type of profile smoothing (see Hartigan, 1975, pp. 28-34; Hubert & Baker, 1978; Wegman, 1990) to display individuals' patterns of involvement and average linkage clustering to represent the structure among the product categories.

More germane to the theme of this volume is the view expressed in Johnston's (1981) review:

> Examination of the various sociometric, and informal, interactions emerging during the industrial buying process as well as the formal organizational hierarchy directed linkages must be accomplished to give a full picture of the

organizational communications network. In addition, there appears to be a relatively low degree of consensus among the various buying center members with respect to their perceptions of the buying center structure (Spekman & Ford, 1977). . . . If the buying center networks were developed, certain matrix algebra concepts of graph theory from the social sciences (e.g., social psychology and sociology) could be used to develop dependent measures of those interrelationships. Patterns of involvement in the buying center . . . are probably affected by structural variables of the specific organization and the particular product class being purchased. Characteristics of the product, such as its newness to the particular firm, its complexity, and its overall importance in relation to other purchases made by the firm can be hypothesized to also affect the buying center's structure and function. (pp. 84-85)

White's (1961) study of management conflict and sociometric structure among 16 staff members in an industrial R&D center could still serve as a model for the collection of social network data in buying centers. White's (1961) questions included the following:

1. Could you list the two or three managers with whom you have the most dealings in the course of your work?
2. Do any of your personal friends work at [firm being studied]? Who? How regularly do you see them away from work?
3. Would you single out the one or two people in [firm being studied] whose ideas about business policy and procedure are most similar and congenial to yours?
4. Who do you guess might single you out as one of those with similar ideas about business policy and procedure?
5. Who is the individual in [firm being studied] whom you most respect for great knowledge? For ability to deal effectively with people?
6. With what persons in [firm being studied] do you find it most uncomfortable to associate?—not that you dislike them, just that you find it awkward to deal with them.
7. Who might think you were one of the people it was most uncomfortable to associate with? (p. 192)

Although more tailored to practices in a buying center, the questions asked by Silk and Kalwani (1982) would seem to yield somewhat different information:

1. If you had to make a change in . . . brands because of problems which were occurring with your usual brand, how likely would each of the following individuals be to suggest the need for a change?

2. How much influence would you expect each of the following individuals to have in evaluating alternative brands?
3. How much influence would you expect each of the following individuals to have in making the final decision as to what brand to change to? (p. 172)

The more recent of these two papers follows Holland and Leinhardt's (1973) injunction against limiting the number of responses/choices allowed respondents and those authors' recommendation that a roster of all members of the group be provided each respondent. On the other hand, White's (1961) study sought to elicit information on *anticipated* responses directed toward the respondent and also included negative types of ties, a practice that the social networks research community has reluctantly recognized as very important (see Arabie, Boorman, & Levitt, 1978; Marsden, 1990, p. 442).

For investigators seeking to compile a set of sociometric questions appropriate to any particular buying center, Wind and Thomas (1980, p. 254) suggested four types of relations to measure: interpersonal influence, personal assignment, authority, and task specialization. A set of sociometric questions emphasizing influence in a buying center was given by Ronchetto, Hutt, and Reingen (1989, p. 56). Also, Marsden and Friedkin (1993) provided an incisive review of network studies of social influence.

Longitudinal Data

A firmly established tenet of organizational buying is that there are three types of situations: new buy, modified rebuy, and straight rebuy (Robinson et al., 1967). Differential familiarity with the products being purchased is a critical determinant of which situation pertains. We would expect sociometric structure and relationships to vary as a function of these three scenarios.

Somewhat more ambiguous is the number and specific sequence of stages in the buying process. For example, Robinson et al. (1967, p. 14) proposed eight stages for industrial buying, but Choffray and Lilien (1980, p. 334) had only five. Depending on how one interprets some of the proposed stages, at most four were common to both lists. As Johnston (1981) summarized the situation: the "specification of a limited number of phases through which all organizations pass in a chronological sequence begins to become suspect when the number of different research studies specifying different stages are examined" (p. 77). Data to support a widely accepted set of stages are lacking, and if the data were available, the problem would be one of *seriation*, which is not a network problem. See Carroll and Arabie (1980, p. 617), Hubert and Arabie (1988), and Arabie and Hubert (1992, pp. 171-172) for technical details. There does seem to be agreement, however, that the composition and functioning of a buying center change depending on the buying situation and as progress is made toward making a purchase. This consideration implies the need for *longitudinal* sampling of sociometric data (see Galaskiewicz & Wasserman, 1981, and Wasserman, 1980, for a careful discussion of the technical issues involved). The agenda is summarized by Nicosia and Wind (1977): We must focus "on the *process* of organizational decisions by people leading to and following the act of purchasing. This calls for the *description* of a buying process over time in great detail: the interactions of people and activities, i.e., who does what, when, and where" (pp. 103-104, emphasis in original).

There is a particularly useful form of longitudinal data that we expect would be available only to in-house researchers at a firm: concurrence data over final purchase decisions. Specifically, one would have an $N \times N$ symmetric matrix C (where N is the number of participants in the buying center, as determined, for example, by exhaustive snowball sampling), where c_{ij} indicates the proportion of times that participants voted for the same outcome in a purchase decision, and $c_{ii} \equiv 1$. Although such data are not, strictly speaking, sociometric, they have proven useful for clustering analyses of coalitions of U.S. Supreme Court justices (Carroll & Arabie, 1983) and multidimensional scaling analyses of the U.S. Senate (Easterling, 1987). Appendix 2 of the latter paper, in particular, shows some of the interesting mathematical properties of such data.

Relevance of Two-Mode Sociometric Data

The discussion thus far has assumed that any sociometric data collected on a buying center would be "one mode." That is, any given two-way sociomatrix would have the same number (N) of rows and columns, with the former depicting choices *sent* and the latter choices *received*, so that the rows and columns correspond to the same set of individuals in the buying center. Such a matrix is said to be *one mode* (Tucker, 1964) because one set of entities corresponds to both of the two *ways* (namely, rows and columns) of the matrix. The focus of analyses using one-mode data is implicitly *intra*organizational. See Wasserman and Faust (1994, chaps. 2-3) for further discussion.

The preoccupation with one-mode, intraorganizational designs for buying center research ignores one of the basic missions of such organizations: to conduct buyer-seller interactions and exchanges (Wind & Thomas, 1980). Wind and Robertson (1982) complained that "interorganizational dynamics (between buying center members and outside organizations) have been ignored in buying center research" (p. 169). A single sociomatrix relevant to the study of interorganizational behavior will have rows corresponding to members of one organization and columns for a different one, so that such data are said to be "*two mode*" and "*two way*." Methodologically, the transition from one- to two-mode data entails considerable changes in traditional analyses developed for intraorganizational data (Breiger, 1974; Doreian, 1979-1980, 1986; Iacobucci & Wasserman, 1990; Wasserman & Faust, 1994, chaps. 8, 15). Hopkins, Henderson, and Iacobucci (in press) illustrate many of the relevant issues, using three sets of data describing interpersonal interactions between buyers and sellers, corporate-industry involvements, and the marketing ties among the major international automobile manufacturers.

Substantively, the shift to two-mode designs confers the benefit of access to a much greater literature, much of it emanating from organizational behavior (e.g., Aldrich & Whetten, 1981; Pfeffer & Salancik, 1978; see Laumann, Galaskiewicz, & Marsden, 1978, and Mizruchi & Galaskiewicz, 1993, for reviews). But the real challenge is to address the research agenda called for by Nicosia and Wind (1977):

> It is increasingly common for a selling organization to be concerned not only with the needs and problems of its immediate customers, but also with the needs and problems of the customers of its immediate customers, including distributors, agents, and brokers. Similarly, the need to assure supplies (quantity, quality, delivery, etc.) leads buyers to worry not only about their own immediate suppliers. In formulating, implementing, and evaluating plans, the managerial horizon extends beyond the single transaction—the result of interactions among only two firms—to include and assess interdependencies among several organizational decision processes. (p. 117)

A demonstration that some of the phenomenology from the organizational behavior literature can be profitably applied to the study of buying centers is given by Wind and Robertson (1982), who demonstrated the importance of the "linking pin" role in buying and selling organizations (although those authors did not use network data). This role is often assumed by purchasing agents, labor negotiators, lobbyists, and other persons involved in interorganizational linkages.

The procedures followed in most *intra*organizational studies may be less useful for *inter*organizational studies of buying and selling centers. Mattsson (1985, p. 265) has listed the types of relations he considers important to interorganizational linkages: technical, time based, knowledge based, social, economic, and legal. These considerations should be noted when formulating questions for a network study of buyer-seller organizations.

Managing Social Networks

The management of social networks in marketing depends on the type of social networks involved. Figure 10.2 highlights some of the major management challenges for each of the four types of social networks in marketing.

In managing consumer networks under the firm's control (or those initiated by the firm) such as MCI's "Friends and Family" or Tupperware parties, the key management tasks are as follows:

developing and implementing a communication program to mobilize the members,
creating an organizational architecture for facilitating the relationship (Figure 10.3 illustrates the key components of an organization's architecture), and
managing the relationships.

Note that, because the social network is "self-created" by the consumers, there is no need for detailed identification of the members of the network. It is helpful, however, if the network is created with a target market segment in mind. Similarly, in the network involving Tupperware parties, pyramid schemes, or referral and user networks, it is very beneficial to focus the effort on an attractive target segment.

In managing consumer networks not under the firm's control, such as "buying centers," the major management tasks are as follows:

identifying the members and their roles in the buying center,
creating a "selling center" to negotiate and manage the relationship with the buying center,

	Consumer Networks		Internal Networks and Networks with Stakeholders Other Than Consumers	
	Under Firm's Control	Not Under Firm's Control	Under Firm's Control	Not Under Firm's Control
Example:	"MCI Friends and Family"	"Buying Center"	Cross-Functional Teams	Strategic Alliances
Key Management *Tasks*:				
a. Identify the members and their roles		x	x	x
b. Mobilize the members	x			
c. Create the contact points and persons		x		x
d. Manage the relationship	x	x		x
e. Create an organizational architecture that will facilitate managing the relationships	x	x	x	x

Figure 10.2. Management Approaches to the Various Types of Social Networks in Marketing

developing an organizational architecture to facilitate managing the relationship with the buying center, and

managing the relationship with the buying center.

Similar decisions have to be made in managing the other social networks of this type, such as affinity groups and buying groups.

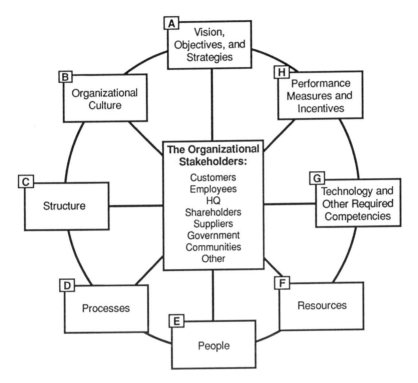

Figure 10.3. The Organizational Architecture

In managing the networks of stakeholders other than consumers under the firm's control such as empowered cross-functional teams, the major management tasks are as follows:

identifying the relevant members of the team and
creating an organizational architecture that will assure the achievement of the team's and organizational vision, objectives, and strategy.

In managing networks of stakeholders other than consumers, which are not under the firm's control, such as strategic alliances, management has to undertake all the management tasks listed in Figure 10.2. Critical in this respect is trying to mold the firm's relationship with the members of the network along the objectives of the firm. This task is not a trivial one and is a major challenge facing companies who aspire to manage an effective network organization.

Marketing Decisions and Social Network
Concepts and Methods

As the previous discussion suggests, social networks can form the basis for a marketing communication and sales strategy. Clear examples of strategies focusing on building a network organization include MCI's "Friends and Family" and attempts to manage effectively the relations with buying centers and suppliers.

In addition to these areas, social network concepts and methods can also be of value to a number of key marketing decision areas. Consider, for example, the following:

Diffusion and adoption of new products (Rogers, 1983; see Mahajan, Muller, & Bass, 1990, for a review) *either to consumers* (see chapters in Mahajan & Wind, 1986) *or among industries* (Martilla, 1971). These "products" can, of course, be services (Reingen & Kernan, 1986). In our opinion, the techniques on which this volume focuses have not been especially successful in studying diffusion processes, probably because suitable data would be very difficult to acquire. Iacobucci and Hopkins (1992), however, have argued that the extant methodology of social networks could be used to identify "market mavens" or "opinion leaders" in the diffusion process. Also, advances (tailored toward marketing) in existing techniques may allow profitable applications to communication networks in marketing (see Cho & DeSarbo, 1991).

Market segmentation (see Wind, 1978a). This is a process of dividing a heterogenous market into a number of homogeneous groups (segments) of consumers and designing products and promotions specifically aimed at each segment. Social networks can be viewed as relevant segments. For example, Reingen, Foster, Brown, and Seidman (1984) found that stronger social ties within a sorority led to greater agreement on brand selections for a variety of consumer goods.

Similarly, Ward and Reingen (1990) sought to show that coherent social groups' shared beliefs led to consistent consumer choices. Also, Rentsch (1990) showed that, within a firm, members who interacted more frequently tended to have similar interpretations of events within the firm.

Introducing a marketing perspective to other business functions. This aspect of the organizational architecture is important to firms adapting to the new management paradigm for successful twenty-first-century enterprises (Wind et al., 1993). It is consistent with the study of the symbiotic relationships between marketing and other functions within the firm (Wind, 1981). Ruekert and Walker (1987) considered a social network approach to the study of interfunctional interactions:

> Conceptually, a network approach seems most appropriate because the relations between the members of two departments may well be influenced by *each* of their relations with representatives of a third department. For example, the level of conflict between a market research project director and an R&D project director is likely to be affected by their individual negotiations with the finance department in attempting to secure shares of available research funds. (p. 4)

But, noting the two major impediments to marketing applications of social network methodology, Ruekert and Walker (1987) concluded:

> However, two practical limitations to the network approach caused us to reject it. First, little theory and even less empirical research is available to provide a sound theoretical foundation for a network approach to interfunctional relationships. Second the complexity of the data collection procedures required for a network analysis constrains the number of . . . variables that can be examined empirically. (p. 4)

While we regard the second problem as the more serious of the two, there can be no denying that these two drawbacks have greatly limited the application of social network analysis to marketing problems.

Relationship marketing. One of the fundamental shifts in current marketing thought is from transactions to relationships. The shift has been one of the key driving forces behind many of the changes in sales training, sales approaches, and marketing strategies and programs.

Understanding the interconnected relations within and among organizations is a key to our ability to design and implement effective relationship marketing programs. This understanding can be anecdotal or ideally can use network models. These models are analytical techniques that explicitly use the relational linkages between actors in a network (i.e., buyer-seller) as the unit of analysis to examine the structure of relationships (Wasserman & Faust, 1994).

Conclusions

Social networks and their patterns of relationships are a fundamental fact of market behavior and can and have been used effectively as a basis for marketing strategies. A major challenge facing marketing strategists is how to increase the effectiveness of social networks-based marketing strategies. This goal requires, however, that marketing researchers and scientists start collecting network-related data and analyze them using social network analyses.

As the chapters (and their references) in this volume demonstrate, the methodology is currently available for making major advances in the study of social networks, but it has not been widely used in marketing, primarily because of the scarcity and difficulty in obtaining the requisite data. We expect, however, that, as management recognizes the power of social networks-based marketing strategies, management will start demanding the collection of social network data focusing on the inter-dependencies among actors (such as buyers and sellers) in all marketing research and as part of the ongoing data the firm collects.

The challenge facing marketing scientists and social network researchers is the simplification of the required data collection task, the creative application of social network models to marketing problems, and the development of graphic ways of portraying the results. The challenge facing marketing strategists is the creative design and management of innovative, effective, social networks-based marketing and business strategies.

References

Aldrich, H., & Whetten, D. A. (1981). Organization sets, action sets, and networks: Making the most of simplicity. In P. C. Nystrom & W. H. Starbuck (Eds.), *Handbook of organizational design* (Vol. 1, pp. 385-408). New York: Oxford University Press.

Arabie, P., Boorman, S. A., & Levitt, P. R. (1978). Constructing blockmodels: How and why. *Journal of Mathematical Psychology, 17,* 21-63.

Arabie, P., & Hubert, L. (1992). Combinatorial data analysis. *Annual Review of Psychology, 43,* 169-203.

Breiger, R. L. (1974). The duality of persons and groups. *Social Forces, 53,* 181-190.

Carroll, J. D., & Arabie, P. (1980). Multidimensional scaling. *Annual Review of Psychology, 31,* 607-649.

Carroll, J. D., & Arabie, P. (1983). INDCLUS: An individual differences generalization of the ADCLUS model and the MAPCLUS algorithm. *Psychometrika, 48,* 157-169.

Cho, J., & DeSarbo, W. S. (1991). A new stochastic path-length tree methodology for constructing communication networks. *Social Networks, 13*, 105-140.

Choffray, J., & Lilien, G. L. (1980). Industrial market segmentation by the structure of the purchasing process. *Industrial Marketing Management, 9*, 331-342.

Doreian, P. (1979-1980). On the evolution of group and network structure. *Social Networks, 2*, 235-252.

Doreian, P. (1986). On the evolution of group and network structure II: Structures within structure. *Social Networks, 8*, 33-64.

Easterling, D. V. (1987). Political science: Using the generalized Euclidean model to study ideological shifts in the U.S. Senate. In F. Young & R. M. Hamer (Eds.), *Multidimensional scaling: History, theory, and applications* (pp. 219-256). Hillsdale, NJ: Lawrence Erlbaum.

Ferber, R. (1977). Applications of behavioral theories to the study of family marketing behavior. In F. M. Nicosia & Y. Wind (Eds.), *Behavioral models for market analysis: Foundations for marketing action* (pp. 80-95). Hinsdale, IL: Dryden.

Galaskiewicz, J., & Wasserman, S. (1981). A dynamic study of change in a regional corporate network. *American Sociological Review, 46*, 475-484.

Hartigan, J. A. (1975). *Clustering algorithms.* New York: Wiley.

Holland, P. W., & Leinhardt, S. (1973). The structural implications of measurement error in sociometry. *Journal of Mathematical Sociology, 3*, 85-111.

Hopkins, N., Henderson, G., & Iacobucci, D. (in press). Actor equivalence in networks: The business ties that bind. *Journal of Business to Business Marketing.*

Hubert, L. J., & Arabie, P. (1988). Relying on necessary conditions for optimization: Unidimensional scaling and some extensions. In H. Bock (Ed.), *Classification and related methods of data analysis* (pp. 463-472). Amsterdam: North-Holland.

Hubert, L. J., & Baker, F. B. (1978). Applications of combinatorial programming to data analysis: The traveling salesman and related problems. *Psychometrika, 43*, 81-91.

Iacobucci, D., & Hopkins, N. (1992). Modeling dyadic interactions and networks in marketing. *Journal of Marketing Research, 29*, 5-17.

Iacobucci, D., & Wasserman, S. (1990). Social networks with two sets of actors. *Psychometrika, 55*, 707-720.

Johnston, W. J. (1981). Industrial buying behavior: A state of the art review. In B. M. Enis & K. J. Roering (Eds.), *Review of marketing 1981* (pp. 75-88). Chicago: American Marketing Association.

Johnston, W. J., & Bonoma, T. V. (1981). The buying center: Structure and interaction patterns. *Journal of Marketing, 45*, 143-156.

Kotler, P. (1991). Philip Kotler explores the new marketing paradigm. *Marketing Science Institute Review, 1*, 4-5.

Laumann, E. O., Galaskiewicz, J., & Marsden, P. V. (1978). Community structure as interorganizational linkages. *Annual Review of Sociology, 4*, 455-484.

Lilien, G. L., & Wong, M. A. (1984). An exploratory investigation of the structure of the buying center in the metalworking industry. *Journal of Marketing Research, 21*, 1-11.

Mahajan, V., Muller, E., & Bass, F. M. (1990). New product diffusion models in marketing: A review and directions for research. *Journal of Marketing, 54*, 1-26.

Mahajan, V., & Wind, Y. (Eds.). (1986). *Innovation diffusion models of new product acceptance.* Cambridge, MA: Ballinger.

Marsden, P. V. (1990). Network data and measurement. *Annual Review of Sociology, 16*, 435-463.

Marsden, P. V., & Friedkin, N. E. (1993). Network studies of social influence. *Sociological Methods & Research, 22,* 127-151.

Martilla, J. A. (1971). Word of mouth communication in the industrial adoption process. *Journal of Marketing Research, 8,* 173-178.

Mattsson, L. (1985). An application of a network approach to marketing: Defending and changing market applications. In N. Dholakia & J. Arndt (Eds.), *Changing the course of marketing: Alternative paradigms for widening marketing theory* (Suppl. 2, pp. 263-288). Greenwich, CT: JAI.

Miller, C. (1991, August 19). Network marketers can shop for distributors at new store. *Marketing News, 25,* 25.

Mizruchi, M. S., & Galaskiewicz, J. (1993). Networks of interorganizational relations. *Sociological Methods & Research, 22,* 46-70.

Moriarty, R. T., & Bateson, J. E. G. (1982). Exploring complex decision units: A new approach. *Journal of Marketing Research, 19,* 182-191.

Nicosia, F. M., & Wind, Y. (1977). Behavioral models of organizational buying processes. In F. M. Nicosia & Y. Wind (Eds.), *Behavioral models for market analysis: Foundations for marketing action* (pp. 96-120). Hinsdale, IL: Dryden.

Perrow, C. (1992). Small network firms. In N. Nohria & R. G. Eccles (Eds.), *Networks and organizations: Structure, form, and action* (pp. 445-470). Boston: Harvard Business School Press.

Pfeffer, J., & Salancik, G. R. (1978). *The external control of organizations: A resource dependence perspective.* New York: Harper & Row.

Reingen, P. H., Foster, B. L., Brown, J. J., & Seidman, S. B. (1984). Brand congruence in interpersonal relations: A social network analysis. *Journal of Consumer Research, 11,* 771-783.

Reingen, P. H., & Kernan, J. B. (1986). Analysis of referral networks in marketing: Methods and illustration. *Journal of Marketing Research, 23,* 370-378.

Rentsch, J. R. (1990). Climate and culture: Interaction and qualitative differences in organizational meanings. *Journal of Applied Psychology, 75,* 668-681.

Robinson, P. J., Faris, C. W., & Wind, Y. (1967). *Industrial buying and creative marketing.* Boston: Allyn & Bacon.

Rogers, E. M. (1983). New product adoption and diffusion. *Journal of Consumer Research, 2,* 290-301.

Ronchetto, J. R., Hutt, M. D., & Reingen, P. H. (1989). Embedded influence patterns in organizational buying systems. *Journal of Marketing, 53,* 51-62.

Ruekert, R. W., & Walker, O. C. (1987). Marketing's interaction with other functional units: A conceptual framework and empirical evidence. *Journal of Marketing, 51,* 1-19.

Silk, A. J., & Kalwani, M. U. (1982). Measuring influence in organizational purchase decisions. *Journal of Marketing Research, 19,* 165-181.

Spekman, R. E., & Ford, G. T. (1977). Perceptions of uncertainty within a buying center. *Industrial Marketing Management, 6,* 395-403.

Tucker, L. R. (1964). The extension of factor analysis to three-dimensional matrices. In N. Frederiksen & H. Gulliksen (Eds.), *Contributions to mathematical psychology* (pp. 109-127). New York: Holt, Rinehart & Winston.

Ward, J. C., & Reingen, P. H. (1990). Sociocognitive analysis of group decision making among consumers. *Journal of Consumer Research, 17,* 245-262.

Wasserman, S. (1980). Analyzing social networks as stochastic processes. *Journal of the American Statistical Association, 75*, 280-294.

Wasserman, S., & Faust, K. (1994). *Social network analysis: Methods and applications.* New York: Cambridge University Press.

Wasserman, S. S., & Galaskiewicz, J. (Guest Eds.). (1993). Advances in sociology from social network analysis [Special issue]. *Sociological Methods & Research, 22*, 1-151.

Webster, F. E., Jr., & Wind, Y. (1972). A general model for understanding organizational buying behavior. *Journal of Marketing, 36*, 12-19.

Wegman, E. J. (1990). Hyperdimensional data analysis using parallel coordinates. *Journal of the American Statistical Association, 85*, 664-675.

White, H. C. (1961). Management conflict and sociometric structure. *American Journal of Sociology, 67*, 185-199.

Wilson, J. W., & Dobrzynski, J. H. (1986, March 3). And now, the post-industrial corporation. *Business Week, 2935*, 64-66, 71.

Wind, Y. (1976). Preference of relevant others and individual choice models. *Journal of Consumer Research, 3*, 50-57.

Wind, Y. (1978a). Issues and advances in segmentation research. *Journal of Marketing Research, 15*, 317-337.

Wind, Y. (1978b). Organizational buying center: A research agenda. In T. V. Bonoma & G. Zaltman (Eds.), *Organizational buying behavior* (pp. 67-76). Chicago: American Marketing Association.

Wind, Y. (1981). Marketing and other business functions. In J. N. Sheth (Ed.), *Research in marketing* (Vol. 5, pp. 237-264). Greenwich, CT: JAI.

Wind, Y., Holland, R., & West, A. P., Jr., with Gunther, R. (1993, June). *Pace-setting 21st century enterprises: A glimpse of what might emerge* (Working paper). Philadelphia: University of Pennsylvania, Wharton School, SEI Center.

Wind, Y., & Robertson, T. S. (1982). The linking pin role in organizational buying centers. *Journal of Business Research, 10*, 169-184.

Wind, Y., & Thomas, R. J. (1980). Conceptual and methodological issues in organizational buying behavior. *European Journal of Marketing, 14*, 239-263.

Wind, Y., & West, A. P., Jr. (1991). Reinventing the corporation. *Chief Executive, 71*, 72-75.

11

Networks of Elite Structure and Decision Making

DAVID KNOKE

Over the past two decades, research on power structures at the community and national levels increasingly benefited by incorporating principles, concepts, and methodologies from the social network perspective. Debate among pluralist, Marxist, elitist, corporatist, and state-centric theorists about state structures and processes fundamentally revolves around the existence of a cohesive ruling class, which effectively dominates all the major decisions made by government officials. Each theoretical perspective conjectures about various mechanisms for creating collaborative and oppositional collective actions among state managers, political parties, corporate organizations, interest groups, social movements, mass publics, class segments, and other social formations. Researchers applying network methods produced new insights into political cleavages and coalition formation. Combining reputational, positional, and decision-making measures, these analysts dissected the personal, organizational, and interorganizational communication and resource exchanges resulting in collective actions aimed at influencing the outcomes of political controversies.

I critically review recent research on local and national power by political scientists and sociologists that applied network techniques to the research design, data collection, and analysis of elite structures and decision making. I emphasize how network methods have refocused the

AUTHOR'S NOTE: My thanks to Joseph Galaskiewicz and two anonymous reviewers for suggestions that improved an earlier manuscript.

substantive issues within this field, raised provocative theoretical questions, and addressed important empirical relationships. For fuller, but more substantively oriented treatments of these topics, see Knoke (1990, 1993).

Specifying Network Contents

Power relationships are asymmetrical actual or potential interactions among social actors that enable one actor to exert greater control over another's behavior. Power conceptualized as a property of interactions among two or more actors (e.g., persons, organizations, classes) is inherently relational, and thus amenable to analysis in network terms. Two fundamental dimensions of power can be exercised via exchange relationships that connect political actors in a system: influence and domination (Knoke, 1990, pp. 11-16).

Influence occurs when one actor provides information to another with the intention of altering the latter's actions (see Gamson, 1968, p. 60). Influence is persuasive information used to change an actor's perception of the connection between an action and its consequences. Influence is a relational dimension of power, because a two-way communication channel must exist between influencer and influencee. Exchanges of information produce differential capacities among elite members to shape the collective policies of a system. Actors who are well connected to other informed actors gain power through their positional ability to tap into larger stores of useful political information. Actors on the periphery of information networks, whose direct and indirect ties link them mainly to other marginal actors, will encounter inadequate quantities and qualities of information. They are in uninformed, hence uninfluential, locations.

In most elite network studies, relational data have usually been collected about structural ties that offer elites direct or short indirect communication opportunities. For example, Floyd Hunter's (1953) innovative effort to trace connections among Atlanta's top leaders mapped their joint memberships in civic committees, corporate boards, and social clubs. Laumann and Pappi (1976), using Parson's four-subsystem paradigm (AGIL: adaptive, goal attainment, integrative, latent pattern maintenance), operationalized the relations among elites in a small German city as three distinct network ties: community affairs discussion, business-professional contacts, and informal social relations. The

American Leadership Study (Moore, 1979), and comparable studies in Australia (Higley & Moore, 1981) and West Germany (Higley, Hoffmann-Lange, Kadushin, & Moore, 1991), asked elite respondents to name other persons with whom they had discussed one national issue of greatest importance to them during the past year. Others have examined overlapping leadership positions among business, government, civic, and cultural organizations as evidence for the existence of a "ruling elite" (Perrucci & Pilisuk, 1970), "ruling class" (Domhoff, 1983; Dye, 1986), or "inner circle" (Useem, 1983). While indicating the presence of latent channels for passing messages or coordinating common political strategies, the mere existence of discussion linkages or interpenetrated boundaries cannot substantiate that overt efforts to influence policy are occurring among actors. Useem (1980) recognized the limits to such interpretations: "Scattered evidence suggests that they can significantly influence institutional policies under certain, specific circumstances . . . but direct verification of the impact of the business elite in these specific areas of outside governance is still needed" (p. 223).

Domination, the second basic type of power relationship, occurs when one actor controls the behavior of another actor by offering or withholding some benefit or harm. In other words, one actor promises, or actually delivers, a *sanction* (reward or punishment) to another actor to gain the latter's compliance with the first's commands. Sanctions may be physical events but may also involve primarily intangible symbols. Domination is clearly an exchange relationship because it involves one actor giving some type of valued (or abhorred) resource to another in return for compliance or obedience. One person or organization dominates others in the network when it becomes a source of scarce resources that are unavailable from alternative suppliers. Imperatively coordinated organizations (bureaucracies) and informal systems of political exchange (patron-client networks) are two familiar political domination structures based primarily on resource exchanges among actors.

Elite network studies of domination structures and processes are much less common than analyses of influence relations. Using secondary data sources ranging from corporate reports to social club rosters, G. William Domhoff (1983) extensively documented the linkages among institutions, organizations, and persons that he believed play a "dominant role in the economy and government" (p. 1), by which he meant not total control but the "ability to set the terms under which other groups and classes must operate" (p. 2). A power elite is established at the intersection of three social formations: a class-conscious upper social class of wealth holders, interlocked directors of major corporations, and a policy-planning network of foundations, research institutes, and nonpartisan organizations that discuss social problems and propose policy solutions. These structural connections form the prerequisites for policy consensus and concerted action by the power elite (Domhoff & Dye, 1987). Likewise, Dye's systematic mappings of positional connections among 400 national organizations spanning a dozen institutional sectors uncovered a core leadership that was heavily overrepresented by upper social class origins (Dye, 1986). Useem (1982) invoked a classwide rationality principle in which elite membership is "primarily determined by position in a set of interrelated networks transecting virtually all large corporations" (p. 202). The fusion of friendship, asset ownership, social club and trade association membership, and interlocking directors generates a dominant segment or inner circle. Because its members simultaneously hold multiple directorships, the core can act politically in the interests of the class, which transcend the parochial concerns of its individual firms. The inner circle "possesses both the cohesion and broader concerns necessary for it to serve as a vehicle for promotion of the interests of business in general" (Useem, 1982, p. 212).

A series of elite analyses guided by network principles underscored the importance of treating influence and domination processes separately. Laumann and Pappi (1976, pp. 193-197) included imputed control over land, jobs, and capital among their operationalizations of community elite resources, but they did not analyze these resources as interelite exchanges. However, the two American community organization studies (Laumann, Marsden, & Galaskiewicz, 1977) constructed three distinct exchange networks, two dealing with influence relations (community affairs discussion and social support) and one that can be interpreted as a domination network (money exchanges). Galaskiewicz (1979) found that the money exchange network was much sparser in both communities than were the communication and social support ties, as did Knoke and Wood (1981, pp. 156-183). Laumann, Knoke, and Kim (1985) treated communication and resource exchanges as separate networks in their U.S. energy and health analyses, finding almost no covariation once organizational interests were taken into account. However, Knoke, Pappi, Broadbent, Kaufman, and Tsujinaka (1991) revealed moderately positive covariations in organizations' centrality in the communication and resource exchange networks within U.S., German, and Japanese labor policy domains. These findings underscore the importance of treating influence and domination as conceptually and empirically separate power relations. The patterns, meanings, and significance of both types of ties vary so greatly among elites that their conflation into a single power network would obscure the distinctive contributions that each makes to system differentiation and structural integration. Rather, researchers must investigate how the influence and domination networks each mutually shape and constrain one another.

Delineating System Boundaries

Before any data collection can begin, a researcher must specify, analytically, which objects are included in the political networks of interest. To designate a system's boundaries, researchers may alternatively focus their attention on the actors, their relations, or the critical policy events as the primary elements delineating a network. Applied to elite research, system boundary specification requires analysts to decide whether they are primarily interested in attributes of elite actors (whether these are persons or organizations), in the political relationships that connect the actors to one another, in these actors' involvements in policymaking activities or events, or in some combination of these elements (Laumann, Marsden, & Prensky, 1983; Pappi, 1984). For example, in launching the classic debate over business domination of urban politics, Hunter (1953) asked his informants to name Atlanta's top leaders "from the point of view of ability to lead others" (p. 265), while Robert Dahl (1961) began his study in New Haven by selecting three decision arenas and tracing backward to uncover the most active participants. Not surprising, such divergent system specifications produced divergent patterns of actor concentration across policy decisions and hence supported fundamental theoretical disagreements about local elite or plural power structures. In proposing their new elite framework, Field, Higley, and Burton (1990) defined elites as "persons who are able, by virtue of their strategic positions in powerful organizations, to affect national political outcomes regularly and substantially" (p. 152). Operationalizing this concept requires precise clarification of what they meant by "strategic positions," "powerful organizations," and "regular and substantial" effects on "national political outcomes." Each choice broadening or narrowing these definitional components shifts the boundaries of elite membership in ways likely to alter the substantive conclusions.

Investigators working from a multiple institutional framework require even more complex boundary specifications. Unfortunately, common-sense labels for these sectors have predominated, although occasional efforts are made to specify the arenas theoretically, such as Parson's AGIL subsystem scheme (Laumann & Pappi, 1976). For example, Hunter asked his informants to nominate the 10 top persons in the civic, government, business, and status-society arenas (Hunter, 1953). Perrucci and Pilisuk (1970) significantly advanced the network perspective in community power structure research by designating as interorganizational leaders (IOLs) those persons holding executive positions in four or more community groups. In West Lafayette, Indiana, a set of 6 organizations linked through 11 IOLs formed the core of the local ruling elite. Dye (1986) cataloged the top 6,000 American national position holders in more than 400 major organizations drawn from a dozen institutional sectors. His framework was one of the few to designate the military as a distinct sector, perhaps because C. Wright Mills had included it in his national power elite triad. The global-mapping approach used in the American, Australian, and German elite network surveys specified the analytic universes as persons holding authoritative positions in powerful public and private organizations and influential movements (Higley et al., 1991). In practice, the top leaders of organizations in seven arenas were included: politics, civil service, business, trade unions, mass media, voluntary associations, and the academic sphere. Analytic rationales were generally missing for deciding on the particular arenas, determining the important organizations, or selecting the key administrative positions within each organization, and researchers have not grappled with the problem of whether all sectors should be treated as equally important. Too often, researchers simply assert that certain arenas and actors are important, consequently leaving unclear their precise conceptualization of a system's "elite."

One analytic effort to delineate elite subsystem boundaries in explicitly relational terms was Knoke and Laumann's (1982) concept of a *policy domain*, consisting of formal organizations identified "by specifying a substantively defined criterion of mutual relevance or common orientation . . . concerned with formulating, advocating, and selecting courses of action" to solve that domain's problems (p. 256). A domain excludes those organizations whose interests and actions are not taken into account by other core participants. Their definition emphasized the priority of interorganizational relations over actor size or attributes, strongly implying that participation in problem-solving activity constitutes the source of the mutual recognition that warrants an organization's inclusion in that subsystem. Numerous national policy domains exist within modern states, and their core organizations interpenetrate to varying degrees (Browne, 1990; Heinz, Laumann, Salisbury, & Nelson, 1990; Laumann & Knoke, 1987, pp. 387-395; Manigart, 1986; Salisbury, Heinz, Laumann, & Nelson, 1987). Whether a specific actor must be included depends both on its own interests in that domain's events and on its ability to make the other domain actors take it into account when collective decisions are made. Thus which actors belong in a national policy domain cannot be specified a priori. They must ultimately be determined empirically.

Finding Key Actors

With the analytic boundaries of a system determined, the researcher's next task is to identify the specific empirical members of the elite population. The actors may be natural persons or formal organizations— such as corporations, unions, professional societies, and government agencies. In either case, comprehensive lists must be assembled that unambiguously locate these entities, including names, mailing addresses, phone numbers, and various descriptive attributes. In practice, four generic techniques have been developed to locate the players:

(1) Positional methods: Persons or organizations occupying the key roles in the analytic system, such as the elected or executive positions in major economic and political units. Published directories for city or national governments, stock and bond services, information clearinghouses, social registries, even telephone books are frequently consulted compendia for identifying those with prima facie interests in the system.

(2) Decisional methods: Actors that participate in making or influencing the collectively binding policy decisions for the system as a whole. These participants often leave public records of their involvement in such accessible sources as newspaper accounts and minutes of board or commission meetings.

(3) Reputational methods: Actors widely believed by knowledgeable observers to have the actual or potential power to "move and shake" the system. Rarely are accounts of power reputations already available; they must be assembled from informant testimonies, such as journalists and academic experts, as well as elites themselves. The list of reputedly powerful nominees can be expanded by snowball sampling; each new

addition is asked for further names until closure is reached. Despite researchers' best efforts to construct comprehensive lists before entering the field, some key actors are likely to be omitted. When such lists are presented for elites to check off their interactions, it is imperative to ask, "Is there anyone [any organization] not on this list whom you believe to be especially powerful/influential? What is that person's [organization's] name?"

(4) Relational methods: Actors who maintain important political relationships with other system members, who were not uncovered during queries about elites' power reputations. The main difference is that relational techniques only pick up additional actors who have direct contacts with those already located: "With which other persons [organizations] not named on this list do you discuss politics/exchange resources/etc.?"

In practice, the four basic methods for finding key actors are difficult to keep separated. For example, many elites' reputations are based on a blending of their current incumbency of major leadership positions with the informants' perceptions of their past actual or anticipated future involvement in major decisions (Knoke, 1983). Similarly, information about who participated in and influenced decisions that occurred out of public sight may only be reconstructed through evidence provided by informants. Unfortunately, no studies of the reliabilities of these alternative approaches have been conducted.

Taking the union of the lists generated by the four identification methods has the advantage of achieving closure on a final elite membership list with reduced possibilities for serious omission or erroneous inclusion. For example, Laumann and Pappi (1976, pp. 271-273) began their study of a small German city with a list of the position holders in the largest organizations of four sectors. They then consulted newspaper archives and informants to eliminate persons not influential in recent community affairs. Other persons were added if they received frequent mentions during interviews by the elite informants (see also Galaskiewicz, 1979, pp. 45-48). Domhoff (1978) identified members of an American national power elite through such secondary data sources as social registers, *Who's Who*, government directories, corporation annual reports, interlocking directorships, and social club membership rosters. Demonstrating that this ruling class actually influenced major national policies required Domhoff to reconstruct the actors' roles in specific historical events. Whitt's (1982) investigation of the class politics behind five California mass transit propositions required

painstaking reconstructions of business organizations' campaign contributions. Clawson, Neustadtl, and Scott (1992) combined data on
corporate donations to 309 political action committees (PACs) with
in-depth interviews of 30 corporate PAC officers to explain the flow of
political money in national elections.

Research on the U.S. national health, energy, and labor policy domains combined multiple lists of organizational participants in policy
decisions, using congressional testimony, newspaper accounts, lobbyist
registrations, and federal appellate and Supreme Court *amicus curiae*
(friend of the court) briefs as well as asking panels of experts to
nominate additional actors not on the lists (Knoke & Pappi, 1991;
Laumann & Knoke, 1987). Because the preliminary listings typically
turned up more than 1,000 organizational names, a prominence criteria
was imposed to reduce the final list to manageable proportions (requiring at least five mentions by all sources typically selected only 100-200
names). During the field periods, additional organizational names were
solicited from the interviewees and were added if at least five mentions
were received (only a couple were included, suggesting that the other
procedures resulted in near closure of the elites). Taken together, these
criteria essentially require that members of an elite have a high level of
network centrality, in the form of either publicly visible participation
in many policy events or a high degree of in-choice from many of their
system peers. Higley et al.'s (1991) surveys of American, Australian,
and German top elites found much larger numbers of position holders
(545, 370, and 497, respectively) and located hundreds of other second-
tier names, through snowball nominations.

For elite network studies that collect data beyond published sources,
high response rates to personal or mail interviews are necessary to
prevent an inaccurate picture of elite relational structures. When individual persons are the actors, their refusal to participate can prove
devastating. For example, the American Leadership Study gained cooperation from only 31% of the "owners of large fortunes" (Barton, 1985).
Hence the degree to which that sector was integrated into the larger
institutional complex remains unclear. Elite research on organizations
can typically attain very high response rates (ranging from 89% to 98%;
see Knoke et al., 1991; Laumann & Knoke, 1987, p. 98). The advantage
is that, in larger organizations, any one of several persons may be
suitable as a knowledgeable informant. Thus, if the executive director
is too busy or uninterested, a governmental affairs expert or lobbyist
may be able to provide the necessary information. Although no study

of informant reliability has been conducted, a potential source of error is staff turnover that results in a loss of institutional memory. My personal experiences in hundreds of such interviews revealed that a far more serious problem is a tendency of the political heads of organizations either not to be well informed about what their subordinates are doing or to engage in ideological posturing rather than to communicate candid insights into what the organization is really trying to accomplish.

Representing Network Structures

Both local community and national elite systems are likely to contain dozens, and possibly hundreds, of important actors, whether individuals or organizations. Attempts to represent these entire networks—as sociograms, matrices, or other graphic images—often result in cluttered and indecipherable figures that conceal far more than they reveal about the internal social structures of the elites. The researcher's goal may be to characterize the global structure of the entire network, to determine the composition of jointly occupied positions within the network, or to locate individual actors in the overall configuration. Thus an important step in analyzing elite networks might be to reduce their complexity by aggregating actors into jointly occupied positions, manipulating these positions to uncover their connections, and interpreting the results in light of theoretical expectations.

The remarkable proliferation of network analysis methods beginning in the mid-1970s placed a large arsenal at researchers' disposal (for methodological overviews, see Burt & Minor, 1983; Knoke & Kuklinski, 1982; Pappi, 1987). With the aid of specialized network programs— such as the personal computer versions of UCINET (Borgatti, Everett, & Freeman, 1992), GRADAP (Sprenger & Stokman, 1989), SONIS (1990), and STRUCTURE (Burt, 1989)—as well as the standard matrix manipulation and multidimensional scaling routines in SAS and SPSS, researchers now routinely subject multiple binary and valued matrices to complicated analyses. Unfortunately, space limits prevent a detailed examination here of the range of applications to political relational data.

To illustrate the kinds of substantive issues underlying network representation, consider the question of whether an elite system has a core subset. In a social analogue to geographic distance, two elites who interact frequently and intensely should be located near one another in a spatial representation of the social interaction "space," but pairs having rare and weak indirect ties should be quite distant. The set of all interactor connections generates the elite's social-spatial map, just as all pairs of intercity mileages yield a geophysical map. A basic network question is this: What global configuration results when a matrix of pairwise transactions are represented as social-spatial structures? Laumann and Pappi (1976, p. 142) proposed two generic structuring principles: sectoral differentiation and integrative centrality. Social space could be divided into relatively homogeneous regions jointly occupied by actors from the same functional subsystem who are likely to share common values, attitudes, and interests. Actors located at a network's center might play key coordination roles in the system, while actors with less integrative importance occupy the periphery. Thus the spatial diagram could resemble a wheel (or, in three dimensions, a sphere), with spokes separating the sectors, radiating out to the peripheral rim from a dense hub containing the core elites. Such patterns were uncovered in a German town and two U.S. cities (Galaskiewicz, 1979, pp. 61-90; Laumann & Pappi, 1976, pp. 133-144), in the U.S. national energy and health policy domain organizations (Laumann & Knoke, 1987, pp. 242-248), and national labor policy domain organizations (Knoke, 1990, pp. 163-171). Laumann and Knoke (1987) succinctly summarized the spatial structure:

> The core is dominated by governmental actors with the most broad-reaching policy mandates; the first circle is dominated by the major special interests of particular sectors; and the peripheries are occupied by the minor claimants. In effect, the aggregative interest groups serve as intermediate communication filters that link the peripheries with the core. (p. 245)

A notable exception was a study of Washington private sector representatives' assistance ties to 72 notables (elite actors) in four policy domains (agriculture, energy, health, and labor). The pattern in each domain was a "sphere with a hollow core" (Heinz et al., 1990). No identifiable sets of autonomous statesmen capable of bridging the empty center were uncovered in any arena. Rather, client type, economic ideology, and political party affiliations produced sharply polarized sectors in which communication "takes place mostly with the elites of adjacent, politically-compatible interest groups. They deal with their allies not with their adversaries" (p. 381). The authors speculated that hollow spheres could be an artifact of omitting government officials who might act as mediators binding the system together.

Participating in Policy Events

Network analyses of elite structures are ultimately valuable only if they improve our understanding of how elites interact to reach policy decisions. Thus analysts must determine if the global structures and actor positions within influence and domination networks are related to those actors' mobilization for participation in policy events. An event is a "critical, temporally located decision point in a collective decision-making sequence that must occur in order for a policy option to be finally selected" (Laumann & Knoke, 1987, p. 251). Events occur in many institutional settings, such as legislatures, regulatory agencies, or courts. They can reference various types of decisions, including new program creation, promulgation of eligibility restrictions, enunciation of legal precedents, funding changes, implementation, oversight, and evaluation. Given the enormous complexity and often ponderous decision-making procedures of liberal democratic states, a potentially infinite number of decision points may occur in any policy process. Unfortunately, conceptualization of the event space and appropriate methods for representatively sampling time points from this space lag far behind the parallel problem of identifying and selecting elite actors. Most researchers resort to purposive selection of highly visible and controversial events, where elite mobilization is exceptionally great. This overemphasis on the exciting rather than the routine runs the risk of a distorted view of how policy participation occurs, nor do we understand the full implications of singular event embeddedness within much larger temporal sequences of events (Abbott & Hrycak, 1990).

Analyses of elite policy participation typically emphasize actor mobilization as a consequence of their interests, resources, and network positions. Domhoff (1978), Whitt (1982), Schneider and Werle (1991), Jansen (1991), and others have produced thick descriptions for specific cases where conflicts over high-stakes issues erupted in publicly visible arenas. But these approaches tend to concentrate on the dramatic details of particular events, at the expense of more systematic structural patterns emerging across numerous events of varied intensity. The policy domain approach of Laumann, Pappi, Knoke, and their colleagues has attempted to characterize the global interactions of political elites across numerous domain policy events. Early studies in one German town and two American cities obtained actors' positions on each of five events (for, against, neutral) (Galaskiewicz, 1979; Laumann & Pappi, 1976; Laumann et al., 1977; Marsden & Laumann, 1977). Not a surprise, those actors holding similar positions tended to be located close to one another in the information, support, and resource exchange networks; opponents clustered in one region, proponents in another portion of the space. Although the fault lines separating antagonists might shift from event to event, the contours still followed the network structure. Galaskiewicz (1979, pp. 91-127) showed that central location in the three exchange networks significantly boosted an organization's involvement in each of the five events, even controlling for various organizational attributes. Community actors' ties to other elites were directly related to their likely participation in events for which they held preferred outcomes. The conclusion that interorganizational network ties promote participation in community decision making is inescapable. The appearance of sharply different pro and con coalitions across separate events refuted claims of a pervasive oppositional configuration that structured all community conflicts into an invariant polarized pattern. Importantly, no evidence was uncovered that an overarching economic class-based cleavage recurred across every controversy.

Similar plural patterns of mobilization were uncovered in national policy domain analyses. Analyzing the energy and health domains, Laumann, Knoke, and Kim (1985) specified a causal model in which an organization's positions in communication and material resource exchange networks mediated between three antecedent factors (the organization's interests in issues, its external monitoring capacity, and its influence reputation) and the organization's policy event participation. Issue interests exerted a large direct effect in both domains, meaning that the broader an organization's issue concerns, the greater the number of events in which it is actively engaged. For energy organizations, neither network measure was significantly related to event participation, supporting a noninstitutionalized interpretation of the energy domain in the 1970s. In contrast, in the health domain, while resource exchange only slightly increased health policy event participation, communication network position substantially raised event participation. This effect was as strong as that for health issue interests. The authors concluded that the greater importance of network position for event mobilization in health than in energy reflected the greater institutionalization of the latter domain. Because policy information is less accessible in such domains, an advantageous network position allows an organization to reduce some of the higher costs of obtaining relevant data. By contrast, the turbulent, highly visible energy domain of the 1970s did not impose serious information impediments to policy involvement. Hence privileged locations in the communication or resource exchange networks did not convey special advantages to mobilizing an organization's policy event participation. Simply having an interest in a policy issue was sufficient to stimulate involvement.

Another major consideration in policy domain analysis is the oppositional structure of domain events. A legislative, executive, or judicial controversy typically attracts opposing sets of organizations, each side seeking an outcome favorable to its interests. But these lines of consensus and cleavage between pro and con organizations generally do not persist across numerous domain events (Laumann & Knoke, 1987, pp. 311-342; Laumann & Marsden, 1979). Rather than the polarized sets of opponents implied by class-conflict or power elite theories, each event seems to attract unique opposing organizational configurations. Because every actor maintains a different portfolio of issue interests and also communicates with distinctive sets of others, very few of these groupings can be exactly reassembled as new events move toward a decision. Analyses of communication networks and policy event participation in the U.S. and German national labor policy domains in the 1980s revealed similar spatial cleavage patterns in three dimensions (Knoke & Pappi, 1991). Opposing business and labor coalitions (collective actors and action sets) structured many of the legislative fights; no central body emerged to coordinate actions; and organizational interests were the driving forces behind coalition formation, with resource capacity playing a minor role in the United States.

Explaining Event Outcomes

The outcomes of public policy controversies are also related to network connections among elites interested in collective decisions. Winning or losing a policy fight depends on which of the opposing sides best uses its network connections to mobilize and coordinate greater quantities of political resources. Galaskiewicz (1979, pp. 140-141) proposed simple but elegant measures of interorganizational resource inflows and outflows. First, each community organization could tap resources from its support system. An organization receiving numerous money, information, and moral support contacts has potentially greater access to the resources of those partners than does an organization with fewer such connections. Second, an organization's resource dependents—the organizations to which it sends money, information, and support—are also potential sources of resources that could be obtained by calling in debts. Galaskiewicz calculated six indices that measured the total amount of money an organization might mobilize through its support and dependency networks. These inflow and outflow linkages significantly explained both an organization's influence reputation and its success in affecting four community events, independent of the organization's funds and personnel as well as its purpose.

Parallel efforts to explain collective decisions applied a collective action model, developed by James S. Coleman, to event data (Coleman, 1973; Marsden, 1983). The essence of Coleman's approach considers how actors with interests in different events exchange resources that influence the event outcomes. Following from resource dependence principles, actors are more powerful and more likely to achieve their preferred outcomes if they possess resources that control events in which other actors have strong interests. Event outcomes depend on the intensity of interests in the various events and the controlling resources held by each actor. In a pure market situation, every pair of actors can directly exchange with one another. But in political elite systems, where mutual trust is required before such transactions take place, resource exchanges most likely occur only through well-established communication networks comprising direct and indirect connections. Brokerage relations may also be critical in bringing potential exchange partners together.

The Coleman exchange model has been applied to only a few real collective action situations. Marsden and Laumann (1977) studied five events (including two hypothetical ones) in an American city. Using 10 types of resources controlled by the community organizations (ranging from money and credit to influence with subgroups), they estimated the power of each actor and the probabilities of the outcome of each event. The correlation between actors' exchange power, predicted by the Coleman model, and direct measures of their influence reputations was .90. Exchange power was also highly correlated with centrality in networks of social relations ($r = .58$) and business-professional ties ($r = .61$). However, the Coleman model correctly predicted only three of the five event outcomes, a result the authors attributed to incorrect assumptions about the closed nature of the community system for all events (Marsden & Laumann, 1977, p. 223; see also Kappelhoff, 1989; Pappi & Kappelhoff, 1984).

Laumann and Knoke with Kim (1987, pp. 343-373) applied a modified version of Coleman's exchange model to 16 American energy and health policy domain event outcomes. A resource deployment model depicted one domain organization as allocating valuable resources to another organization to achieve a favorable event outcome. The deployer delivers resources to a deployee, or its agent, to create the latter's dependence on the former. The analysts combined the candid-confidential communication network with the money, staff, and facilities exchange network to identify the presumed equilibrium pattern of restricted exchanges among government and private sector organizations in the energy and health domains. Power in the resource deployment model was estimated simultaneously for all organizations as a system of equations. Thus this concept of power is a function of pairwise dependence, exchange network volume or centrality, and the quality of relations among organizations. Power estimates were strongly correlated with the independently measured reputed influence standings of the organizations ($r = .58$ and $.73$ in energy and health, respectively). For each of the 16 events analyzed, the model quite accurately predicted the collective outcome, failing in only one of the eight health events to designate correctly the actual result (Laumann & Knoke with Kim, 1987, pp. 362-363; however, one of the eight energy events was erroneously reported as accurately predicted). Pappi and Knoke (1991) also applied the exchange model to analyze organizational demand and supply of control across 12 German and 9 U.S. labor policy subfields. They found that, the more concentrated an actor's interests on a few subfields, the higher the chances of realizing its interests.

Stokman and Van den Bos (1992) proposed a general model of policymaking that integrates a preliminary stage of mutual interactor influence and a final stage of decision only by the actors entitled to vote on the binding decision (i.e., governmental authorities). Applied to the U.S. energy domain data, it demonstrated that the positional power of various types of organizations was especially dependent both on the organizations' resources and on their voting power, indicating that the distinction between governmental and nongovernmental actors is important to preserve. Another intriguing development is Peter Kappelhoff's (1989) development of power in exchange networks beyond the Marsden reformulation, taking into account clientelistic dependency and barter-exchange relations among actors. Exchange analysts continue to develop the dynamic and predictive aspects of their models, to the ultimate improvement of knowledge about how political elites shape collective policy outcomes.

Seeking New Directions

Researchers have made significant strides in recent years toward understanding networks of elite structure and decision making. Developments in data collection strategies and analysis methods were indispensable in providing suitable tools for specifying and testing propositions that relate influence and domination structures to the mobilization of political resources and the collective resolution of policy events.

The community and national power studies discussed above led to several important conclusions about the structural foundations of such collective action systems:

- The principal political actors in elite systems are organizations, not individual natural persons. As systems increase in size and complexity, organizational imperatives surpass family and class interests as the principal structuring dimension of domination and influence.
- A major problem for all actors is reduction of resource dependency. Actors try to use their interorganizational relations to acquire necessary inputs and dispose of outputs, while avoiding control by other actors. Structural autonomy (low resource dependence) within networks enables an actor to pursue its goals with fewer constraints.
- The most important feature of a power structure is its multiple networks of interactor influence and domination. Actors' locations within networks of information and resource exchange affect their abilities to achieve both individual and collective objectives.
- An actor's ability to get the resources essential for its political purposes is increased by its access through multiple networks to other resourceful actors.
- An actor's influence reputation varies with its centrality in the information and resource exchange networks. Influence reputation reflects others' perceptions of an actor's past and future capacity to persuade other actors to support its interests.
- Formation of coalitions on a specific event is helped by ties of sponsorship and obligation through exchange networks. Actors having common interests and short communication linkages form coalitions that can more easily undertake coordinated action to achieve a collective outcome.
- Activation on policy events and success or failure in controversies involves exchanges of control over resources and coordinating actions through restricted interactor networks.
- Most elite power structures are decentralized bargaining systems rather than hierarchical systems controlled by a central economic elite.

Evidence to support these assertions comes from a handful of community and national studies that examined influence and domination networks among actors and events. Warrant for generalizing to a wider scope of elite systems is narrow. Because the collection of primary data on elite networks is costly in money and time, the cumulation of empirical support is unfortunately slow. More rapid progress might be made through closer relations between the natural elite system tradition and the small group experimental tradition. The much greater precision and control over exchange structures that is possible in artificial systems has the advantage of isolating important causes from extraneous effects. One potentially fruitful topic is how network explanations can be augmented by the laboratory findings on coalition formation, mostly developed in a rational-choice game theory paradigm (Pridham, 1986). By manipulating actors' interests, resources, and locations in exchange networks, experimenters can assess the effects of centralization, cohesion, structural equivalence, and other relational phenomena on actor participation in coalitions and their contributions to the production of collective action outcomes. Findings produced in laboratory and computer-simulated settings subsequently would need to be verified by analogous tests with natural elite systems before their generalizability could be confirmed.

Beyond research focused solely on elite structures and decision making, analysts should turn to a larger set of questions about the functions of elites in mass political systems, their contributions to stability and stagnation, and the enduring issues of justice, equity, and well-being for all members of the political community. The impact of citizen discontent in the rapid collapse of communism in eastern Europe and the Soviet Union, in the impending upheavals in China, Cuba, and other oligarchic societies, and even in the persistent malaise pervading advanced liberal democracies suggests much fertile terrain available to be plowed by innovative investigators. Except for a brilliant effort by Laumann and Pappi (1976, pp. 217-253) to map, comprehensively, the interface between one community's elite and its population subgroups, network researchers have made little progress toward solving the knotty problems of data collection and analysis of such large systems. These opportunities should only spur us on to greater creative theoretical and methodological efforts.

References

Abbott, A., & Hrycak, A. (1990). Measuring resemblance in sequence data: An optimal matching analysis of musicians' careers. *American Journal of Sociology, 96*, 144-185.

Barton, A. H. (1985). Determinants of economic attitudes in the American business elite. *American Journal of Sociology, 91*, 54-87.

Borgatti, S., Everett, M., & Freeman, L. (1992). *UCINET IV, Version 1.0*. Columbia, SC: Analytic Technologies.

Browne, W. P. (1990). Organized interests and their issue niches: A search for pluralism in a policy domain. *Journal of Politics, 52*, 477-509.

Burt, R. S. (1989). *STRUCTURE, Version 4.1*. New York: Columbia University, Center for the Social Sciences.

Burt, R. S., & Minor, M. J. (1983). *Applied network analysis: A methodological introduction*. Beverly Hills, CA: Sage.

Clawson, D., Neustadtl, A., & Scott, D. (1992). *Money talks: Corporate PACs and political influence*. New York: Basic Books.

Coleman, J. S. (1973). *The mathematics of collective action*. Chicago: Aldine.

Dahl, R. A. (1961). *Who governs? Democracy and power in an American city*. New Haven, CT: Yale University Press.

Domhoff, G. W. (1978). *The powers that be: Processes of ruling class domination in America*. New York: Vintage.

Domhoff, G. W. (1983). *Who rules America now? A view for the '80s*. Englewood Cliffs, NJ: Prentice-Hall.

Domhoff, G. W., & Dye, T. R. (Eds.). (1987). *Power elites and organizations*. Newbury Park, CA: Sage.

Dye, T. R. (1986). *Who's running America: The conservative years* (4th ed.). Englewood Cliffs, NJ: Prentice-Hall.

Field, G. L., Higley, J., & Burton, M. G. (1990). A new elite framework for political sociology. *Revue européenne des sciences sociales, 28*, 149-182.

Galaskiewicz, J. (1979). *Exchange networks and community politics*. Beverly Hills, CA: Sage.

Gamson, W. A. (1968). *Power and discontent*. Homewood, IL: Dorsey.

Heinz, J. P., Laumann, E. O., Salisbury, R. H., & Nelson, R. L. (1990). Inner circles or hollow cores? Elite networks in national policy systems. *Journal of Politics, 52*, 356-390.

Higley, J., Hoffmann-Lange, U., Kadushin, C., & Moore, G. (1991). Elite integration in stable democracies: A reconsideration. *European Sociological Review, 7*, 35-53.

Higley, J., & Moore, G. (1981). Elite integration in the United States and Australia. *American Political Science Review, 75*, 581-597.

Hunter, F. (1953). *Community power structure*. Chapel Hill: University of North Carolina Press.

Jansen, D. (1991). Policy networks and change: The case of high-tech superconductors. In B. Marin & R. Mayntz (Eds.), *Policy networks: Empirical evidence and theoretical considerations* (pp. 137-174). Frankfurt: Campus Verlag.

Kappelhoff, P. (1989, June). *Power in exchange networks: An extension and application of the Coleman model of collective action*. Paper presented at First European Conference on Social Network Analysis, Groningen, the Netherlands.

Knoke, D. (1983). Organization sponsorship and influence reputation of social influence associations. *Social Forces, 61*, 1065-1087.

Knoke, D. (1990). *Political networks: The structural perspective.* New York: Cambridge University Press.

Knoke, D. (1993). Networks as political glue: Explaining public policy making. In W. J. Wilson (Ed.), *Sociology and the public agenda* (pp. 164-183). Newbury Park, CA: Sage.

Knoke, D., & Kuklinski, J. H. (1982). *Network analysis.* Beverly Hills, CA: Sage.

Knoke, D., & Laumann, E. O. (1982). The social organization of national policy domains: An exploration of some structural hypotheses. In P. V. Marsden & N. Lin (Eds.), *Social structure and network analysis* (pp. 255-270). Beverly Hills, CA: Sage.

Knoke, D., & Pappi, F. U. (1991). Organizational action sets in the U.S. and German labor policy domains. *American Sociological Review, 56*, 509-523.

Knoke, D., Pappi, F. U., Broadbent, J., Kaufman, N., & Tsujinaka, Y. (1991, June). *Policy networks and influence reputations in the U.S., German, and Japanese labor policy domains.* Paper presented to Second European Social Networks Conference, Paris.

Knoke, D., & Wood, J. R. (1981). *Organized for action: Commitment in voluntary associations.* New Brunswick, NJ: Rutgers University Press.

Laumann, E. O., & Knoke, D. (1987). *The organizational state: A perspective on national energy and health domains.* Madison: University of Wisconsin Press.

Laumann, E. O., Knoke, D., & Kim, Y. (1985). An organizational approach to state policymaking: A comparative study of energy and health domains. *American Sociological Review, 50*, 1-19.

Laumann, E. O., & Knoke, D., with Kim, Y. (1987). Event outcomes. In E. O. Laumann & D. Knoke, *The organizational state* (pp. 343-373). Madison: University of Wisconsin Press.

Laumann, E. O., & Marsden, P. V. (1979). The analysis of oppositional structures in political elites: Identifying collective actors. *American Sociological Review, 44*, 713-732.

Laumann, E. O., Marsden, P. V., & Galaskiewicz, J. (1977). Community influence structures: Replication and extension of a network approach. *American Journal of Sociology, 31*, 169-178.

Laumann, E. O., Marsden, P. V., & Prensky, D. (1983). The boundary specification problem in network analysis. In R. S. Burt & M. J. Minor (Eds.), *Applied network analysis: A methodological introduction* (pp. 18-34). Beverly Hills, CA: Sage.

Laumann, E. O., & Pappi, F. U. (1976). *Networks of collective action: A perspective on community influence systems.* New York: Academic Press.

Manigart, P. (1986). The Belgian defense policy domain in the 1980s. *Armed Forces and Society, 13*, 39-56.

Marsden, P. V. (1983). Restricted access in networks and models of power. *American Journal of Sociology, 88*, 686-717.

Marsden, P. V., & Laumann, E. O. (1977). Collective action in a community elite: Exchange, influence processes, and issue resolution. In R. J. Liebert & A. Imershein (Eds.), *Power, paradigms, and community research* (pp. 199-250). London: Sage.

Moore, G. (1979). The structure of a national elite network. *American Sociological Review, 44*, 673-692.

Pappi, F. U. (1984). Boundary specification and structural models of elite systems: Social circles revisited. *Social Networks, 6*, 79-95.

Pappi, F. U. (Ed.). (1987). *Methoden der Netzwerkanalyse.* Munich: R. Oldenbourg Verlag.

Pappi, F. U., & Kappelhoff, P. (1984). Abhaengigkeit, Tausch und kollektive Entsheidung in einer Gemeindeelite. *Zeitschrift fuer Soziologie, 13,* 87-177.

Pappi, F. U., & Knoke, D. (1991). Political exchange in the German and American labor policy domains. In B. Marin & R. Mayntz (Eds.), *Policy networks: Empirical evidence and theoretical considerations* (pp. 179-208). Frankfurt: Campus Verlag.

Perrucci, R., & Pilisuk, M. (1970). Leaders and ruling elites: The interorganizational bases of community power. *American Sociological Review, 35,* 1040-1057.

Pridham, G. (Ed.). (1986). *Coalition behaviour in theory and practice.* Cambridge: Cambridge University Press.

Salisbury, R. H., Heinz, J. P., Laumann, E. O., & Nelson, R. L. (1987). Who works with whom? Interest group alliances and opposition. *American Political Science Review, 81,* 1217-1234.

Schneider, V., & Werle, R. (1991). Policy networks in the German telecommunications domain. In B. Marin & R. Mayntz (Eds.), *Policy networks: Empirical evidence and theoretical considerations* (pp. 97-136). Frankfurt: Campus Verlag.

SONIS. (1990). *Benutzerhandbuch, PC-Version 2.0.* Kiel, Germany: Institut fuer Soziologie.

Sprenger, C. J. A., & Stokman, F. N. (1989). *GRADAP: Graph definition and analysis package: User's manual, Version 2.0.* Groningen, the Netherlands: Iec ProGRAMMA.

Stokman, F. N., & Van den Bos, J. (1992). A two-stage model of policy making with an empirical test in the U.S. energy-policy domain. *Research in Politics and Society, 4,* 219-253.

Useem, M. (1980). Which business leaders help to govern? In G. W. Domhoff (Ed.), *Power structure research* (pp. 199-226). Beverly Hills, CA: Sage.

Useem, M. (1982). Classwide rationality in the politics of managers and directors of large corporations in the United States and Great Britain. *Administrative Science Quarterly, 27,* 199-226.

Useem, M. (1983). *The inner circle: Large corporations and business politics in the U.S. and U.K.* New York: Oxford University Press.

Whitt, J. A. (1982). *Urban elites and mass transportation: The dialectics of power.* Princeton, NJ: Princeton University Press.

About the Contributors

Phipps Arabie is Chair of Marketing and Professor of Management and Psychology at the Rutgers Faculty of Management. Formerly Professor of Psychology and Sociology at the University of Illinois, he has also been visiting Professor of Computer Science at University College, Dublin. His research interests include multidimensional scaling, clustering and other forms of combinatorial data analysis, models of judgment, and social networks. He is founding editor of *Journal of Classification*.

Daniel J. Brass is Associate Professor of Organizational Behavior in the Smeal College of Business Administration at the Pennsylvania State University. He received his M.A. in labor relations and Ph.D. in business administration from the University of Illinois. His research interests focus on the relationship between organizational technology and structure (viewed from a social network perspective) and individual jobs, attitudes, behaviors, and power. Much of his research deals with social networks and power.

Malcolm M. Dow is Professor of Anthropology and Sociology at Northwestern University. Over the past decade he has published a series of papers on the statistical analysis of network data, using both continuous and categorical statistical models. He is the Editor for Social/Cultural Anthropology for the *Journal of Quantitative Anthropology*. Currently he is examining integrator role behaviors across formal subgroup boundaries within a multinational network organization.

Noah E. Friedkin is Professor of Education and Sociology at the University of California, Santa Barbara. Recent articles include "Theoretical Foundations for Centrality Measures" in the *American Journal of Sociology* (1991, Vol. 96, pp. 1478-1504) and "Social Networks in Structural Equation Models" in the *Social Psychology Quarterly* (1990, Vol. 53, pp. 316-328). Currently he is examining the accuracy and applications of a formal theory on how networks of interpersonal power and influence enter into the formation of opinions and agreements.

Joseph Galaskiewicz is Professor of Sociology and Strategic Management and Organization at the University of Minnesota. He is the author of *Exchange Networks and Community Politics* (Sage, 1979) and the *Social Organization of an Urban Grants Economy* (Academic Press, 1985). He is currently working on a monograph with Wolfgang Bielefeld on the growth and decline of nonprofit organizations in Minneapolis-St. Paul during the Reagan years. He is also continuing his work on corporate giving and network methodology.

Jeffrey C. Johnson is Associate Scientist at the Institute for Coastal and Marine Resources and Associate Professor in the Department of Sociology and the Department of Biostatistics, East Carolina University. He received his Ph.D. from the University of California, Irvine, and is currently working on a long-term research project on the group dynamics of the winter-over crews in the South Pole Station in Antarctica. Research interests include the application of quantitative and qualitative methods in ethnographic research, social networks, diffusion models of innovation, small group dynamics, and relationships between social structure and cognition. He has published extensively in anthropological, sociological, and marine journals and is the current Editor-in-Chief of the *Journal of Quantitative Anthropology*.

David Knoke is Professor of Sociology at the University of Minnesota. His main research interests are in organizations and in political sociology. His current projects include the human resources policies of U.S.

organizations (with Arne L. Kalleberg, Peter V. Marsden, and Joe L. Spaeth) and a comparative study of labor policy networks in the United States, Germany, and Japan (with Franz Urban Pappi, Jeffrey Broadbent, and Yutaka Tsujinaka). His recent books include *Political Networks* (1990), *Organizing for Collective Action* (1990), and *Statistics for Social Data Analysis,* 3rd ed. (with George W. Bohrnstedt, 1994). In 1992-1993 he was Chair of the Organizations and Occupations Section of the American Sociological Association and a Fellow at the Center for Advanced Study in the Behavioral Sciences.

David Krackhardt is Associate Professor of Organizations and Public Policy at the H. John Heinz III School of Public Policy and Management, Carnegie Mellon University. Since receiving his Ph.D. in 1984, his research has focused on how the theoretical insights and methodological innovations of network analysis can enhance our understanding of how organizations function. His interests range from cognitive representations of networks to the global, structural aspects of social networks in organizations. His published works have appeared in a variety of journals in the fields of psychology, sociology, management, and statistical methodology. His current research agenda includes developing models of diffusion of controversial innovations, predicting organizational outcomes from global network structures, and understanding the roles of "Simmelian ties" in organizations.

Peter V. Marsden is Professor of Sociology at Harvard University, where he is currently serving as Chair. He is the Editor of *Sociological Methodology,* an annual methodology volume sponsored by the American Sociological Association. His academic interests lie in organizations, social networks, and methodology. He is currently studying the recruitment and selection practices of U.S. employers, as measured in a national employer-employee survey.

Mark S. Mizruchi is Professor of Sociology and Business Administration at the University of Michigan. His research focuses on the economic and political behavior of large American corporations. His books include *The American Corporate Network, 1904-1974* (Sage, 1982), *Intercorporate Relations* (Cambridge University Press, 1987; coedited with Michael Schwartz), and *The Structure of Corporate Political Action* (Harvard University Press, 1992).

Martina Morris is Assistant Professor of Sociology at Columbia University. Her research examines the effects of network structures on infectious disease transmission. She is currently investigating the role of sexual networks on the spread of AIDS in the United States, Thailand, and Uganda, using egocentric network data.

Philippa Pattison is Associate Professor and Reader in the Department of Psychology at the University of Melbourne. Her major research interests include algebraic and statistical models for social networks, discrete models for binary data, and models for mathematical cognition. Her work on algebraic network models is described in her book *Algebraic Models for Social Networks* (Cambridge University Press, 1993).

Ronald E. Rice received his Ph.D. in Communication Research from Stanford University and is currently Associate Professor, School of Communication, Information & Library Studies, Rutgers University. He has coauthored or coedited *Public Communication Campaigns* (first edition, 1981; second edition, 1989), *The New Media: Communication, Research and Technology* (1984), *Managing Organizational Innovation* (1987), and *Research Methods and the New Media* (1989). He has conducted research and published widely in communication science, public communication campaigns, computer-mediated communication systems, methodology, organizational and management theory, information systems, information science and bibliometrics, and social networks. He has been elected divisional officer in both the ICA and the Academy of Management.

Donald Stone Sade received his Ph.D. in anthropology from the University of California, Berkeley, in 1966. Currently he is Professor of Anthropology at Northwestern University and President of the North Country Institute for Natural Philosophy in Mexico, New York. His research since 1960 has been on social networks of nonhuman primates, including rhesus monkeys at Cayo Santiago, Puerto Rico, and emperor tamarins in cooperation with the Lincoln Park Zoological Gardens. More recently, he has also been researching the socioendocrinology of emperor tamarins, the Westernization of martial arts (JuJutsu) systems, and vocalizations of common crows.

Michael E. Walker is Assistant Professor in the Department of Psychology at Ohio State University. He recently received his Ph.D. from the University of Illinois at Urbana. His dissertation was on the statistical analysis of social network data. Methodological interests include the assessment of similarity using the method of sorts as well as categorical data analysis. Other interests include ethnic group relations and social distance, and dispute resolution.

Stanley Wasserman is Professor of Psychology, Statistics, and Sociology, and Professor, Beckman Institute for Advanced Science and Technology, at the University of Illinois. He is the coauthor (with Katherine Faust of the University of South Carolina) of *Social Network Analysis: Methods and Applications* (Cambridge University Press, 1994). His current research interests include categorical data analysis, social networks, and applied statistics (in general). He is Associate Editor of *Journal of the American Statistical Association, The American Statistician, Psychometrika,* and the *Journal of Quantitative Anthropology* and the Book Review Editor of *CHANCE: New Direction in Statistics and Computing.* He is also the Secretary/Treasurer of the Classification Society of North America.

Barry Wellman is Professor of Sociology at the Centre for Urban and Community Studies, University of Toronto. He founded the International Network for Social Network Analysis in 1976 and headed it until 1988. Born in the Bronx, he soon realized that supportive communities thrive in cities—but as social networks. After receiving his Ph.D. from Harvard in 1969, he spent his academic career studying the nature of social support in personal community networks. He coedited *Social Structures: A Network Approach* (Cambridge University Press) and has recently written *Men in Networks,* an account of the move of community ties from male-dominated public spaces to female-dominated domestic spaces.

Yoram Wind is the Lauder Professor and Professor of Marketing at the Wharton School of the University of Pennsylvania. He is also the founding director of the SEI Center for Advanced Studies in Management. He has written 10 books and about 200 papers, articles, and monographs encompassing marketing strategy, marketing research, new product and market development, international marketing, and consumer and industrial buying behavior.

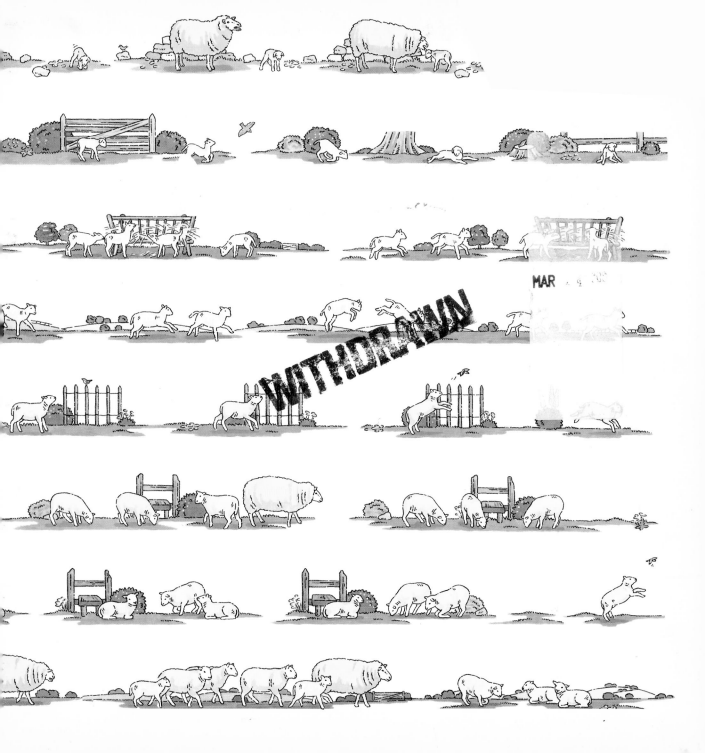

Library of Congress Cataloging-in-Publication Data

Royston, Angela.
  Lamb / written by Angela Royston; photographed by Gordon Clayton.
—1st American ed.
    p. cm.—(See how they grow)
  Summary: Photographs and text depict the growth and development of
a lamb from its first hours of life to twelve weeks old.
  ISBN 0-525-67359-8
  1. Lambs—Juvenile literature.   2. Sheep—Development—Juvenile
literature. [1. Sheep. 2. Animals—Infancy.]   I. Clayton,
Gordon, ill.   II. Title.   III. Series.
SF375.2.R67 1992
636.3' 07—dc20
                                                                91–16372
                                                                    CIP
                                                                    AC

First published in the United States in 1992 by Lodestar Books,
an affiliate of Dutton Children's Books, a division of
Penguin Books USA Inc.
375 Hudson Street
New York, New York 10014

Originally published in Great Britain in 1992 by
Dorling Kindersley Limited, 9 Henrietta Street, London WC2E 8PS

Printed in Italy by L.E.G.O.   ISBN 0-525-67359-8
First American Edition   10 9 8 7 6 5 4 3 2 1

Written by Angela Royston
Editor Mary Ling
Art Editor Helen Senior
Production Louise Barratt
Illustrator Jane Cradock-Watson

Color reproduction by J. Film Process Ltd, Singapore